# **ZAGAT**SURVEY®

# **2005**

# **AMERICA'S TOP RESTAURANTS**

**Editors: Daniel Simmons
and Caren Weiner Campbell**

**Published and distributed by
ZAGAT SURVEY, LLC
4 Columbus Circle
New York, New York 10019
Tel: 212 977 6000
E-mail: americastops@zagat.com
Web site: www.zagat.com**

# Acknowledgments

Our special thanks to the thousands of surveyors who have shared their views with us and made this nationwide *Survey* possible, as well as our editors and coordinators in each city: Ron Beigel, Olga Boikess, Nikki Buchanan, Miriam Carey, Lauren Chapin, Suzi Forbes Chase, Ann Christenson, Andrea Clurfeld, Chris Cook, Pat Denechaud, Victoria Elliott, Jeanette Foster, Rona Gindin, Meesha Halm, Lynn Hazlewood, Carolyn Heller, Jill Hensley, Marty Katz, Michael Klein, Marilyn Kleinberg, Rochelle Koff, Gretchen Kurz, Sharon Litwin, Jennifer Mathieu, Christina Melander, Lori Midson, Maryanne Muller, David Nelson, Cynthia Nims, Jan Norris, Ann Lemons Pollack, Joe Pollack, Nicole Prentice, Virginia Rainey, Laura Reiley, Heidi Knapp Rinella, Shelley Skiles Sawyer, Helen Schwab, Maura Sell, Deirdre Sykes Shapiro, Merrill Shindler, Mary Stagaman, Ruth Tobias, John Turiano, Jill V    Cleave, Alice Van Housen, Carla Waldemar, Julie Wilson and Kay Winzenried. We also thank our associate editor, Kelly Sinanis, and junior editor, Michael Gitter, as well as the following members of our staff: Betsy Andrews, Catherine Bigwood, Reni Chin, Larry Cohn, Carol Diuguid, Griff Foxley, Schuyler Frazier, Jeff Freier, Shelley Gallagher, Curt Gathje, Randi Gollin, Katherine Harris, Natalie Lebert, Mike Liao, Dave Makulec, Donna Marino, Laura Mitchell, Emily Parsons, Robert Poole, Benjamin Schmerler, Troy Segal, Robert Seixas, Yoji Yamaguchi and Sharon Yates.

# Contents

# About This Survey

Here is our *2005 America's Top Restaurants Survey,* covering 1,383 restaurants in 41 major U.S. markets. We've created this guide to ensure that anyone can sample the best dining in virtually every major American city. For each area, we have included a list of the top restaurants (based on the results of our most recent *Surveys* in that area) as well as "Additional Noteworthy Places."

This marks the 26th year that Zagat Survey has reported on the shared experiences of diners like you. What started in 1979 in New York as a hobby involving 200 of our friends rating local restaurants has come a long way. Today we have over 250,000 surveyors and now cover entertaining, golf, hotels, resorts, spas, movies, music, nightlife, shopping, sites and attractions as well as the theater. Our *Surveys* are also available on wireless devices and by subscription at zagat.com, where you can vote and shop as well.

By regularly surveying large numbers of avid, educated customers, we hope to have achieved a uniquely current and reliable guide. For this book, nearly 110,000 restaurant-goers throughout the country participated. Our editors have done their best to summarize our surveyors' opinions, with their exact comments shown in quotation marks. Divided roughly 50-50 between men and women and spread evenly among all age groups, these surveyors also come from every imaginable background and employment category. The one thing they have in common is that they are all restaurant lovers. We sincerely thank each of these surveyors; this book is really "theirs."

We are also grateful to our local editors, many of whom are professional food writers in their home cities. They helped us choose the restaurants to be listed and were responsible for editing the *Survey* results.

While all the restaurants listed here were chosen for their high quality, we have prepared two separate lists to facilitate your search: see Top Food Rankings by Area (pages 7–9) and Most Popular by Area (pages 10–12). To assist you in finding the cuisine you want in any region, we have also provided handy indexes.

**To join any of our upcoming *Surveys,* just register at zagat.com.** Each participant will receive a free copy of the resulting guide when published. Your comments and even criticisms of this guide are also solicited. There is always room for improvement with your help. You can contact us at americastop@zagat.com. We look forward to hearing from you.

New York, NY
October 18, 2004

Nina and Tim Zagat

# What's New

Diversity and quality continue to define America's fine-dining scene. At the top of the market, we've seen an explosion of upscale venues charging higher prices than ever before (a 4.1% inflation rate over the last year). At the same time, owners have been investing megabucks in deluxe settings by world-class designers.

**BATH Time:** Overall, however, restaurant prices outside of the fast-food segment have shown very modest inflation. This is because the industry's main growth has been and continues to be in BATH (Better Alternative to Home) places: casual restaurants serving a wide choice of homey, hearty food at prices designed to compete with the cost of shopping, cooking and cleaning up after a meal at home. This year, these affordable spots have helped keep the average national cost of dining down to $31.51 per meal, an increase of 3.1% since last year.

**The Rising Sun:** Americans continue their fascination with Asian cuisines, particulary Japanese. This has long been true in the western part of the U.S., with Japanese topping our survey charts in several West Coast cities. However, it is now emerging as an East Coast favorite as well, receiving top honors in such Eastern cities as Boston and Washington, DC. Meanwhile, Thai has supplanted Chinese as our surveyors' second Asian choice.

**Dieters' Dictates:** With the Federal government finally talking about obesity as a health issue, restaurateurs are putting new emphasis on dietary concerns. Menus are being tweaked to reflect the carb-counting craze still sweeping the nation. Fueled by Atkins-ites, a new wave of steakhouses is attracting a younger clientele. And establishments increasingly feature the highest possible–quality produce, often identifying specific farm sources.

**Portion Control:** From tapas to meze, dim sum to antipasti, little dishes have always had their place on the table, but lately small plates have become big business, taking center stage as chefs apply the concept to a wide range of cuisines. Foodies find it fun to share with friends and family while exercising control over their intake.

**Slamming Service:** If there's one lesson restaurateurs have yet to learn, it's that front-of-house concerns can make or break the meal. A whopping 72% of our surveyors nationwide cite service shortcomings as their top complaint – more than noise, food, prices, parking, crowding, smoking and cell phones cumulatively. Even the absence of a server's smile too often diminishes the dining experience.

New York, NY
October 18, 2004

Nina and Tim Zagat

# Ratings & Symbols

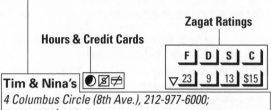

**Name, Address, Phone Number & Web Site**

**Zagat Ratings**

**Hours & Credit Cards**

| F | D | S | C |
|---|---|---|---|
| ▽ 23 | 9 | 13 | $15 |

**Tim & Nina's** ◐ 🖾 ⊅

*4 Columbus Circle (8th Ave.), 212-977-6000;
www.zagat.com*

☑ "You're the tapas" croon connoisseurs of the "less-is-more" Chinese-Castilian canapés at this "bustling" concrete-clad eatery within the Columbus Circle roundabout, where diners can select "savory" small plates from passing dim sum carts to assemble a "tasting menu that's just to their taste"; however, detractors dislike "service with a snarl" and declare Tim and Nina "push the concept too far" ("one sweet-and-sour sardine?"), complaining "they take the phrase 'going out for a bite' literally."

**Review, with surveyors' comments in quotes**

Restaurants with the highest overall ratings and greatest popularity and importance are printed in CAPITAL LETTERS.

Before reviews a symbol indicates whether responses were uniform ■ or mixed ☑.

**Hours:** ◐ serves after 11 PM
🖾 closed on Sunday

**Credit Cards:** ⊅ no credit cards accepted

**Ratings** are on a scale of **0** to **30**. Cost **(C)** reflects our surveyors' estimate of the price of dinner with one drink and tip.

| F | Food | D | Decor | S | Service | C | Cost |
|---|---|---|---|---|---|---|---|
| 23 | | 9 | | 13 | | $15 | |

| | | |
|---|---|---|
| **0–9** poor to fair | **20–25** very good to excellent | |
| **10–15** fair to good | **26–30** extraordinary to perfection | |
| **16–19** good to very good | ▽ low response/less reliable | |

For places listed without ratings, such as a newcomer or survey write-in, the price range is indicated as follows:

| **I** | $25 and below | **E** | $41 to $65 |
|---|---|---|---|
| **M** | $26 to $40 | **VE** | $66 or more |

# Top Food Rankings by Area

## Atlanta
- **29** Bacchanalia
- **28** Ritz-Carlton Buck. Din. Rm.
- **27** Tamarind
  - Aria
  - Sia's

## Atlantic City
- **25** White House
  - Chef Vola's
- **24** Capriccio
- **23** Girasole
- **22** Brighton

## Baltimore/Annapolis
- **28** Charleston
- **27** Prime Rib
  - O'Leary's
  - Joss Cafe
  - Hampton's

## Boston
- **29** Oishii
- **28** L'Espalier
- **27** Aujourd'hui
  - Il Capriccio
  - Olio

## Charlotte
- **27** Barrington's
  - Toscana
  - McNinch House
  - McIntosh's
- **26** Sullivan's

## Chicago
- **29** Ritz-Carlton Din. Rm.
- **28** Tallgrass
  - Les Nomades
  - Carlos'
  - Tru

## Cincinnati
- **29** Jean-Robert at Pigall's
- **28** Daveed's at 934
- **27** Boca
  - BonBonerie
  - Palace, The

## Cleveland
- **28** Johnny's Bar
- **27** Chez François
  - Phnom Penh
  - Lola Bistro/Wine Bar
  - Blue Point Grille

## Connecticut
- **27** Restaurant du Village
  - Jean-Louis
  - Da Pietro's
  - Coromandel
  - Métro Bis

## Dallas
- **28** French Room
  - Lola
- **27** York Street
  - Teppo
  - Cafe Pacific

## Denver/Mtn. Resorts
- **28** Mizuna
- **27** Highlands Garden
  - Del Frisco's
  - L'Atelier
  - Sweet Basil

## Detroit
- **28** Rugby Grille
  - Lark, The
  - Emily's
- **27** Zingerman's
  - Tribute

## Ft. Lauderdale
- **27** Eduardo de San Angel
  - Sunfish Grill
  - La Brochette
  - Casa D'Angelo
  - Mark's Las Olas

## Ft. Worth
- **28** Lonesome Dove
- **27** Saint-Emilion
  - La Piazza
- **26** Boi NA Braza
  - Kincaid's

# Top Food

## Honolulu
28 Alan Wong's
27 La Mer
   Hoku's
   3660 on the Rise
26 Roy's

## Houston
28 Mark's
   Chez Nous
27 Pappas Bros.
26 Cafe Annie
   Indika

## Kansas City
27 Bluestem
26 Stroud's
   Oklahoma Joe's
   Le Fou Frog
   American Rest.

## Las Vegas
28 Nobu
   Renoir
27 Picasso
   Malibu Chan's
   Le Cirque

## Long Island
28 Mill River Inn
27 Kotobuki
   Peter Luger
   Mirko's
26 Mirabelle

## Los Angeles
28 Sushi Nozawa
   Matsuhisa
   Water Grill
   Mélisse
27 Saddle Peak Lodge

## Miami
28 Chef Allen's
   Shibui
   Nobu Miami Beach
27 Norman's
   Tropical Chinese

## Milwaukee
29 Sanford
   Watermark
27 Dream Dance
   Ristorante Bartolotta
26 Immigrant Room/Winery

## Minneapolis/St. Paul
28 Bayport Cookery
   La Belle Vie
27 Goodfellow's
   D'Amico Cucina
   Vincent

## New Jersey
28 Ryland Inn
27 Nicholas
   DeLorenzo's
   Cafe Panache
   Whispers

## New Orleans
27 Peristyle
   Bayona
   Jacques-Imo's
   Dick and Jenny's
   Brigtsen's

## New York City
28 Le Bernardin
   Bouley
   Daniel
   Gramercy Tavern
   Sushi Yasuda

## Orange County, CA
28 Picayo
27 Ramos House Cafe
   Aubergine
   Studio
   Basilic

## Orlando
27 Le Coq au Vin
   Victoria & Albert's
   Chatham's Place
   Del Frisco's
26 Manuel's on the 28th

## Palm Beach
28 11 Maple Street
   Chez Jean-Pierre
   Four Seasons
26 Cafe L'Europe
   New York Prime

## Philadelphia
28 Fountain
   Le Bec-Fin
   Le Bar Lyonnais
   Django
   Birchrunville Store

## Phoenix/Scottsdale
**27** T. Cooks
Michael's at the Citadel
Pizzeria Bianco
Mastro's
**26** Mary Elaine's

## Portland, OR
**27** Genoa
Paley's Place
Higgins
Saburo's
Heathman

## Salt Lake City/Mtn. Resorts
**27** Tree Room
Red Iguana
Mariposa
**26** Michelangelo
Seafood Buffet

## San Diego
**27** Pamplemousse Grille
El Bizcocho
**26** Tapenade
Sushi Ota
WineSellar & Brasserie

## San Francisco Bay Area
**29** Gary Danko
**28** French Laundry
Masa's
Fleur de Lys
**27** Le Papillon

## Seattle
**29** Mistral
**28** Cafe Juanita
Nishino
Herbfarm, The
Tosoni's

## St. Louis
**27** Tony's
Sidney Street Cafe
Trattoria Marcella
**26** Crossing, The
Dominic's

## Tampa/Sarasota
**28** Beach Bistro
Café B.T.
**27** SideBern's
**26** Six Tables
Selva Grill

## Tucson
**28** Dish, The
**27** Grill at Hacienda del Sol
**26** Vivace
Ventana Room
Janos

## Washington, DC
**28** Makoto
Inn at Little Washington
Maestro
Citronelle
L'Auberge Chez François

## Westchester/HRV
**29** Xaviar's at Piermont
Freelance Café
**28** Arch
La Panetière
**27** Il Cenàcolo

# Most Popular by Area

**Atlanta**
1. Bacchanalia
2. Bone's
3. Chops/Lobster Bar
4. BluePointe
5. Nava

**Atlantic City**
1. White House
2. Chef Vola's
3. Dock's Oyster House
4. Capriccio
5. Brighton

**Baltimore/Annapolis**
1. Charleston
2. Ruth's Chris
3. McCormick & Schmick's
4. Cheesecake Factory
5. Clyde's

**Boston**
1. Legal Sea Foods
2. Blue Ginger
3. Aujourd'hui
4. Hamersley's Bistro
5. L'Espalier

**Charlotte**
1. Upstream
2. Sullivan's
3. LaVecchia's
4. Guytano's
5. Mickey & Mooch

**Chicago**
1. Tru
2. Charlie Trotter's
3. Frontera Grill
4. Everest
5. Gibsons

**Cincinnati**
1. Jean-Robert at Pigall's
2. Montgomery Inn
3. Maisonette
4. Palomino
5. Jeff Ruby's

**Cleveland**
1. Blue Point Grille
2. Lola Bistro/Wine Bar
3. Johnny's Bar
4. Hyde Park Prime
5. Baricelli Inn

**Connecticut**
1. Thomas Henkelmann
2. Jean-Louis
3. City Limits
4. Rebeccas
5. Ching's Table

**Dallas**
1. Abacus
2. Bob's
3. Mansion on Turtle Creek
4. P.F. Chang's
5. French Room

**Denver/Mtn. Resorts**
1. Sweet Basil
2. Adega Rest./Wine
3. Flagstaff House
4. Mizuna
5. Del Frisco's

**Detroit**
1. Lark, The
2. Tribute
3. Zingerman's
4. Emily's
5. Common Grill

**Ft. Lauderdale**
1. Cheesecake Factory
2. Mark's Las Olas
3. Ruth's Chris
4. Houston's
5. Outback

**Ft. Worth**
1. Del Frisco's
2. Reata
3. Joe T. Garcia's
4. Texas de Brazil
5. Bistro Louise

**Honolulu**
1. Alan Wong's
2. Roy's
3. Hoku's
4. La Mer
5. 3660 on the Rise

**Houston**
1. Mark's
2. Brennan's
3. Cafe Annie
4. Churrascos
5. Américas

## Kansas City
1. McCormick & Schmick's
2. Fiorella's Jack Stack
3. Plaza III
4. Lidia's
5. Grand St. Cafe

## Las Vegas
1. Picasso
2. Michael Mina
3. Aureole
4. Bellagio Buffet
5. Emeril's New Orleans

## Long Island
1. Peter Luger
2. Cheesecake Factory
3. Coolfish
4. Bryant & Cooper
5. Mill River Inn

## Los Angeles
1. Café Bizou
2. Water Grill
3. Spago
4. Campanile
5. A.O.C.

## Miami
1. Joe's Stone Crab
2. Cheesecake Factory
3. Norman's
4. Chef Allen's
5. Blue Door

## Milwaukee
1. Maggiano's
2. Sanford
3. P.F. Chang's
4. Lake Park Bistro
5. Eddie Martini's

## Minneapolis/St. Paul
1. Oceanaire
2. Manny's
3. Kincaid's
4. Vincent
5. Goodfellow's

## New Jersey
1. Scalini Fedeli
2. Ryland Inn
3. Saddle River Inn
4. Amanda's
5. River Palm Terrace

## New Orleans
1. Commander's Palace
2. Galatoire's
3. Bayona
4. Brennan's
5. Emeril's

## New York City
1. Gramercy Tavern
2. Union Square Cafe
3. Daniel
4. Gotham Bar & Grill
5. Blue Water Grill

## Orange County, CA
1. Houston's
2. Cheesecake Factory
3. Ruth's Chris
4. P.F. Chang's
5. Il Fornaio

## Orlando
1. California Grill
2. Emeril's Orlando*
3. Victoria & Albert's
4. Flying Fish Café
5. Cheesecake Factory

## Palm Beach
1. Cheesecake Factory
2. Ke-e Grill
3. Cafe L'Europe
4. Ruth's Chris
5. Chez Jean-Pierre

## Philadelphia
1. Buddakan
2. Le Bec-Fin
3. Fountain
4. Lacroix/Rittenhouse
5. Django

## Phoenix/Scottsdale
1. P.F. Chang's
2. T. Cooks
3. Roy's
4. Mary Elaine's
5. Houston's

## Portland, OR
1. Jake's Famous Crawfish
2. Higgins
3. Heathman
4. Wildwood
5. McCormick & Schmick's

---

* Tied with restaurant above

# By Popularity Rank

## Salt Lake City/Mtn. Resorts
1. Market St. Grill
2. New Yorker Club
3. Wahso
4. Chimayo
5. Red Iguana

## San Diego
1. George's at the Cove
2. Ruth's Chris
3. Sammy's Woodfired
4. Pamplemousse Grille
5. Roppongi

## San Francisco Bay Area
1. Gary Danko
2. Boulevard
3. French Laundry
4. Chez Panisse
5. Aqua

## Seattle
1. Wild Ginger
2. Dahlia Lounge
3. Metropolitan Grill
4. Canlis
5. Rover's

## St. Louis
1. Tony's
2. Sidney Street Cafe
3. Trattoria Marcella
4. Annie Gunn's
5. Harvest

## Tampa/Sarasota
1. Bern's
2. Columbia
3. Armani's
4. Bijou Café
5. SideBern's

## Tucson
1. Grill at Hacienda del Sol
2. Ventana Room
3. Vivace
4. Janos
5. Cafe Poca Cosa

## Washington, DC
1. Kinkead's
2. Jaleo
3. Citronelle
4. L'Auberge Chez François
5. TenPenh

## Westchester/HRV
1. Crabtree's Kittle House
2. Xavier's at Piermont
3. La Panetière
4. Rest. X & Bully Boy Bar
5. Harvest on Hudson

# Restaurant Directory

# Atlanta

## TOP 20 FOOD RANKING

| Restaurant | Cuisine |
|---|---|
| **29** Bacchanalia | New American |
| **28** Ritz-Carlton Buck. Din. Rm. | New French |
| **27** Tamarind | Thai |
| Aria | New American |
| Sia's | Asian/Southwestern |
| Bone's | Steakhouse |
| MF Sushibar | Japanese |
| Floataway Cafe | French/Italian |
| Chops/Lobster Bar | Steakhouse/Seafood |
| **26** Park 75 | New American |
| Pano's & Paul's | Continental |
| Nan | Thai |
| Seeger's | Continental |
| Nikolai's Roof | French/Continental |
| McKendrick's | Steakhouse |
| Joël | French |
| di Paolo | Northern Italian |
| Sotto Sotto | Northern Italian |
| La Grotta | Northern Italian |
| South City Kitchen | Southern |

## ADDITIONAL NOTEWORTHY PLACES

| | |
|---|---|
| Atlanta Fish Market | Seafood |
| Babette's Café | European |
| BluePointe | Asian/New American |
| Blue Ridge Grill | Southern |
| Brasserie Le Coze | French Bistro |
| Buckhead Diner | New American |
| Canoe | New American |
| dick & harry's | New American |
| Food Studio | New American |
| Hsu's Gourmet | Chinese |
| Iris | Continental |
| La Tavola | Italian |
| Madras Saravana | Indian/Vegetarian |
| Nava | Southwestern |
| ONE.midtown kitchen | New American |
| Rathbun's | New American |
| Sushi Avenue | Japanese |
| Thumbs Up | American |
| Tierra | Pan-Latin |
| Wisteria | Southern |

### ARIA ☒    27 | 25 | 26 | $49

*490 E. Paces Ferry Rd. (Maple Dr.), 404-233-7673;*
*www.aria-atl.com*

■ Surveyors sing the praises of this "suave Buckhead" boîte with an "entirely original and elegant" aura that "continues to shine" thanks to the "superlative, creative" New American cuisine of chef-owner Gerry Klaskala, who "gets it" when it comes to "making customers feel welcome", setting an example for the "outstanding, unobtrusive" staff; it's set in a "glamorous" "renovated house" with "dynamite contemporary decor" that's "heavy on the comfort factor" and, despite somewhat "poor acoustics", "perfect for a special evening."

### Atlanta Fish Market    23 | 19 | 20 | $36

*265 Pharr Rd. (bet. Peachtree St. & Piedmont Rd.), 404-262-3165;*
*www.buckheadrestaurants.com*

☑ Enthusiasts exclaim "holy mackerel, this place rocks" – at this "warehouse-size" Buckhead seafooder a "huge variety" of "eerily fresh fish" prepared "any way you want it" reels in "schools" of finatics; service is "solid" but "long waits" are to be expected in the "fun-filled" setting that's "too damn noisy" for many, and fretful foes feel this fin-fare "factory" "for the masses" has "lost its freshness."

### Babette's Cafe    24 | 20 | 23 | $30

*573 N. Highland Ave. (Freedom Pkwy.), 404-523-9121;*
*www.babettescafe.com*

■ Chef-owner "Marla Adams never disappoints"; her midpriced Poncey-Highlands European "staple" is "highly recommended" for "well-seasoned", "casual" fare that's a "superb blend of fancy and simple", as well as for "one of the best Sunday brunches in town"; the "renovated Victorian cottage" is "comfy" and *très, très* homey", and the "fantastic" "servers are as pleasant as the food."

### BACCHANALIA ☒    29 | 25 | 28 | $69

*Westside Mktpl., 1198 Howell Mill Rd. (bet. 14th St. & Huff Rd.),*
*404-365-0410; www.starprovisions.com*

■ A "feast for the senses", this Westside "culinary shrine", Atlanta's Most Popular destination, was also voted the city's No. 1 for Food; chef-owners Anne Quatrano and Clifford Harrison's "exquisitely prepared" New American creations are a "joy to serious foodies" "without scaring off amateurs" and the service is "exquisite" "but subtle", while the "lovely, contemporary" space in a former "meatpacking plant" "betrays its industrial roots"; "the only bad thing is how hard it is to get in."

### BLUEPOINTE    24 | 26 | 21 | $47

*3455 Peachtree Rd. (Lenox Rd.), 404-237-9070;*
*www.buckheadrestaurants.com*

☑ "Quintessential new Atlanta – sleek, hip and better than you expect" is how groupies describe this "upscale" Buckhead showcase for chef Ian Winslade's "vibrant, terrific" Asian-accented New American cuisine, where "movers and shakers" mingle with "tremendous eye candy" at the "electrifying neon bar" and the "wow factor" extends to the "sharp room" with "high ceilings", towering windows and a "sweeping staircase"; the jaded, however, jeer at "cheesy crowds" and "snooty", "slow-as-molasses" service and lament "if only the customers and staff were as cool as the place."

### Blue Ridge Grill
23 | 25 | 23 | $40

*1261 W. Paces Ferry Rd. (Northside Pkwy.), 404-233-5030;*
*www.blueridgegrill.com*

■ "Aspen meets Atlanta" is how some geography-challenged fans describe this Buckhead homage to the Blue Ridge Mountains, thanks to its "ritzy moose-lodge" decor with stacked stone fireplace, exposed beams and a "restful" wicker- and antique-strewn indoor porch, but "pitch-perfect Southern cuisine with polish" and "well-mannered, informed servers" put it on the map as a "favorite" dining "destination" of many; the "prime location" next to I-75 is another plus.

### BONE'S
27 | 22 | 27 | $53

*3130 Piedmont Rd. (Peachtree Rd.), 404-237-2663;*
*www.bonesrestaurant.com*

■ No bones about it – carnivores counsel "bring a big appetite and lots of money" to this "ridiculously decadent power steakhouse" in Buckhead that "beats those national chains" "hands down" with "consistently superb", "soft and buttery" steaks and a "comprehensive wine list"; a "warm, knowledgeable and accommodating" staff will make you feel like an "old friend who has been away too long" at this "dark" and "elegant" "old-school" setting where "dealmakers and hotshot business types" abound.

### Brasserie Le Coze ⊠
24 | 21 | 22 | $38

*Lenox Sq., 3393 Peachtree Rd. (Lenox Rd.), 404-266-1440*

■ "Don't let the mall location fool you"; this "worthy" Buckhead offshoot of NYC's Le Bernardin ("at a much lower cost") is "as close to Paris as Atlanta gets without Delta", offering "classic French done right with a modern twist" and "first-class" service to celebrities and "ladies who lunch" in a "charming", "sunny yellow bistro setting"; while the staff can be "a bit snooty" at times, fans still exclaim "*c'est magnifique!*"

### Buckhead Diner ◑
22 | 21 | 22 | $32

*3073 Piedmont Rd., NE (E. Paces Ferry Rd.), 404-262-3336;*
*www.buckheadrestaurants.com*

■ "A diner for people who wouldn't normally be caught dead in one", this "upscale" Buckhead production is "no Mel's", offering a "gourmet yet grounded" all-day menu of New American "classics" that "never disappoint" in a "streamlined", "stainless-steel" space; there's "something for everybody", from "families" to "Elton John" – including "excessive waits" (though "lunch is a lot less busy"); while a few feel it's "not what it used to be", loyalists insist it's still "holding its own."

### Canoe
25 | 26 | 23 | $41

*Vinings on the River, 4199 Paces Ferry Rd. (I-75), 770-432-2663;*
*www.canoeatl.com*

■ "The Southern charm is infectious" at this "well-loved" "special-occasion" destination in Vinings that surveyors say has "got it all"; chef Gary Mennie's "excellent" New American cuisine that makes "exceptional use of fresh local ingredients", "idyllic" "riverside" surroundings featuring "stellar gardens" and an "inviting" atmosphere that's "more comfortable than home", and "attentive" service from a staff that's "knowledgeable" "without being long-winded"; in sum, it's a "super-romantic" spot to "impress a date" or "out-of-town visitors."

### CHOPS/LOBSTER BAR   27 | 24 | 26 | $52 |
*Buckhead Plaza, 70 W. Paces Ferry Rd. (Peachtree Rd.), 404-262-2675;*
*www.buckheadrestaurants.com*
■ "Superlatives" abound around this "exceptional" Buckhead
steakhouse that's "ground zero for meat eaters" who "slash away"
at "beautiful", "melt-in-your-mouth" cuts in a "tony", "masculine"
setting; meanwhile, downstairs in the "more intimate" Lobster
Bar, afishionados tuck into "sophisticated, fabulous", "always-
fresh" fin fare in a "fab art deco" room with a "younger feel" to it;
an "efficient", "impeccable" staff "makes you feel like Trump"
at both, which are "buzzing" to the "power pulse" of "expense-
account" meals and "special occasions."

### dick and harry's ☒   25 | 18 | 23 | $38 |
*Holcomb Woods Vlg., 1570 Holcomb Bridge Rd. (½ mi. east of GA 400),*
*Roswell, 770-641-8757; www.dickandharrys.com*
■ "Exceptional" fish dishes are the "highlight" of the "superb"
New American cuisine (the "spicy" crab cakes are "some of the
best around") at this "upscale" Roswell production where "classy
service" makes "well-dressed" diners "feel special", and "sitting
at the chef's counter" near the back of the "stainless steel"–
accented dining room is always a "great experience" (even if critics
sigh it looks "so '90s") ; budget hawks grouse about the "pricey"
tabs, but many feel it's "worth the drive" to suburbia.

### di Paolo   26 | 21 | 24 | $33 |
*Rivermont Sq., 8560 Holcomb Bridge Rd. (Nesbitt Ferry Rd.),*
*Alpharetta, 770-587-1051*
■ "As good as any inside the Perimeter", this "friendly" Alpharettan
is "worth the drive from wherever you are" for an "educated" menu
of "upscale" Northern Italian cuisine that's "unique and filling"
"without being weighty"; there's "always a warm welcome" from
"outstanding" owner Susan Thill, and her "superb" staff delivers
"wonderful", "personalized" service in a "dark" and "sexy" yet
"homey" dining room; intowners say the "only improvement" it
needs is to move "closer to the city."

### Floataway Cafe ☒   27 | 24 | 23 | $41 |
*Floataway Bldg., 1123 Zonolite Rd. (Briarcliff & Johnson Rds.),*
*404-892-1414; www.starprovisions.com*
■ "You'll need a GPS to find" "Bacchanalia's little sister", located
"in the middle of an industrial park" near Emory, but it's "well worth
the excursion" for chef Anne Quatrano's "stunning" French-Italian
cuisine that fans swear is "every bit as good" as (and "more
affordable" than) its elder sibling's; the "serious", "if not always
friendly", staff "can't be beat" for "professional" service, while
the "airy", "post-industrial" space is "relaxing" (notwithstanding
grumbles about the "noise"), framing an "ultracool" scene for an
"arty crowd" that's "top of the line and quite divine."

### Food Studio   25 | 26 | 25 | $42 |
*King Plow Art Ctr., 887 W. Marietta St. (bet. Ashby St. & Howell Mill Rd.),*
*404-815-6677; www.thefoodstudio.com*
■ Foodies "drop bread crumbs" so they can "find their way back"
to this Westside New American "favorite" that "feels a world
away", and not just because of its "obscure location"; exec chef
Chip Ulbrich's "spectacular" creations are served in a "dark,
luxurious" space that's "all candles and fireplace" ("even the

food makes you want to smooch"), while "smooth" service adds to the "special-occasion" atmosphere.

### Hsu's Gourmet
25 | 16 | 23 | $23

*192 Peachtree Center Ave. (International Blvd.), 404-659-2788;*
*www.hsus.com*
■ Arguably the "best authentic Chinese cuisine in the Southeast" according to local loyalists, this Downtown Szechuan serves up "generous portions" of "fabulous" dishes (e.g. Spicy Anna seafood noodle soup) that are "worth every penny"; "multiple servers" "cater to your every need" and pay "attention to detail", making it a "popular" lunch choice with visiting conventioneers and the business crowd.

### Iris
25 | 21 | 22 | $32

*1314 Glenwood Ave. (Haas Ave.), 404-221-1300;*
*www.irisatlanta.com*
■ An "oasis of big-city chic with a small-town attitude", this "top-notch addition" to East Atlanta offers a Continental-inspired organic menu of "sublime flavors" that are "creative" "without being alienating", as well as "professional" service by an "earnest, attentive" staff and the "modernist" digs of a "dressed-up gas station"; an "interesting clientele" of "locals" mixes with those willing to "venture" into this "gentrifying part of town", though most agree this newcomer "could work anywhere."

### Joël ⊠
26 | 26 | 25 | $54

*The Forum, 3290 Northside Pkwy. (W. Paces Ferry Rd.), 404-233-3500;*
*www.joelrestaurant.com*
■ At Joël Antunes' "haute" Buckhead establishment, "flawless" "high-concept" French cuisine (with Asian and Med inflections) by a "world-class talent" and an "extensive wine list" that "reads like *War and Peace*" are proffered by an "excellent" staff in a "sizzling", "stunning, modern" space with "awesome" bathrooms and a "gorgeous" bar; dissenters may grimace at the "odd location", "haughty" attitude and "big dollars", but most agree "many cities would be happy to have this one"; P.S. the "$29 prix fixe is an outstanding value."

### La Grotta ⊠
26 | 22 | 26 | $46

*Crowne Plaza Ravinia Hotel, 4355 Ashford Dunwoody Rd. (Hammond Dr.),*
*770-395-9925*
*2637 Peachtree Rd. (bet. Lindbergh Dr. & Wesley Rd.), 404-231-1368*
*www.la-grotta.com*
■ This "old-world" Northern Italian duo is many mavens' "top choice" for "consistently excellent", "flawless" cuisine from a "deep and satisfying menu" and "impeccable" service from a "well-trained" staff that'll "do anything to make you feel comfortable"; while some prefer the "gorgeous room" and "outstanding views" of the Dunwoody location, others are partial to the "relaxing, luxurious" ambiance of the "original" "grande dame" in Buckhead, but whichever spot you choose, it's a "pleasure from start to finish."

### La Tavola
24 | 21 | 23 | $30

*992 Virginia Ave., NE (N. Highland Ave.), 404-873-5430;*
*www.latavolatrattoria.com*
■ A "bright spot in the Va-Highlands dining scene", this trattoria "has found its groove" with "delicious, inventive" Italian cooking

that's "heaven on a plate" for ardent fans who also laud the "impeccable" wine list and "attentive", "but not overbearing" service; the "sleek" room is "refreshing and cool" but "always packed"; fortunately, those who feel "cramped" can retreat to the "comfortable" patio for a more "relaxing" repast.

### Madras Saravana Bhavan    25 | 11 | 15 | $15

*Cub Foods Shopping Ctr., 2179 Lawrenceville Hwy. (N. Druid Hills Rd.), Decatur, 404-636-4400; www.madrassaravanabhavan.net*

■ Delhi ho – this Decatur dining destination dazzles diners with "unbelievably good" and "savory" vegetarian dishes that represent "some of the best" subcontinental cooking "this side of Madras"; "bountiful portions" ("don't miss the six-foot-long dosai" for a group) are always "satisfying" and the "lunch buffet is a bargain"; meanwhile, the service is "friendly" and the "kitschy" space has a "funky-bamboo" and "vinyl-booth" "flair" to it; P.S. it's "MSB to those in-the-know."

### McKendrick's Steak House    26 | 22 | 24 | $46

*Park Place Shopping Ctr., 4505 Ashford Dunwoody Rd., NE (bet. Hammond Dr. & Perimeter Ctr.), 770-512-8888; www.mckendricks.com*

■ A "suburban Bone's" "without the markup" crow carnivores concerning this "top-notch" Dunwoody "old faithful" where an "attentive" staff serves up "tender" "brontosaurus"-size steaks and seafood "to savor" in a "clubby", "noisy" setting; though it's "less pretentious" and somewhat "easier to get into" than similarly "upscale" intown venues, wallet-watchers still advise "bring lots of $$$" or a "corporate charge card."

### MF Sushibar    27 | 24 | 19 | $35

*265 Ponce de Leon Ave. (Penn St.), 404-815-8844; www.mfsushibar.com*

■ "In a world of McSushi", "this is the real deal" swear "completely addicted" "slaves" of this "unsurpassed" Midtown Japanese that's "raised the bar" for sushi savants with "amazing" raw fin fare "so fresh it gives you a buzz"; the "wicked cool", "minimalist" decor "matches" the "cosmopolitan" crowd, and while cold fish carp about "appalling prices" and "too much attitude", a sea of supporters are "saving up their cash", since it's "worth every penny" (the "free valet parking" helps).

### Nan Thai Fine Dining    26 | 28 | 24 | $40

*1350 Spring St., NW (17th St.), 404-870-9933; www.nanfinedining.com*

■ The "absolutely stunning", "dramatic" space of this "refined, elegant" Midtown Thai newcomer was designed by the Johnson Studio (Canoe, BluePointe, Joël, among others) for maximum "wow factor", which is complemented here by the "perfect", "superbly presented" cuisine and "kind", "warm" service; chef/co-owner "Nan [Niyomkul] has outdone herself" at this "upscale sibling" of Tamarind where acolytes come to "worship her in all her glory", while others "would love to make this a regular spot, if [they] could afford it."

### NAVA    25 | 25 | 22 | $39

*Buckhead Plaza, 3060 Peachtree Rd., NW (W. Paces Ferry Rd.), 404-240-1984; www.buckheadrestaurants.com*

■ A "sophisticated" stalwart, this Buckhead Southwesterner satisfies with "creative", "vibrant" cuisine that's "fan-freakingtastic" "from beginning to end", served in a "pleasing", "upscale Santa Fe"–esque setting where "alfresco dining" by the babbling fountain is always a "treat"; the staff is "friendly yet thoroughly professional" and gives you the "royal treatment" – in sum, "they know what they're doing here."

### Nikolai's Roof　　　26 26 27 $72
*Hilton Atlanta, 255 Courtland St. (bet. Baker & Harris Sts.),*
*404-221-6362; www.nikolaisroof.com*
■ "Splurge on caviar" and "sip flavored vodkas" like a "noble" at this "elegant" "treat" atop Downtown's Hilton where the "fine" French and Continental cuisine with a Russian accent is simply "impeccable"; a "knowledgeable" staff "is on top of everything" in the "wonderful" room ("beautiful table settings"), which is overshadowed somewhat by "breathtaking" views of the skyline; it's a "spectacular" experience (and "tab") "you'll never forget."

### ONE.midtown kitchen ◗　　　21 26 19 $33
*559 Dutch Valley Rd. (Monroe Dr.), 404-892-4111;*
*www.onemidtownkitchen.com*
■ "Veteran restaurateur" Bob Amick "has done it again" with this "cooler-than-thou" Midtown New American "über-bistro" where there's "atmosphere to spare" in the "happening" bar and "edgy" dining room with "smokin'" decor; a "charming staff" serves up "superb" small plates and entrees that reflect chef Joey Masi's "cutting-edge prowess", and oenophiles and "novice enthusiasts" alike laud the "terrific" tiered wine list and "bottomless-glass" concept; "brush up on your sign language", wags warn, because "you can't hear a thing over the roar of the crowd."

### Pano's & Paul's ⊠　　　26 23 24 $56
*West Paces Ferry Shopping Ctr., 1232 W. Paces Ferry Rd.*
*(Northside Pkwy.), 404-261-3662;*
*www.buckheadrestaurants.com*
■ "Worth the splurge" for a "platinum-dining" experience, this "simply timeless" Buckhead beauty features chef Gary Donlick's "phenomenal" Continental cuisine ("nothing short of spectacular") and "flawless service"; the "rich and sumptuous" setting is like a "home away from home" for the "old-money crowd" and a "perfect celebration" spot, and while some find the scene "stuffy", others marvel how it "manages to stay fresh" after 25 years.

### Park 75　　　26 24 27 $54
*Four Seasons Atlanta, 75 14th St. (bet. Peachtree & W. Peachtree Sts.),*
*404-253-3840; www.fourseasons.com*
■ Fumbling fans give all "10 thumbs up" to this "elegant" New American in Midtown's Four Seasons for "unsurpassed service" from a "professional and caring staff"; meanwhile, "each bite" of the "superior" cuisine "melts in your mouth" (the "incredible brunch" is a "lesson in decadence"), and the "luxurious" room is "intimate" and "quiet" enough for either a "power lunch" or "special occasion"; P.S. for an "over-the-top dining experience", "try to eat in the kitchen."

### Rathbun's ⊠　　　– – – M
*Stove Works, 112 Krog St. (bet. Edgewood & Lake Aves.),*
*404-524-8280; www.rathbunsrestaurant.com*
Gratified gourmets gather to graze at this Inman Park newcomer, a striking industrial-chic space in a circa-1890 building that

also boasts a year-round patio with fountain; in the kitchen, chef-owner Kevin Rathbun (formerly with Nava) turns out New American specialties with a frequent foreign flair (such as his signature dish, lobster soft taco with poblanos and cascabel cream), while on-site pastry chef Kirk Parks (also of Nava) provides the happy endings (e.g. malted milk brûlée); the select cellar holds 90 boutique wines.

### RITZ-CARLTON BUCKHEAD DINING ROOM ⧄
| 28 | 27 | 28 | $76 |

*Ritz-Carlton Buckhead, 3434 Peachtree Rd., NE (Lenox Rd.), 404-237-2700; www.ritzcarlton.com*

■ "Those who like pampering" call this "jacket-only" special-occasion place at the Ritz-Carlton Buckhead the "gold standard" for "world-class dining"; the uniformly lauded locale showcases "endlessly creative" French cuisine "with a Japanese accent", "paired perfectly" with selections from an "extensive wine list"; the service is "flawless" from a staff that seems to "anticipate your every thought" and "not a thing is overlooked" as you sit in the "beautiful", "magical room", so although you need a "fat wallet" ("too expensive for an expense account!"), it's "well worth every penny."

### Seeger's ⧄
| 26 | 24 | 23 | $86 |

*111 W. Paces Ferry Rd. (E. Andrews Dr.), 404-846-9779; www.seegers.com*

☑ "Gastronauts" reach "nirvana" at this "world-class" Buckhead Continental where "über-chef" Guenter Seeger's "spectacular", "inspiring", "knockout" cuisine "pushes the edge" in a "romantic, quiet" setting; "stratospheric prices" and staffers seemingly "too in love with themselves" inspire "active hatred" in clamorous critics, but ardent admirers "can't say enough" about this destination and declare it one of "the finest dining experiences in any city."

### SIA'S ⧄
| 27 | 24 | 25 | $44 |

*The Shoppes of St. Ives, 10305 Medlock Bridge Rd. (Wilson Rd.), Duluth, 770-497-9727; www.siasrestaurant.com*

■ "Hats off to the kitchen" exclaim enamored enthusiasts of this "memorable" Asian-Southwestern in Duluth that "lays to rest the notion that you can't find gourmet food outside the Perimeter" with "excellent, innovative creations" that effervesce with "skillfully blended", "fantastic" flavors; owner "Sia [Moshk] is a charming and attentive host", and "friendly" "servers know what they're doing" in a "beautiful" room graced with "white tablecloths and candlelight" that "makes you forget you're in a strip mall."

### Sotto Sotto ⧄
| 26 | 19 | 21 | $34 |

*313 N. Highland Ave. (Elizabeth St.), 404-523-6678; www.sottosottorestaurant.com*

■ At this Inman Park "treasure", *amici* advise just "close your eyes and point" at the "well-rounded menu" of "modern" Northern Italian "heaven on a plate" ("divine homemade pastas", "risotto that shines"), presented in "perfect portions" and brought to table by an "efficient, knowledgeable" (though sometimes "snooty") staff; a "diverse, arty crowd" flocks to the "relaxed", "sexy" space for a "fashionable night out", and though "bad acoustics and close tables make for major noise on busy nights", the "great food makes it tolerable."

**South City Kitchen**  26 │ 22 │ 23 │ $34
*1144 Crescent Ave., NE (14th St.), 404-873-7358;*
*www.southcitykitchen.com*

■ "You don't even have to like Southern cooking" to appreciate the "unconventional" "taste of the New South" at this "excellent" Midtown "staple" where the "inventive, flavor-packed offerings" are said to be "suitable for royalty"; the staff is "pleasant" and "knowledgeable", and there's an "energetic" "let-your-hair-down atmosphere" in the "sleek", "ultramodern" renovated "old house", but the downstairs room can get "irritatingly loud", so many insiders "try to get a table upstairs."

**Sushi Avenue**  24 │ 14 │ 18 │ $22
*131 Sycamore St. (Church St.), Decatur, 404-378-0228*
*The Shops of West Ponce, 308 W. Ponce de Leon Ave.*
*(Ponce de Leon Pl.), Decatur, 404-378-8448*

◪ This Decatur Japanese twosome "has more than its share of regulars", thanks to "outstanding", "mega-fresh" sushi meals at "reasonable prices", served in "clean, casual" settings by a "super-friendly" staff ("even when we bring toddlers"); when it gets "crowded on weekends", though, service can be "terribly slow"; P.S. sources say the new branch on the Square boasts "significantly better" decor.

**TAMARIND**  27 │ 20 │ 24 │ $29
*80 14th St., NW (bet. Spring & Williams Sts.), 404-873-4888*

■ "Year after year", this "upscale", "dependable treat" located in Midtown has "maintained its reputation" as the "best Thai in town", with "simply superb", "perfectly prepared and presented" "food for the gods"; it's run by a "husband-and-wife team" who lend a "personal touch" to the "exotic", "uplifting setting", with help from a "friendly", "gracious" crew, and though it's "expensive" and the "parking's difficult", devotees agree it's "worth it"; P.S. new sibling Nan is located "just a few blocks north" in Midtown.

**Thumbs Up**  25 │ 16 │ 20 │ $11
*573 Edgewood Ave. (Bradley St., SE), 404-223-0690*

■ Inman Park's "classic diner" "makes it look easy" with "scrumptious", "serious" "all-American breakfasts" ("heavenly" pancakes, "fluffy" biscuits, "homemade jellies") and "friendly" service; there's a "neighborhood feel" and plenty of "people-watching" possibilities in the space, which is graced with "nice artwork", but "get there early to avoid weekend crowds", and don't forget to hit the ATM first.

**Tierra**  25 │ 19 │ 23 │ $31
*1425 Piedmont Ave., NE (Westminster Dr.), 404-874-5951;*
*www.tierrarestaurant.com*

■ At this "cozy" Pan-Latin "tucked away" in a Piedmont strip shopping mall, the array of "creative, sublime flavors" from an "ever-changing" yet "consistently delightful" seasonal menu "defies description" (though a "handy dandy glossary" helps); there's also an "interesting selection of South American wines", and if you "leave without dessert", cognoscenti caution, you will be "committing a serious crime"; the chefs/co-owners are "very involved" and their "friendly" staff "goes out of its way" to make your experience "pleasant and exceptional."

**Wisteria**                    25 | 22 | 23 | $33

*471 N. Highland Ave. (bet. Colquitt Ave. & Freedom Pkwy.), 404-525-3363*

■ The "food speaks for itself" at this "incredible" Inman Park "nouveau Southern" production, but fans can't help weighing in to praise chef Jason Hill's "extraordinary", "fabulously prepared" cuisine featuring "in-season ingredients and local specialties"; meanwhile, the "low-key" service is "spot-on", and the "intimate" space, "hidden from the hubbub", shines with an "understated elegance" – all of which leads groupies to gush "you can twist me around this vine anytime."

# Atlantic City

## TOP 5 FOOD RANKING

| | Restaurant | Cuisine |
|---|---|---|
| *25* | White House | Sandwich Shop |
| | Chef Vola's | Italian |
| *24* | Capriccio | Italian |
| *23* | Girasole | Southern Italian |
| *22* | Brighton | Steakhouse |

## ADDITIONAL NOTEWORTHY PLACES

|  |  |
|---|---|
| Alfonso's City Grill | American |
| Babalu Grill | Cuban |
| Dock's Oyster House | American/Seafood |
| Mixx | Latin/Asian Fusion |
| Suilan | Chinese/French |

| F | D | S | C |
|---|---|---|---|

**Alfonso's City Grill**    | – | – | – | E |
*3426 Atlantic Ave. (S. Boston Ave.), 609-340-0045*
In decadent AC, a city where simple isn't seen as chic, this new paean to American favorites set in a serene, non-casino space is a delightful surprise; the focused menu features meatloaf, chops and seafood, all given alluring accents.

**Babalu Grill**    | – | – | – | M |
*2020 Atlantic Ave. (Arkansas Ave.), 609-572-9898;*
*www.serioussteaks.com*
Deep in the heart of Casinoville, this newbie offers real Cuban family recipes, as well as potent mojitos and a colorful, spirited atmosphere; crowds are also coming to this AC trendsetter for the clever Cuba-tinis and dancing on Friday and Saturday nights.

**BRIGHTON STEAKHOUSE**    | 22 | 22 | 21 | $56 |
*Sands Hotel & Casino, Indiana Ave. (Brighton Park), 609-441-4300;*
*www.acsands.com*
☑ "One of the best AC steakhouses", this "upscale" spot in the Sands Casino Hotel is the place to go "if you're a beef eater" who's worked up an appetite at the gaming tables for "fabulous" cuts "cooked to perfection", "classy" earth-and-wine-toned decor and "pampering" service; while most maintain it's "worth the price", "coupon"-clippers cavil it's "overpriced" "unless you're comped."

**CAPRICCIO**    | 24 | 24 | 24 | $53 |
*Resorts Atlantic City Casino & Hotel, 1133 Boardwalk*
*(North Carolina Ave.), 609-340-6789*
■ Count on "guaranteed odds you'll hit the restaurant jackpot" at this "high-class" "hangout" in the Resorts Atlantic City that's "so great you'll forget you're in a casino"; the "delicious" Italian dishes are "lovingly prepared", "service is efficient", the "ambiance is pleasant", "the ocean view alone is worth the trip" and so what if it's "pricey" – "isn't that what AC is about?"

### CHEF VOLA'S ⊉    | 25 | 10 | 22 | $45 |
*111 S. Albion Pl. (Pacific Ave.), 609-345-2022*
■ "Getting in is part of the experience" at this "hidden" "cash-only" AC BYO (you "almost need a reference to be considered for a reservation"), but once you "find it and get seated" you'll be "treated like a high roller" with "humongous portions" of "some of the best traditional Italian food ever" served in a "memorable" "throwback-to-the-'50s" setting.

### DOCK'S OYSTER HOUSE    | 22 | 19 | 18 | $39 |
*2405 Atlantic Ave. (Georgia Ave.), 609-345-0092;*
*www.docksoysterhouse.com*
☑ "AC's grande dame of dining got a face-lift and – voilà! – she's a beauty" say admirers of this "old-fashioned seafood house" (circa 1897) who "escape the gambling scene" here, enjoying "fresh" fish and other "Traditional" American fare that "beats" "the usual casino" "buffets by a mile"; some say "service suffers when it's crowded", but the "pianist adds a nice touch" most nights.

### GIRASOLE ⊠    | 23 | 23 | 19 | $44 |
*Ocean Club Condos, 3108 Pacific Ave. (bet. Chelsea & Montpelier Aves.),*
*609-345-5554; www.girasoleac.com*
■ "After a spectacular night at the tables", dice-tossers "tired of casino food" head to this "hip and happening" Southern "Italian establishment (with a full bar)" whose name "translates as sunflower – and it does shine" with its "incredibly flavorful dishes"; an "off-the-boardwalk" location means it's "not as convenient as some other AC spots", but it's nevertheless an "unexpected pleasure in a mad resort town."

### Mixx    | – | – | – | VE |
*Borgata Hotel, Casino & Spa, 1 Borgata Way (Atlantic City Expwy., exit 1),*
*609-317-7249; www.theborgata.com*
Snuggled in the billion-dollar Borgata Casino, this Latin-Asian fusion nightclub-cum-restaurant falls under the culinary jurisdiction of Aaron Sanchez and Edwyn Ferrari; the setting of hot pinks, rich purples and cool blues seduces, the dishes sport come-hither monikers and the sushi is served on thick-cut glass plates.

### Suilan    | – | – | – | VE |
*Borgata Hotel, Casino & Spa, 1 Borgata Way (Atlantic City Expwy., exit 1),*
*609-317-7725; www.theborgata.com*
Philadelphia's queen of Chinese-French fusion, Susanna Foo, brings her culinary act to Atlantic City, where she's set a swanky stage for *très-chic* fare inside the plush Borgata Casino; Neptune reigns in the Frette-draped dining room set off by arches and dramatic art, especially in the seasonal seafood-box starters and roasted-fish entrees, but don't skip over the tea-smoked birds and Mongolian lamb pots on your way to the homemade sorbets.

### WHITE HOUSE ⊉    | 25 | 7 | 14 | $12 |
*2301 Arctic Ave. (Mississippi Ave.), 609-345-1564*
■ "One word – legendary" – is how succinct supporters sum up this "must-stop" sub shop in AC whose sandwiches (made with "delicious lean meat and soft, fresh bread") are beloved from "coast to coast"; "you may find a showbiz personality" seated next to you or among the "fabulous pictures of famous and not-so-famous customers that adorn the walls."

# Baltimore/Annapolis

## TOP 10 FOOD RANKING

| Restaurant | Cuisine |
|---|---|
| **28** Charleston | New American |
| **27** Prime Rib | Steakhouse |
| O'Leary's | Seafood |
| Joss Cafe | Japanese |
| Hampton's | New American |
| Les Folies | French Bistro |
| Bicycle | Eclectic |
| Linwoods | New American |
| Helmand | Afghan |
| Boccaccio | Northern Italian |

## ADDITIONAL NOTEWORTHY PLACES

| | |
|---|---|
| Cheesecake Factory | American |
| Clyde's | American |
| Corks | New American |
| Lewnes | Steakhouse |
| McCormick & Schmick's | Seafood |
| Mr. Bill's Terrace Inn | Seafood |
| Paul's Homewood Cafe | New American/Greek |
| Ruth's Chris | Steakhouse |
| Samos | Greek |
| Soigné | Asian/Mediterranean |

| F | D | S | C |
|---|---|---|---|

**Bicycle** ⬧ — 27 | 22 | 23 | $42

*1444 Light St. (bet. Birckhead St. & Fort Ave.), Baltimore, 410-234-1900; www.bicyclebistro.com*

☑ "Brilliant" chef-owner Barry Ramsey rolls right along with "amazing" Asian-tinged tastes that are "creative but not too out there" at this "dynamic" South Baltimore Eclectic; there's an "electric vibe" to the "funky" interior ("vastly improved" by a recent renovation), but ask the "attentive" if "oh-so-cool" staff "for a table in the courtyard" for truly "comfortable" dining, and if you think the "prices are frightening", "don't forget the 18 bottles of wine for $18."

**Boccaccio** — 27 | 22 | 24 | $51

*925 Eastern Ave. (bet. Exeter & High Sts.), Baltimore, 410-234-1322*

■ "Even simple dishes speak lovingly" at Baltimore's Top "Italian stallion", "Little Italy's most sophisticated" "institution", where "superior Northern" items ("have one of everything") and "old-style service" "turn any meal into" a "special occasion"; "formal", "elegant and unhurried", it "caters to upscale, loyal regulars" and "big-event celebrants" who sometimes "dine in the private wine room for small-group intimacy."

**CHARLESTON** ⌷  28 | 26 | 27 | $64
*1000 Lancaster St. (Exeter St.), Baltimore, 410-332-7373;*
*www.charlestonrestaurant.com*
■ Expect "culinary heaven" at this Inner Harbor East "favorite",
a "national-class" New American that's ranked No. 1 for Food
and Most Popular among Baltimore/Annapolis restaurants; chef-
owner Cindy Wolf's kitchen "fires on all cylinders", conjuring
"magical creations" with a "Southern touch" such as "divine
fried oysters" (not to mention "a to-die-for tasting menu" and an
"outstanding cheese cart"), while "highly professional service",
"posh environs" and co-proprietor Tony Foreman's "phenomenal"
wine list further secure its reputation as a place "to impress
and be impressed."

**CHEESECAKE FACTORY**  19 | 17 | 16 | $25
*Harborplace Pratt St. Pavilion, 201 E. Pratt St. (South St.), Baltimore,*
*410-234-3990; www.thecheesecakefactory.com*
⌷ At this mall-based, midpriced American, "everything is huge" –
"menu, portions, slabs of cheesecake and the lines" – but that
sums up its "gluttonous" appeal; "tons of choices", plenty of
"leftovers" "and, of course", their "amazing" signature dessert
have legions of hungry fans shrugging at the "get 'em in, get 'em
out" game plan and strategizing to cope with the "interminable"
waits ("put your name in and shop awhile").

**CLYDE'S** ◐  18 | 19 | 18 | $28
*10221 Wincopin Circle (Little Patuxent Pkwy.), Columbia, 410-730-2829;*
*www.clydes.com*
■ A "local tradition", this popular American bistro "gets the
basics right" with "affordable", "updated" tavern "classics",
"seasonally appropriate specials", a "hopping bar" and some of
the "best brunches", making it a "go-to place" for virtually any
age or occasion; the "warm, brass-and-wood", "Ralph Lauren–
fantasy" atmosphere is also a plus.

**Corks**  26 | 20 | 25 | $45
*1026 S. Charles St. (bet. E. Cross & W. Hamburg Sts.), Baltimore,*
*410-752-3810; www.corksrestaurant.com*
■ The "home away from home" for local "wine connoisseurs
(and those pretending to be)" is this "unassuming", "narrow"
South Baltimore row house, "transformed" into a restaurant
"unlike any other in town", where the "singing" New American
fare "rises to the challenge" of a 200-plus all-domestic list of
"unusual" selections "from small vintners"; with a "knowledgeable
staff" and printed "suggested pairings for each menu item",
"you'll not be at a loss for a delicious" sip with each "bite of
the sublime creations."

**HAMPTON'S**  27 | 28 | 27 | $68
*Harbor Court Hotel, 550 Light St. (bet. Conway & Lee Sts.),*
*Baltimore, 410-347-9744*
■ "Extraordinary in all respects", this "cultured" venue in the
"exquisite" Harbor Court Hotel boasts a "beautiful room" with
water views matched by "sublime" New American fare created by
a "master chef" and "beautifully presented" "under silver domes"
by a "thoughtful" staff that makes guests "feel so pampered"; to
many, it's "the ultimate place for the meal of a lifetime" – especially
"if someone else is paying."

### Helmand     27   20   23   $26

*806 N. Charles St. (bet. Madison & Read Sts.), Baltimore,
410-752-0311; www.helmand.com*

■ "Expand your mind" at this "effortlessly exotic" Mt. Vernon
"legend" that "herbivores and carnivores" alike "dream about";
the "polished, urban Afghan" offers an "explosion of flavors" in
"transforming" dishes like the "don't-miss" *kaddo borawni*
(pumpkin in garlic yogurt) at "reasonable, even cheap prices";
with "dressy theater adventurers" joining "casual" students in
"gustatory bliss", it's "very busy", so service is "a bit rushed."

### JOSS CAFE & SUSHI BAR     27   18   23   $31

*195 Main St. (Church Circle), Annapolis, 410-263-4688;
www.josscafe-sushibar.com*

☑ "Wait in line" to sit practically "on each others' laps, fighting for
attention" at this "odd, little" "upbeat" "place in the tourist zone"
where the raw fish "can turn non–sushi eaters into devotees"; the
"fresh and fabulous, world-class" cuts, "inventive concoctions"
and "delicious" "selection of cooked Japanese food" are "worth
the drive in rush-hour traffic."

### Les Folies Brasserie     27   22   25   $43

*2552 Riva Rd. (Aris Allen Blvd.), Annapolis, 410-573-0970;
www.lesfoliesbrasserie.com*

■ The "raw oysters are from all the best areas", and so is the
"dress-and-spend crowd" at this "slice of Paris" in Annapolis
serving a "daily selection of fresh shellfish", as well as other
"sumptuous" French "comfort food"; it's a "class act" "with great
attention to detail", where everything from the "copper-topped bar"
to the cassoulet is "authentic", except the staff – unlike your typical
Gallic servers, "they'll treat your valentine better than you do."

### Lewnes' Steakhouse     27   21   24   $47

*401 Fourth St. (Severn Ave.), Eastport, 410-263-1617*

☑ "Head and shoulders [and ribs and loins and flanks] above",
this "locally owned" Eastporter is "everything a steakhouse should
be": "classic", "clubby" and "comfy", serving "butter-topped
beef" "so good it'll make vegetarians regretful" – until they get
to those "divine" sides; "true Annapolitans sip drinks" at the
bar, skipping the "overpriced wine list" and shrugging over the
sometimes "uninspired service."

### Linwoods     27   25   25   $49

*McDonogh Crossroads, 25 Crossroads Dr. (McDonogh &
Reisterstown Rds.), Owings Mills, 410-356-3030; www.linwoods.com*

■ A "suburban-chic" "destination" for "haute Owings Mills"
denizens and "captains of industry", this "sleek", "sophisticated"
New American manages to be "trendacious" "without pretense",
thanks to "high-caliber", "hands-on management"; sit around the
central exhibition kitchen at the "chef's bar to watch them prepare"
"top-drawer" dishes for both the "fine dining and light fare" sides
– in other words, "you can spend megabucks or not."

### MCCORMICK & SCHMICK'S     21   20   19   $38

*Pier 5 Hotel, 711 Eastern Ave. (President St.), Baltimore, 410-234-1300;
www.mccormickandschmicks.com*

☑ There's "nothing fishy" about this "classy" chain outpost that
hooks fans with "seafood at its best", cooked in seemingly "a

hundred different ways"; some mutineers malign the "spotty" service and "lackluster presentation", but the "hands-down best" happy-hour "bargains" go over swimmingly well.

### Mr. Bill's Terrace Inn    ▽ 24 | 9 | 18 | $30
*200 Eastern Blvd. (Helena Ave.), Essex, 410-687-5996*
■ "Away from the tourists", "locals" work through "steamed crabs the real MD way – piled hot on brown paper, with beer", at this "true" joint; it's not one of those "cleanish, upscale-ish fancy places" – "it literally has no windows", and the only things passing for decor are the "kudos from sports legends all over the walls" – but "all that is set aside once you crack a claw"; P.S. "call ahead to check that day's" catch, and "go on weeknights or very early, or wait."

### O'LEARYS SEAFOOD    27 | 22 | 25 | $46
*310 Third St. (Severn Ave.), Eastport, 410-263-0884;*
*www.olearys-seafood.com*
■ "The staff's knowledge" is so "stellar" it's "almost not human" at this "seriously good" Eastporter where the waiters' many "suggestions on preparation of their ultra-fresh seafood choices are fabulous" and the "wine list is well chosen" to go with the "glorious" crispy grouper and other "excellent" piscatorial pleasures (the "lobster in cream will have you fumbling for your belt buckle"); "just make sure your credit-card limit is high."

### Paul's Homewood Cafe ⊠    21 | 14 | 20 | $24
*919 West St. (Taylor Ave.), Annapolis, 410-267-7891*
■ You can "feel the warmth" at this Annapolis New "American with Greek overtones" that's "not on the tourist path"; a reinvention of the "owners' dad's old lunch counter", it now boasts a "new dining room" where folks enjoy "good comfort food" and "watch all the action" as "happy regulars banter"; in short, it proves the adage that "good things come in small packages" – though its "big, rich cakes" are a "great" "exception to the rule."

### PRIME RIB    27 | 26 | 27 | $56
*Horizon House, 1101 N. Calvert St. (Chase St.), Baltimore,*
*410-539-1804; www.theprimerib.com*
■ "For a night of red meat and romance", put on "your little black dress" or jacket (mandatory, gentlemen) then "take your credit card and somebody sexy" to this "classic steakhouse" where "excellent jazz" musicians entertain and "tuxedoed waiters" "satisfy your ravenous appetite" with "gargantuan cuts" amid the "plush" if "faded glory" of "leopard-print-and-mirrors" decor that "makes you feel like the Rat Pack will walk in at any moment"; P.S. expect "long waits [even] with reservations."

### RUTH'S CHRIS STEAK HOUSE    24 | 22 | 23 | $53
*600 Water St. (bet. Gay St. & Market Pl.), Baltimore, 410-783-0033*
*301 Severn Ave. (3rd St.), Eastport, 410-990-0033*
*1777 Reisterstown Rd. (Hooks Ln.), Pikesville, 410-837-0033*
*www.ruthschris.com*
◪ It's "all about the beef and nothing but the beef" at these "excellent" chain links where "sinful steaks swimming in butter" are served by a "phenomenal" staff in a setting of "dark woodwork" with an "old-school boys' club–meets–power scene" "charm"; be forewarned, though, that you'll "pay big-time for the privilege" of partaking in that "divine" "mountain of meat."

### Samos ☒⌿   26  12  21  $18
*600 S. Oldham St. (Fleet St.), Baltimore, 410-675-5292*

■ "It's a minor miracle that a short-order kitchen can provide some of the area's best food" say supporters of this "real Greek for real Greeks" in (where else?) Greektown; the spartan decor is "not fancy", and "no reservations and wild popularity" mean a "long wait", but the cash-only BYO "will blow your taste buds away" with "outstanding gyros", "delicious salad" and "excellent calamari", prepared with a "warm spirit" in "big portions at reasonable prices" – just "be ready to bus your table to help."

### Soigné ☒   26  22  23  $46
*554 E. Fort Ave. (Jackson St.), Baltimore, 410-659-9898*

■ "Understanding food as an art" form, "au courant" chef-owner Edward Kim "pleases" patrons of this "gem" with a "dazzling" array of "phenomenal" Asian-Mediterranean "fusion" dishes from a menu that's "interesting" and "exciting" "but never weird" – and "not too exotic for blue-collar [South] Baltimore"; be warned, though, that the "intimate space" "can get a bit overwhelmed" at times "by crowds of cognoscenti", especially during "Wednesday night omakase tastings."

# Boston

## TOP 20 FOOD RANKING

| Restaurant | Cuisine |
|---|---|
| 29 Oishii | Japanese |
| 28 L'Espalier | New French |
| 27 Aujourd'hui | New French |
| Il Capriccio | Northern Italian |
| Olio | New American |
| Lumière | New French |
| Hamersley's Bistro | French Bistro/New American |
| Salts | New American |
| Coriander | French Bistro |
| Caffe Bella | Mediterranean |
| 26 Terramia | Italian |
| Blue Ginger | Asian Fusion |
| No. 9 Park | French/Italian |
| Trattoria a Scalinatella | Italian |
| Le Soir | French |
| Troquet | French Bistro |
| Radius | New French |
| Clio | New French/New American |
| Mistral | New French/Med. |
| Rialto | Mediterranean |

## ADDITIONAL NOTEWORTHY PLACES

| | |
|---|---|
| Bricco | Italian |
| Craigie Street Bistrot | French Bistro |
| Dalí | Spanish/Tapas |
| East Coast Grill | Seafood/Barbecue |
| Excelsior | New American |
| Franklin Café | New American |
| Helmand | Afghan |
| Icarus | New American |
| Jumbo Seafood | Chinese/Seafood |
| Lala Rokh | Persian |
| Legal Sea Foods | Seafood |
| Locke-Ober | Continental |
| Meritage | New American |
| Oleana | Mediterranean |
| Pigalle | French Bistro |
| Restaurant L | Asian Fusion |
| Ritz-Carlton Din. Rm. | French |
| Sage | Italian |
| Taranta | Southern Italian |
| UpStairs on the Square | New American |

## AUJOURD'HUI
27 | – | 27 | $72

*Four Seasons Hotel, 200 Boylston St. (bet. Arlington & S. Charles Sts.), 617-351-2071; www.fourseasons.com*

■ Now that this "luxe-to-the-max" "special-occasion" destination has reopened following a complete revamp, dinner at the Four Seasons is an even more "serenely" "transcendent experience" than before; indeed, it's "worth the mortgage on the house" to indulge in the "imaginative", "flawless" New French favorites, accompanied by a "sublime" wine selection and proffered with "unmatched" "refinement" in "gorgeous" surroundings; N.B. chef Edward Gannon left the kitchen post-*Survey*, and has been replaced by Jérôme Le Gras, fresh from the Four Seasons Tokyo.

## BLUE GINGER Ⓢ
26 | 22 | 24 | $47

*583 Washington St. (Rte. 16), Wellesley, 781-283-5790; www.ming.com*

■ "Actually surpassing all the hype", "celebrity" chef-owner Ming Tsai's "bustling" Asian fusion "winner" in Wellesley "wittily blends Eastern and Western cuisines" into "inspired" dishes that taste "even better than they look on the Food Network"; his "delectable offerings bring joy to the foodie in all of us", while the "cosmopolitan" ambiance and feng shui–correct layout provide a "refreshing break from the dime-a-dozen bistros" around town; the "only problem": "getting a reservation is torture", but you'll (eventually) be rewarded with a blue-ribbon experience.

## Bricco
22 | 20 | 19 | $40

*241 Hanover St. (bet. Cross & Richmond Sts.), 617-248-6800; www.bricco.com*

◪ At this "modern" ristorante/enoteca in the North End, there's a "good bar scene" that "begs you to come with friends" – and, even better, "food that's the equivalent of sex", from "tasty" antipasti to handmade pasta to the signature bread pudding, attracting gourmets as well as singles looking for a "great date place" (though penny-pinchers may blanch: "the tab adds up quickly"); N.B. Beantown culinary stars Rita d'Angelo and Marisa Iocco returned from their native Abruzzo post-*Survey* to revamp the menu.

## Caffe Bella Ⓢ
27 | 19 | 23 | $39

*19 Warren Ave. (Main St.), Randolph, 781-961-7729*

■ "Wow!" exclaim enthusiasts of this Mediterranean "jewel" set in ("surprise!") a Randolph strip mall; it's a "consistent winner" thanks to chef-owner Patrick Barnes' "fabulous", "absolutely tops" cooking ("complex without being fussy" and "innovative without straying from its true roots"), brought to table in a "rustic" room by a staff that "knows its business"; the only downsides: the "noise level" and "inevitable wait" to get seated (though a newly expanded bar area makes the delay more comfortable).

## Clio
26 | 25 | 24 | $66

*Eliot Suite Hotel, 370A Commonwealth Ave. (Mass. Ave.), 617-536-7200; www.cliorestaurant.com*

■ "World-class" chef-owner Ken Oringer is a "god" in the "food laboratory" (aka "the kitchen"), where he "invents" "absolutely divine" ways to "delight the palate"; the result is "Boston's most cutting-edge cuisine", an "extraordinary combination of taste sensations" that's "amazing from beginning to end" (despite portions so "skimpy" you may need to "have a sandwich" later);

his New French–New American creations are "served with class" by a "knowledgeable" staff in a "chic" Back Bay room; N.B. raw-fish finatics flip for its Uni sashimi bar.

### Coriander Bistro 🗷 | 27 | 21 | 25 | $45 |

*5 Post Office Sq. (bet. Billings & S. Main Sts.), Sharon, 781-784-5450; www.corianderbistro.com*

■ In the vast wasteland of the southern suburbs, this Sharon storefront stands out as a "lovely oasis"; chef-owner Kevin Crawley is "one of the most talented chefs" in the Boston area, which is evident after one bite of his "fantastic", "imaginative" French bistro dishes, and along with his spouse and co-owner, Jill, he "makes you feel like a million bucks"; the "wine list deserves kudos" too, as does the "intelligent and warm" staff, so though it's "pricey by neighborhood standards, if it were in the city it'd be a steal."

### Craigie Street Bistrot | ▽ 24 | 20 | 22 | $35 |

*5 Craigie Circle (bet. Brattle St. & Concord Ave.), Cambridge, 617-497-5511; www.craigiestreetbistrot.com*

◪ Fast embraced as a "promising" "new treasure" in the "02138 neighborhood", this "hidden" "reward" outside Harvard Square is a "real find" for "creative, urbane and satisfying" French fare (chef-owner Tony Maws has "got it right"); it's an "authentic re-creation of a Parisian bistro" through and through, from the "memorable", daily changing menu to the "cozy" "European"-style quarters to the service with a "Continental flair", though some early reports say it needs to "work out a few kinks."

### Dalí | 25 | 24 | 22 | $31 |

*415 Washington St. (Beacon St.), Somerville, 617-661-3254; www.dalirestaurant.com*

■ With its "sexy", "surrealistic" scene, this "tapas paradise" in Somerville manages to be "outrageous and romantic at the same time"; whether you come for a "memorable" "dinner for two" or a "boisterous" fiesta "for 12", you'll be treated to the "best" "authentic" Spanish cuisine in Boston, presented with "gracious, old-world" style; if you're on a budget, just watch what you order because the check "adds up fast."

### East Coast Grill & Raw Bar | 25 | 17 | 20 | $35 |

*1271 Cambridge St. (Prospect St.), Cambridge, 617-491-6568; www.eastcoastgrill.net*

■ Even "after all these years", this "dressed-down" Inman Square grill remains one of the "biggest food thrills in the Boston area", because chef-owner Chris Schlesinger's "passion comes through in each dish" – from the "way-cool raw bar" selections to the "amazing" "spiced-up seafood" to the "incredible" oak-smoked pit BBQ, all served by an "exceptionally friendly" staff that's "efficient" "even under pressure"; though it "gets so loud you can't hear yourself think", this "exciting" "hot spot" is an "entrenched fave" for good reason; N.B. check out the Latin brunch on Sundays.

### Excelsior | – | – | – | E |

*272 Boylston St. (bet. Arlington & S. Charles Sts.), 617-426-7878; www.excelsiorrestaurant.com*

Designer Adam Tihany revamped a Back Bay site overlooking the Public Garden to create this ultra-luxe showcase – dominated by a jaw-dropping, 600-label-strong "wine tower" – for Lydia Shire (über-chef of Locke-Ober) and her playfully sophisticated New

American fare; a ritzy crowd ranging from debutantes to grandes dames (and gents) gathers here to indulge in her lusty creations incorporating edible exotica from all over the globe, while old faithfuls return regularly for her legendary lobster pizza.

**Franklin Café** ◗                                    25 | 17 | 19 | $31
*278 Shawmut Ave. (Hanson St.), 617-350-0010*
■ "Dark, difficult and delicious" say the "city folk" who love this "hip" yet "unpretentious" South End "hangout" that's always packed with a "lively crowd" lined up for its "incredible" New American dishes; the "wait can be unbearable", though once you finally secure a table, "you're never rushed out" by the "friendly" servers; what's more, the "prices are so reasonable", and the kitchen's open till 1:30 AM every night.

**HAMERSLEY'S BISTRO**                           27 | 24 | 24 | $54
*553 Tremont St. (Clarendon St.), 617-423-2700;*
*www.hamersleysbistro.com*
■ "Much like the fabled *Mary Poppins*", this "perennial favorite" in the South End is "practically perfect in every way"; chef-owner Gordon Hamersley's "passion for great food" is obvious after one bite of his "stellar" yet "earthy" French–New American fare (his signature roast chicken "pleases even fancy-food fanatics"), served by a "welcoming" staff in an "intimate", "inviting" space; "haute prices" notwithstanding, this "neighborhood star turned world-class restaurant" "continues to shine."

**Helmand**                                         26 | 22 | 20 | $30
*143 First St. (Bent St.), Cambridge, 617-492-4646*
■ Promising a most "enchanting" evening, this "unique dining experience" in East Cambridge entices eaters with its "magical" Afghan specialties infused with "out-of-this-world flavors"; from the "outstanding flatbread" to the "divine" baby pumpkin appetizer to the "unbelievable" *qabelee* (rice baked with lamb shanks and raisins), the dishes accurately "reflect" the motherland's location "halfway between the Middle East and India"; after all, the "owner's brother is Afghanistan's president" – "how can it not be authentic?"

**Icarus**                                          26 | 24 | 24 | $51
*3 Appleton St. (bet. Arlington & Berkeley Sts.), 617-426-1790;*
*www.icarusrestaurant.com*
■ While it seems to be drawing "less attention than its trendier neighbors", "all restaurants should strive" to be as "classy" as this "winged wonder", an "elegant" "institution" in the South End that "soars head and shoulders above most"; chef-owner Chris Douglass' "sophisticated" New American dishes are "deftly conceived and executed", and they're served by a "fabulous" staff that always "goes the extra bit to please" in a "refined" room that's "ideal for quiet conversation."

**IL CAPRICCIO** ⊠                                 27 | 22 | 25 | $50
*888 Main St. (Prospect St.), Waltham, 781-894-2234*
■ "Even the pickiest gourmets love" this Waltham Italian "gem"; it "totally wows" foodies with Richard Barron's "meticulously prepared" specialties from the Northern region of The Boot ("do not miss the mushroom soufflé"), "spectacular wine list" and "accommodating" service; though the space is a "little cramped" and the prices are "fairly tough on the wallet", "oh, mama mia" is it "worth it."

### Jumbo Seafood
24 | 10 | 18 | $22

*7 Hudson St. (bet. Beach & Kneeland Sts.), 617-542-2823* ◐
*10 Langley Rd. (Center St.), Newton, 617-332-3600*
*www.jumboseafoodrestaurant.com*

■ "Seafood is the name of the game" at this "authentic" Chinatown "favorite", voted the "best Chinese restaurant in Boston"; the "fish could not be any fresher", as it "goes from swimming in the tank to your plate in minutes" (and the place is "justifiably famous for its lobster preparations" and "scrumptious" "salty, spicy squid"); "don't look too closely around" the bare-bones digs – just focus on all the "fabulous" "traditional" dishes with "jumbo taste" brought by "quick and efficient" servers at "very reasonable prices"; N.B. a second location opened post-*Survey* in Newton.

### Lala Rokh
23 | 22 | 24 | $37

*97 Mt. Vernon St. (Charles St.), 617-720-5511; www.lalarokh.com*

■ As if "you've come to eat" in a private home, the staff "bends over backward to make patrons happy" at this "old townhouse on Beacon Hill", where the "adventurous are rewarded" with "lovingly prepared" Persian food; the "extremely attentive servers help customers navigate" the "exotic" menu, presented in an "inviting", "tranquil oasis" (with "original artwork") that's "recommended for a romantic dinner."

### LEGAL SEA FOODS
22 | 17 | 19 | $33

*Copley Pl., 100 Huntington Ave. (bet. Dartmouth & Exeter Sts.), 617-266-7775*
*Long Wharf, 255 State St. (Atlantic Ave.), 617-227-3115*
*26 Park Plaza (Columbus Ave.), 617-426-4444*
*South Shore Plaza, 250 Granite St. (I-95, exit 6), Braintree, 781-356-3070*
*Burlington Mall, 1131 Middlesex Tpke. (Rte. 128), Burlington, 781-270-9700*
*5 Cambridge Ctr. (bet. Main & 6th Sts.), Cambridge, 617-864-3400*
*20 University Rd. (Eliot St.), Cambridge, 617-491-9400*
*The Mall at Chestnut Hill, 43 Boylston St. (Hammond Pond Pkwy.), Chestnut Hill, 617-277-7300*
*50-60 Worcester Rd./Rte. 9 (Ring Rd.), Framingham, 508-766-0600*
*Northshore Mall, 210 Andover St./Rte. 114 (Rte. 128), Peabody, 978-532-4500*
*www.legalseafoods.com*

◪ Voted the Most Popular restaurant in town, this "quintessential Boston seafood experience" "won't let you down" when you're looking for finny fare prepared "just the way you want it"; whether you're "taking out-of-town visitors" or "mom and dad", you can "depend" on this "solid performer"; sure, it's a "chain", but if you can "ignore the tourists" and "wade through" the sea of "crowds" to "catch a table", you'll get "good, fresh fish – enough said."

### Le Soir
26 | 23 | 24 | $52

*51-53 Lincoln St. (bet. Chester & Columbus Sts.), Newton, 617-965-3100; www.lesoirbistro.com*

■ "Escoffier would be proud" of chef-owner Mark Allen (ex Ritz-Carlton Dining Room), because "this guy can cook", and what comes out of his Newton Highlands kitchen is "out-of-this-world" French fare that "rivals almost any in Boston"; the Gallic "classics" are proffered in a "classy manner" in an "intimate", "elegant" bistro environment, leaving the smitten swooning "thank heaven" for this "memorable" taste of "Paris in the suburbs."

## L'ESPALIER 图 28 | 27 | 27 | $87

*30 Gloucester St. (bet. Commonwealth Ave. & Newbury St.),*
*617-262-3023; www.lespalier.com*

■ "To remind yourself that elegance still exists in the world", "indulge" in the "pure luxury" provided by this "exceptional" "class act" set in an "exquisite" townhouse in the Back Bay; chef-owner Frank McClelland is a "genius", "layering textures and flavors in such brilliant ways" that "you're almost intoxicated" by his "sublime" "haute" New French masterpieces; the "flawless" staff "treats everyone like a VIP", so despite prices that could rival "airfare to Paris", this is the "crème de la crème" of Boston.

## Locke-Ober 图 21 | 24 | 22 | $60

*3 Winter Pl. (bet. Tremont & Washington Sts.), 617-542-1340;*
*www.locke-ober.com*

◪ "It's not your father's Locke-Ober", but it still "tastes of old money", but "you're transported back in time" to "Brahmin Boston at its best", yet owner Lydia Shire has "revitalized" this "elegant" Downtown "landmark" by adding some modern touches to the Continental menu while "maintaining some traditional favorites"; still, trendoids find it "too stuffy" and gripe tabs "break the bank."

## Lumière 27 | 23 | 24 | $51

*1293 Washington St. (Waltham St.), Newton, 617-244-9199;*
*www.lumiererestaurant.com*

■ "Everything sparkles" at this "suave", "sophisticated" West Newton star that "shines like a beacon in the suburbs"; chef-owner Michael Leviton's "stellar" New French preparations guarantee an "amazing culinary experience" that's enhanced by the "gorgeous surroundings" and "gracious" service; granted, it's awfully "tough to get a reservation", but if you're lucky enough to snag a booking, you'll "thank heaven" for this "high-class" "enchantress."

## Meritage 图 – | – | – | VE

*Boston Harbor Hotel, 70 Rowes Wharf (Atlantic Ave.), 617-439-3995;*
*www.meritagetherestaurant.com*

Reinventing the Boston Harbor Hotel's dining room, chef Daniel Bruce indulges his passion for pairing vino with victuals; his creative, seasonally changing New American menu is organized by type of wine, such as 'sparklers' (ideal with oysters), 'full-bodied whites' (with, say, lobster) or 'fruity reds' (poultry, perhaps?); what's more, each dish is available as a small or large plate, the better for oenophiles to sample more well-matched options.

## Mistral 26 | 25 | 23 | $58

*223 Columbus Ave. (bet. Berkeley & Clarendon Sts.), 617-867-9300;*
*www.mistralbistro.com*

◪ "Where the elite meet to greet and eat", this "see-and-be-seen" scene pulls in "sexy" "hipsters" to the South End–Back Bay border, because "you just can't help feeling fabulous" here; chef-owner Jamie Mammano continues to produce "outstanding", "innovative" French-Med dishes, though surveyors suspect some servers "think they're the star attraction."

## No. 9 Park 图 26 | 23 | 25 | $58

*9 Park St. (bet. Beacon & Tremont Sts.), 617-742-9991; www.no9park.com*

■ At her "tony" Beacon Hill "class act", "first-rate" chef-owner Barbara Lynch's "impeccable" cooking "sparkles" like the golden dome of the "nearby State House"; she "works magic" with her Country French and Italian dishes, constantly creating "new wonders", and the "talented sommelier" has assembled "one of Boston's most adventurous wine lists"; enhancing the "memorable" experience are the "stylish" setting and "exquisite" service, making any meal "feel like a celebration."

### OISHII 29 | 13 | 19 | $34
*612 Hammond St. (Boylston St.), Chestnut Hill, 617-277-7888*
*Mill Vlg., 365 Boston Post Rd./Rte. 20 (Concord Rd.), Sudbury, 978-440-8300*
■ Even "sushi snobs" agree that the "heaven on rice" at this "tiny" twosome in Chestnut Hill and Sudbury is the "best" around – in fact, with the "freshest fish in town", the pair was voted No. 1 for Food in the Boston area; the "creative maki and hand rolls are exceptional", "taking a favorite item to a whole new level", while the omakase extravaganza elicits a chorus of "oh my Gods"; "seating is sardinelike" to the extreme, but it's worth it to "watch the chef create works of art" that rival even "Nobu's."

### Oleana 26 | 21 | 22 | $41
*134 Hampshire St. (bet. Columbia & Prospect Sts.), Cambridge, 617-661-0505; www.oleanarestaurant.com*
■ "Carried away on a magic carpet ride" of "exotic" Mediterranean flavors, enchanted enthusiasts of this "delightful" spot near Inman Square exclaim it's "as though our taste buds won the lottery"; indeed, chef-partner Ana Sortun is clearly "not afraid to challenge your palate", and she "succeeds" with "well-conceived" dishes that evoke "sun-soaked" climes; what's more, the atmosphere indoors is "sophisticated, yet warm and comfortable", though the hottest tables are outside, on a patio that feels like an urban "oasis."

### OLIO ☒ 27 | 16 | 23 | $44
*655 Washington St. (Rte. 128, exit 2A), Canton, 781-821-2396; www.oliorestaurant.com*
■ "Lucky Canton" – with chef-owner Paul Turano now in charge, this "exquisite" fave "hasn't skipped a beat"; the New American fare is still "on par with the best Downtown", making grateful guests glad to have "such a quality" "find" south of Boston, while the service is "casual yet professional"; the olive-green scene is "relaxing", though with only 30 seats, it's not much bigger than a "sardine can."

### Pigalle 26 | 21 | 24 | $54
*75 S. Charles St. (bet. Stuart St. & Warrenton Pl.), 617-423-4944*
■ "Ooh-la-la", "this is a winner" coo devotees of this acclaimed "performer" in the Theater District, a "sophisticated" bistro that's a "testament to doing it right"; Marc Orfaly "really cares" about pleasing his guests, which he does "beautifully" by "seductively" putting a "contemporary twist" on timeless French classics; his "outstanding" creations are turned out by a "smart, well-informed" staff in an "intimate" room, a "romantic hideaway" that's best enjoyed with "someone you love"; "bravo!"

### Radius ☒ 26 | 25 | 25 | $62
*8 High St. (bet. Federal & Summer Sts.), 617-426-1234; www.radiusrestaurant.com*
■ "Feel like a master of the universe" at this "sumptuous" spot in the Financial District; chef-owner Michael Schlow "deserves to

wear the tall hat" because his "cutting-edge" New French interpretations are "exquisite"; "top-notch" "across the board", the place pulls in a "stylish crowd" and power "suits" with its "high-energy", "minimalist" design and "professional" service; "be prepared to drop some dough", but dinner here is "not just a meal – it's an event" that "everyone should indulge in" since it's "one of the best in the city."

### Restaurant L ☒　　　　　　　– | – | – | E
*Louis Boston, 234 Berkeley St. (Newbury St.), 617-266-4680; www.louisboston.com*
Located on the first floor of swanky Back Bay department store Louis Boston, this sleek Asian-oriented eatery replaces the breezier, Mediterranean-influenced Café Louis; in a spare, angular setting of black, white and russet hues with brushed stainless-steel accents, exec chef Pino Maffeo whips up whimsically presented delicacies (sake-cured salmon, wok-seared lobster in coconut broth) for chic, black-clad forty- and fiftysomethings as they sip the high-end sakes that round out an otherwise traditional wine list.

### Rialto　　　　　　　　26 | 25 | 25 | $57
*Charles Hotel, 1 Bennett St. (University Rd.), Cambridge, 617-661-5050; www.rialto-restaurant.com*
■ "Be still my beating heart" swoon the smitten who've just savored a "knock-your-socks-off" dinner at the Charles Hotel's flagship dining room, an "ethereal" experience that's "lost none of its sparkle" over the years; the "elegantly understated" eatery attracts an "upper-crust-meets-Cambridge-academic" crowd for "sublime" Mediterranean fare that "sings with every bite"; you may need to "bring an extra credit card", but it's "worth every penny" to "worship" at "Jody Adams' shrine."

### Ritz-Carlton Dining Room　　　　– | – | – | VE
*Ritz-Carlton Boston, 15 Arlington St. (Newbury St.), 617-536-5700; www.ritz-carlton.com*
After a multimillion-dollar face-lift last year, the Back Bay's grande dame is back with a brighter, more youthful look (though, rest assured, its famous cobalt-blue crystal chandeliers remain); new top toque Tony Esnault confidently executes a French menu that intersperses beloved classics (such as the legendary Grand Marnier soufflé) with contemporary creations, while early reports indicate that the polished Ritz service remains ever so white-gloved; N.B. jacket required, *naturellement*.

### Sage ☒　　　　　　　　26 | 19 | 23 | $43
*69 Prince St. (Salem St.), 617-248-8814; www.sageboston.com*
■ "Good things come in small packages" is a proverb proved by this "teeny" "treasure" "tucked away" in the North End; a "chef's chef", Anthony Susi tantalizes taste buds with his "changing menu" of "fabulous", "gourmet" Northern Italian and New American fare, and he'll make you feel "like you've come to his home and he's cooking just for you"; the "downside: tight seating."

### Salts ☒　　　　　　　　27 | 22 | 25 | $45
*798 Main St. (Windsor St.), Cambridge, 617-876-8444; www.saltsrestaurant.com*
■ Even under new ownership, this Cambridge bistro remains its old, "intimate" self: though its Eastern European accents have given way to French overtones, the New American menu is still

"inventive enough to delight without being overwrought", while the interior is as "tasteful, understated" and, well, "cramped" as ever.

### Taranta
24 | 20 | 24 | $40

*210 Hanover St. (Cross St.), 617-720-0052; www.tarantarist.com*
■ "Not your run-of-the-mill" "red-sauce" factory in the North End, this "adorable" "gem" of a triplex thrills the taste buds with "highly imaginative" Southern Italian dishes that "reach the heights"; appreciative admirers attest that "everything is made with care", and enhancing the "lovely" dining experience is a "knowledgeable" staff that's always "ready to help."

### Terramia
26 | 17 | 23 | $41

*98 Salem St. (Parmenter St.), 617-523-3112; www.terramiaristorante.com*
■ "Go next door if you want spaghetti and meatballs", but if you're seeking more "inventive" Italian fare in the North End, keep this "outstanding" ristorante "on your short list"; the homemade pastas are "incredible" and other dishes "expertly" prepared, so even though you're "scrunched" into a "phone booth–sized" storefront, admirers assert "we love it – no matter how crowded."

### Trattoria a Scalinatella
26 | 23 | 25 | $48

*253 Hanover St., 2nd fl. (bet. Cross & Richmond Sts.), 617-742-8240*
■ Get "as romantic as two people can in a public place" at this "intimate" cocoon "hidden one story up from the hubbub of Hanover Street"; "superb in every way", it pairs "fabulous", "gourmet" Italian fare (including "pastas that taste like heaven") with an "exceptional wine list" and a "first-class" staff well versed in "old-country hospitality", making for a "special treat" in the North End; N.B. minor changes may be in store for the place now that owner Paolo Diecidue has opened his new venture, Via Valverde, two doors down.

### Troquet ◗
26 | 21 | 25 | $48

*140 Boylston St. (bet. S. Charles & Tremont Sts.), 617-695-9463*
■ A "must" for "anyone who loves wine", this "charming" French bistro in the Theater District is an "oenophile's delight", "perfectly matching" "fabulous" plates (including an "exquisite cheese course") with "flights of wine"; owners Chris and Diane Campbell are "wonderful hosts", and their "unpretentious", "savvy" staff is "truly interested" in helping "diners enjoy a good evening"; "Bacchus would be proud."

### UpStairs on the Square ◗
– | – | – | VE

(fka UpStairs at the Pudding)
*91 Winthrop St. (JFK St.), Cambridge, 617-864-1933; www.upstairsonthesquare.com*
The former UpStairs at the Pudding relocated to this dramatically over-the-top space in the heart of Harvard Square last year; the casual Monday Club Bar downstairs serves lighter meals while the upstairs Soirée Room pulls out all the stops with creative New American fare; co-owners Mary-Catherine Deibel and Deborah Hughes recently lured local lights Amanda Lydon and Susan Regis into the kitchen.

# Charlotte

## TOP 10 FOOD RANKING

| Restaurant | Cuisine |
|---|---|
| **27** Barrington's | New American |
| Toscana | Northern Italian |
| McNinch House | Eclectic |
| McIntosh's | Steakhouse/Seafood |
| **26** Sullivan's | Steakhouse |
| Volare | Italian |
| **25** Coffee Cup | Soul Food |
| Upstream | Seafood |
| Noble's | Med./New French |
| Carpe Diem | New American |

## ADDITIONAL NOTEWORTHY PLACES

| | |
|---|---|
| Blue Rest. & Bar | Mediterranean |
| Bonterra | New American |
| Guytano's | N. Italian/New American |
| LaVecchia's | Seafood |
| Luce | Northern Italian |
| Mickey & Mooch | Steakhouse |
| Pewter Rose | Eclectic |
| Sonoma | Californian |
| Woodlands | Indian/Vegetarian |
| Zebra Rest./Wine Bar | New French |

| F | D | S | C |
|---|---|---|---|

### BARRINGTON'S ☒

| 27 | 21 | 24 | $40 |
|---|---|---|---|

*FoxCroft Shopping Ctr., 7822 Fairview Rd. (bet. Carmel & Colony Rds.), 704-364-5755; www.barringtonsrestaurant.com*

■ Rated No. 1 for Food in Charlotte, this "tiny gem tucked away on the side of a strip center" near SouthPark is the brainchild of "talented" chef-owner Bruce Moffett, whose "innovative" New American menu "will capture your loyalty after just one visit"; his "simply marvelous" dishes are served in a "charming", rustic-chic room with a "friendly" vibe by a "helpful, informative" staff; even if the "tight quarters may promote eavesdropping", it's "all worth it when the food packs such a powerful punch."

### Blue Restaurant & Bar ☒

| – | – | – | M |
|---|---|---|---|

*Hearst Tower, 214 N. Tryon St. (5th & 6th Sts.), 704-927-2583; www.bluerestaurantandbar.com*

Few are blue at this Uptown yearling in the Hearst Tower; as a matter of fact, foodies are fond of its broader-than-usual Med-mix menu, on which Moroccan and Tunisian dishes mingle with Italian, French and Spanish specialties (there's an equally far-flung 250-label wine list as well); stained-glass oil lamps and bronze sculptural flourishes lend an exotic feel to the spacious sunken dining room, and live jazz keeps toes tapping five nights a week.

**Bonterra Dining & Wine Room** ⌧        23 | 25 | 22 | $45
*1829 Cleveland Ave. (E. Worthington Ave.), 704-333-9463;*
*www.bonterradining.com*
■ "We love the New South!" sing acolytes who worship at this
"beautifully redone old church" in Dilworth, which draws the
faithful with its "fabulous" wine list (400 selections by the bottle,
"200 by the glass – oh my!") and a "creative" New American
menu that's "exceptional from beginning to end" (don't miss
the "dynamite fried lobster tail"); enhanced by a "wonderfully"
"unique" atmosphere and "knowledgeable, personable" service,
it's "the place to be for all bons vivants in Charlotte."

**Carpe Diem** ⌧        25 | – | 22 | $34
*1535 Elizabeth Ave. (Travis Ave.), 704-377-7976;*
*www.carpediemrestaurant.com*
■ A "well-heeled, hip" crowd gathers at this Elizabeth "gem" for
"distinctive, sophisticated" New American dinners ("scrumptious
appetizers", pistachio-encrusted trout, "decadent desserts")
that are "interesting without being scary"; though a post-*Survey*
move finds sibling proprietors Tricia Maddrey and Bonnie Warford
now overseeing a sunny, sleek art-nouveau space, their enterprise
remains "one of the truly original places in Charlotte", so supporters
simply state "seize the meal!"

**Coffee Cup, The**        25 | 8 | 19 | $9
*914 S. Clarkson St. (W. Morehead St.), 704-375-8855;*
*www.coffeecupsoul.com*
■ "Buttoned-down bankers meet the hard-hat crowd" at this
"down-home" Uptown "institution" over "superior" meat-and-two
(vegetables, that is, "the way they're supposed to be – cooked
to death") and fried chicken so "good" "we'd put it up against
anyone's, even mom's"; it may be a "don't-look-in-the-kitchen"
kind of place, but it prepares the "best soul food in Charlotte" and,
besides, "where else can you order pig's feet?"

**GUYTANO'S** ⌧        23 | 24 | 22 | $38
*6000 Fairview Rd. (J.A. Jones Dr.), 704-554-1114;*
*www.guytanos.com*
◪ Its "flashy" "Vegas-like" atmosphere (the "dining room ceiling
alone is worth a visit") distinguishes this "upscale" SouthPark
destination, which presents "imaginative" Tuscan and New
American dishes in "artful" ways; supporters praise it as a
"much-needed injection of modernity" into the city's restaurant
scene, but skeptics who find the decor as "overwrought" (if not
"gaudy") as the "overblown" food ("oversauced, overgarlicked")
ask "can you say 'overpriced?'"

**LAVECCHIA'S SEAFOOD GRILLE** ⌧        24 | 23 | 21 | $39
*225 E. Sixth St. (College St.), 704-370-6776;*
*www.lavecchias.com*
◪ Accented with enormous "sculptures of fish hanging from the
ceiling", this "happening", "energetic" Uptown seafood sanctuary
is where the "beautiful people" "dress to impress", "guzzle
martinis" and dine on "amazing, melt-in-your-mouth" finny
fare "prepared with verve"; fans urge "don't miss it" (you'll
"feel like you're in New York City"), but foes frown it's "like eating
in a barn, only not as quiet" ("bring your earplugs and forget
about meaningful conversation").

## Luce ☒    – | – | – | VE
*214 N. Tryon St. (bet. 5th & 6th Sts.), 704-344-9222*
The small and stylish sibling of Toscana, this Uptown Northern Italian newcomer (pronounced 'loo-cheh') is decked out with Murano glass and travertine tiles and peopled with patrons nearly as beautiful as the imported fixtures; handmade pastas and grilled meats star on its Tuscan menu, which ranges from traditional to contemporary and is accompanied by a handsome list of wines from The Boot.

## MCINTOSH'S STEAKS & SEAFOOD ☒    27 | 23 | 27 | $47
*1812 South Blvd. (East Blvd.), 704-342-1088; www.mcintoshs1.com*
■ Locally owned and offering the "best steaks in Charlotte" ("eat your heart out, Morton's"), this "warm, personal" South End surf 'n' turfer is a perennial "favorite" because owner Greg McIntosh "knows how to treat his guests"; though you "can't beat" the beef, schools of surveyors urge "don't pass up the seafood either" (the "fried lobster tail is a must"); "they do things the right way" here (the "professional" "staff goes beyond" the call of duty), making for an "all-around wonderful" evening that's "worth" the "big dollars."

## MCNINCH HOUSE ☒    27 | 27 | 28 | $89
*511 N. Church St. (bet. 8th & 9th Sts.), 704-332-6159*
■ Utterly "romantic" and "intimate", this "exquisite" "Victorian" "jewel" quartered in a "private home" Uptown is where many prospective grooms in Charlotte "pop the question"; all patrons, though, can expect "total pampering", from the host who "tells stories of the local history" to the "attentive" staff that serves an "outstanding" six-course prix fixe Eclectic menu; "from soup to dessert", this is a "uniquely" "memorable" experience where "everything is taken care of for you", so just "sit back and enjoy."

## MICKEY & MOOCH ❶    23 | 23 | 21 | $31
*Arboretum, 8128 Providence Rd. (Pineville-Matthews Rd.), 704-752-8080*
*9723 Sam Furr Rd. (I-77), Huntersville, 704-895-6654; www.mickeyandmooch.com*
■ A "chophouse that's like a ray of sunshine in the valley of mediocre chains" is how partisans describe this pair of '40s-style "finds" with "slick Rat Pack–era" decor ("you almost expect Frank Sinatra to come strolling around the bar"); it's a "great place for a great meal" – "everything we tried was excellent", plus the portions are "large" (expect to "bring a doggy bag" home) – and because it "feels like fine dining without the high prices", it's one of the "best values in town."

## Noble's ☒    25 | 26 | 24 | $45
*3 Morrocroft Ctr. at SouthPark, 6801 Morrison Blvd. (Cameron Valley Pkwy.), 704-367-9463; www.noblesrestaurant.com*
■ "So many things are going on in the decor and on the plate" that you may be "exhausted by the time you leave" this "lavish" SouthPark "heavy hitter", but it's worth the effort because the European "country"-style setting is so "stunning" and the Mediterranean–New French fare "superb" and "innovative" (the "fried oyster salad is a must-try"); enhanced by an "excellent wine list" and "knowledgeable yet not overbearing" service, it adds up to a "charming" experience.

### Pewter Rose
23 | 24 | 21 | $30

*1820 South Blvd. (East Blvd.), 704-332-8149; www.pewterrose.com*

■ "Delightfully funky", this South End bistro quartered in a turn-of-the-(last)-century textile warehouse is a "bohemian" haunt appointed with massive wood beams, soaring 30-ft. ceilings, walls of paned glass and lots of colorful knickknacks; it's a "cool" backdrop for a "contemporary" Eclectic menu and equally "astounding wine list" served by a "solid" staff; "very popular" and a "great meeting place to people-watch", it's become a "Charlotte tradition."

### Sonoma ☒
24 | 23 | 23 | $38

*129 W. Trade St. (Church St.), 704-377-1333; www.sonomabistro.com*

■ Demonstrating a "great vision for food", this "super", "wine-centric" Uptown bistro features a menu so "witty" that it "makes you want to eat here every day"; that wouldn't be difficult, as its roster of "exciting", "modern" Californian dishes changes almost every week, though it's always based on "outstanding" local ingredients; just as "stylish" as the cooking is the spare, "almost edgy" interior, populated by a "truly dedicated" staff.

### SULLIVAN'S STEAKHOUSE
26 | 25 | 26 | $45

*1928 South Blvd. (Tremont Ave.), 704-335-8228; www.sullivansteakhouse.com*

■ The "bar is attractive, as are the regulars", at this "blow-out red-meat extravaganza" in the South End that showcases "melt-in-your-mouth steaks" and a "fantastic wine list"; the portions are "huge", so you may want to "skip lunch (and breakfast too)", the better to tuck into an "exceptional" bone-in Kansas City strip hauled out by "attentive" servers who "treat you real nice"; "upbeat" and "atmospheric", this is a "great place for a hungry, happy table of carnivores."

### TOSCANA ☒
27 | 24 | 25 | $41

*Specialty Shops on the Park, 6401 Morrison Blvd. (Roxborough Rd.), 704-367-1808*

■ Worth a visit just "for the basket of crusty warm bread and white beans, garlic and herbs drenched in olive oil that start every meal", this "comfortable, welcoming" Northern Italian in SouthPark will "make you feel like you're back in the homeland" thanks to "sublime", "authentic" cooking served by "charming waiters with accents"; a "real treat" ("coming here is as much an escape as a mini-vacation"), it's also a "great date place", especially "out on the romantic patio."

### UPSTREAM
25 | 25 | 23 | $43

*Phillips Pl., 6902 Phillips Place Ct. (bet. Colony & Sharon Rds.), 704-556-7730; www.upstreamit.com*

■ Voted the Most Popular restaurant in Charlotte, this "beautiful" "aquatic wonderland" near SouthPark is "inventive without being weird", luring in afishionados with its "magnificent" selection of "artfully prepared" seafood (the "bass is so good you'll want to lick the plate clean") and "ornate" presentations; tended by a "polished", "hospitable" crew, it garners "a lot of buzz", so "if there are any celebrities in town, this is where you'll find them"; it's not inexpensive, but it's "worth the money and you'll leave satisfied."

## Volare ⌧  26 | 20 | 26 | $42
*545-B Providence Rd. (Laurel Ave.), 704-370-0208*
■ "Intimate and incredible", this "hidden treasure" tucked away in an "unassuming storefront" in Myers Park is "one of the most romantic rendezvous around"; it appeals with an "interesting" seasonal menu of "authentic", "accomplished" Italian food, accompanied by a "respectable wine list" and delivered by a "marvelous", "cordial" staff; "seriously, don't miss this one", and be sure to "make reservations early, as it fills up quickly."

## Woodlands Pure Vegetarian  ▽ 28 | 12 | 21 | $16
*7128A Albemarle Rd. (Harris Blvd.), 704-569-9193;*
*www.woodlands-usa.com*
■ "*The* place to eat Indian in Charlotte", this "vegetarian's nirvana" turns out dishes so "top-notch" (including the "best ever samosas") that even hard-core carnivores "won't miss the meat"; these "excellent cheap eats" are a "must" for "adventurous seekers" of ethnic cooking because they're "different from the standard fare that you get elsewhere", allowing even seasoned palates to experience the "joy of discovering" what the subcontinent has to offer; N.B. no liquor.

## Zebra Restaurant & Wine Bar ⌧  24 | 24 | 22 | $48
*4521 Sharon Rd. (bet. Fairview Rd. & Morrison Blvd.), 704-442-9525;*
*www.zebrarestaurant.com*
■ "New and worth watching", this "sophisticate" near SouthPark will "challenge your palate" with "inventive", "delectable" New French cuisine (the "tasting menu is especially inspired") executed by a "witty chef" who "loves to mingle with his diners"; the "beautifully presented" plates and an "awesome" wine list that may be the "best in town" are brought to table by a "personable", "at-the-ready" staff in "refined" environs that are "elegant without being stuffy"; fans only "hope they never change their stripes."

# Chicago

## TOP 20 FOOD RANKING

| Restaurant | Cuisine |
|---|---|
| **29** Ritz-Carlton Din. Rm. | New French |
| **28** Tallgrass | New French |
| Les Nomades | New French |
| Carlos' | New French |
| Tru | New French |
| Ambria | New French |
| Mirai Sushi | Japanese |
| Seasons | New American |
| **27** Charlie Trotter's | New American |
| Le Titi de Paris | New French |
| 302 West | New American |
| Everest | New French |
| mk | New American |
| Arun's | Thai |
| Topolobampo | Mexican |
| Le Vichyssois | French |
| Bistro Banlieue | French |
| Oceanique* | New French/New American |
| Kevin | New American/New French |
| **26** Avec | Mediterranean |

## ADDITIONAL NOTEWORTHY PLACES

| | |
|---|---|
| Blackbird | New American |
| Chicago Chop Hse. | Steakhouse |
| Courtright's | New American |
| Frontera Grill | Mexican |
| Gibsons | Steakhouse |
| Green Zebra | New American |
| Hugo's Frog Bar | Seafood |
| Japonais | Japanese |
| Joe's Seafood | Seafood |
| Le Francais | New French |
| Lou Malnati's | Pizza |
| Morton's | Steakhouse |
| Naha | New American/Med. |
| NoMI | New French |
| North Pond | New American |
| Red Light | Asian Fusion |
| Salpicón | Mexican |
| Shanghai Terrace | Pan-Asian |
| Spiaggia | Italian |
| Spring | New American/Seafood |

---

\* Indicates a tie with restaurant above

### Ambria 🖪                    28 | 26 | 27 | $72
*Belden-Stratford Hotel, 2300 N. Lincoln Park W. (Belden Ave.),
773-472-5959; www.leye.com*
■ "A gem for years", this "culinary delight" "in a top-end Lincoln
Park residential hotel" has created "many wonderful memories"
with its "unbelievably delicious" New French cuisine served by a
"battalion of waiters" who "make you feel like royalty" within a
"quiet, wood-paneled room that speaks of old money"; a few
find the "jackets-required" policy "stuffy", but most say this is
"what a restaurant should be"; P.S. sommelier Bob Bansberg is a
"guru – trust him."

### Arun's                    27 | 23 | 26 | $86
*4156 N. Kedzie Ave. (bet. Belle Plaine & Berteau Aves.),
773-539-1909; www.arunsthai.com*
■ Chef-owner Arun Sampanthavivat "brings you to a unique and
enchanting world" with his "ultimate Thai food" at this "refined"
Northwest Side Siamese; "plan to spend a few hours" "blowing
the budget" on the "fixed-price" "tasting menu" (no à la carte),
"one exquisitely prepared course after another" "customized
to your tastes"; the "personalized service" is "smooth" and
"accommodating", the "vast wine list has many unexpected
choices" and the "quiet" space with "gorgeous artwork" has "nice
niches for conversation" – in short, "these folks got it" right.

### Avec ❶                    26 | 19 | 23 | $37
*615 W. Randolph St. (Jefferson St.), 312-377-2002;
www.avecrestaurant.com*
■ "Foodies" feel that Koren Grieveson's "profound" "merry-go-
round of Med" small plates "blows the competition away" at this
West Loop wunderkind (spin-off of Blackbird), where oenophiles
enjoy "lovely big pours" of "unusual" wines and service is
"energetic" and "attentive"; "you have to like minimalism to get"
the "stark", "sauna" decor, and the "elbow-to-elbow" "communal"
"table setup" isn't for introverts, but it does "enable" social-ists
"to meet sexy, interesting and sophisticated people."

### Bistro Banlieue                    27 | 21 | 24 | $40
*44 Yorktown Convenience Ctr. (bet. Butterfield Rd. & Highland Ave.),
Lombard, 630-629-6560; www.bistrobanlieue.com*
■ Advocates aver this "lovely" West Suburban bistro offers
"outstanding", "innovative French cuisine" (a rising Food score
justifies the claim that it's "getting better with age"); expect "an
impeccable experience" with "attentive, friendly service" and
"reasonable prices" (especially since they "offer half portions –
a great idea"), but allow yourself plenty of time to find its "hidden
strip-mall location."

### Blackbird 🖪                    26 | 20 | 22 | $53
*619 W. Randolph St. (bet. Desplaines & Jefferson Sts.), 312-715-0708;
www.blackbirdrestaurant.com*
☑ Faithful fans "flock" to this "absolute pinnacle of hip" in the
West Loop where chef Paul Kahan's "outstanding" "seasonal"
New American fare "will knock your socks off", "service is
unexpectedly friendly" and the "modern, austere" surroundings
are part of the "high concept"; contrarily, critics crow that the
"cold", "sterile decor", "noise" and "too-close tables" "detract
from the food."

### CARLOS'
| 28 | 24 | 27 | $80 |

*429 Temple Ave. (Waukegan Ave.), Highland Park, 847-432-0770;*
*www.carlos-restaurant.com*

■ "Bring a Polaroid camera" (and gentlemen, wear a jacket) to Carlos and Debbie Nieto's "beautiful!" North Shore "temple" of "inspired" "New French cuisine" to capture the "meticulous presentation" of its "fabulous food"; also expect "personalized service" from a "courteous staff" that's "knowledgeable about" the "outstanding list" of "amazing wines", but be warned that "high prices" make this "a special-occasion favorite" for penny-wise pen pals.

### CHARLIE TROTTER'S ⌧
| 27 | 25 | 27 | $119 |

*816 W. Armitage Ave. (Halsted St.), 773-248-6228;*
*www.charlietrotters.com*

☑ "If food can be poetic, orgasmic or intoxicating", you'll find it at this "benchmark" New American in Lincoln Park, where "master" chef and owner Charlie Trotter "still reigns", creating cuisine that "can change your life"; believers "bow down before" the "perfect harmony" of "sublime" "food-as-art", a "wonderful wine list" "as thick as a phone book" and "unbelievably attentive", "top-tier service" – even if a few infidels insinuate it's "a bit full of itself" and are "not sure it's worth the price."

### Chicago Chop House
| 25 | 19 | 22 | $49 |

*60 W. Ontario St. (bet. Clark & Dearborn Sts.), 312-787-7100;*
*www.chicagochophouse.com*

☑ "Testosterone-laced" (though you may see "women smoking cigars"), this "old-school" River North steakhouse with "piano bar" rouses raves from red-meat-eaters for its "superb beef" selections – such as roasted or "char-grilled prime rib" – that are "not à la carte" (potato and salad included) and for servers with "lotsa hustle" "who remember what being a waiter is all about"; still, unkind cattlemen call it "touristy" and "cramped."

### Courtright's
| 25 | 27 | 24 | $53 |

*8989 S. Archer Ave. (Willow Springs Rd.), Willow Springs, 708-839-8000;*
*www.courtrights.com*

■ Take an "easy drive out" to the Southwest Suburbs for a "tranquil dining experience" amid "gorgeous", "understated decor" at this "warm, friendly place" where "picture windows" allow you to "watch the forest wildlife while you dine"; not only is "innovative" chef Jonathan Harootunian's New American cooking "terrific", but a "knowledgeable staff" and an "extensive list" of "excellent" vintages make it a "wine lover's paradise."

### EVEREST ⌧
| 27 | 26 | 27 | $86 |

*One Financial Pl., 440 S. La Salle Blvd., 40th fl. (Congress Pkwy.),*
*312-663-8920; www.leye.com*

☑ High-minded Francophiles seeking "the summit of Chicago dining" say "chef [Jean] Joho continues to weave magic" with his "world-class", Alsatian-accented New French cuisine at this "special place" with a "million-dollar view" above the Loop; "noble service", a "posh setting" and sommelier Alpana Singh, a "wonderful guide" to the "extraordinary wine list", also help justify the "steep prices", though a segment says the "polished staff" can be "stiff" and the "room needs updating"; N.B. remember, gentlemen, jacket suggested.

## FRONTERA GRILL 🗷    26 | 21 | 22 | $37
*445 N. Clark St. (bet. Hubbard & Illinois Sts.), 312-661-1434;*
*www.fronterakitchens.com*

☑ "Genius" Rick Bayless' "more casual alternative to its swankier [sibling] Topolobampo" "remains spirited, fresh and fun" for "amazing" "non-gringo" "regional Mexican" cooking "that lives up to the hype" and "changes with the seasons" (and oh, "those incomparable margaritas" and that "wide variety of tequila"), all in a "boisterous" setting filled with "festive art"; a soupçon of surveyors submits that "service can vary greatly" when it's "crowded", while "long waits" have some sighing "if only they took [advance] reservations" for parties of fewer than five.

## GIBSONS STEAKHOUSE ❶    25 | 19 | 23 | $54
*1028 N. Rush St. (Bellevue Pl.), 312-266-8999*
*Doubletree Hotel, 5464 N. River Rd. (bet. Balmoral & Bryn Mawr Aves.),*
*Rosemont, 847-928-9900*
*www.gibsonssteakhouse.com*

☑ This "A-list" Gold Coast steakhouse "is da place" for "pretty people" (including "locals, tourists, conventioneers", "politicos" and those "looking for a mistress" or a "sugar daddy") who hanker for "a hunka hunka burnin'" "prime-aged beef" in a "high-energy" "boys'-club" atmosphere (the "bar scene is jumping"); those who eschew this "expense-account" "meatery" say "service suffers" from "crowding" and "reservations are rarely on schedule"; P.S. the O'Hare area spin-off is "a nice sibling."

## Green Zebra    – | – | – | E
*1460 W. Chicago Ave. (Greenview Ave.), 312-243-7100;*
*www.greenzebrachicago.com*

Spring chef-partner Shawn McClain gives his upscale New American cuisine a vegetarian slant at this Wicker Park encore named for an heirloom tomato variety; the menu showcases organic and locally raised produce (with a few fish and poultry items), the wine list emphasizes artisanal producers and the soothing, harvest-hued space (a former hat shop) is accented with stainless steel and live greenery.

## Hugo's Frog Bar & Fish House ❶    25 | 20 | 22 | $46
*1024 N. Rush St. (bet. Bellevue Pl. & Oak St.), 312-640-0999;*
*www.hugosfrogbar.com*

■ "Loud, fun and friendly" with "fantastic" aquatic fare ("best crab cakes around", "great frogs' legs", "excellent raw oyster selection") plus "humongous desserts", this "clubby" Gold Coast "fish version of Gibson's" also offers the latter's meat-centric menu from their mutual kitchen; it's "brash", "packed to the gills" and "pricey but still manages to feel like" a "fairly reasonable" "alternative to the hustle bustle next door"; P.S. folks "love the [nightly] piano" music.

## Japonais    24 | 27 | 19 | $56
*600 W. Chicago Ave. (Larrabee St.), 312-822-9600;*
*www.japonaischicago.com*

☑ Superlatives surrounding this "ultrachic" Near West Japanese newcomer, "one of the brightest lights on the scene", cover the "drop-dead gorgeous" decor that "transports" "the 'it'-crowd" patrons "out of Chicago", the "amazing sushi and innovative menu items" and the "Indochine-sexy" "bar"-cum-"patio that opens up to the river"; still, unswayed raters report that all that "style comes at a high price" and the "service is not the best."

### Joe's Seafood, Prime Steak & Stone Crab
**25 | 21 | 23 | $51**

*60 E. Grand Ave. (Rush St.), 312-379-5637; www.leye.com*

◪ "Power diners and tourists" pour into this "good imitation" of its Miami "namesake" in River North for its "deliciously simple" surf 'n' turf menu ("terrific" "for those times you can't decide between fish and meat"), "consistently" "excellent service" from "well-trained professionals" and "sophisticated masculine atmosphere", including a "nice-looking bar" with lots of "action"; still, vice cops vent that it's "a madhouse at peak hours", which leads to "long waits despite reservations", and claim "prices leave you crabby."

### Kevin ⊠
**27 | 23 | 24 | $55**

*9 W. Hubbard St. (State St.), 312-595-0055; www.kevinrestaurant.com*

◪ Kindred spirits contribute kudos for Kevin Shikami's "beautifully prepared", "inventive" New American–New French "fusion cuisine with definite Asian overtones", the basis of a "superb experience" at his "high-power" River North namesake where the "spare and elegant" environs glow in "flattering low lighting"; still, skeptical scribes suggest it's "pricey" and pick up a whiff of "attitude."

### Le Français ⊠
**26 | 23 | 26 | $89**

*269 S. Milwaukee Ave. (Dundee Rd.), Wheeling, 847-541-7470; www.lefrancaisrestaurant.com*

■ "It's b-a-c-k!" bellow believers beguiled by new chef-partner Michael Lachowicz's "superb" New French fare that's "creative yet harkens back to the old days" of this North Suburban "classic" after "a series of chef and personnel changes"; service is "outstanding", "changes in decor" make the "beautiful room" "more comfortable" and the "fantastic wine list" is both "substantial" and "delightful"; N.B. gentlemen, jackets are required.

### LES NOMADES ⊠
**28 | 26 | 28 | $89**

*222 E. Ontario St. (bet. Fairbanks Ct. & St. Clair St.), 312-649-9010; www.lesnomades.net*

■ Refined ramblers revel in this "sophisticated" Streeterville "jewel", where chef-partner Roland Liccioni's "superb" New French prix fixe menus change monthly; a "solicitous" staff "unobtrusively" provides "impeccable service" within the "civilized" "townhouse atmosphere" (jackets required), which still retains the "members-only feel" from its days as a "private dining club"; P.S. the "wine list is top-notch" and "the sommelier knows his stuff."

### Le Titi de Paris
**27 | 24 | 25 | $64**

*1015 W. Dundee Rd. (Kennicott Ave.), Arlington Heights, 847-506-0222; www.letitideparis.com*

■ "A suburban treasure" that "maintains excellence year after year", this "rare find in the Northwest Suburbs" is a "fine-dining" oasis according to die-hard fans of chef Michael Maddox's "fantastic" New French fare "at a fair" price, a "fantastic wine list", "exceptional service" and a "quiet", "intimate" setting; N.B. the Food rating may not reflect a post-*Survey* change of ownership, with Pierre Pollin passing the restaurant to his longtime, above-referenced chef, who is incorporating New American influences into the menu.

### Le Vichyssois
27 | 21 | 21 | $48

*220 W. Rte. 120 (2 mi. west of Rte. 12), Lakemoor, 815-385-8221; www.levichyssois.com*

■ "If you want to understand the way French food was intended to be", head for the Northwest Suburbs to this "true family-run" "favorite" that's "still excellent after all these years" thanks to new and "classic cuisine prepared by a real pro", chef-owner Bernard Cretier; throw in "good service", a "quaint" ambiance and "great prices" that make it "a nice value", and you'll see why most contributors proclaim it's "worth the drive."

### Lou Malnati's Pizzeria
23 | 12 | 16 | $18

*439 N. Wells St. (Hubbard St.), 312-828-9800*
*3859 W. Ogden Ave. (Cermak Rd.), 773-762-0800*
*958 W. Wrightwood Ave. (Lincoln Ave.), 773-832-4030*
*85 S. Buffalo Grove Rd. (Lake Cook Rd.), Buffalo Grove, 847-215-7100*
*1050 E. Higgins Rd. (bet. Arlington Heights & Busse Rds.), Elk Grove Village, 847-439-2000*
*1850 Sherman Ave. (University Pl.), Evanston, 847-328-5400*
*6649 N. Lincoln Ave. (bet. Devon & Pratt Aves.), Lincolnwood, 847-673-0800*
*131 W. Jefferson Ave. (Washington St.), Naperville, 630-717-0700*
*1 S. Roselle Rd. (Schaumburg Rd.), Schaumburg, 847-985-1525*
*www.loumalnatis.com*

■ Chi-town pizza fanaticism is alive and well, with delirious devotees dubbing this "enduring" "institution's" "dangerously addictive deep-dish" pies the "only Chicago-style 'za worth eating" ("you won't be disappointed" by the "fantastic thin crust", either); whether it's the "just-right mix of ingredients" or the optional "butter crust to die for", fans are "sure that if there's a heaven, they serve Lou's there"; P.S. it "ships well, too."

### Mirai Sushi
28 | 21 | 20 | $45

*2020 W. Division St. (Damen Ave.), 773-862-8500; www.miraisushi.com*

☑ "The fish swim down Division to get" to this "always-amazing" "trendy Japanese", officially the "best in Chicago" thanks to its "fresh", "creative" and "adventurous sushi" ("love the rare varieties they have") and "cool" "scene" (especially the "great bar upstairs"); nonconformists nag that they "need to work on the service" and pout about the "premium price" you'll pony up for the "edible art", though ayes aver "you get what you pay for."

### mk
27 | 24 | 24 | $56

*868 N. Franklin St. (bet. Chestnut & Locust Sts.), 312-482-9179; www.mkchicago.com*

■ "Long adored" and "still among the best", this River North New American proffers chef-owner Michael Kornick's "creative menu", which "delivers on the promise" of "subtle", "sophisticated" cuisine "with minimal pretension" (it "looks simple, but a lot of work went into these dishes") accompanied by "stupendous desserts" and "wonderful wines"; "service is stellar", and the "sleek", "swanky" space is "elegant in that urban warehouse loft kind of way", even if "a bit noisy."

### Morton's, The Steakhouse        26 | 21 | 24 | $56

*Newberry Plaza, 1050 N. State St. (Maple St.), 312-266-4820*
*9525 W. Bryn Mawr Ave. (River Rd.), Rosemont, 847-678-5155*
*1470 McConnor Pkwy. (Meacham Rd.), Schaumburg,*
*847-413-8771*
*1 Westbrook Corporate Ctr. (22nd St.), Westchester,*
*708-562-7000*
*www.mortons.com*

☑ Still edging out some stiff competition in its carnivorous category, "Chicago's original" "genteel" "king of the steakhouse chains" "continues to reign supreme" "in a town famous for steak" with the "best" "prime beef", "clubby" digs and "service as crisp as the hash browns"; a note to wallet-watchers, though: everything's "huge", including the "big prices"; P.S. "save room for" the "must-have" "hot Godiva cake."

### Naha ☒        26 | 24 | 24 | $57

*500 N. Clark St. (Illinois St.), 312-321-6242;*
*www.naha-chicago.com*

☑ "Creative" chef-partner Carrie Nahabedian's "amazing" New American "dining with daring Mediterranean touches" tempts travelers to her "flat-out superb" River North "keeper", where "the *Queer Eye* guys would be proud of" the "streamlined", "simple" "Zen-like" decor; sure, her "food is pricey" but most meditate it's "worth the splurge" – though what's a "great buzz" to some is just plain "noisy" to others.

### NoMI        26 | 27 | 24 | $66

*Park Hyatt Chicago, 800 N. Michigan Ave. (Chicago Ave.), 312-239-4030;*
*www.nomirestaurant.com*

☑ Beguiled boulevardiers believe "they built the Park Hyatt hotel around this" "fabulous" "first-class" "favorite" where a "table by the window" offers a "celestial" Gold Coast view and the "stunning modernist decor" sets the stage for chef Sandro Gamba's "superb", "innovative" New French fare and selections from the "top-notch sommelier"; still, those who aren't "loaded" lament the "inflated prices" and say "the staff needs to loosen up"; P.S. the "outdoor [seating] is smashing in the summer."

### North Pond        25 | 27 | 21 | $53

*2610 N. Cannon Dr. (bet. Diversey & Fullerton Pkwys.), 773-477-5845;*
*www.northpondrestaurant.com*

☑ "Nestled" "lagoon-side" in a "breathtaking" Lincoln Park locale, this "beautiful remodel" of a "historic" "ice-skating shelter" features a "fantastic" "Prairie School interior", which provides a suitable setting for "gifted chef" Bruce Sherman's "phenomenal" New American fare employing "local artisan ingredients" and paired with a "unique wine selection"; still, perfectionists point out that the "stiff staff" is "not always as attentive" as you'd expect considering the "top-of-the-line prices."

### Oceanique ☒        27 | 20 | 23 | $51

*505 Main St. (bet. Chicago & Hinman Aves.), Evanston, 847-864-3435;*
*www.oceanique.com*

■ Putting his "creativity on display nightly", "personable" "chef-owner Mark Grosz continues to amaze" at this "unpretentious" but "absolutely fabulous" North Suburban New French–New American "favorite" serving "excellent" seafood so "inventive and outstanding" it "should be illegal"; kudos, too, for the "understated storefront" space with "fabric-draped ceiling", as well as the "knowledgeable staff" that's "attuned to the needs of the diner"; P.S. "the three-course $30 menu" is a "great deal."

### Red Light 23 | 24 | 21 | $41
*820 W. Randolph St. (Green St.), 312-733-8880;*
*www.redlight-chicago.com*
☑ "Amiable chef" Jackie Shen has "raised the bar several notches" with her "imaginative", "fantabulous Asian fusion" fare at this "kinky", "clublike" "haunt" in the Market District; the sometimes "spicy" offerings come with "sassy service" and "knockout drinks", but some rueful raters are red in the face from "shouting over the loud", "pulsating music" and aren't willing to shell out the "serious money."

### RITZ-CARLTON DINING ROOM 29 | 28 | 28 | $79
*Ritz-Carlton Hotel, 160 E. Pearson St. (Michigan Ave.), 312-573-5223;*
*www.fourseasons.com*
■ "In a class by itself", this "tony" Streeterville New French boasts an "encyclopedic wine list" and "superb" cuisine (rated No. 1 for Food in Chicago) that "consistently excites the palate" and is "stunningly presented" by a "solicitous" staff within a "luxurious", "old-world setting" where patrons are "treated like royalty"; no wonder supplicants would "put on the Ritz any day, if [they] could afford it"; N.B. the Food rating may not reflect the post-*Survey* departure of chefs Sarah Stegner and George Bumbaris, as well as pastry toque En-Ming Hsu.

### Salpicón 25 | 20 | 23 | $40
*1252 N. Wells St. (bet. Goethe & Scott Sts.), 312-988-7811;*
*www.salpicon.com*
■ Owners "Vince and Priscila [Satkoff] rock" at this Old Town "gem", and the latter "gets it right" with her "high-end", "gourmet" fare, "a whole different level" of Mexican cuisine with "sauces you want to lick off the plate"; the "tequila menu is as extensive as" the "impressive wine list", and the "festive", "intimate" setting includes the option to "sit outside under the canopy" in warm weather.

### Seasons 28 | 27 | 27 | $77
*Four Seasons Hotel, 120 E. Delaware Pl., 7th fl.*
*(bet. Michigan Ave. & Rush St.), 312-649-2349;*
*www.fourseason.com*
■ "Excellent chef" Robert Sulatycky's "top-flight" seasonal New American cuisine "is always refined but has an edge" at this "formal-dining" "power scene" in the Gold Coast's Four Seasons Hotel, a "haven of culinary delights" where the substantial "expense is worth it" thanks to "outstanding food", "exceptional atmosphere" (the decor "defines elegance") and the "sensitive", "unobtrusive" staff's "superb timing"; P.S. don't forget about the "incredible brunch" on Sundays.

### Shanghai Terrace Ⓢ 26 | 26 | 26 | $54
*Peninsula Hotel, 108 E. Superior St., 4th fl. (bet. Michigan Ave. &*
*Rush St.), 312-573-6744*
■ Surveyors say this "very special", "sophisticated" "jewel within the magnificent Peninsula" serves "the highest available caliber of inventive Pan-Asian cuisine" around, with "clean, fresh,

delicate" flavors featured in its "pricey but perfect" provender, which is "impeccably" "presented" with "flawless service" in a "posh" "little lacquered jewel-box of a room" (or "outdoors on the rooftop in summer").

### Spiaggia                    26 | 26 | 25 | $72

*One Magnificent Mile Bldg., 980 N. Michigan Ave., 2nd fl. (Oak St.), 312-280-2750; www.spiaggiarestaurant.com*

■ Pleased patrons say "pinch me" as they pontificate about this Gold Coast "epitome of sophisticated dining" and "special place for special times" that "serves its fair share of glitterati", where chef Tony Mantuano's "heavenly and luxurious" Italian cuisine deserves its "stunning setting" with a "great view of the lake", and a "professional" staff "anticipates any need" ("sommelier [Henry Bishop] is first rate"); N.B. jackets are required.

### Spring                    26 | 24 | 24 | $55

*2039 W. North Ave. (Damen Ave.), 773-395-7100; www.springrestaurant.net*

◪ A "multi-sensory experience" that's "everything a gourmet restaurant should be", this Wicker Park New American seafood "standout" has satisfied surveyors swooning over chef-partner Shawn McClain's "subtle, savory" and "sublime" dishes, which are offered with "high-class service" in an "über-cool", "Zen" "converted bathhouse"; a few rain on this parade, though, calling the "austere" setting "cold" and "noisy" and the experience "a bit overpriced."

### TALLGRASS                    28 | 22 | 25 | $62

*1006 S. State St. (10th St.), Lockport, 815-838-5566; www.tallgrassrestaurant.com*

■ Grateful gastronomes "thank goodness there's a real restaurant" in the Southwest Suburbs – especially an "intimate" one where "creative chef" and partner Robert Burcenski's "memorable" New French fare is "out of this world", the "fantastic wine list" is "extensive" and the "staff is very knowledgeable"; N.B. both jackets and reservations are de rigueur.

### 302 West Ⓢ                    27 | 26 | 26 | $49

*302 W. State St. (3rd St.), Geneva, 630-232-9302*

■ Superlatives abound for this "romantic" New American "dining treasure" where "adventurous", "terrific, modern city fare" from a "creative" daily changing menu belies the "far-outpost" setting of its "unique", "elegant-yet-casual" "old bank building" within a "postcard-perfect little town" in the Western Suburbs; there's also a "great wine list", and the "yummy", "homemade desserts" alone "are worth the trip"; N.B. the Food rating may not reflect the recent death of chef-owner Joel Findlay, whose wife, Catherine, continues to operate the restaurant.

### Topolobampo ⓈS                    27 | 23 | 25 | $53

*445 N. Clark St. (bet. Hubbard & Illinois Sts.), 312-661-1434; www.fronterakitchens.com*

■ This "upscale" "regional Mexican" in River North ("Frontera's higher-end partner") is nothing short of a "national treasure" that "expands eaters' horizons" thanks to "master chef" Rick Bayless' "parade of tastes" exhibiting "creativity and respect for ingredients" ("do they do it this well in Mexico?"); plus, "they've achieved margarita perfection", the "savvy sommelier" picks "wonderful wine pairings", the helpful staff is "informative and unassuming" and the ambiance is "festive" yet "elegant."

**TRU** ⌧                                          28 | 27 | 27 | $107

*676 N. St. Clair St. (bet. Erie & Huron Sts.), 312-202-0001;*
*www.trurestaurant.com*

■ The "one-two punch of talented [toque Rick] Tramonto and [pastry chef Gale] Gand" has grateful gastronomes gushing about this "extraordinary" New French "event-dining" "extravaganza", the Most Popular restaurant in our *Survey*; from the "serene, minimalist decor" and "choreographed service" to the "help of knowledgeable sommelier" Scott Tyree, it's a "seamless" Streeterville "food-as-theater" "spectacle", and if a soupçon of "nitpickers" find it "over the top" ("you can easily spend four hours for dinner") and beyond "expensive", the majority nevertheless advises you to just "spend the money and do it."

# Cincinnati

## TOP 10 FOOD RANKING

| | Restaurant | Cuisine |
|---|---|---|
| **29** | Jean-Robert at Pigall's | New French |
| **28** | Daveed's at 934 | Eclectic |
| **27** | Boca | Italian |
| | BonBonerie | Bakery |
| | Palace, The | Continental/New American |
| **26** | Maisonette | New French |
| | Precinct | Steakhouse |
| | Sturkey's | Eclectic |
| | Jeff Ruby's | Steakhouse |
| **25** | Morton's | Steakhouse |

## ADDITIONAL NOTEWORTHY PLACES

| | |
|---|---|
| Aioli | Eclectic |
| Beluga | Asian Fusion |
| China Gourmet | Chinese |
| Chokolate Morel | Pan-Latin |
| Cumin | Indian |
| Dewey's | Pizza |
| JeanRo | French |
| Montgomery Inn | Barbecue |
| Nicola's | Northern Italian |
| Palomino | New American/Med. |

| F | D | S | C |
|---|---|---|---|

**Aioli** 🅢  **23 20 19 $36**
*700 Elm St. (7th St.), 513-929-0525; www.aiolibistro.com*
■ "Unpretentious" and "relaxed", this Downtown Eclectic is an "every-night kind of place", smile satisfied supporters of chef-owner Julie Francis, saying the "forward-thinking" toque deserves props for her "wonderful, inventive" and "always unexpected" Southwestern- and Asian-inspired cuisine, which may be paired with European and Californian vintages; the eatery's location on a corner near Music Hall makes it convenient for a pre-concert supper, but if you've got a curtain to make, you may have to goose the "slow" staff.

**Beluga** 🅢  **25 23 20 $42**
*3520 Edwards Rd. (Erie Ave.), 513-533-4444*
■ A whale of a nightspot, this "as-hip-as-it-gets" Asian fusion fave in monied Hyde Park serves up "amazing sushi" and much more during dinner hours, then "shifts into high gear" when the DJ starts spinning house and hip-hop music and the famed martinis start flowing; a "delightfully meandering floor plan" and "minimalist" white rooms help put the focus on the "gorgeous clientele", while "accommodating" service helps compensate for the Tokyo-esque prices.

### BOCA ⌂
27 | 20 | 24 | $48

*4034 Hamilton Ave. (bet. Blue Rock St. & Spring Grove Ave.), 513-542-2022; www.bocarest.com*

■ Boca, right on! cheers the "impassioned local following" of gregarious chef/co-owner David Falk, whose "utter devotion to sharp, distinctive flavors" gives rise to "contemporary Italian cuisine" with the "perfect balance of color, taste and texture"; his "relaxed and friendly" converted storefront "off the beaten path" in Northside has consequently become a "foodie mecca", with a "smallish" but "nevertheless excellent" wine list that has inspired the $90, four-course tasting menu with pairings; diners are divided on service, though – some call it "superb", others "spotty."

### BONBONERIE ⌂
27 | 17 | 18 | $14

*2030 Madison Rd. (Grandin Rd.), 513-321-3399; www.thebonbon.com*

■ "They could charge just for the aroma" of the "decadent desserts" in this East Side "sweet-tooth heaven", coo carbophiles who claim the cakes constitute a "reason to look forward to your birthday"; what's more, the bakery's "quirky" tearoom offers light breakfasts and lunches, and an "excellent selection" of leaves "from jasmine green to cherry sencha" plus the "world's best scones" make it a "great place to meet a friend" for a cuppa (reserve 24 hours in advance).

### China Gourmet ⌂
24 | 17 | 23 | $37

*3340 Erie Ave. (Marburg Ave.), 513-871-6612*

■ Sino-style specialties (whole steamed fish, "five-spice oysters" in season) are prepared and served "with flair and uncommon elegance" at this Hyde Park "fixture" beloved by an "upscale crowd"; proprietors from the Moy family dynasty "are always present and it shows": "they know you by name" and "make you feel right at home", while the "accommodating" staff "will adapt a dish to any desire"; a small minority calls prices "inscrutably high", but most feel the "total experience justifies the cost."

### Chokolate Morel ⌂
25 | 21 | 21 | $44

*101 E. Main St. (Mason Montgomery St.), Mason, 513-754-1146; www.chokolatemorel.com*

■ Patrons posit "personable" chef-owners Dave Avalos and Pam Kennedy are "building something really special" with their "very different, very contemporary" Pan-Latin in a "historic" suburban Mason manse that now houses 65 dinner guests (plus a "friendly ghost"); the intrepid are intrigued by its "cutting-edge" cuisine ("seasonal" tapas, espresso-seared tenderloin, 'conquistador stew'), as presented by "knowledgeable" servers; however, a hidebound handful feels the kitchen's "trying a little too hard" ("eccentric dishes that are more odd than tasty").

### Cumin
25 | 17 | 19 | $27

*3514 Erie Ave. (Pinehurst St.), 513-871-8714*

◪ Cumin and sit down at this Hyde Park "nouveau" Indian bistro to savor "lots of unusual taste mixtures" from chef-owner Yajan Upadhyaya, whose "superlative", "cutting-edge" subcontinental dishes ("delicious dosas") demonstrate his "creativity and flair"; with portions "on the small side", you can "try a bit of many things"; however, the "minimalist, Ikea-like" space is diminutive as well, which makes claustrophobes feel "cramped" and "crowded", and the "service needs a bit of help."

### DAVEED'S AT 934 ☒    28 | 20 | 24 | $58
*934 Hatch St. (Louden St.), 513-721-2665*

■ At this "romantic, inventive and intimate" 65-seat "hideaway" in trendy Mt. Adams, chef/co-owner David Cook lives up to his name, cooking up an Eclectic menu that "mixes the familiar and the innovative" to create an "adventure for the palate"; wife Liz "lovingly" manages the "comfortable", colorful dining rooms, "delightful back patio under the trees" and "considerate" crew (a few do find them "condescending" to non-"connoisseurs"); as a result, respondents report it's "terrific for special occasions."

### Dewey's Pizza    23 | 16 | 20 | $17
*265 Hosea Rd. (Clifton Ave.), 513-221-0400*
*Oakley Sq., 3014 Madison Rd. (Markbreit Ave.), 513-731-7755*
*Shops at Harper's Point, 11338 Montgomery Rd. (Kemper Rd.),*
*Symmes, 513-247-9955*
*Newport on the Levee Mall, 1 Levee Way (E. 3rd St.), Newport, KY,*
*859-431-9700*
*www.deweyspizza.com*

■ "Why can't all pizza be this good?" wonder 'za zealots who zip over to this local chain of pie palaces for the "perfect formula" of "great crust", "top-notch toppings and good value" rolled into "exotic", "garlic-laden" combinations (e.g. the "incredible Bronx Bomber"); you can also opt to "build your own" or dig into "excellent", "very shareable salads"; staffers are "friendly" and "lively", and "kids love watching" the "chefs toss and top" the dough in the open-windowed kitchen, while parents appreciate the "terrific wines" and "good beers on tap."

### JeanRo ☒    25 | 24 | 23 | $36
*413 Vine St. (bet. 4th & 5th Sts.), 513-621-1465; www.bistrojeanro.com*

■ "Like everything else Jean-Robert [de Cavel] touches", this new Gallic is "golden", report city "power brokers" who peg this "low-cost offspring of [Jean-Robert at] Pigall's" as Downtown's "new star"; at the "chummy yet sophisticated" bistro, "casual but not lax" servers proffer "authentic", "not over-fussy" "French comfort foods" and a "wine list full of values"; the deep and narrow room has walls of "Provençal yellow" with "cafe-style posters" of old Paris, plus a copper bar ideal for "meeting friends" and pretending "you've escaped" to the City of Light.

### JEAN-ROBERT AT PIGALL'S ☒    29 | 28 | 29 | $83
*127 W. Fourth St. (bet. Elm & Race Sts.), 513-721-1345; www.pigalls.com*

■ "Alain Ducasse, look out for Jean-Robert" de Cavel (formerly of Maisonette), whose Downtown New French two-year-old, Cincinnati's Most Popular restaurant, was also voted the city's No. 1 for Food in this *Survey*, demonstrating "impeccable taste", the maestro's "ethereal" cuisine (offered only as a three-course prix fixe or a five-course tasting menu) "stimulates the eye as much as it does the palate", against the backdrop of an "elegant but understated" room where the "welcoming" servers "read your mind"; in short, according to the "upper-crust" "society-crowd" clientele, the whole experience is simply "world-class."

### JEFF RUBY'S ☒    26 | 22 | 24 | $59
*700 Walnut St. (7th St.), 513-784-1200; www.jeffruby.com*

■ Living large is the motif at this Downtown meatery, a "celebrity hot spot" where "everything is super-sized" from the "great martinis" and "deep wine list" to the "shrimp on steroids" and "aged-on-the-premises" "roasts disguised as steaks" that will "fill you up with beef happiness"; meanwhile, the "well-done" art deco–influenced interiors are "flashy" but "not over-the-top gaudy", and servers "never miss a beat"; all agree you'll need a "fat wallet" or an "expense account" to dine here, though the unimpressed couldn't care less: "overrated, overpriced, overdone – I'm over it."

## MAISONETTE 🖂

26   25   27   $73

*114 E. Sixth St. (bet. Main & Walnut Sts.), 513-721-2260;*
*www.maisonette.com*

☑ "For more than half a century" this "bona fide classic" in Downtown has been the city's "grande dame of cuisine", offering "Grade A everything": New French fare that's "consistently excellent" ("you can bring Parisians and not be embarrassed"), luxurious environs hung with paintings by area artists and "efficient", "tried-and-true" staffers; overall, the "ambiance is old-world" and the "old-money" clientele "a bit old-fashioned", leading trendier types to tsk it's "dated, overrated" and "a little stuffy" – though traditionalists harrumph "style and graciousness are always in"; N.B. jacket required.

## MONTGOMERY INN

22   19   20   $31

*925 Eastern Ave. (Pete Rose Way), 513-721-7427*
*9440 Montgomery Rd. (bet. Cooper & Remington Rds.), Montgomery, 513-791-3482* 🖂
*400 Buttermilk Pike, Ft. Mitchell, KY, 859-344-5333* 🖂
*www.montgomeryinn.com*

☑ "I'd like to be committed into this local institution" pun pork-loving partisans of this "venerable" BBQ mini-chain known for "steamed, not smoked, ribs"; they praise "melt-in-your-mouth" meat ("no gnawing necessary") and "sauce so good you won't mind wearing it" as you perch in the "crowded", "bustling" dining rooms (Downtown's recently spiffed-up Boathouse location offers sports artifacts and "nice evening views of the Ohio River"); however, the reluctant rib "it's living on its rep" and reject the "factory" feel, the "ordeal" of "long waits" and the "fatty, greasy", "heavy and boring" eats.

### Morton's, The Steakhouse

25   20   24   $59

*Tower Place Mall, 28 W. Fourth St. (Vine St.), 513-241-4104*

■ "Expense-accounters" know there are "mountains of meat" and "Paul Bunyanesque" vegetables to be had at this "very reliable" Downtown chainster, a "traditional steakhouse" that's always "good for business" bread-breaking; the dining room is "big, open and bright", and staffers exhibit the amiability that earned "the Midwest its friendly reputation", but the restaurants' standard pre-meal display of ingredients leaves some wondering "who wants to meet their dinner before they eat it?"

### Nicola's 🖂

25   21   22   $44

*1420 Sycamore St. (Liberty St.), 513-721-6200*

■ "You may stay" in "Porkopolis", but "your taste buds leave for Firenze" when you dine Downtown at this Tuscan with its "expertly crafted food", "strong" 1,200-label Italian wine list and "marvelous sauces" ("you'll never want to touch another jar of Ragu"); what's more, since arriving in June 2004, new chef Christian Pietoso (son of Nicola) has "added contemporary flair" and new tasting menus; meanwhile, the spacious setting, a "transformed old trolley barn" with a "pleasant patio", provides a "nice atmosphere", but "friendly" service can be "painfully slow."

### PALACE, THE                                   27 | 25 | 25 | $63

*Cincinnatian Hotel, 601 Vine St. (6th St.), 513-381-6006;*
*www.palacecincinnati.com*

■ "Attention to detail" is the hallmark of this "first-rate" longtimer in Downtown's Cincinnatian Hotel, where "talented" toque Guy Hulin turns out "extraordinary", "artfully presented" Continental–New American cuisine, complemented by a cellar that boasts some "truly wonderful gems"; meanwhile, even commoners feel like "royalty" here thanks to "exquisite service", live music and a stately dining room with "civility", "elegance and style."

### PALOMINO                                      22 | 23 | 20 | $36

*Lazarus Ctr., 505 Vine St. (5th St.), 513-381-1300; www.palomino.com*

■ Its "primo location" ensures quick access to the Convention Center and the Aronoff Center for the Arts plus "excellent views" of "Fountain Square skaters" at holiday time – but that's hardly the only reason "beautiful people" "abound" at this "slick" Downtown chain link; a "piece of Seattle in Cincy", it turns out "extraordinarily consistent" New American–Mediterranean fare ("good thin-crust pizzas", rotisserie chicken), served by a "courteous and professional staff"; the "lively", "loud and vibrant" atmosphere is generally a plus, though occasionally the "din" makes it hard to "enjoy your dinner."

### Precinct                                      26 | 21 | 24 | $52

*311 Delta Ave. (Columbia Pkwy.), 513-321-5454; www.jeffruby.com*

☑ Carnivores (including "local celebs" and "pro ballplayers") cop to craving the "mammoth portions" of "aged-to-perfection" steak dispatched at Jeff Ruby's "white-tablecloth" East Side beefhouse, once a district police station; also singing a siren song are the raw bar, "fabulous cellar" and "outstanding service", all fit for "boys' night out" or to "impress a date"; however, a uniform complaint is that "tables are too close together" ("busy nights can be ear-shattering"), which leaves even loyalists a little blue.

### Sturkey's                                     26 | 19 | 23 | $41

*400 Wyoming Ave. (Oak St.), Wyoming, 513-821-9200;*
*www.sturkeys.com*

■ "Personable" proprietors "Pam and Paul" perennially please patrons of their popular eponymous Eclectic, located in the suburban village of Wyoming; the "innovative", "fabulous food" is "beautifully presented" ("even the house salad is magnificent", "desserts are works of art in their own right"), "friendly" staffers foster a "very pleasant" atmosphere and the decor is colorful and uncluttered – even if a few aesthetes assess it as a little too "South Florida."

# Cleveland

## TOP 10 FOOD RANKING

| Restaurant | Cuisine |
|---|---|
| **28** Johnny's Bar | N. Italian/Continental |
| **27** Chez François | French |
| Phnom Penh | Cambodian |
| Lola Bistro/Wine Bar | New American |
| Blue Point Grille | Seafood |
| Giovanni's Ristorante | Northern Italian |
| Flying Fig | American/Eclectic |
| **26** Battuto | Italian |
| Classics | French |
| Sans Souci | French/Mediterannean |

## ADDITIONAL NOTEWORTHY PLACES

| | |
|---|---|
| Baricelli Inn | Continental |
| Blake's Seafood Grille | Seafood |
| Century | New American |
| fire | New American |
| Fulton Bar & Grille | Eclectic |
| Ginza Sushi House | Japanese |
| Grovewood Tavern | Eclectic |
| Hyde Park Prime | Steakhouse |
| Theory | Steakhouse |
| Three Birds | New American |

| F | D | S | C |
|---|---|---|---|

**BARICELLI INN** 🖻     26 | 25 | 25 | $57

*Baricelli Inn, 2203 Cornell Rd. (Murray Hill Rd.), 216-791-6500; www.baricelli.com*

■ *Fromage* fanatics smile and "say cheese" when focusing on the "exceptional" artisanal wedges paired with pours from a "great" 400-label wine list at this "elegant" East Side Continental, where Paul Minnillo's cuisine is "creative and ever-changing" yet "consistently excellent"; diners also deem the "comfortable, quiet" setting in a "gracious" mansion-turned-B&B "conducive to talking, meeting or celebrating special occasions" with the help of "impeccably" "attentive" staffers; some lament "the size of the check" but others regard rates as "reasonable" for a "very special" evening.

**Battuto Restaurant** 🖻     26 | 20 | 23 | $43

*12405 Mayfield Rd. (125th St.), 216-707-1055*

■ At his East Side "oasis on a street of ketchup and egg noodles", chef-owner Mark Daverio conjures up "incredible", "inventive" variations on Italian classics (game, seafood, "excellent fresh" pasta) that servers present with "style and panache"; another "nice change" from nearby eateries is a "cozy" interior tinged with "modern-Euro coolness" instead of Little Italy "kitsch"; as a result, pleased patrons are prone to pick this "relaxing place" when they aim to "linger over dinner with friends."

### Blake's Seafood Grille
23 | 23 | 20 | $44

*17 River St. (West St.), Chagrin Falls, 440-893-9910;*
*www.hydeparkgrille.com*

◪ Location, location, location is the lure of this "always packed" chain seafooder – a "mini-getaway" within an "easy [25-mile] drive" of Downtown – because the "dramatic" view of the 50-ft. Chagrin Falls cascade (plus its "quaintest-of-the-quaint" namesake village) is "what postcards are made of"; indoors, the "doozy of a room" is "upscale but not stuffy", and pescavores praise "perfectly prepared" (if "plain") fish dishes served by a "knowledgeable staff"; still, a few find the place "noisy" and "overpriced", much to their chagrin.

### BLUE POINT GRILLE
27 | 25 | 24 | $47

*700 W. Saint Clair Ave. (6th St.), 216-875-7827;*
*www.hospitalityrestaurants.com*

■ Fin fans have a merry time at this maritimer in the Warehouse District, voted Cleveland's Most Popular in this *Survey*; all this "terrific fresh seafood" ("so many oysters, my wife found me attractive") in such a landlocked locale is a "rare treat", the nautical-themed, lofty room with floor-to-ceiling windows is "stunning" for "special celebrations" and the ministrations of "attentive" servers fall "just short of palm-frond fans and hand-fed grapes" – so surveyors simply tune out or tolerate "noise" from an often-"boisterous" business-class crowd.

### Century
26 | 26 | 25 | $51

*Ritz-Carlton Hotel, 1515 W. Third St. (Huron Rd.), 216-902-5255*

■ Call it the "Orient Express on the Cuyahoga": the Ritz-Carlton's "spectacular" yet "comfortable" railroad-style New American recalls the "days of luxury train travel" – complete with attendants who provide "stellar" "white-glove service with a smile" – so reviewers make tracks Downtown for its "Asian-inspired" fin fare ("superb, fresh sushi") and post-prandial bowl of cotton candy; since the fare is "pricey", the cash-crunched come for lunch, confiding "there's no cheaper way to feel like a million bucks."

### CHEZ FRANÇOIS
27 | 26 | 28 | $63

*555 Main St. (Liberty Ave.), Vermilion, 440-967-0630;*
*www.chezfrancois.com*

■ "Exemplary" service from an "experienced staff" and "the best French food within 100 miles" ("foie gras to die for") make this "high-end special-occasion eatery" about 40 minutes west of Downtown "worth the hike"; the converted sailmakers' loft on the Vermilion River boasts a "charming" exposed-brick interior and a patio for "great alfresco dining", and provides docking to those who barge in – but even the yachtsmen who weigh anchor here admit it's "kinda pricey"; N.B. jacket required.

### Classics ⌀
26 | 28 | 26 | $67

*InterContinental Hotel & Conference Ctr., 9801 Carnegie Ave.*
*(E 100th St.), 216-707-4157; www.classicsrestaurant.com*

◪ Revived in early 2003, this "new incarnation" of a "special-occasion" culinary classic now resides at the Cleveland Clinic's Intercontinental Hotel east of Downtown; "wowed" admirers attest to "first-class" "fairy-tale evenings" that are "worth the splurge", citing an "opulent" atmosphere that's "polished in every way", "fanciful" yet "exacting" French preparations, "stellar desserts" and "impeccable service" ("so many servers, you wonder who gets the tip") – yet to the less impressed it "lacks the excitement of its predecessor" and sometimes even "borders on the pretentious"; N.B. no children under 10.

### fire     25   21   22   $42
*13220 Shaker Sq. (N. Moreland Blvd.), 216-921-3473;*
*www.firefoodanddrink.com*

☑ Shaker Square's flickering fortunes notwithstanding, "talented chef" Doug Katz's "lively" New American is still hot; foodies are fired up about his "simply prepared" but "imaginative" seasonal cuisine cooked in "brick ovens and tandoors" ("phenomenal pork chops") and servers who are "usually" "downright charming"; meanwhile, the exposed-brick, open-kitchen environs spark heated debate – some term them "upscale" and "chic", others "noisy" and "cramped" (with chairs so "uncomfortable" they "should be burned"); regardless, elbow-roomers will appreciate "alfresco" patio dining in summer.

### Flying Fig     27   21   24   $40
*2523 Market Ave. (W. 25th St.), 216-241-4243*

■ Foodies give far more than a flying fig for this "undiscovered gem" in trendy Ohio City; in fact, they lick their chops over chef-owner Karen Small's "brilliant", "unconventional" and "thoroughly satisfying" American-Eclectic concoctions, presented by servers "as entertaining as the menu"; though it's set on "one of the coziest streets in Cleveland", the dining room's sleek, minimalist decor "captures the feel of a Lower Manhattan eatery" – complete with "reverberating acoustics", so silence-seekers may want to sup "out on the streetside patio."

### Fulton Bar & Grill     22   20   20   $37
*1835 Fulton Rd. (Bridge Ave.), 216-694-2122*

■ Though it's no longer the "chef-driven spot it once was", this "great neighborhood bar" in Ohio City still delivers "inventive" Eclectic eats from a "kitchen that is open late"; the "cozy" space, adorned with murals and housed in a historic 1880 building, has a "warm", "fun" vibe and "friendly servers", making it a "perfect place to take a date", "hang out with pals" or just "grab a cocktail."

### Ginza Sushi House ☒     24   16   21   $30
*1105 Carnegie Ave. (E. 9th St.), 216-589-8503;*
*www.ginzasushi.com*

■ When they want "the most authentic Japanese in town with the least Midwestern flair", aficionados angle to attend this "best-value" sushi specialist situated "close to Jacobs Field" Downtown; they savor its "amazing", "fresh" fin fare and say "personable proprietors" provide a "true Tokyo experience" within a simple setting (larger parties can even choose "traditional" sunken seating); the "quality-rather-than-flash" philosophy makes for a "pleasant" meal "without too much fuss"; N.B. wine and beer only.

### Giovanni's Ristorante ☒     27   24   27   $62
*25550 Chagrin Blvd. (Richmond Rd.), Beachwood, 216-831-8625;*
*www.giovanniscleveland.com*

■ "Don't be fooled by the location" in a "suburban office building"; this "expensive" Beechwood "grande dame" is one of "Cleveland's classiest places", where "traditional" Tuscan dishes are "prepared to perfection" and paired with any of 700 wines; within the "lush", chandeliered and paneled main room, a "skilled" "black-tie" staff provides "superb" "old-school service" ("it's rumored the headwaiter came over on the Mayflower"); cutting-edgers call the place a "throwback" that's "formal to the point of distraction" but well-wishers willing to "wear a jacket" (not required, but preferred) deem it "divine."

### Grovewood Tavern and Wine Bar  22 | 12 | 17 | $30
*17105 Grovewood Ave. (E. 172nd St.), 216-531-4900;*
*www.grovewoodtavern.com*

☑ Oenophiles especially enjoy this "funky and popular" East Side "neighborhood fave" because "staffers know their wine" and the "extensive" cellar contains some 150 vintages "in all categories", plus about 60 hard-to-find beers; even better, point out partisans, the "minuscule kitchen" turns out "innovative", "upscale" and "delicious" Eclectic eats in a "casual atmosphere" ("only the food here is snobby"); however, "unimpressed" customers call the big, "bowling alley-like" tavern a "cavern" and caution of "alarmingly inconsistent service."

### HYDE PARK PRIME STEAKHOUSE  25 | 22 | 24 | $49
(fka Hyde Park Grille)
*123 Prospect Ave. (W. 2nd St.), 216-344-2444*
*26300 Chagrin Blvd. (Park East Dr.), Beachwood, 216-464-0688*
*www.hydeparkgrille.com*

■ The meat-eating elite take a seat at these Downtown and Beachwood outposts of the statewide chophouse chain, where a menu of "delectable", "mouthwatering" steaks (some "named after Cleveland sports figures") accords with the "masculine" feel of handsome "wood-accented" rooms populated by a "business crowd" ("old guys with their trophy dates"); "superb service" from "personable" staffers makes patrons feel they "really count" – but some bean-counters have a beef with "lofty", "expense-account" prices; N.B. West Prospect serves lunch during the week.

### JOHNNY'S BAR ☒  28 | 22 | 25 | $51
*3164 Fulton Rd. (Trent Ave.), 216-281-0055*

■ No Johnny-come-lately, this "outstanding" 80-year-old patriarch just south of Downtown has once again been voted Cleveland's No. 1 for Food; the "sophisticated" Northern Italian–Continental cuisine provides so many "twists and surprises" "you'll never tire" of it, let alone the "high-end" 1,000-label wine list; paneled interiors with "faux-leopard carpets" give off a vintage vibe (like "dining with the Great Gatsby") and "knowledgeable" staffers treat you "like a regular even if it's your first visit", so "dress up" and dine with the "'in' crowd"; N.B. lunch Thursdays–Fridays only.

### LOLA BISTRO & WINE BAR  27 | 23 | 24 | $46
*900 Literary Rd. (Professor Ave.), 216-771-5652; www.lolabistro.com*

■ "I would eat shoe leather if Michael Symon cooked it for me", vow votaries of the chef/co-owner's "fantastic", "inventive" New American victuals (a "revelation" in a "pierogi and kielbasa town") and 500 "well-valued" wines; meanwhile, his "cool-cat" Tremont 65-seater "pleases more than just your palate", since the "hip, chic", exposed-brick main room has "lots of energy" (read: "can get loud") and "professional service" is usually "excellent"; still, a vocal minority found this "local foodies' sacred cow" fell "a little short of expectations."

## PHNOM PENH ⊅ 27 | 8 | 19 | $16

*13124 Lorain Ave. (131st St.), 216-251-0210; www.ohiorestaurant.com*
◪ Ok, the "atmosphere is not luxurious" and it "looks like a dump from the outside", but this "quiet" West Side BYO delivers "tremendous value", turning out "exquisite" Cambodian rice and noodle dishes whose "brilliant flavors" put your "taste buds on sensory overload"; the "owners make you feel like family" and staffers "help you order" so chances are "once you dine here, you'll join the cult" of fervent fans frequenting this phnom-enon.

## Sans Souci 26 | 26 | 25 | $47

*Cleveland Renaissance Hotel, 24 Public Sq. (bet. Superior Ave. & 3rd St.), 216-696-5600*
■ A culinary "Old Faithful" just off the lobby of Downtown's Renaissance Hotel, this "classy", "romantic" special-occasioner evokes a Provençal farmhouse via an enormous stone fireplace, beamed wooden ceiling and "murals with countryside themes"; "marvelous" French-Med fare demonstrates the "kitchen's attention to detail", a "strong cellar" boasts 400 wines and "helpful, kind" staffers help create a "warm ambiance" where diners can usually "converse without shouting" – but "because this is a place where people go to celebrate", you may encounter "some noisy folks."

## Theory ⊠ 23 | 21 | 23 | $47

*2221 Professor St. (Literary Rd.), 216-621-2301; www.theorydining.com*
◪ Tremont trendies make an educated guess that this "new favorite" (founded 2003) has a "bright future"; a brick-walled eatery with Arts and Crafts interiors, it's "billed as a steakhouse but the fish is just as good"; partisans postulate "delicious sauces", "dyn-o-mite" appetizers, a wine list as "creative" as the "funky menu" and "timely" service from a "friendly", "attentive" staff; refuters respond this Theory doesn't yet work in practice ("more imitation than inspiration"), but acknowledge it's "trying very hard to improve."

## Three Birds ⊠ 25 | 24 | 22 | $47

*18515 Detroit Ave. (Riverside Dr.), Lakewood, 216-221-3500; www.3birdsrestaurant.com*
■ "Even East Siders will cross the Cuyahoga" to take a flyer on Lakewood's "new kid in town" (opened 2003), which has feathered friends chirping about the "whimsical", "well-executed" New American entrees and what they call "Cleveland's prettiest garden patio" (with "fresh herbs grown" nearby); inside, big windows and brightly colored walls and booths add "energy to the room", where eagle-eyed eaters enjoy "people-watching" and "friendly", casually attired staffers flit to and fro; N.B. dinner only.

# Connecticut

## TOP 20 FOOD RANKING

| Restaurant | Cuisine |
|---|---|
| **27** Restaurant du Village | French |
| Jean-Louis | New French |
| Da Pietro's | French/N. Italian |
| Coromandel | Indian |
| Métro Bis | New American |
| Ibiza | Spanish |
| Meigas* | Spanish |
| Thomas Henkelmann | French |
| Alta | Seafood |
| **26** La Colline Verte | French |
| Rebeccas | New American |
| Frank Pepe | Pizza |
| Max's Oyster Bar | Seafood |
| Bravo Bravo | Italian |
| Mako of Japan | Japanese |
| Bernard's | French |
| Le Petit Cafe | French Bistro |
| Union League Cafe | French Bistro |
| Jeffrey's | New American/Continental |
| Harry's | Pizza |

## ADDITIONAL NOTEWORTHY PLACES

| | |
|---|---|
| Ann Howard | New American |
| Bentara | Malaysian |
| Carmen Anthony | Steakhouse |
| Carole Peck's | New American |
| Cavey's | N. Italian/New French |
| Ching's Table | Pan-Asian |
| City Limits | Diner |
| Esteva American | American/Eclectic |
| Il Palio | Northern Italian |
| L'Escale | French |
| Max Downtown | New American/Steakhouse |
| Mayflower Inn | New American |
| Ondine | French |
| Peppercorn's Grill | Italian |
| Piccolo Arancio | Italian |
| Restaurant Bricco | Italian |
| Roomba | Nuevo Latino |
| Sally's Apizza | Pizza |
| Valbella | Northern Italian |
| Zanghi on Summer Street | French/Italian |

---

* Indicates a tie with restaurant above

## Alta Restaurant ☒    27 | 23 | 23 | $51
*363 Greenwich Ave. (Fawcett Pl.), Greenwich, 203-622-5138*
■ Though Christer Larsson's Christer's in NYC is no more, his "exquisite" seafooder in Fairfield County is still going strong; surveyors say "you can never go wrong with his outstandingly fresh fish" ("the best salmon in the history of the world") and other "imaginative" and "unique" dishes served in a "sleek", "quiet" setting; just be prepared for "prices fit for Greenwich millionaires."

## Ann Howard Apricots    25 | 23 | 22 | $44
*1593 Farmington Ave. (Highwood Rd.), Farmington, 860-673-5405*
■ With a "picturesque setting on the Farmington River", this "consistent", "elegant, yet comfortable" New American is "the best place in the Hartford area to take your mother for a special occasion", "impress those you need to" or have "a casual weekend dinner with friends"; whether upstairs in the "formal", "white-glove", "de-crumb-your-table-between-courses" dining rooms or downstairs in the "easy-on-the-pocketbook" pub, "try the duck" or "fabulous homemade soups", all served by a "first-rate" staff.

## Bentara    25 | 24 | 20 | $33
*76 Orange St. (Center St.), New Haven, 203-562-2511; www.bentara.com*
■ This "snazzy" Malaysian "gem" "tucked away" on New Haven's Orange Street is the "place to drink fine wines and eat" "fabulous" "spicy fare" that "will burn your palate but not your wallet"; a "knowledgeable and engaging staff" presides over a "hip", "open" setting punctuated with Asian artifacts like shadow puppets.

## Bernard's    26 | 25 | 23 | $57
*20 West Ln. (Rte. 35), Ridgefield, 203-438-8282;*
*www.bernardsridgefield.com*
■ Devotees dub this Ridgefield French in a "great old New England inn" "a dream come true", with lunches and dinners that are "absolutely delicious" and a "perfect" "prix fixe Sunday brunch with piano music that's the greatest bargain in Fairfield County"; a few critics complain about "tired decor" and "inconsistent service", but they're outvoted by proponents who proclaim it's a "beautiful place for a special occasion."

## Bravo Bravo    26 | 15 | 19 | $38
*Whalers Inn Bldg., 20 E. Main St./Rte. 1 (Holmes St.), Mystic, 860-536-3228; www.whalersinnmystic.com*
■ Enthusiastic exclamations for the "fantastic food" with "big flavors" ("wow!") are heard at this high-energy Mystic Italian located in the Downtown Whaler's Inn; even though it's "noisy", with "tables too close together", the cuisine and "personable service" "are worth the turmoil."

## Carmen Anthony Steakhouse    25 | 20 | 22 | $47
*496 Chase Ave. (Thomaston Ave.), Waterbury, 203-757-3040;*
*www.carmenanthony.com*
■ Lending "true New York style" to Waterbury is this "classic steakhouse with all the trimmings": "hearty servings" of "tender, mouthwatering" beef "cooked exactly as ordered", an "affordable, super wine list", a "warm", "clubby atmosphere" of "dark wood and white tablecloths", "first-class service" from a "snappy, well-dressed staff" and "even a wise guy here or there to sneak a peek at"; all in all, carnivores concur it's an "excellent place to

eat"; N.B. at press time, a new New Haven branch is slated to debut in late 2004.

### Carole Peck's Good News Cafe
25 | 18 | 19 | $41

*694 Main St. S./Rte. 6 (Rte. 64), Woodbury, 203-266-4663;*
*www.good-news-cafe.com*

■ "It's love at first bite" sigh smitten surveyors about this Woodbury New American where the "well-renowned" chef-owner transforms "the freshest ingredients from local farmers" into "ultra-creative" "homey" dishes "with an edge"; "ever-changing artwork" plus celebrities like "Cyndi Lauper at the next table" help make this "a memorable experience" before or after "going up the road to Antique Row for expensive furniture."

### Cavey's ⊠
25 | 24 | 25 | $59

*45 E. Center St. (Main St.), Manchester, 860-643-2751*

■ CT's culinary version of *Upstairs, Downstairs,* this "remarkable" "family-run" tandem spot in Manchester is *magnifique* as well as *magnifico,* i.e. it's "superb" in any language; "warm but formal service and excellent food" in the "basement's" New French "makes you reminisce about Gay Paree", while "abundance" and a staff that makes you feel "at home" enlivens the "vibrant Northern Italian" at street level; in short, either floor is "delightful."

### CHING'S TABLE
25 | 18 | 19 | $33

*64 Main St. (Locust Ave.), New Canaan, 203-972-8550;*
*www.chingsrestaurant.com*

■ A "mix of mild and hot" dishes "satisfies both the yins and yangs" of "yuppie-to-the-core" New Canaanites in their "de rigueur camel coats and blue jeans" at this "super" spot serving "inspired Pan-Asian" fare such as "incredible Szechuan dumplings with peanut sauce", "excellent Vietnamese salad" and "fantabulous Thai curry chicken"; be warned, though, that service can be "sloppy", the space is often "crowded and noisy" and you may have to "stand in line" – "even with a reservation."

### CITY LIMITS DINER
18 | 15 | 15 | $23

*135 Harvard Ave. (I-95, exit 6), Stamford, 203-348-7000;*
*www.citylimitsdiner.com*

■ "Frenetic" but "friendly", these "justifiably popular" eateries have reached "institution" status as "the most un-diner-like diners around"; everyone from "first dates" to families gives kudos to this "crowd-pleaser", applauding the "inventive food", "easygoing" atmosphere and "whimsical decor" with a "little kitsch thrown in"; just remember, you may have to "wait to be seated" and "for your meal to arrive", since they're "always" jam-packed.

### Coromandel
27 | 15 | 22 | $32

*Goodwives Shopping Ctr., 25-11 Old Kings Hwy. N. (Sedgewick Ave.), Darien, 203-662-1213*

■ "Near-perfect", "outrageously delicious" Southern Indian dishes made with "fresh ingredients and spices" make devotees of this Darien delight declare it "the best in the tri-state area"; P.S. the lunch buffet is a "great deal."

### Da Pietro's ⊠
27 | 18 | 24 | $59

*36 Riverside Ave. (Boston Post Rd.), Westport, 203-454-1213*

■ "Redford or the Newmans may be on hand, but the real star is in the kitchen" rave reviewers about this "micro" (24 seat) Westport

French–Northern Italian that "feels like someone's crowded house" (or "like dining in a phone booth with 20 other people"), where Pietro Scotti, the "great" chef-owner, prepares "elegant" dishes like rack of lamb; just remember that "getting in is tough", and though the experience is "precious", it's "pricey."

### Esteva American Cafe　　　24 │ 23 │ 21 │ $42 │
*25 Whitfield St. (Guilford Green), Guilford, 203-458-1300;*
*www.estevaamericancafe.com*
■ Restaurateur Steve Wilkinson's Guilford Green American-Eclectic features "fresh, seasonal", "new-fashioned New England cooking"; moreover, the "cheerful setting", "lovely" views and "great outdoor patio" ensure you'll "dine in style."

### Frank Pepe Pizzeria ⊅　　26 │ 11 │ 14 │ $18 │
*157 Wooster St. (bet. Brown & Olive Sts.), New Haven, 203-865-5762*
■ "As good as legend has it", this 78-year-old is New Haven's "crown jewel of pizza"; fans have come to "expect a line around the block", "sometimes surly service" and "crummy decor", but "no one seems to care" when the prize is "the best pie on the planet", with a "crackling, charred crust" (and don't miss the "obscenely delicious", "fresh-shucked and sweet tasting whole clam" version); N.B. no credit cards.

### Harry's Pizza　　　　　26 │ 14 │ 19 │ $17 │
*West Hartford Ctr., 1003 Farmington Ave. (bet. LaSalle Rd. &*
*Woodrow St.), West Hartford, 860-231-7166*
■ Pizza proponents wax poetic about this West Hartford "leader" that makes "ultra-thin crusts" with "just the right texture" then adds "fresh, flavorful toppings"; the "limited menu works in their favor" say fans, and "quick and efficient service" keeps things moving even when it's "very busy" and "crowded", which is often; of course "the decor is irrelevant", but some find those wooden booths "surprisingly comfortable."

### Ibiza ⊠　　　　　　　27 │ 23 │ 26 │ $41 │
*39 High St. (bet. Chapel & Crown Sts.), New Haven, 203-865-1933*
■ The "absolutely wonderful" "old-world service and new-world re-creation of elegant Spanish cuisine" from executive chef Louis Bollo have patrons "glowing with pleasure" and raving about this Downtown New Haven redo of the former Pikas Tapas (same owner); throw in "sophisticated decor" and a "good wine list" and it's a "lovely experience all around."

### Il Palio ⊠　　　　　　24 │ 26 │ 21 │ $46 │
*5 Corporate Dr. (Enterprise Dr.), Shelton, 203-944-0770*
■ This "classically elegant" chef-owned, office-park Northern Italian is "popular at lunch" among business types "on large expense accounts", but surveyors say it's even "better for dinner", when there's more time to enjoy the "excellent food" and "beautiful decor"; locals are laughing that "it proves Shelton is no longer a backwater town."

### JEAN-LOUIS ⊠　　　　27 │ 23 │ 26 │ VE │
*61 Lewis St. (bet. Greenwich Ave. & Mason St.), Greenwich,*
*203-622-8450; www.restaurantjeanlouis.com*
■ Acclaimed chef-owner Jean-Louis Gerin "makes you feel as though he's cooking just for you" at this "intimate and elegant" "*très magnifique*" Greenwich French "gem"; since the five-course

tasting menu ($69) is "excellent" ("truly spectacular foie gras terrine"), the award-winning wine list "fabulous" and the service "supreme", "near perfection" sums up the experience for most.

### Jeffrey's ⊠　　　　　26　21　25　$43
*501 New Haven Ave. (Old Gate Ln.), Milford, 203-878-1910*
■ "Anything" on the New American–Continental menu "is a great choice" say surveyors citing the "subtle mélange of flavors" marking "always perfectly cooked and seasoned meat dishes" and the signature seared tuna at this Milford favorite; "truly gracious" staffers who treat even first-timers "like old friends" add to this "oasis of class" in a "lackluster" "industrial" area; P.S. it's even better if you "time it to dine while watching the sun set over the salt marshes."

### La Colline Verte　　　　　26　25　27　$61
*Greenfield Hill Shopping Ctr., 75 Hillside Rd. (Bronson Rd.), Fairfield, 203-256-9242*
■ Even "Charles de Gaulle would have been impressed" by the "quintessential" French dishes ("with a stick of butter per course") and "to-die-for" dessert soufflés at this Fairfield shopping-center "jewel"; *amis* also appreciate the "gracious, unobtrusive" staff and "beautiful, intimate setting", making it a "special place for special occasions."

### Le Petit Cafe　　　　　26　20　25　$40
*225 Montowese St. (Main St.), Branford, 203-483-9791; www.lepetitcafe.net*
■ Surveyors "show up hungry" at this "*très* chic, *très* French", yet "homey" "bargain" Branford bistro where the "charming" owner is also a "skilled chef"; the "fabulous" four-course $38.50 prix fixe dinner is prepared with "the style and flair of a place costing twice the price"; N.B. dinner served Wednesday–Sunday, with two seatings nightly.

### L'Escale　　　　　–　–　–　VE
*Delamar Hotel, 500 Steamboat Rd. (I-95, exit 3), Greenwich, 203-661-4600; www.lescalerestaurant.com*
A glamorous addition to Greenwich Harbor, this French sophomore attached to the Delamar Hotel (formerly the legendary Showboat Inn) dazzles with delectable Provençal dishes, which are slanted toward such seafood specialties as raw shellfish platters and bouillabaisse, but include carnivore comestibles like filet mignon; water views from the terrace or the soft-hued, antiqued dining room might make you feel you're in Antibes.

### Mako of Japan　　　　　26　–　23　$29
*222 Post Rd. (Rte. 130), Fairfield, 203-259-5950*
■ Relatively "new digs" in a "much more cheerful", "bigger location" mean this already esteemed Fairfield Japanese is even better, since it already dazzles devotees with the "highest-grade sashimi", "superb sushi" and "wonderful, personable servers who treat first-timers as though they were regulars."

### Max Downtown　　　　　25　24　22　$46
*City Place, 185 Asylum St. (bet. Ann & Trumbull Sts.), Hartford, 860-522-2530; www.maxrestaurantgroup.com*
■ Still "the toast of the town" after eight years, this "cult-status" Hartford New American "steak- and chophouse" "maintains the

energy and buzz of a yearling", with "the best martinis in town" and a menu to "satisfy the carnivore and stun even the most jaded bon vivant"; "hallmark attention to detail" and a prime location across from the Civic Center make it the "leader of the pack" for "power lunching", "pre- or post-show dining" or the "place to go when you want to treat yourself or others."

**Max's Oyster Bar**　　　　　26 | 24 | 23 | $43 |
*964 Farmington Ave. (S. Main St.), West Hartford, 860-236-6299; www.maxrestaurantgroup.com*
■ An "impeccable" "selection of succulent oysters" as well as other examples of "stellar seafood" ("the shellfish tower is amazing") have critics claiming that this West Hartford "pearl in the Max dynasty" is "great"; even the "noisier-than-a-boiler-factory" atmosphere doesn't keep "beautiful suburbanites" and "singles" from diving in here.

**Mayflower Inn, The**　　　　　24 | 26 | 24 | $59 |
*The Mayflower Inn, 118 Woodbury Rd./Rte. 47 (Rte. 109), Washington, 860-868-9466; www.mayflowerinn.com*
☑ A "gracious hideaway in the woods", this "charming", "pricey" and "in-its-prime" Washington Relais & Châteaux inn is "filled with the local elite and visiting dignitaries", who come to "sit by the fireplace and have a drink" before enjoying "flawless service" and "first-rate" New American fare in the "romantic" dining room or out on the patio overlooking "beautifully manicured grounds" and "fabulous gardens"; while foes find the "food inconsistent" and the overall experience "pretentious" ("there's not an unaffected bone in its body"), they're outvoted; N.B. the Food rating may not reflect a post-*Survey* chef change.

**Meigas**　　　　　27 | 22 | 25 | $56 |
*10 Wall St. (bet. High & Knight Sts.), Norwalk, 203-866-8800; www.meigasrestaurant.com*
■ On the site of the former Meson Galicia, owner Ignacio Blanco and "genius" executive chef Louis Bollo are creating "the best Spanish cuisine this side of Madrid"; factor in a "wonderful wine list" and "outstanding service" and it's "the perfect place for something out of the ordinary."

**Métro Bis** ☒　　　　　27 | 19 | 24 | $41 |
*Simsburytown Shops, 928 Hopmeadow St./Rte. 202 (Massaco St.), Simsbury, 860-651-1908; www.metrobis.com*
■ He's "as close as there is to a cooking star in central CT" assert acolytes of "highly acclaimed" chef-owner Chris Prosperi, whose "sumptuous", "inventive-without-being-gimmicky" New American dishes include pan-seared scallops with lobster potatoes; this "sleeper" in a Simsbury shopping center also offers "warm service and inviting ambiance"; N.B. his wife and co-owner, Courtney Febbroriello, authored *Wife of the Chef.*

**Ondine**　　　　　26 | 25 | 26 | VE |
*69 Pembroke Rd./Rte. 37 (Wheeler Dr.), Danbury, 203-746-4900*
■ "Romantic" and "refined without being pretentious", this chef-owned Classic French in "a beautiful old" home on the outskirts of Danbury dazzles diners with à la carte entrees and a four-course, $52 prix fixe menu of "luxurious" choices like ebony-roasted duckling and "delightful soufflés" that is enhanced by "superlative service"; N.B. jacket required.

### Peppercorn's Grill 🅈          24 | 19 | 20 | $43

*357 Main St. (bet. Buckingham St. & Capital Ave.), Hartford,*
*860-547-1714; www.peppercornsrestaurant.com*

■ The "palate-pleasing Italian dishes" – including "terrific osso buco" and "top tiramisu" – flame the ardor of Hartford fans who find this spot "great for a date or a pre/post Bushnell Theater" visit; "you'll want to spend more than you budgeted" on the "imaginative dishes" at this "chic place", though a few peppery patrons are put off by the "substandard location" and service that can "seem snobbish"; N.B. although normally closed on Sundays, it opens for dinner when the Theater has scheduled shows.

### Piccolo Arancio 🅈          25 | 18 | 22 | $40

*819 Farmington Ave./Rte. 4 (Rte. 10), Farmington, 860-674-1224;*
*www.piccoloarancio.com*

■ "Set on the outskirts of Farmington" ("pay attention or you'll drive right past it"), this "Italian jewel" (and sibling of Hartford's Peppercorn's Grill) serves "top-notch", "rustic" "comfort food with a twist" – ravioli al Arancia, chocolate bread pudding – in a "quiet room" populated by groups of good friends; just a few find the decor a bit "sterile."

### REBECCAS 🅈          26 | 19 | 22 | $62

*265 Glenville Rd. (Riversville Rd.), Greenwich, 203-532-9270*

■ Greenwich gourmands gravitate to this New American "hot spot" for "incredible" foie gras dumplings in black truffle broth, grilled Dover sole that's the "best anywhere" and other "outstanding" dishes "fabulously presented"; the eponymous co-owner "makes sure your experience is great", and the "minimalist decor" and "jumping" vibe further entice eaters; sure it's "loud" and "pricey", but "the food, setting and service are worth the money."

### Restaurant Bricco          25 | 20 | 20 | $36

*78 LaSalle Rd. (Farmington Ave.), West Hartford, 860-233-0220;*
*www.restaurantbricco.com*

■ Chef-owner Billy Grant ("the Mario Batali of Hartford County") is liable to serve up "one of the best meals" you've ever had at his West Hartford Italian, judging from reviewers recollections of the "depth of flavor" in his "absolutely fabulous" fare; there's also an "excellent" wine list, a "busy bar scene" and a staff that "does a good job explaining the selections"; it's "always full", so be "prepared to wait."

### Restaurant du Village          27 | 25 | 26 | $53

*59 Main St. (Maple St.), Chester, 860-526-5301*

■ There's truly "something special" about this "romantic, little softly lit" French "treasure" in "incredibly quaint" Chester, whose "delectable" dishes such as tournedos of beef au poivre and "unique" desserts that make you "swoon" were voted No. 1 for Food among Connecticut restaurants; on top of it all, the staff "honors your wishes with a smile", making this "charming" "destination" "just as good as you ever thought it would be."

### Roomba          26 | 23 | 20 | $42

*1044 Chapel St. (bet. College & High Sts.), New Haven, 203-562-7666*

■ "Ay!" critics cheer, "if you can get in, go again and again" to this "wild, fun" chef-owned Nuevo Latino in a Downtown New Haven basement where the "room shouts, and so does the food" – with "presentations as vertical and flamboyant as Carmen Miranda's headdresses"; though the service can be "a bit slow", it's also "extremely friendly", and you can escape the "deafening" decibels by heading to the "outdoor tents" for summer dining.

### Sally's Apizza ♥    26 | 9 | 12 | $18
*237 Wooster St. (Olive St.), New Haven, 203-624-5271*
■ The "amazing" "pie hasn't changed in 66 years and neither has the attitude" at this "no-frills" New Haven pizza "standard" that's "heaven for those who dream of an eternity with red sauce and mozzarella"; but "if you're not a regular" you'll probably be waiting for an eternity in the "long lines", and "don't be surprised if locals get served before you do."

### THOMAS HENKELMANN 🗷    27 | 27 | 26 | $73
*Homestead Inn, 420 Field Point Rd. (bet. Bush Ave. & Horseneck Ln.), Greenwich, 203-869-7500; www.thomashenkelmann.com*
■ Voted Most Popular among Connecticut restaurants is this "perfect-in-every-way" French in a "beautiful" Relais & Châteaux inn in Greenwich's "dripping-rich Belle Haven section"; "wizard" chef-owner Thomas Henkelmann's "amazing" cuisine is served in a "warm, rustic", "country-elegant" setting by a "solicitous" staff, making it "the luxury of luxuries for those ultra-special occasions"; N.B jacket required.

### Union League Cafe 🗷    26 | 27 | 25 | $46
*1032 Chapel St. (bet. College & High Sts.), New Haven, 203-562-4299; www.unionleaguecafe.com*
■ "Yalies with visiting parents", "professors and other intellectual types" and "regulars" like Jacques Pépin gather at this "refined" New Haven French bistro "overlooking Chapel Street and the campus", where "the union of food and service puts [it] in a league of its own"; chef-owner Jean-Pierre Vuillermet's "top-notch" cuisine is served in a "gorgeous room" with "wood paneling" and a fireplace "where history seeps through."

### Valbella 🗷    24 | 23 | 24 | $64
*1309 E. Putnam Ave./Rte. 1 (Sound Beach Ave.), Riverside, 203-637-1155*
■ Insiders advise "sit in" the "enchanting wine cellar if possible", though the "main room near the fireplace" is better for "celeb-spotting" ("tell Regis we said hello") at this "pricey" Riverside Northern Italian where "expense-account types" and "the Greenwich who's who" gather; "outstanding" seasonal seafood specials "customized to order", a "stellar" 1,400-bottle vino list and a "discreet staff" add up to a "magical evening."

### Zanghi on Summer Street 🗷    25 | 22 | 22 | $52
*201 Summer St. (bet. Broad & Main Sts.), Stamford, 203-327-3663; www.zanghionsummerstreet.com*
■ "Compliments" to "charming" chef-owner Nicola Zanghi for his Downtown Stamford "winner" where "expertly prepared, perfectly balanced fare with Italian flair or a French twist" (think woodland mushrooms or seared foie gras) is the order of the day; the "serene setting" also makes for an "evening to cherish."

# Dallas

## TOP 20 FOOD RANKING

| Restaurant | Cuisine |
|---|---|
| **28** French Room | French/American |
| Lola | New American |
| **27** York Street | New American |
| Teppo | Japanese |
| Cafe Pacific | Seafood |
| Abacus | Eclectic/New American |
| Tei Tei Robata Bar | Japanese |
| Del Frisco's | Steakhouse |
| Café on the Green | New American |
| Mansion on Turtle Creek | Southwestern |
| **26** Nana | New American |
| Green Room | New American |
| Bob's | Steakhouse |
| Hôtel St. Germain | French/Continental |
| Suze | Mediterranean |
| Al Biernat's | Steakhouse |
| **25** Chamberlain's | Steakhouse |
| Tramontana | New American |
| Pappas Bros. | Steakhouse |
| Old Warsaw | Continental/French |

## ADDITIONAL NOTEWORTHY PLACES

| | |
|---|---|
| Aurora | New American |
| Capital Grille | Steakhouse |
| Chow Thai | Thai |
| Fogo de Chão | Brazilian/Steakhouse |
| Grape, The | New American |
| Il Mulino | Italian |
| Il Sole | Italian |
| Iris | New American |
| La Duni Latin Café | Pan-Latin |
| L'Ancestral | French Bistro |
| Lavendou | French Bistro |
| Mercury Grill | New American |
| Mi Piaci Ristorante | Northern Italian |
| Modo Mio Cucina | Italian |
| Nick & Sam's | Steakhouse |
| Oceanaire | Seafood |
| P.F. Chang's | Chinese |
| Roy's | Hawaii Regional |
| Steel | Japanese/SE Asian |
| 2900 | New American |

## ABACUS ☒  27 | 27 | 26 | $56

*4511 McKinney Ave. (Armstrong Ave.), 214-559-3111;*
*www.abacus-restaurant.com*

☑ Chef Kent Rathbun "choreographs the perfect East-meets-West dance" at this "trendy" Knox Henderson Eclectic where "exciting specials" emerge from the open kitchen and the "hip-to-the-max" decor is "an elegant version of *The Jetsons*"; factor in an "exceptional wine list", "established movers and shakers" and "attentive, down-to-earth" servers and you have the Most Popular restaurant in Dallas.

### Al Biernat's  26 | 24 | 25 | $53

*4217 Oak Lawn Ave. (Herschel Ave.), 214-219-2201; www.albiernats.com*

■ "Consummate host" Al Biernat "always remembers a repeat customer" (not to mention the "local business executives", "socialites", sports heroes and other headline grabbers sitting two tables away) at this Oak Lawn steakhouse known for "fabulous salads", a "killer rib-eye" and "surprisingly wonderful seafood"; an "artistic", "contemporary" setting that's quite "pretty", a "cool bar scene" and "snappy service" are other inducements.

### Aurora ☒  – | – | – | VE

*4216 Oak Lawn Ave. (Wycliff Ave.), 214-528-9400; www.auroradallas.com*

At his new Oak Lawn domain, chef/co-owner Avner Samuel constructs intricate New American dishes with French inflections (the adventurous opt for his 10- to 12-course tasting menu); fascinated foodies can watch him – and vice versa – as he works in an exposed stainless-steel kitchen, separated by an etched-glass wall from the 56-seat ultrasuede-walled dining room hung with Peter Max art; Limoges china, Cristofle flatware and the cellar's 380 wines are all handled deftly by the staff; N.B. lunch served Wednesday–Friday.

## BOB'S STEAK & CHOP HOUSE ☒  26 | 20 | 24 | $53

*4300 Lemmon Ave. (Wycliff Ave.), 214-528-9446*
*The Shops at Legacy, 5760 Legacy Dr. (Dallas N. Tollway), Plano,*
*972-608-2627*
*www.bobssteakandchop.com*

■ "Bring your hearing aid" to these "dark, clubby" "hangouts" on Lemmon Avenue and in Plano, where a mix of "celebrities", "real Dallasites" and "conventioneering" "expense-account types" begin meals over "the best blue-cheese salad" then segue to "perfectly cooked steaks" ("the *côte de boeuf* is outstanding") perhaps with an "oversized glazed carrot"; truth be told, they may be "the city's best restaurants with TVs in the dining rooms."

### Café on the Green  27 | 26 | 26 | $46

*Four Seasons Resort & Club Dallas at Las Colinas,*
*4150 N. MacArthur Blvd. (Northgate Dr.), Irving, 972-717-2420;*
*www.fourseasons.com*

■ "Quiet, calming" and "casually elegant", this New American at the Four Seasons Las Colinas is lauded for an "impeccable" staff that doesn't disturb the Zen-like setting, and a "fabulous rotating menu" of "inventive" Asian-accented dishes that is sure to "impress even jaded diners"; in addition to being a "wonderful venue for holidays and special events", it's also "one of the most pleasant Sunday brunch experiences in existence"; N.B. child-care services are available while you dine.

## CAFE PACIFIC ⊠     | 27 | 25 | 25 | $45 |
*Highland Park Vlg., 24 Highland Park Vlg. (bet. Mockingbird Ln. & Preston Rd.), 214-526-1170*
■ "If Dallas had an ocean this restaurant would be on the beach" avow admirers of this "swanky" seafood bistro in Highland Park where patrons know to "dress the part" if they want to convincingly "rub elbows with the city's elite"; insiders insist "try the short-smoked salmon", the "unbelievable three-onion sea bass" and the "addictive sweet potato fries" and like to watch how "maitre d' Jean-Pierre Albertinetti runs the dining room in a no-nonsense, efficient Gallic manner" that ensures "polished service."

## Capital Grille, The     | 25 | 25 | 25 | $53 |
*Crescent Shops & Galleries, 500 Crescent Ct. (bet. Cedar Springs Rd. & McKinney Ave.), 214-303-0500; www.thecapitalgrille.com*
■ The opposite of a boring Texas-style meatery, this "masculine" McKinney Avenue "power-dining center" (part of a chain, but with only a "faint whiff" of one) is an "investment-banker heaven" for "top-quality beef", "wood-paneled" rooms that breathe "old-style class" and staffers who "know how to pace a great meal" with "fabulous wines" that are "properly served"; just "don't let your guest select unless you've struck oil, are celebrating" or have a "liberal expense account."

## Chamberlain's Steak and Chop House     | 25 | 22 | 24 | $48 |
*5330 Belt Line Rd. (east of Dallas N. Tollway), Addison, 972-934-2467; www.chamberlainsrestaurant.com*
■ "Gracious" chef-owner Richard Chamberlain is both "wonderful cook and consummate host" ("he will prepare anything you request") at this "classy" Addison steakhouse that puts out "one of the best rib-eyes you will ever have" as well as "excellent" slow-roasted prime rib (in three portion sizes); "smooth, unobtrusive service", "heavy wood paneling" and handsome lithographs on the walls are other reasons some "enjoy giving gift certificates to this restaurant."

## Chow Thai     | 24 | 21 | 20 | $28 |
*5290 Belt Line Rd. (east of Dallas N. Tollway), Addison, 972-960-2999*
*3309 Dallas Pkwy. (Parker Rd.), Plano, 972-608-1883*
*www.mangosdallas.com*
■ A family affair that "does Thai right" sums up reactions to these Addison and Plano sibs where "innovative" big bowls of noodles, "magnificent curries" and owner Vinnie Virasin's fusion specialties ("excellent tea-smoked pork chops") "have patrons running back for more"; the clan's recipes, moreover, are showcased in "upscale", "contemporary" settings that are thankfully "free of the usual Asian clichés."

## Del Frisco's Double Eagle Steak House     | 27 | 25 | 26 | $58 |
*5251 Spring Valley Rd. (N. Dallas Pkwy.), 972-490-9000; www.delfriscos.com*
■ "That ultimate beef and lobster you promised your doctor you'd cut back on" is here at this two-story North Dallas "Mercedes of steakhouses", a "masculine" mecca with dark-wood paneling, fireplaces, eight dining rooms, a cozy upstairs salon and a "wine cellar that's terrific for parties"; the "entire staff does a superb job" too – however, the á la carte menu means many can only go for "special occasions" or "on an expense account."

### Fogo de Chão
25 | 20 | 24 | $48

*4300 Belt Line Rd. (Midway Rd.), Addison, 972-503-7300;*
*www.fogodechao.com*

■ "Bring a huge appetite" to this expansive Brazilian churrascaria in Addison, where meals begin with an "awe-inspiring salad buffet" then segue into a "carnivore's orgy" of traditional and exotic meats that are brought on skewers by "charming", gaucho-wearing waiters and "carved tableside"; it's quite a show (note the fire pit at the entrance) for both locals and "tourists" – just remember to "pace yourself" at this single-price extravaganza and don't fill up on the "wonderful" cheese bread.

### FRENCH ROOM ⊠
28 | 29 | 28 | $77

*Hotel Adolphus, 1321 Commerce St. (Akard St.), 214-742-8200;*
*www.hoteladolphus.com*

■ No. 1 for Food among Dallas restaurants, this "incomparable French-American" in a "historic Downtown hotel" is where William Koval sets a "standard of excellence" with his "outstanding" dishes; expect an "elegant experience from start to finish" where gentlemen wear jackets, the staff "treats patrons like royalty" and the "stunning", "romantic" interior includes "exquisite frescoes" reminiscent of "Versailles"; "you will need to sell family silver to pay the bill", but that's a small price given you're dining at the "finest restaurant in town."

### Grape, The
25 | 22 | 23 | $35

*2808 Greenville Ave. (Vickery Blvd.), 214-828-1981;*
*www.thegraperestaurant.com*

■ "Always interesting, always good" wax loyal disciples of this "longtime" Greenville Avenue New American located on a strip of ephemeral nightclubs and tequila bars; expect "outstanding" "seasonal feasts" from a "creative", often-changing menu, as well as an "awesome", "smart wine list"; as a "charming", "romantic" "little nook" with "small tables", it's a "perfect first-date place" so long as you're "prepared to get to know your neighbors" too.

### Green Room
26 | 20 | 23 | $44

*2715 Elm St. (Crowdus St.), 214-748-7666;*
*www.thegreenroom.com*

■ "Hip" foodies wade through the "tattooed crowd" outside this "dark", "funky" Deep Ellum venue to "have a drink on its rooftop bar" then sample chef Marc Cassel's "fabulous" New American cooking that "works the outer edge of the envelope", particularly the "awesome 'Feed Me, Wine Me' multicourse menu" ("a great value"); "pierced" servers, sometimes with "green hair", and "lots of rock 'n' roll memorabilia" further fuel the "Hendrix-like haze of great food, drink and music."

### Hôtel St. Germain ⊠
26 | 27 | 26 | $72

*2516 Maple Ave. (bet. Cedar Springs Rd. & McKinney Ave.),*
*214-871-2516; www.hotelstgermain.com*

■ "Pack the kids off to grandma's", put on the heels or the jacket and tie, then call a limousine to take you and the spouse to this "romantic", "antique-filled", "neat old" mansion Uptown where "white-gloved waiters" provide "silver service" as patrons partake of "impeccable" seven-course French-Continental meals in a "tiny", "extremely quiet" dining room overlooking a courtyard; P.S. "top off the evening by staying in one of the fabulous rooms."

### Il Mulino ⊠
_ _ _ VE

*2408 Cedar Springs Rd. (Fairmont St.), 214-855-5511*

An offshoot of NYC's perennially packed Italian institution, this Uptown upper-cruster has created an uproar with its identical menu of indulgently rich classic cuisine (served in stereotypically enormous portions); a legion of suave white-tie waiters will prepare pasta and debone fish tableside in a dimly lit old-world dining room featuring oil paintings, draperies, chandeliers and even marble-accented loos; given the hefty prices, it's especially excellent for expense-accounters.

### Il Sole ◐
24 23 22 $40

*Travis Walk, 4514 Travis St. (Knox St.), 214-559-3888;*
*www.ilsole-dallas.com*

■ "Wonderful Tuscan decor" is the backdrop for "a lovely evening" at this "quaint, romantic" second-story Italian "overlooking one of the city's hippest areas", Knox Henderson; loft-dwellers and townhouse owners meander though the neighborhood of trendy boutiques, then head here for "people-watching", "perfectly scrumptious meals" ("fabulous sea bass"), "outstanding" wines by the glass and "professional service"; if the weather is right, ask for a "table on the patio – oh yeah."

### Iris ⊠
_ _ _ E

*5405 W. Lovers Ln. (Inwood Rd.), 214-352-2727;*
*www.irisdallas.net*

Owner Susie Priore (ex Suze) and her handpicked partner, chef Russell Hodges, lure the diva-designer–discerning-diner crowd to this much-praised New American with creative organic cuisine like seared foie gras and pistachio-crusted rack of lamb; meanwhile, the West Lovers site (which has seen a host of eateries come and go) underwent an extreme makeover this time around, resulting in a serene scene of putty-colored walls, dark-wood tables and iris-themed original works by renowned Texas artists.

### La Duni Latin Café
24 22 21 $29

*4264 Oak Lawn Ave. (Herschel Ave.), 214-520-6888* ⊠
*4620 McKinney Ave. (Knox St.), 214-520-7300*
*www.laduni.com*

■ You "won't believe how little it costs to treat your taste buds" at these "cute", "lively" Pan-Latin Americans, where the "super" dishes are complemented by "imaginative cocktails" and "the best collection of South American wines in the Metroplex", sometimes poured by "owners who hang around and chat"; regulars rave about "first-rate", "lip-smacking desserts" (particularly the "to-die-for" cuatro leches cake) and the "novel Sunday brunch"; N.B. the Oak Lawn kitchen and bakery, which begins serving coffee and pastries at 6 AM on weekdays, opened post-*Survey.*

### L'Ancestral ⊠
24 21 21 $42

*4514 Travis St. (Knox St.), 214-528-1081*

■ "Slow down and enjoy the pace" at this "beautiful", "never-too-crowded-or-loud" French bistro in the showy Knox Henderson area; classical music is piped softly through the blond-wood and lace-curtain dining room as diners partake in "timeless" standards like "well-prepared escargots", "excellent steak tartare" and "great pommes frites"; it's also, thankfully, a place for "those not on an expense account."

### Lavendou Ⓢ 24 23 23 $40

*19009 Preston Rd. (bet. Frankford Rd. & Rte. 190), 972-248-1911;*
*www.lavendou.com*

■ The "next best thing to being in France" is a visit to this "unstuffy" North Dallas bistro with a reputation for "reasonable prices" on "first-rate" Gallic goodies ("don't-miss soufflés", "the best" roast duck); so soak up the Provençal atmosphere, ask the "attentive", "friendly" waiters to pour you a second glass of Burgundy and savor another bite of crusty bread dipped in olive oil.

### LOLA Ⓢ 28 24 27 $51

*2917 Fairmount St. (Cedar Springs Rd.), 214-855-0700;*
*www.lola4dinner.com*

■ "Dallas's most creative bills of fare" await visitors to this "quaint, little cottage" Uptown where the "deft culinarians" produce "amazing [two- to four-course] prix fixe" New American meals, complemented by an "incredible", 800-label, "fairly priced" wine list; a "uniformly knowledgeable" and "passionate front-of-the-house team" and a "charming patio" are added attractions; N.B. the adjacent eight-table Tasting Room offers "to-die-for" 10- and 14-course petite-portion menus that can be paired with wines.

### MANSION ON TURTLE CREEK 27 27 27 $70

*2821 Turtle Creek Blvd. (Gillespie St.), 214-559-2100;*
*www.mansiononturtlecreek.com*

☑ Southwestern "flavors you can't imagine anywhere else" are found at "Texas icon" and "master-inventor" chef Dean Fearing's "venerable" Uptown destination, an art and antique-filled "grand place for a special occasion" where jacketed "old-money" "regulars" enjoy "sublime lobster tacos" and "must-try tortilla soup" brought by tuxedoed staffers, all part of a "well-orchestrated production"; quibblers say it's "no longer cutting-edge" and "you're paying for the reputation", but more love that "it just keeps rolling."

### Mercury Grill 25 23 22 $44

*11909 Preston Rd. (Forest Ln.), 972-960-7774; www.restaurantlife.com*

■ "Awesome food" (the "pepper-crusted seared ahi is as good as ever") from "a great menu" generates positive reviews for Chris Ward's "winning" New American, a "great find in a strip mall" in Preston Forest, below LBJ; with its "sleek", "sophisticated" vibe, it reminds Big Apple aficionados of "being in Manhattan" and draws a loyal crowd of local luminaries.

### Mi Piaci Ristorante Ⓢ 24 25 23 $44

*14854 Montfort Rd. (Belt Line Rd.), Addison, 972-934-8424*

■ "Ask for a patio table overlooking the pond" at this "sleekly serene" "Addison–meets–Northern Italy" classic where everything is "exceptional", from the "top-notch" staffers who could double as Armani models to the "fabulous" wine list and "handmade pastas with perfectly balanced sauces" ("the veal ragout was wonderful"); P.S. epicureans know to mark their calendar for truffle season, which brings the "best risotto in Texas."

### Modo Mio Cucina Rustica Italiana 24 19 23 $35

*Frankford Crossing, 18352 Dallas Pkwy. (Frankford Rd.), 972-713-9559;*
*www.modomio.net*

■ Dressy-casual patrons of this "small" North Dallas Italian *cucina* know to look for its camouflaged entrance within a bustling "suburban shopping center"; the venue's "serious following" is attributable to an "efficient staff" and "high-quality dishes" that are "a break from the formulas used elsewhere"; while this is definitely "the place for pasta", including a ravioli menu, the "sea bass is a standout" too; N.B. the wine list has tripled in size over the last few years.

### Nana　　　　　　　　　　26　27　26　$62
*Wyndham Anatole Hotel, 2201 Stemmons Frwy., 27th fl.*
*(Market Center Blvd.), 214-761-7470; www.nanarestaurant.com*
☑ What a "calmly elegant", "romantic" room and "panoramic view" declare diners dazzled by this Market Center "sky-high" dining venue; "from its height you can look down at all the lesser restaurants in town" while enjoying "scintillating" New American fare served on Versace place settings; he-men hail it as a "place to make your woman happy", and if you don't have one just swagger over to "the bar [that] swings with jazz on weekends."

### Nick & Sam's　　　　　　　24　23　23　$53
*3008 Maple Ave. (Carlisle St.), 214-871-7444; www.nick-sams.com*
☑ "Larger-than-life steaks reflect the larger-than-life personality of owner" Phil Romano at this "hip" Uptown beefhouse; it's "unlike the traditional, stuffy ones" thanks to a "speakeasy vibe", arched ceilings and "lively open kitchen" flanked by a piano; visits begin with "phenomenal martinis" (with spoons of caviar gratis) from the bar, a prelude to "fine" "expense-account" cuts of meat, "damn-good fries" and "build-your-own wine flights."

### Oceanaire Seafood Room　　　　25　24　24　$49
*Westin Galleria Hotel, 13340 Dallas Pkwy. (LBJ Frwy.), 972-759-2277;*
*www.theoceanaire.com*
■ "Finally, great seafood comes to this landlocked town", declare piscatorily partial partisans of this multilevel "upscale" chain link located in the Westin Galleria; decorated with horseshoe-shaped, fire-engine-red banquettes and a "nautical-but-nice" motif, it makes patrons feel like they're "dining on a five-star liner" from the '30s "with everyone at your service"; "crab cakes are a must", as are the "incredible selection of oysters" from the raw bar.

### Old Warsaw　　　　　　　　25　24　25　$57
*2610 Maple Ave. (bet. Cedar Springs Rd. & McKinney Ave.),*
*214-528-0032; www.theoldwarsaw.com*
☑ "One hates to admit liking the same Uptown restaurant one's parents did a generation ago, but it's hard not to enjoy a meal" at this "elegant", "dress-up" Continental-French, which is "still a grand dining venue" for a "well-heeled crowd" looking to celebrate "special occasions" over "classic haute cuisine" ("wonderful soufflés"); "personalized service" from tuxedoed waiters, a piano player and "strolling violinist" add to the "charm", so when trendies call it "tired" and "out of touch", defenders blithely boast that "it will probably be open for another 100 years."

### Pappas Bros. Steakhouse ⌧　　　25　24　24　$55
*10477 Lombardy Ln. (bet. I-35 & Northwest Hwy.), 214-366-2000;*
*www.pappasbros.com*
■ Further evidence that "Texas is about 'big'" is this Love Field area surf 'n' turf outpost from the Pappas Bros., which is "not as much of a see-and-be-seen steakhouse as other places in town" (though it does get "famous people") but boast a "'30s-style art

deco" interior with "great private rooms", an "amazing cellar", the "largest rock lobster tails you've ever seen" and "great steaks."

### P.F. CHANG'S CHINA BISTRO    23 | 21 | 20 | $27

*225 NorthPark Ctr. (Northwest Hwy.), 214-265-8669*
*18323 N. Dallas Pkwy. (Frankford Rd.), 972-818-3336*
*www.pfchangs.com*

☑ "Addictive lettuce wraps", "to-die-for Mongolian beef" and "spicy dishes galore" headline the "high-quality" Chinese menu at these "expansive", "stylish" and "still wildly popular" upmarket chain outposts in NorthPark and North Dallas; they're "extremely noisy and crowded" and you can "grow old waiting for a table" ("takeout is a brilliant solution"), but "they sure beat your local delivery place"; N.B. reservations now accepted.

### Roy's    24 | 23 | 22 | $45

*2840 Dallas Pkwy. (bet. Park Blvd. & Parker Rd.), Plano, 972-473-6263;*
*www.roysofplano.com*

☑ "If I can't be in [the islands], at least I can come here" assert admirers of Roy Yamaguchi's Hawaii Regional entry where the "architectural", "zippy mixtures" (like the signature macadamia nut–crusted whitefish) from the huge open kitchen are "something different and exotic"; some snipe about "a little food for a lot of money", but hey, after one of the "fun", fruity cocktails and a gander at the tropical plantation decor you'll think "all that's missing is the Maui coast."

### Steel ●    24 | 26 | 20 | $48

*Centrum Bldg., 3102 Oak Lawn Ave. (Cedar Springs Rd.), 214-219-9908;*
*www.steeldallas.com*

☑ Cloaked in an "alluring", dark, mysterious", "early-industrial" interior, this Oak Lawn Japanese–Southeast Asian showplace – a "see-and-be-seen runway" for fashionistas, elite athletes and aspiring moguls – pairs "delicious sushi" and "excellent cooked dishes" ("outstanding sea bass") with an "unbelievable selection of wines and sakes" (1,600 and 60, respectively); dissenters dis it as "flash and dash" with a "condescending" staff and prices so "high" it's "a great place to rack up frequent-flier miles."

### Suze ☒    26 | 17 | 24 | $36

*4345 W. Northwest Hwy. (Midway Rd.), 214-350-6135*

■ It's safe to say "you won't just stumble onto" Gilbert Garza's "cozy, neighborhood" Mediterranean in an "out-of-the-way" strip center near Love Field, but it's worth seeking out; this "little gem" exemplifies "all the quality and personal attention you'd expect from a chef-owner" applied to dishes such as the signature veal Bolognese and a "well-chosen wine list"; patrons pray for a decor "upgrade", including relief from "cramped" seating.

### Tei Tei Robata Bar    27 | 23 | 22 | $45

*2906 N. Henderson Ave. (Willis Ave.), 214-828-2400;*
*www.teiteirobata.com*

■ "If you've just gotten paid" and are seeking "out-of-this-world sushi" ("including crazy stuff you can't get elsewhere"), "amazing Kobe beef" and other "delicious grilled meat and fish", head to this "unassuming" Knox Henderson "Japanese jewel box" where owner Teiichi Sakurai is a "perfectionist" and "tables are a hot commodity"; not surprisingly, "you'll see all the pretty people", as well as DJs and an "Elvis look-alike chef."

### TEPPO

| 27 | 24 | 23 | $39 |

*2014 Greenville Ave. (Prospect Ave.), 214-826-8989; www.teppo.com*

■ "Stylish" types who frequent this "small", "minimalist" Greenville Avenue Japanese say the "hip" sushi ("great" "for pros and amateurs") "might make you forget to order the grilled items", which would be a shame since the "yakitori here is not to be missed"; yes, many "wish the place were bigger" because "it's a hassle to get a table", but it's "worth the wait", especially since its sibling Tei Tei Robata Bar is just as tough a ticket.

### Tramontana ⊠

| 25 | 19 | 23 | $39 |

*Preston Ctr. West, 8220B Westchester Dr. (bet. Luther & Sherry Lns.), 214-368-4188; www.mybistro.net*

■ "A neighborhood dining spot with an edge" sums up this Italian- and Gallic-influenced New American where James Neel's large menu (including a prix fixe option) of "distinctive", "creative" cuisine is "consistently enjoyable"; surveyors say he and his staff "go the extra mile" to ensure you get "personal attention", and add that the space feels like a "charming bistro in Paris", overcoming its location in the older part of Preston Center.

### 2900 ●⊠

| 25 | 21 | 23 | $41 |

*2900 Thomas Ave. (Allen St.), 214-303-0400*

◩ Set in a former Uptown office space that's been converted to a "sleek", "dark" and "romantic" eatery with black-and-white photographs and a bar aglow with flickering candles, this "great place to take a date" is a "hip, little neighborhood sleeper" that serves "delicious", "innovative" New American fare (grilled artichokes, stuffed tenderloin); P.S. the "live jazz band is a nice touch" on some evenings, so long as you're prepared to "yell at your neighbor" to communicate.

### YORK STREET ⊠

| 27 | 22 | 28 | $54 |

*6047 Lewis St. (Skillman St.), 214-826-0968*

■ Chef-owner Sharon Hage "has more talent in one finger than the rest of us have in 10" swear acolytes of this East Dallas New American set in a tiny house in a "funky, old neighborhood", where her "imaginative", "exciting" "market-driven" menu employs "the freshest ingredients" and the staff "would rather help than hurry" ("they even gave my daughter a tour of the kitchen"); epicureans beg "please don't tell anyone, it's already" too "crowded."

# Denver Area & Mountain Resorts

## TOP 20 FOOD RANKING

| Restaurant | Cuisine |
|---|---|
| **28** Mizuna | New American |
| **27** Highlands Garden | New American |
| Del Frisco's | Steakhouse |
| L'Atelier | French |
| Sweet Basil | New American |
| Cafe Brazil | Brazilian/Colombian |
| Sushi Den | Japanese |
| Adega Rest./Wine | New American |
| Flagstaff House | New American/Eclectic |
| **26** Six89 Kitchen/Wine | New American |
| Matsuhisa | Japanese |
| Tante Louise | French |
| Keystone Ranch | New American |
| John's | New American |
| 240 Union | New American |
| Montagna | New American |
| Kevin Taylor | New American |
| Alpenglow Stube | Bavarian/American |
| Opus* | New American |
| Capital Grille | Steakhouse |

## ADDITIONAL NOTEWORTHY PLACES

| | |
|---|---|
| Barolo Grill | Northern Italian |
| Emma's | New American |
| Full Moon Grill | Northern Italian |
| Grouse Mountain Grill | Regional American |
| Jax Fish House | Seafood |
| Left Bank | French |
| Luca D'Italia | Italian |
| Mel's | New American |
| Morton's | Steakhouse |
| New Saigon | Vietnamese |
| Panzano | Northern Italian |
| Parisi | Italian |
| Piñons | Regional American |
| Potager | New American |
| Q's | New American |
| Solera Rest./Wine | New American |
| Splendido | New American |
| Syzygy | New American |
| Wildflower | New American |
| Zengo | Nuevo Latino/Asian Fusion |

---

* Indicates a tie with restaurant above

### ADEGA RESTAURANT + WINE BAR    | 27 | 27 | 25 | $59 |
*1700 Wynkoop St. (19th St.), 303-534-2222;*
*www.adegadenver.com*
■ Taking its name from the Portuguese word for 'cellar', this
"contemporary, citified" Lower Downtown lair centers on an
"awesome", "glass-encased" vino vault containing some 800
labels; in the kitchen, Bryan Moscatello's "audacious concepts"
result in "stunning" New American "culinary adventures" (e.g. a
"phenomenal" six-course prix fixe and "extraordinary chef's
table") brought to you by an "attentive", "accommodating staff";
though a few "finicky" folks find portions "startlingly small" and
the menu sometimes "obscure", everyone agrees this is "one of
Denver's hottest scenes."

### Alpenglow Stube    | 26 | 28 | 27 | $73 |
*Keystone Resort, 21996 Hwy. 6 (top of North Peak Mtn.), Keystone,*
*970-496-4386; www.keystone.snow.com*
■ "Both the altitude and the food take your breath away" at this
lodge atop the North Peak of Keystone (elevation: 11,444 ft.)
reachable only by gondola; the "romantic" old-world aerie with
roaring fireplace boasts "exquisite panoramas", plus "outstanding"
staffers who provide "nice sheepskin slippers" and "wonderful,
creative" Bavarian-American cuisine; for this "peak experience",
"bring a fat wallet" and be sure to bundle up ("you freeze on the
way up and down"); N.B. limited hours in summer.

### Barolo Grill ☒    | 25 | 23 | 24 | $48 |
*3030 E. Sixth Ave. (bet. Milwaukee & St. Paul Sts.), 303-393-1040*
☑ "Warm and intimate" yet always "bustling", this Cherry Creek
dinner-only "class act" "could hold its own anywhere", thanks
to "consistently excellent", "belt-expanding" Northern Italian
favorites ("fabulous duck"), an "extensive", "expensive" list of
630 regional wines and an "attentive" staff that travels to The
Boot regularly for educational tastings; some surveyors find the
"upsell, upsell, upsell" approach too "pushy", yet happily take a
"seat by the fireplace" to "watch the sparks fly . . . literally."

### Cafe Brazil ☒⊅    | 27 | 16 | 22 | $32 |
*4408 Lowell Blvd. (44th Ave.), 303-480-1877*
■ Chef/co-owner Tony Zarlenga's "exciting", "exotic" Brazilian-
Colombian fare "astonishes the taste buds" at this "bright",
"unpretentious" 70-seater, now in a "slightly folky", "good-looking
new location" in "not-quite-gentrified" Berkeley Park; "warm,
friendly" and "super laid-back" servers also add to the place's
"personality"; regulars advise reservations, reporting "it's well
worth the wait" for such a "magical experience" – just "don't get
caught without cash", since plastic is not accepted; N.B. the Decor
score may not reflect a mid-*Survey* move.

### Capital Grille, The    | 26 | 26 | 26 | $50 |
*1450 Larimer St. (15th St.), 303-539-2500; www.thecapitalgrille.com*
■ A new battleground in "Denver's steakhouse wars", this
"carnivore's-dream" chain link in LoDo yields "marvelous" chops,
"very good seafood" and more than 400 wines via the ministrations
of an "inspired" staff that "makes everyone feel like a VIP";
"clubby" quarters are "chic, sleek and sophisticated" "without
the stuffiness" of some competitors, and the "see-and-be-seen"
"bar excels"; even those with expense accounts admit that "your

wallet will get a workout, but who cares when you're treated like royalty?"; N.B. free valet parking.

## DEL FRISCO'S
## DOUBLE EAGLE STEAK HOUSE
27 | 25 | 26 | $58

*Denver Tech Ctr., 8100 E. Orchard Rd. (I-25), Greenwood Village, 303-796-0100; www.delfriscos.com*

■ "Denver's elite" – including "pro ballplayers" (e.g. "the Broncos' defensive unit") and other "celebs" – are among the "testosterone-charged" "faithful" of this Greenwood Village chain meatery; they consider it "well worth the coronary risk" to chow down on the "succulent" "slabs of steer" and sides at this "clubby" "Western parlor" where an "impeccable" staff is "out to please"; bellyachers beef about a "loud crowd that likes to show off their money", apparently preferring fellow diners to be seen and not herd.

### Emma's 🏠
25 | 24 | 24 | $41

*603 E. Sixth Ave. (Pearl St.), 720-377-3662; www.emmasrestaurant.com*

■ Habitués hail this "charming", "homey" New American 50-seater in a central Denver Victorian as "one of the friendliest places in town", thanks to "delightful" owners Garen and Linda Austin and their "accommodating" crew; what's more, chef Brian Sack's "ultra-competent kitchen" turns out "terrific" seasonal entrees "rich with creative sauces" and homegrown herbs yet "without pretension"; in short, it's a "true find."

## FLAGSTAFF HOUSE
27 | 26 | 27 | $64

*1138 Flagstaff Rd. (on Flagstaff Mtn.), Boulder, 303-442-4640; www.flagstaffhouse.com*

◪ The "breathtaking views overlooking Boulder" from Flagstaff Mountain are by themselves "worth the high price of admission" to this "classic" hillside haven, but wait, there's more: loyalists laud the "imaginative, delicious" "French- and Asian-accented" New American–Eclectic fare, the "elegant", "romantic" dining room, the "spectacular" 20,000-bottle wine cellar and the "white-glove" service, though a miffed minority finds the "whole experience" "hoity-toity" and "stuffy to the point of claustrophobia."

### Full Moon Grill
25 | 19 | 23 | $38

*Village Shopping Ctr., 2525 Arapahoe Ave. (bet. Folsom & 28th Sts.), Boulder, 303-938-8800; www.fullmoongrill.com*

■ For a "guaranteed happy eating experience", Boulderites roll over to this "cozy" shopping-center "gem" where the "excellent" seasonal Northern Italian cuisine ("try the pear-and-polenta appetizer", "wonderful desserts") pleases both neighbors and visiting "urbanites"; picky eaters appreciate "knowledgeable" servers who "cheerfully honor custom requests", while tipplers toast "spectacular wine dinners"; a few elbow-roomers sigh the "tables are uncomfortably close" and take solace in patio seating.

### Grouse Mountain Grill
26 | 25 | 25 | $59

*Beaver Creek Resort, 141 Scott Hill Rd. (Village Rd.), Avon, 970-949-0600; www.beavercreek.snow.com*

■ When they want a "first-rate" "fine-dining" experience, the cognoscenti "come back" to this Beaver Creek stalwart for Rick Kangass' "monstrous portions" of "creative", "outrageously delicious" Regional American fare ("fantastic without being too fancy") and 450 vintages, all "wonderfully presented" by an "attentive and professional" staff; the "elegant" yet "kid-friendly" setting offers a fireplace and "gorgeous views" plus the "most comfortable chairs in the universe" from which to enjoy them; P.S. "ask for a table in the bar" near the jazz pianist.

### HIGHLANDS GARDEN CAFE 🗷          | 27 | 27 | 25 | $43 |

*3927 W. 32nd Ave. (bet. Osceola & Perry Sts.), 303-458-5920; www.highlandsgardencafe.com*

■ The "quintessential place for ladies of a certain age" ("take your mom"), this "impeccable" North Denver "Victorian manor" is a "treat for all the senses"; chef-owner Patricia Perry proffers a "shockingly huge" New American menu of "creative", "challenging flavor combos" executed with "talent and style" plus 300 wines; "luscious flora" blooming in "charming" "courtyard gardens" make for a "lovely summer meal on the patio", especially when you're doted on by a "delightful waitstaff."

### Jax Fish House          | 24 | 18 | 20 | $34 |

*1539 17th St. (Wazee St.), 303-292-5767; www.jaxfishhousedenver.com*
*928 Pearl St. (bet. 9th & 10th Sts.), Boulder, 303-444-1811; www.jaxfishhouseboulder.com*

☑ Everyone agrees the quarters are "tight" and the noise level is "way over the top" ("you'll need to use the crayons on the table to communicate"), but even so, most are swept away by the "lively" "party atmosphere" at these "happening" Boulder and LoDo "cult fish houses for locals"; finatics file in to feast on "scrumptious seafood" (the "oysters rock") that's ferried to the table by "hotties" who navigate the "cool" environs swimmingly; P.S. the hooked beseech "please start taking reservations!"

### John's 🗷          | 26 | 19 | 25 | $46 |

*2328 Pearl St. (bet. 23rd & 24th Sts.), Boulder, 303-444-5232; www.johnsrestaurantboulder.com*

☑ For an "intimate respite" from Boulder's "hectic Pearl Street Mall", epicures opt for this New American "classic charmer" set in a "delightfully quiet" cottage; they love "longtime faves" ("incredible Stilton filet mignon") combined with "inventive" and "eclectic" "new offerings", all of which are served "gracefully" and with "professional" aplomb; a 2003 ownership change for this "standby" has apparently "kept things going well" – though to some, that means decor is "dated" and the menu "stale."

### Kevin Taylor 🗷          | 26 | 25 | 25 | $60 |

*Hotel Teatro, 1106 14th St. (Arapahoe St.), 303-820-2600; www.ktrg.net*

☑ Downtown Denver's Hotel Teatro is the stage for this "posh" Parisian-style haute house, an "elegant" and "rather formal" "special-occasion place"; foodies effervesce over chef-owner Kevin Taylor's "delicately balanced" and "innovatively presented" New American cuisine ("perfection on a plate"), the "great" 1,000-label cellar and "truly dedicated" staffers who "cater to your every need" – even if naysayers nitpick that prices are "ridiculous" and the scene "pretentious."

### Keystone Ranch Restaurant          | 26 | 25 | 25 | $70 |

*Keystone Ranch Golf Course, 1437 Summit County Rd. 150 (Rd. D), Keystone, 970-496-4386*

■ Keystone cognoscenti crow about this "consistently exceptional" lodge with its "elegant" "Western ambiance" ("your own cabin in the hills, if your name happens to be Trump"); the "first-class" Colorado-style New American vittles (bison, rack of lamb, wild game) are complemented by some 500 "interesting wines"; afterwards, in a "sitting room" complete with "roaring fireplace", the "tremendous" crew brings guests "wonderful desserts" and coffee; sure, it's "expensive", but just "bring a fat wallet", "forget about" the cost and enjoy a "true mountain experience."

### L'ATELIER    27  23  23  $44

*1739 Pearl St. (18th St.), Boulder, 303-442-7233; www.latelierboulder.com*

■ Chef-owner Radek Cerny is once again a culinary "artiste-in-residence", "cooking up French-inspired eats" for "NY–wanna-bes" at his "charming" two-year-old Boulder cafe; well-wishers wallow in the "dazzling", "imaginative" fare ("colorful essences and reductions") served on "beautiful art-glass dishes" in "good-size portions"; however, claustrophobes cluck this 50-seater has "tables too close together", resulting in "too many people in too small a space."

### Left Bank ♥    25  21  24  $62

*Sitzmark Lodge, 183 Gore Creek Dr. (Bridge St.), Vail, 970-476-3696; www.leftbankvail.com*

☑ Gallic gourmet "classics" ("fantastic bouillabaisse", "don't-miss tomato soup", "sauces that make you want to lick your plate") without the "phony nouveau frills" make this "sophisticated" stop at Vail's Sitzmark Lodge a must for Francophiles ("*sans les enfants*", *s'il vous plaît*) who also ooh-la-la over the "outstanding wine list" and "relaxed" but "meticulous" service; sure, the "old-fashioned" decor might be a mite "dated", and you'll need to "run to the ATM" beforehand (no cards), but "it's all worth it."

### Luca d'Italia ☒    25  20  25  $42

*711 Grant St. (bet. 7th & 8th Aves.), 303-832-6600; www.lucadenver.com*

■ "Hey Dorothy, we're in Italy now", swear smitten surveyors who swoon over this "high-on-the-buzz-chart" Capitol Hill spot from chef-owner Frank Bonanno (Mizuna); foodies feast on "fabulous" five-course tasting menus, crab gnocchi "to make your Italian grandmother smile" and "wonderful 'rabbit three ways'", while an "outstanding" staff that's "caring but not stuffy" traverses the "upscale", "minimalist", modern dining room; though a few fret that the menu's "quirky" and "confusing", most maintain the experience is "hip, happening and heavenly."

### Matsuhisa    26  21  21  $64

*303 E. Main St. (Monarch St.), Aspen, 970-544-6628; www.nobumatsuhisa.com*

■ "Omakase . . . oh my goshe", gasp gourmets who gather at this Aspen outpost of the "Nobu empire", where "refined Japanese chow" and "world-class sushi" constitute a "culinary experience not to be missed"; decor is comparatively "down-home" vis à vis the coastal siblings, comprising a "tasteful" "basement" dining room and a "swanky" upstairs lounge for sipping "tasty saketinis"; though there's a groundswell of grumbling about "indifferent service", overall the cognoscenti consider a dinner here "worth the wound" on your "bleeding wallet."

### Mel's Restaurant & Bar    24  20  23  $40

*235 Fillmore St. (bet. 2nd & 3rd Aves.), 303-333-3979; www.melsbarandgrill.com*

■ The "mature 'in' crowd" hangs in and "hangs out" at this Cherry Creek "hardy perennial"; they report "kitchen magician" Tyler

Wiard "keeps reinventing the menu" with an "ever-changing" roster of "delicious and satisfying" New American dishes, staffers who "take their jobs seriously" pour selections from a "stellar" wine list, and live music at the "terrific bar" "brings in both young city slickers and old-timers" – but decor detractors demand a "makeover" of the "dated" dining room.

### MIZUNA ☒    28 | 22 | 27 | $49 |
*225 E. Seventh Ave. (bet. Grant & Sherman Sts.), 303-832-4778;*
*www.mizunadenver.com*
■ "Let's be frank": Frank Bonanno's "exceptional" Capitol Hill New American, rated No. 1 for Food in Colorado, is "best in breed, class and show"; gourmets are "dizzy with glee" over the "globe-trotting" goodies ("exquisite lobster mac 'n' cheese", "salads almost too pretty to eat") and "stunning wines" proffered by Denver's "most polished kitchen", and the "superb" service is "not just responsive but anticipatory"; a recent expansion of the "lovely and intimate setting" to include a bar and private dining nook "means even more happy diners" at this "winner."

### Montagna    26 | 26 | 27 | $66 |
*The Little Nell Hotel, 675 E. Durant St. (Spring St.), Aspen,*
*970-920-6330; www.thelittlenell.com*
■ "Upscale, classy" and even a touch "formal" (you'll find "few snowboarders here"), this "brightly shining star" at Aspen's Little Nell Hotel is known for its "legendary service" – but what's more, regulars report, "Paul Wade's cooking has never been better"; he's concocting "unbelievably creative", "indescribably delicious" New American cuisine (plus "spectacular desserts") while "treasured master sommelier" Richard Betts proposes perfect pairings; sure, "it's expensive, but worth it."

### Morton's, The Steakhouse    25 | 22 | 25 | $60 |
*1710 Wynkoop St. (17th St.), 303-825-3353*
*Denver Crescent Town Ctr., 8480 E. Belleview Ave. (DTC Blvd.),*
*Englewood, 303-409-1177*
*www.mortons.com*
■ "Chockablock" with "devoted carnivores" and "local celebrities" who store "their own personal wine collections", this "old-school, clubby" cow palace chainster brings in beef eaters for "dinner and show": an "impeccable" "tag-team" staff presents a "food tour" of "massive", "plump and juicy" slabs later "seared to perfection" and served with "diabolically rich sides"; of course, as the "sizzling" meat "melts in your mouth", "funds in the wallet melt at a similar pace", so "cash in a bond before you go" or "enjoy it on a corporate expense account."

### New Saigon    26 | 11 | 17 | $21 |
*630 S. Federal Blvd. (bet. Center & Exposition Aves.), 303-936-4954;*
*www.newsaigon.com*
☑ With an "enormous" menu the "size of a Tolstoy novel" (there's "an entire section devoted to frogs' legs"), this "awesome" "old-timer" in a small South Denver strip mall remains an "inexpensive" way to "take your tongue on a trip to Vietnam"; "attentive" if sometimes "surly" servers will "guide you" to a "truly wonderful" meal (the "best spring rolls", "outrageous noodle soups", "fantastic smoothies"), and though "fancy folk" fret the "nothing-special" interiors are "starting to fray", the "food makes up for it."

---

**Opus**     26 | 23 | 25 | $44

*2575 W. Main St. (Curtice St.), Littleton, 303-703-6787*

■ "Yes, Virginia, there really is great" fare in the "land of the bland chain restaurants" announce "pleasantly surprised" diners who've found this "quaint" "storefront in downtown Littleton"; they talk up its "adventuresome", "exciting" and "wonderful" New American entrees presented with "panache" by "professional" servers in an "urban-chic" setting some call "stark"; a vocal minority maintains the place "still feels like a work in progress", but all admit this "up-and-comer" is "trying hard."

**Panzano**     25 | 23 | 22 | $41

*Hotel Monaco, 909 17th St. (Champa St.), 303-296-3525;*
*www.panzano-denver.com*

☑ "Even with the loss of chef Jennifer Jasinski", this sunny, "centrally located" Downtown "hotel restaurant" has "kept its status as a great Northern Italian bastion"; the "awesome" "open kitchen makes it fun to watch the action" as new top toque Elise Wiggins creates her "hearty yet sophisticated" and "delicious" cuisine (Sunday brunch is "unusual and terrific") for "power-lunchers", "special visitors" and "relatives from NY"; still, some say it's been "hit-or-miss lately", with service that can be "slow."

**Parisi** ☒     25 | 18 | 17 | $17

*4401 Tennyson St. (44th St.), 303-561-0234; www.parisidenver.com*

■ "There's a good reason for the line out the door" at this "always packed" Berkeley Park Italian, swear swooning surveyors: "it's all about" the "superb and sophisticated", "authentic and delicious" food ("fantastic lasagna", "peerless focaccia sandwiches", "thin-crusted" "pizzas to dream about"); the "spacious" new location's "warm atmosphere" appeals to lingerers who "love topping off a fine dinner with gelato or espresso", while for time-challenged types, there's a "knockout deli" stocking "specialty foods" and "prepared dishes for takeout."

**Piñons**     25 | 24 | 25 | $62

*105 S. Mill St. (E. Main St.), Aspen, 970-920-2021*

■ "No trip" to Aspen "is complete" without dining at this "always excellent and reliable" Regional American "classic", according to admirers; in a "comfortable" room that feels like a "Southwestern art gallery", "cordial" staffers extend a "wonderful welcome" before "knowledgeably" discoursing on chef Rob Mobilian's "Colorado cuisine" for the "gourmet Western palate" ("perfect elk chops") and sommelier Jeff Walker's "superb wines"; "off-the-charts" tabs have some grumbling "overrated and overpriced" and others countering "even if the total bill comes to $5 per bite, it's worth every penny."

**Potager** ☒     24 | 20 | 22 | $40

*1109 Ogden St. (bet. 11th & 12th Aves.), 303-832-5788*

■ Clearly a "Chez Panisse devotee", chef Terry Rippeto fashions her "eclectic, seasonal" New American fare from "sublime", "freshest-of-the-fresh" ingredients at this "funky" Capitol Hill "charmer"; add in a "breezy", "bohemian", "Euro-distressed" dining room, a "delightful garden" ideal for "romantic interludes" and a "friendly", "wine-savvy staff" that's up on the "thoughtful" "boutique" list and you get a "Berkeley"-style "bistro that could – and does"; still, some sticklers' "high expectations" were

---

"disappointed" by "loud acoustics" and "indifference" from the crew; N.B. no reservations.

### Q's     25 | 23 | 23 | $42

*Boulderado Hotel, 2115 13th St. (Spruce St.), Boulder, 303-442-4880; www.qsboulder.com*

■ An "oasis within the People's Republic of Boulder" that's "far from the tree-hugging crowd", this "classy", "historic" New American in the Hotel Boulderado is a "great place to take your parents or have a business dinner"; servers "really care", and "outstanding" chef John Platt's "inspiring" seasonal menu is "heavenly" (though acrophobes assert his "artistic presentations" are "a little heavy on the towers"); "breakfast is awesome" too, especially if you sit on the "nice porch" overlooking the Pearl Street pedestrian mall.

### Six89 Kitchen & Wine Bar     26 | 22 | 24 | $45

*689 Main St. (7th St.), Carbondale, 970-963-6890; www.six89.com*

■ Tight-lipped tastemakers "hate to share the secret" of chef-owner Mark Fischer's Carbondale New American, but admit they "owe it" to him to spill the beans; in fact, his "passionate", "creative" "culinary artistry" ("each dish is more delicious than the last") has won over flocks of foodies willing to journey "from Denver just for the meal and then home the same night"; "genius sommelier" Bill Bentley's "stellar cellar" and "hospitable", "well-trained" servers who make everything "look effortless" also contribute to this "uplifting" "down-valley" experience.

### Solera Restaurant and Wine Bar     25 | 22 | 23 | $45

*5410 E. Colfax Ave. (Grape St.), 303-388-8429; www.solerarestaurant.com*

■ "Rising star" Goose Sorensen took a "tough location" on a "seedy strip" in East Denver and elevated it to a "superb local eatery" with his "innovative, playful" and "utterly fantastic" New American fare and an "incredible selection" of "reasonably priced wines"; thanks to "snappy service", a "quiet and calming" atmosphere and a "beautifully appointed patio" perfect for "starlit summer nights", it's "a delicious experience" for those "interested in food, not scenes"; P.S. "Wednesday wine tastings are a treat."

### Splendido     26 | 26 | 25 | $67

*The Chateau at Beaver Creek Resort, 17 Chateau Lane. (Scott Hill Rd.), Beaver Creek, 970-845-8808; www.splendidobeavercreek.com*

■ "Chef David Walford puts out one amazing meal after another", at this "first-class" Beaver Creek New American, an "outrageously beautiful" "château" where window tables provide "fantastic views" and the piano bar and central fireplace "make you want to never leave"; "spectacular wines" and "top-notch service" also add allure, but "very expensive" rates have some slamming the scenario as strictly for those "who like to light their cigars with $100 bills."

### Sushi Den     27 | 23 | 20 | $39

*1487 S. Pearl St. (E. Florida Ave.), 303-777-0827; www.sushiden.net*

☑ "Beverly Hills meets the Rockies" at this "sleek", "modern" sushi specialist in Washington Park where "beautiful people galore" gather for "artful and inventive" "ultra-fresh" fare ("creative rolls", "must-eat" sashimi) made from fish that's "flown in from Japan daily", along with "amazing banana cream pie"; some snipe that "service is pompous and pretentious" but admit the "food is worth the 'tude – barely" ("I wish it weren't so good, so I could stop going"); P.S. no reservations, so "be prepared" for "long waits" during "prime time."

### SWEET BASIL                    27   22   24   $51
*193 E. Gore Creek Dr. (Bridge St.), Vail, 970-476-0125;*
*www.sweetbasil-vail.com*

■ "After so many [27] years", this "super place" still "satisfies and stimulates", declare devotees of this "dynamic" Vail Village "landmark", voted Colorado's Most Popular in this *Survey*; respondents "never tire" of Bruce Yim's "clever, innovative" New American cuisine with "Asian touches", the "caring" staff, "great après-ski scene" or "beautiful views" of Gore Creek; sure, service can be "spotty", the reservation list fills "months in advance" and you might have to "sell your seat at the bar" to "help defray the cost", but the place's "energy and verve" endures; P.S. "insider's tip: go for lunch."

### Syzygy                         25   23   23   $58
*520 E. Hyman Ave. (bet. Galena & Hunter Sts.), Aspen, 970-925-3700*

■ "Syzygy – a word constructed from sizzle and energy?" wonder wordsmiths who in any event agree this "great Aspen secret" "has both"; "wild-game master" Martin Oswald conjures up "terrific" New American dishes that aren't "drenched in sauces" for pairing with bottles from a "superb wine list"; the setting "has it all", with an "elegant", "tastefully simple" dining room and a lively bar offering "jumping jazz" on weekends; it may be "expensive", yet most feel this "hip", "happening place" is "worth every dollar."

### Tante Louise    26   24   27   $52
*4900 E. Colfax Ave. (Eudora St.), 303-355-4488; www.tantelouise.com*

■ "You owe it to yourself to go" to this East Denver "grande dame", where "charming" owner and "ultimate host" Corky Douglas "glides through his domain", "elegant surroundings" that are "as warm as your own living room"; "splendid service", "first-class" Gallic specialties ("amazing bread pudding"), an "extensive", "diverse" 500-label *carte du vin* and "great patio dining" all contribute to the "long-standing excellence" that makes this "special-occasioner" a perfect place "to pop the question" – though wags wink "Tante Louise must be French for 'overpriced.'"

### 240 Union                      26   20   24   $36
*240 Union Blvd. (bet. W. Alameda Pkwy. & 6th Avenue Fwy.),*
*Lakewood, 303-989-3562; www.240union.com*

☑ This "beacon of exciting food in the culinary desert" of the Western suburbs is "alive, exciting and always busy" boast boosters who believe it's "a bargain for the quality of food you get"; the "modern" dining room is overseen by "superb" servers, and chef Matt Franklin's "a genius with seafood", creating "bright, innovative" and "consistently excellent" New American fin fare and "seasonal menus" whose "flavors sing on the plate"; perhaps that's one reason the sound-sensitive snipe it's "too darn loud."

### Wildflower                     25   25   24   $58
*The Lodge at Vail, 174 E. Gore Creek Dr. (base of Vail Mountain),*
*Vail, 970-476-5011; www.rockresorts.com*

☑ Two decades after its founding, it's still "a pleasure to return" to this "high-class" New American in the Lodge at Vail; loyalists laud the "delicious", "interesting" New American fare, 1,000-label cellar and "superb summer lunches on the patio" amid "spectacular wildflowers"; diners differ on decor, however, with supporters sticking up for the "charming", "elegant" environs and snipers slamming an "absurdly flowery" "tearoom" "from the '60s"; other observers opine that overall things have "slipped recently", perhaps due to a chef change.

**Zengo**                                26 | 27 | 24 | $44

*1610 Little Raven St. (15th St.), 720-904-0965; www.modernmexican.com*
■ Whether or not it's actually "the coolest-looking eatery in the West", it's certainly "unlike any other restaurant in Denver", rave respondents about Richard Sandoval's new "sassy", "bodaciously" "sexy" "urban hot spot" in Platte River; take in the loungey lair's vibrant colors and textures or "snatch a seat at the chef's counter" to watch the busy kitchen, then let the "exotic", "bizarre" and "deliciously unique" Nuevo Latino–Asian fusion concoctions, "sublime drinks" and "smooth service" do the rest; still, grumblers growl that "deafening noise" deters "dinner conversation."

# Detroit

## TOP 10 FOOD RANKING

| Restaurant | Cuisine |
|---|---|
| **28** Rugby Grille | American/Continental |
| Lark, The | Continental |
| Emily's | New French/Med. |
| **27** Zingerman's | Deli |
| Tribute | New French/Asian Fusion |
| Bacco | Italian |
| Common Grill | Seafood |
| **26** Five Lakes Grill | New American |
| West End Grill | New American |
| Il Posto Ristorante | Italian |

## ADDITIONAL NOTEWORTHY PLACES

| | |
|---|---|
| Beverly Hills Grill | New American |
| Cafe Bon Homme | New French |
| Capital Grille | Steakhouse |
| Grill at the Ritz Carlton | New American |
| No. VI Chop House | Steakhouse |
| Opus One | American/Continental |
| Ristorante Café Cortina | Italian |
| Rochester Chop House | Steakhouse |
| Ruth's Chris | Steakhouse |
| Steve's | Deli |

| | F | D | S | C |
|---|---|---|---|---|

**Bacco** ⌧      27 | 25 | 25 | $52
*29410 Northwestern Hwy. (W. 12 Mile Rd.), Southfield, 248-356-6600; www.baccoristorante.com*
■ "Delectable food" filled with "wonderful flavors" from a "pure-Italian" kitchen that pays "attention to detail" has regulars ranking this "rather elegant", "pricey", "upscale" Southfield spot among the "best in Detroit"; other attributes include "top-notch service" from a "knowledgeable and friendly staff", as well as "great people-watching" at the bar and a "gorgeous", "contemporary" interior, all of which makes it "a place to be seen with the 'in' crowd."

**Beverly Hills Grill**      26 | 19 | 23 | $33
*31471 Southfield Rd. (W. 13 Mile Rd.), Beverly Hills, 248-642 2355*
■ "Always reliable", this "lively" Beverly Hills New American "favorite" "never disappoints" with its "amazing breakfasts", but it also gets "raves" for its "creative brunches", "delicious lunches" and "outstanding dinners" thanks to a "consistently stellar" kitchen and an "expertly trained staff"; true, the "casual" space is "crowded, small and noisy", but most insist the "quality" "makes up for" the "drawbacks" – now "if only they would take reservations."

### Cafe Bon Homme ⊠    26 │ 20 │ 23 │ $55 │
*844 Penniman Ave. (bet. Harvey & Main Sts.), Plymouth,*
*734-453-6260*
■ "A lovely, welcoming experience" awaits at this "charming
restaurant" "in the great little town of Plymouth", where "superb"
New French fare (including "sensational desserts") is paired with
a "great wine list" and served by an "outstanding" staff in a "cozy",
"quiet" setting; a few feel the "outdated decor" "is tired", but more
maintain that the "quaint", "intimate atmosphere" helps "make
every dinner there a special occasion."

### Capital Grille, The    25 │ 25 │ 24 │ $52 │
*Somerset Collection, 2800 W. Big Beaver Rd.*
*(bet. Coolidge & Crooks Rds.), Troy, 248-649-5300;*
*www.thecapitalgrille.com*
■ Set in Troy's "tony Somerset Collection" mall, this "busy" bastion
of a "first-rate" national "steakhouse chain" is a "carnivore's
delight", offering a "clubby atmosphere" and "enormous portions"
of "old-school cuisine" that, of course, includes some of the
"best steak in town" (from a "kitchen that knows what rare is");
it's a "power"-lunch and -dinner "favorite of auto execs" and
"ad-agency biggies", and in the evening the "lively", "smoky bar"
hops with a "fun crowd."

### COMMON GRILL, THE    27 │ 20 │ 24 │ $34 │
*112 S. Main St. (bet. Middle & South Sts.), Chelsea, 734-475-0470;*
*www.thecommongrill.com*
■ It's "worth the trip" to this "off-the-beaten-path" storefront spot
"in the wonderful town of Chelsea", an "hour's drive" from Detroit,
thanks to "great chef" and owner Craig Common's "excellent
seafood" menu, which offers "variety, freshness" and fish "as
good as at an East Coast restaurant"; a "fun, bistro-like bustle"
pervades the "always-crowded" dining room, but be warned that
the atmosphere is decidedly "high decibel" (and "expect to wait
to be seated").

### EMILY'S ⊠    28 │ 22 │ 27 │ $63 │
*505 N. Center St. (8 Mile Rd.), Northville, 248-349-0505;*
*www.emilysrestaurant.com*
■ "A cute house in Northville" is the setting of this "charming"
50-seater, an "absolute gem" where "new chef Gabe" Lacouture
creates a "seasonal" menu of "imaginative" New French–Med
dishes, which "warm and welcoming" owner Rick Halberg
"exceptionally matches" with "an excellent wine list"; the
"outstanding service" and "unpretentious", "intimate atmosphere"
also contribute to "a thoroughly enjoyable experience" that
epitomizes "fine dining at its best."

### Five Lakes Grill ⊠    26 │ 20 │ 23 │ $42 │
*424 N. Main St. (Commerce St.), Milford, 248-684-7455*
■ Fortunate fans feel they've "died and gone to heaven" after
a visit to this "fairly priced" New American where "excellent
chef"-owner Brian Polcyn's "innovative" menu emphasizes "fresh,
fresh, fresh" Michigan ingredients and includes "delightful twists
on old favorites"; it's "food you'll find nowhere else", and the
storefront space offers a surprisingly "urbane atmosphere"
given its location "in the quaint old town" of Milford, 30 minutes
north of Detroit.

### Grill at the Ritz-Carlton, The
26 | 26 | 27 | $57

*Ritz-Carlton Dearborn, 300 Town Center Dr. (bet. Hubbard Dr. & Southfield Frwy.), Dearborn, 313-441-2100; www.ritzcarlton.com*

■ A "gracious", "attentive" staff provides "refined", "first-class service" at this "top-notch" Dearborn hotel near Ford's world headquarters, a "special-occasion" favorite that's "guaranteed to impress" with an "amazing" New American menu of "wonderful food" made from the "highest-quality ingredients"; P.S. a "recent renovation" has rendered the "beautiful, elegant room" "even more luxurious", and the Food rating may not reflect the post-*Survey* arrival of chef Robert Wilson.

### Il Posto Ristorante ⊠
26 | 24 | 24 | $51

*29110 Franklin Rd. (Northwestern Hwy.), Southfield, 248-827-8070*

■ "When you want to splurge", "dress up" and dash to this "expensive, elegant Italian" in Southfield, where "classic" cuisine that "never disappoints" is "prepared flawlessly" from "the noblest of ingredients", accompanied by a "great wine list" and "formally" served by "bona fide waiters [from The Boot]" in a "fabulous room"; some purport it's "pretentious", saying certain staffers are "supercilious", but more maintain it's a must for "memorable meals" of the "highest quality."

### LARK, THE ⊠
28 | 26 | 28 | $81

*6430 Farmington Rd. (W. Maple Rd.), West Bloomfield, 248-661-4466; www.thelark.com*

■ "Romance abounds" at this "still-superb" West Bloomfield "legend" "modeled after a Portuguese country inn" that remains the Most Popular of Detroit-area restaurants; "consummate hosts" and owners "Jim and Mary Lark treat you like guests in their home", while their "educated, professional staff" provides "superior service"; in the kitchen, "new chef Kyle Ketchum" is now "at the helm", "providing freshness to the outstanding menu" of "divine" Continental fare and "adding to an already fabulous dining experience."

### No. VI Chop House & Lobster Bar
26 | 24 | 25 | $56

*27790 Novi Rd. (12 Mile Rd.), Novi, 248-305-5210; www.uniquerestaurants.com*

◪ "Fantastic food" is featured at this "first-class" surf 'n' turfer that has fans "salivating" with "some of the best steaks going", "divine morel bisque" and "wonderful" "sautéed lobster tails with whipped potatoes", plus "top-notch service to match"; some find the "dark-wood" environs too "dimly lit" and the "manly prices" "sinful", but most feel this "favorite" is "worth the drive" to its "far-out" location; P.S. the "catchy name is actually" a play on the town's moniker – "get it?"

### Opus One ⊠
26 | 25 | 25 | $53

*565 E. Larned St. (Beaubien St.), 313-961-7766; www.opus-one.com*

◪ "Still a favorite" with "business- and theater-crowd" "movers and shakers", this "Downtown institution" "delivers on all levels" thanks to chef-partner Tim Giznsky's "interesting, varied menu" offering "a mix of Traditional American" and Continental dishes, "owner Jim Kokas' superb wine list", a "professional staff" that "makes every guest feel special" and recently "updated decor" with "a refreshing, modern look"; a few feel "there are better values", but more insist it's "fine dining the way it was meant to be."

### Ristorante Café Cortina 🅱  26 | 24 | 24 | $53
*30715 W. 10 Mile Rd. (Orchard Lake Rd.), Farmington Hills, 248-474-3033; www.cafecortina.com*

☑ "When you crave" "true Italian flavor", find your way to this "fabulous" Farmington Hills "favorite", a "beautiful cafe" where the "classic" cuisine (including "superb pastas") is "wonderfully prepared" using vegetables and "herbs grown in an [on-site] garden", and the "attentive", "smartly dressed" staff "makes you feel like family"; some fault the "high prices" and feel "the food and service can be a bit uneven at times", but a majority is won over by the "insanely romantic" ambiance.

### Rochester Chop House  26 | 21 | 24 | $39
*306 N. Main St. (3rd St.), Rochester, 248-651-2266; www.kruseandmuerrestaurants.com*

■ Though "beef rules" at this Rochester "Kruse & Muer operation" with "a private-club" feel and "gracious" staff, it's "not your typical chophouse", as it's actually two restaurants under one roof, with the "lively" "Kabin Kruser's Oyster Bar up front" and a "warm, friendly, intimate" dining room featuring "live piano" music (most nights) "in the rear"; it's known for "tempting chops and steaks" and "great lobster", but devotees insist that "everything is wonderful" – including the "great martinis."

### RUGBY GRILLE  28 | 26 | 28 | $60
*Townsend Hotel, 100 Townsend St. (Pierre St.), Birmingham, 248-642-5999*

■ "You may have to mortgage your house, but it's worth it" for the "old-fashioned dining experience" at this "classy", "clubby" Traditional American–Continental that's rated No. 1 for Food among Detroit-area restaurants; "housed in the Townsend Hotel" ("where out-of-town celebs", "stars and musicians stay"), it's "reminiscent of the best intimate European restaurants", and its "exceptional" fare and "elegant service" are "worth every penny" according to "everyone who's anyone in Birmingham"; P.S. "you'll want to be seated inside" "the tiny grille" "rather than the hallway outside."

### Ruth's Chris Steak House  25 | 20 | 24 | $50
*755 W. Big Beaver Rd. (I-75), Troy, 248-269-8424; www.ruthschris.com*

☑ Among the "best of the meat houses", this Troy cow palace strikes supporters as a "top-notch" outpost of a "can't-miss chain" that's "surely worth a visit"; some detractors decry the "noisy atmosphere" as "a little down-market", suggesting "the decor does not compare to the competition's", but the "generous portions" of "delicious beef" "that come sizzling in butter" and "literally melt in your mouth" have more wondering "how can you go wrong?"

### Steve's Deli  25 | 11 | 18 | $17
*Bloomfield Plaza, 6646 Telegraph Rd. (Maple Rd.), Bloomfield Hills, 248-932-0800*

☑ "As close to a New York deli as you can get", this "wonderful delicatessen" "in a strip mall" in Bloomfield Hills "turns out" a "phenomenal selection" of "consistently good", "fast eats", including "the best chicken noodle soup in town" and "fabulous corned beef"; some recommend you "avoid the seating", though, claiming the "cramped, crowded", "unappealing room" and "perennial wait for tables" "make carry out a better choice."

**TRIBUTE** ☒                    27 | 27 | 25 | $76

*31425 W. 12 Mile Rd. (Orchard Lake Rd.), Farmington Hills,*
*248-848-9393; www.tributerestaurant.com*

■ Acolytes "cannot say enough about" the "one-of-a-kind", "remarkable experience" at this "shining star" in Farmington Hills that "deserves all of its acclaim"; "everything is impeccable", from "superb chef" Takashi Yagihashi's "innovative menu" of "delicious", "decadent [New] French–Asian fusion" fare to the "phenomenal ambiance" of its "breathtakingly" "beautiful" space to the "wonderfully attentive staff" – even if "small portions", "over-the-top" prices and certain "haughty staffers" have some "saving" this "culinary masterpiece" "for a special-occasion" "splurge."

**West End Grill** ☒                    26 | 23 | 26 | $47

*120 W. Liberty St. (Ashley St.), Ann Arbor, 734-747-6260*

■ "Make reservations well in advance" for a spot within the "quiet, candlelit setting" of this "romantic, intimate", "white-tablecloth" 65-seater located in the "heart of the action" in Downtown Ann Arbor; reviewers call it "a jewel" for "exquisitely prepared" New American cuisine "impeccably served" by a "solidly trained", "knowledgeable staff" and accompanied by a "fantastic wine list"; true, it's "always crowded" and "occasionally noisy", but you'll be "treated as if you're the only ones dining at the restaurant."

**ZINGERMAN'S DELI**                    27 | 16 | 21 | $17

*422 Detroit St. (Kingsley St.), Ann Arbor, 734-663-3354;*
*www.zingermans.com*

■ "Long lines" "out the door" mark this "legendary" Ann Arbor "institution", "a national treasure" that locals laud as the "best deli in America"; don't be dismayed by the "dizzying array of sandwiches", as the "personable staff" will "guide you through the huge selection" (though you may also need "help" handling the "humongous portions" and "high prices"), or by "the dreary sit-down area" "where your meal is brought to you", as you can always "carry out."

# Ft. Lauderdale

## TOP 10 FOOD RANKING

| | Restaurant | Cuisine |
|---|---|---|
| 27 | Eduardo de San Angel | Mexican |
| | Sunfish Grill | New American/Seafood |
| | La Brochette | Mediterranean |
| | Casa D'Angelo | Italian |
| | Mark's Las Olas | Floribbean |
| 26 | Cafe Martorano | Italian |
| | Darrel & Oliver's | New American/Eclectic |
| | By Word of Mouth | New American |
| | Silver Pond | Chinese |
| | Canyon | Southwestern |

## ADDITIONAL NOTEWORTHY PLACES

| Restaurant | Cuisine |
|---|---|
| Black Orchid | Continental |
| Cafe Vico/Vico's Downtown | Italian |
| Cheesecake Factory | American |
| Chima | Brazilian/Steakhouse |
| Houston's | American |
| Johnny V's | Floribbean |
| Le Bistro | Eclectic |
| Outback | Steakhouse |
| Ruth's Chris | Steakhouse |
| Trina | Mediterranean |

| F | D | S | C |
|---|---|---|---|

**Black Orchid Cafe** — 25 | 21 | 24 | $50

*2985 N. Ocean Blvd. (Oakland Park Blvd.), 954-561-9398; www.blackorchidcafe.com*

■ Chef-owner George Telles has definitely got game, serving such "daring", "exquisitely prepared" specialties as buffalo, elk, pheasant and ostrich along with "outstanding" Continental fare at his "exotic" Ft. Lauderdale cafe; the service is "pampering", the "romantic", "intimate" atmosphere's made more so by a "great" jazz guitarist and even though it's "expensive", "you won't find another experience like it in South Florida."

**By Word of Mouth** 🗷 — 26 | 13 | 23 | $41

*3200 NE 12th Ave. (E. Oakland Park Blvd.), 954-564-3663; www.bywordofmouthfoods.com*

■ "Connoisseurs" just can't help mouthing off about this "hideaway nestled in the depths" of Northeast Lauderdale, where the "daily changing" New American offerings are "fabulous" and the "to-die-for" desserts and baked goods are "the best"; there's no printed menu, but the helpful staff "takes you to a display case to show you the selections", creating a "bonding experience", and despite (or because of) the "small", "snug" setting, it's a "good date place."

### Cafe Martorano ● ⊠      26 | 16 | 20 | $57 |
*3343 E. Oakland Park Blvd. (N. Ocean Blvd.), 954-561-2554*

☑ "It's a real trip, but what a way to go" say legions of loyalists who endure "long waits" to dine at this "tiny" no-reservations, no-menu Lauderdale Italian; "spectacular" standards like "the best meatballs" and "wonderful scampi" have supporters "singing along" with the "blaring Sinatra tunes", and later in the evening the "disco ball" descends and there's "dancing in the aisles"; even if the staff can err on the side of "arrogance" and prices are "outrageous", it's still the "coolest place" in town.

### Cafe Vico/Vico's Downtown      23 | 20 | 23 | $34 |
*IHOP Plaza, 1125 N. Federal Hwy. (NE 11th Ave.), 954-565-9681*
*1 E. Broward Blvd. (NE 1st St.), 954-463-4414 ⊠*
*www.cafevico.com*

■ "White linens at checkerboard [tablecloth] prices" create a "satisfying experience" at this "fine Italian" cafe "treasure" "tucked away" in a Northeast Ft. Lauderdale shopping center; the "expanded" interior provides a "lovely" setting for "outstanding" fare including "superb" seafood, and the "excellent" service rounds out an "enjoyable" evening; N.B. its woodwork-filled Downtown sibling is unrated.

### Canyon      26 | 22 | 23 | $42 |
*1818 E. Sunrise Blvd. (N. Federal Hwy.), 954-765-1950;*
*www.canyonfl.com*

■ The "incredible" prickly pear margaritas sparkle at this "small" "gem" in Ft. Lauderdale, but it's the "unique", "elegant" Southwestern cuisine that has burnished its reputation for a decade; it's still "trendy" and "popular" (and doesn't take reservations), however, so seasoned surveyors suggest "go early to avoid the crowds and noise", "ask for a private booth" and enjoy sampling the "heavenly" fare served by a "knowledgeable" staff in subdued comfort.

### CASA D'ANGELO      27 | 21 | 25 | $46 |
*Sunrise Sq. Plaza, 1201 N. Federal Hwy. (bet. E. Sunrise Blvd. &*
*NE 13th St.), 954-564-1234; www.casa-d-angelo.com*

■ "Master" chef-owner Angelo Elia brings a "touch of Tuscany" to Lauderdale with his "fantastic" Italian fare, from "divine" "homemade pastas" and "exceptional risottos" to "sublime fish", along with "terrific (if pricey) wines"; the "wonderful" staff along with a "classy yet unpretentious" interior contribute to the "fantastic dining experience", but it's the "dependably" "top-flight" food prepared in a wood-burning stove that accounts for the fact that "it's always busy."

### CHEESECAKE FACTORY ●      20 | 19 | 18 | $25 |
*600 E. Las Olas Blvd. (S. Federal Hwy.), 954-463-1999*
*Sawgrass Mills Oasis, 2612 Sawgrass Mills Circle (Flamingo Rd.),*
*Sunrise, 954-835-0966*
*www.thecheesecakefactory.com*

☑ With its fabled "menu longer than the latest Harry Potter" and portions large enough "to serve an entire canasta" group, these "dependable" chain links attract "masses" who "line up" for "good" American fare and "dynamite desserts" earning them the collective title of Most Popular among Ft. Lauderdale area restaurants; sure, they're "noisy" and the lines can be "prohibitively long", but the staff's "quick and efficient" and the "well-done corporate formula" is "great for the kids."

### Chima Brazilian Steakhouse   – | – | – | VE
*2400 E. Las Olas Blvd. (SE 25th Ave.), 954-712-0580; www.chima.cc*
Gourmand gauchos gorge on skewer after skewer of lamb, pork, chicken and *linguica* (Brazilian pork sausages) in a carnivore's parade of a dozen types of meat at this sleek, seductive new South American steakhouse; the all-you-can-eat decadence is rounded out by a salad bar, scrumptious desserts, a sophisticated wine list and, of course, copious caipirinhas.

### Darrel & Oliver's Cafe Maxx   26 | 19 | 24 | $54
*2601 E. Atlantic Blvd. (east of N. Federal Hwy.), Pompano Beach, 954-782-0606; www.cafemaxx.com*
■ A longtime Pompano Beach "favorite", this "superb" New American–Eclectic in an "unpretentious" storefront offers "consistent", "exceptional" cuisine that "blends" flavors from "Florida and the rest of the world"; the interior's "comfortable" (if "plain"), the service is "outstanding" and though it's "pricey", "every bite's worth the premium cost"; P.S. "no cocktails", but the wines are "top-notch."

### EDUARDO DE SAN ANGEL ⌧   27 | 22 | 26 | $46
*2822 E. Commercial Blvd. (bet. Bayview Dr. & 28th Ave.), 954-772-4731; www.eduardodesanangel.com*
■ Chef-owner Eduardo Pria will "change your views of south-of-the-border cuisine" with the "sublime" fare proffered at this Mexican, which garners Ft. Lauderdale's No. 1 Food rating; from "fresh fish to mango crème brûlée", the "unique", "delicate" dishes are "artfully" presented (accompanied by "great wines" but "no margaritas"), and the "solicitous service" is equally "refined"; the "romantic", "old-world" setting in a "small" storefront adds to the "wonderful experience" where, naturally, "reservations are a must during the season."

### HOUSTON'S   21 | 20 | 20 | $29
*1451 N. Federal Hwy. (13th St.), 954-563-2226*
*2821 E. Atlantic Blvd. (Federal Hwy.), Pompano Beach, 954-783-9499*
*www.houstons.com*
■ These "trendy" chain links are "real standouts", thanks to "consistently good" American fare like the "wonderful spinach-artichoke dip" and "great salads and steaks"; the "warm", "wood"-lined interiors and "excellent" service contribute to their "popularity" (though Pompano's "beautiful" waterfront setting doesn't hurt), and an "unbeatable bar scene" ameliorates the "long waits" for a table.

### Johnny V's   – | – | – | VE
*625 E. Las Olas Blvd. (Federal Hwy.), 954-761-7920*
Elevating Ft. Lauderdale's dining and nightlife scene, hot chef Johnny Vinczencz (known for his culinary wizardry in South Beach and beyond) has moved his magic to Las Olas, bringing a bag of delicious Floribbean tricks with touches of Spanish and Mediterranean alchemy to a handsome, urban dining room; the kitchen conjures signatures like wild mushroom short stack and corn-crusted yellowtail snapper, while the gastronomic juju at the bar includes tapas and cheeses teamed with wicked wines.

## LA BROCHETTE BISTRO  | 27 | 18 | 25 | $37 |
*Embassy Lakes Plaza, 2635 N. Hiatus Rd. (Sheridan St.), Cooper City, 954-435-9090*
■ "New innovations and classic favorites" plus "a solid wine list" set apart this "quaint" Cooper City charmer championed for its "memorable" Mediterranean cuisine, particularly the juicy meats served on a skewer and "the freshest seafood" specials "at reasonable prices"; despite its strip-mall setting, the interior's "elegant" but "homey", and the "professional", "informed" staff helps make this "the perfect place to celebrate a special occasion."

### Le Bistro  | – | – | – | M |
*4626 N. Federal Hwy. (bet. NE 44th & 47th Sts.), Lighthouse Point, 954-946-9240; www.lebistrorestaurant.com*
Husband-wife team Elin and chef Andy Trousdale treat patrons at this Lighthouse Point Eclectic to fine dining in a classy but homey space uplifted by the owners' gracious and talented showcasing of their 'One World, One Cuisine' motto with specialties like Thai rack of lamb, chicken kurri korma and a *gambas y tostonas* plantain basket; ask about their great-value tasting menu, cooking classes and parties.

## MARK'S LAS OLAS  | 27 | 24 | 23 | $54 |
*1032 E. Las Olas Blvd. (SE 11th Ave.), 954-463-1000; www.chefmark.com*
☑ This "crown jewel of Las Olas" in Downtown Ft. Lauderdale shines with "beautiful food for beautiful people" from chef Militello, one of the "oft-copied but rarely matched originators of Floribbean" cuisine; the food's "always fabulous" and "innovative", the wines are "unbelievable" and the "chic", "modern" decor's "magical"; foes feel it misses the mark, with "snooty service", a "noisy" atmosphere and "stiff tabs", but they're overruled by those who insist it "exceeds expectations."

## OUTBACK STEAKHOUSE  | 19 | 14 | 18 | $26 |
*6201 N. Federal Hwy. (Bayview Dr.), 954-771-4390*
*1801 SE 10th Ave. (SW 18th St.), 954-523-5600*
*650 Riverside Dr. (Ramblewood Dr.), Coral Springs, 954-345-5965*
*7841 Pines Blvd. (N. University Dr.), Pembroke Pines, 954-981-5300*
*1823 Pine Island Rd. (Sunrise Blvd.), Plantation, 954-370-9956*
*www.outback.com*
☑ "The Aussie theme is worked a little hard" but devotees of this "dependable", "child-friendly" steakhouse chain don't mind undergoing "ridiculous" waits for its "always-delicious" beef at "fair prices" and "fall-off-the-bone ribs" cooked on the barbie; bored blokes, however, blast the "noisy", "crowded" settings and suggest you "stop at the bloomin' onion, 'cuz the bloom is off the rest of the menu."

## RUTH'S CHRIS STEAK HOUSE  | 25 | 22 | 23 | $52 |
*2525 N. Federal Hwy. (bet. Oakland Park & Sunrise Blvds.), 954-565-2338; www.ruthschris.com*
■ Staunch members of this "elegant" chain's gang argue it serves the "best steak north of Argentina" ("signature" beef on "sizzling hot, butter-coated platters") and "great seafood" in "ample portions"; the "sophisticated, country club"–style scene and "experienced" staff that "treats customers like royalty" also please partisans, though a few ruthless sorts slam the "stiff prices."

### Silver Pond
26 | 10 | 15 | $25

*4285 N. State Rd. 7 (south of Commercial Blvd.), Lauderdale Lakes, 954-486-8885*

■ "It's the real thing" cheer champions of this bit of "Chinatown in the tropics" serving "affordable", "authentic", "superb" Hong Kong–style cuisine in a Lauderdale Lakes strip mall; sure, the decor's "average", but "big portions" of "outstanding", "unusual" dishes ensure this "popular" "find" is "packed during winter."

### SUNFISH GRILL ⌧
27 | 15 | 24 | $45

*2771 E. Atlantic Blvd. (Intracoastal Waterway), Pompano Beach, 954-788-2434; www.sunfishgrill.com*

■ "A tiny place with big ambitions", this "fantastic" New American seafooder is tucked into a "nondescript" Pompano Beach strip mall but offers "the best fish in town" thanks to "terrific" chef/co-owner Anthony Sindaco, whose "scrumptious" appetizers, "inventive" entrees and "sinful desserts" are enhanced by "super wines"; the staff's "extraordinarily knowledgeable", and the setting, though "modest", is "relaxed"; even if it's "expensive", sun worshipers insist "it's worth every penny."

### Trina
– | – | – | VE

*The Atlantic, 601 N. Ft. Lauderdale Beach Blvd. (Terramar St.), 954-567-8070; www.trinarestaurant.com*

Fashionable foodies are freaking over hip, new beachfront hotel The Atlantic's hip, new eatery by two New Yorkers – chef Don Pintabona and partner Nick Mautone of Manhattan's Gramercy Tavern – who fuse Big Apple sensibilities with tropical flair; the interior is sexy in chocolate browns (from the leather seating to the walls and plank flooring), but the true star is the Med cuisine, with dinner featuring curried cauliflower soup, homemade ricotta cavatelli and lavender-crusted rack of lamb.

# Ft. Worth

## TOP 10 FOOD RANKING

| | Restaurant | Cuisine |
|---|---|---|
| 28 | Lonesome Dove | Regional American |
| 27 | Saint-Emilion | French |
| | La Piazza | Italian |
| 26 | Boi NA Braza | Brazilian |
| | Kincaid's | Burgers |
| 25 | Del Frisco's | Steakhouse |
| | Classic Cafe | New American |
| | Pegasus | Mediterranean |
| | Cacharel | French |
| | Bistro Louise | New American/Med. |

## ADDITIONAL NOTEWORTHY PLACES

| | |
|---|---|
| Angelo's | Barbecue |
| Babe's Chicken | American |
| Cafe Aspen | New American |
| Chop House | Steakhouse |
| Joe T. Garcia's | Mexican |
| Piccolo Mondo | Italian |
| Reata | Southwestern |
| Rough Creek Lodge | New American |
| Silver Fox | Steakhouse |
| Texas de Brazil | Brazilian |

| F | D | S | C |
|---|---|---|---|

**Angelo's Barbecue** ☒⇎    24 | 13 | 16 | $13
*2533 White Settlement Rd. (University Dr.), 817-332-0357;
www.angelosbbq.com*
■ The "sound of a knife chopping beef and the girl behind the counter yelling for beer" is music to the ears of patrons of this legendary "rustic" Westsider, a "cheap date heaven" whose management "doesn't worry about decor, service" or atmosphere that "reeks of smoke" because they serve "the best BBQ on earth", including ribs and brisket with "lots of napkins"; P.S. lunch on Saturdays, when the lines are shorter, is "a tradition among the well-heeled crowd."

**Babe's Chicken Dinner House**    24 | 14 | 22 | $13
*104 N. Oak St. (Main St.), Roanoke, 817-491-2900*
■ Gather round the "friendly" community table, "loosen your belt" and prepare for "the best darn fried chicken in the Metroplex" at this Roanoke clucker specialist; sure, there's "not a lot of selection" (poultry pooh-poohers can opt only for chicken-fried steak), but there are "bottomless bowls" of sides and buttermilk biscuits, all "perfect comfort food" served family-style and at a "great food-dollar ratio"; just be prepared for a "long, long wait", and remember to BYO if iced tea and soft drinks are not your thing.

## BISTRO LOUISE
25 | 23 | 23 | $39

*Stonegate Commons, 2900 S. Hulen St. (Oak Park Ln.), 817-922-9244;*
*www.bistrolouise.com*

■ You'll "feel like you've wandered into Provence" upon entering Louise Lamensdorf's New American–influenced Mediterranean on the southwest side of town, where she "strolls through the aisles soliciting opinions" while delighted diners compliment her on the "attentive service" and "consistently excellent" food – "no matter what [they] order" from the menu ("we could live on her gazpacho" and "the chicken salad is to die for"); it's also endorsed as a "ladies' lunch" spot and the new "Sunday brunch is simply the best."

## BOI NA BRAZA
26 | 23 | 26 | $50

*4025 William D. Tate Ave. (Hall Johnson Rd.), Grapevine, 817-251-9881;*
*www.boinabraza.com*

■ Bring your appetite, drop off the Hummer with the valet and prepare for an all-you-can-eat spectacle of "expertly prepared" fare (meaning "meat, meat and more meat") at this warmly atmospheric Grapevine Brazilian churrascaria where "roving", "friendly" gaucho-clad waiters ferrying giant skewers sometimes make you forget there's also a "wonderful salad bar"; tip: "come at lunch when virtually the same offerings are available at a lower price."

## Cacharel ⊠
25 | 22 | 25 | $46

*Brookhollow Tower Two, 2221 E. Lamar Blvd. (Ballpark Way),*
*Arlington, 817-640-9981; www.cacharel.net*

■ Reviewers report this "quiet, low-key" French veteran atop a nondescript Arlington office tower works for both "a bad week, because it's the place to go for an attitude adjustment", and "during a good week, to celebrate" "special occasions"; an "absolute culinary delight" (featuring a separate steak menu and the "best soufflés around") with "attentive and courteous" staffers, this is "by far the classiest and most romantic dining spot in town"; P.S. "ask for a window table with great views."

## Cafe Aspen ⊠
24 | 18 | 23 | $33

*6103 Camp Bowie Blvd. (Bryant Irvin Rd.), 817-738-0838;*
*www.cafeaspen.com*

■ This "sparsely decorated" but "cozy" Westsider has a split personality: by day it's a "fast" unfussy lunch outlet, where "pumpkin-seed–crusted catfish is a favorite" and the dessert display is "fabulous" ("it's impossible to pass without making a selection"), while at night it morphs into a "romantic", candlelit New American where live jazz is featured in the back room; at either time, voters applaud the "reasonable prices", "delicious" food and "top-quality service"; N.B. there's now an expansive, air-conditioned patio as well.

## Chop House
24 | 22 | 23 | $43

*301 Main St. (2nd St.), 817-336-4129*

■ A menu overhaul by chef Chris Ward has spiffed up the selections at this "comfortable", brick-walled steakhouse near Sundance Square's epicenter; the "great steaks", veal chops and seafood here are presented with flavorful *jus*, rich reductions and elegant *garni,* and "wonderful treatment" from the staff confirms this is "no hurry-up-and-eat place."

**Classic Cafe** Ⓢ　　　　　　　25 ⎢ 20 ⎢ 25 ⎢ $39
*504 N. Oak St. (Denton St.), Roanoke, 817-430-8185;*
*www.theclassiccafe.com*
■ "A culinary oasis in a sea of burger joints", this "classy" Roanoke American is a rare "white-linen gourmet" experience in the suburbs, complete with "personalized service" and an "intimate", "relaxing" interior; it's ideal for businessmen and "ladies who lunch" on "unusual salads and sandwiches" or dine on dishes both traditional and "creative"; N.B. a slate of special steaks includes T-bones, rib-eyes and porterhouses enhanced with chimichurri, Stilton cheese and more.

**DEL FRISCO'S**　　　　　　　　25 ⎢ 22 ⎢ 24 ⎢ $56
**DOUBLE EAGLE STEAK HOUSE**
*812 Main St. (8th St.), 817-877-3999; www.delfriscos.com*
◪ "Wonderful", "enormous steaks and prices to match" are the rule "at this "loud", "cavernous", "definitive" Downtown beefhouse, which has a "classy men's club" look that attracts "power diners" wearing "boots and creased jeans" (hang your cowboy hat at the entrance) and conventioneers willing to drop big bucks on the "comprehensive wine list"; since it's the Most Popular in Ft. Worth, expect "waits, even with reservations."

**JOE T. GARCIA'S** ⊭　　　　　20 ⎢ 20 ⎢ 20 ⎢ $20
*2201 N. Commerce St. (22nd St.), 817-626-4356; www.joets.com*
◪ Amigos shout "*olé*" for this "not-to-be-missed", cash-only Northside Mexican "institution" where they take "out-of-town guests" for enchiladas, fajitas and margaritas that "knock their socks off"; "on a warm summer night" its lush, resortlike, 600-seat "tropical garden" with swimming pool makes for fine "people-watching" too, though critics insist the place is "overrated" and strictly "for drinks."

**KINCAID'S HAMBURGERS** Ⓢ⊭　　26 ⎢ 15 ⎢ 17 ⎢ $10
*4901 Camp Bowie Blvd. (Eldridge St.), 817-732-2881*
■ Patty piners "rearrange their schedules" to accommodate the "limited hours" (till 6 PM) of this West End mecca because they adore its "fantastic", "big", "juicy" burgers served in white paper bags; a "legend" in the state since 1946, it's set in a converted grocery store whose "communal" tables are often so crowded many have to "stand up to eat" off of "countertops", a small price to pay for "the best hamburger anywhere."

**LA PIAZZA**　　　　　　　　　27 ⎢ 24 ⎢ 22 ⎢ $44
*University Park Vlg., 1600 S. University Dr. (I-30), 817-334-0000*
■ Owner Vito Ciraci has "mellowed" some but still "serves up one heck of a true Italian meal" (especially "the definitive veal") – plus he occasionally sings opera too – at this University mainstay that's a "class act from beginning to end"; since the soft-hued rooms are the "place to rub shoulders with Ft. Worth's upper crust" and spot celebs like "Van Cliburn", remember to "dress properly" ("it's the perfect spot to air out your mink on a cold day") or you may get snubbed by a "snooty" waiter.

**LONESOME DOVE WESTERN BISTRO** Ⓢ 28 ⎢ 23 ⎢ 25 ⎢ $43
*2406 N. Main St. (24th St.), 817-740-8810; www.lonesomedovebistro.com*
■ Don't be afraid to "wear your cowboy boots" as you "step from the Old West stockyards into the tasteful New West atmosphere"

of this "comfortable" Northside Regional American (rated No. 1 for Food among Ft. Worth restaurants); working out of a "tiny open kitchen", chef Tim Love and his "warm" staff create "innovative" Western dishes "emphasizing beef and game" that are an "adventure in upscale dining"; P.S. if you have to wait for a table, lean against the "rustic bar" and order a glass from the small, "carefully chosen" wine list.

### Pegasus, The    25 | 21 | 24 | $41

*2443 Forest Park Blvd. (Park Hill Dr.), 817-922-0808;*
*www.thepegasus.net*

■ "One could live on the meze menu alone" at this "sophisticated", "family-run" Forest Park Mediterranean, but doing so would preclude your trying other items on the "extensive menu" like "crab cakes, any number of phyllo-wrapped goodies" and a signature baklava ice cream sandwich; while its "off-street" location may be a tad hard to find, the place itself is "great for de-stressing" because of its clean lines and oversized windows looking out onto treetops.

### Piccolo Mondo    24 | 18 | 23 | $32

*829 Lamar Blvd. E. (Collins St.), Arlington, 817-265-9174;*
*www.piccolomondo.com*

■ Loyalists of the Arlington Italian ("one of the best-kept secrets" around, despite being in the neighborhood for more than 20 years) advise that you don't let the "strip-center location keep you away"; environs notwithstanding, this "steady-in-all-things" "gem" is a "friendly, romantic oasis" where the "food delights the mouth", particularly such specialties as eggplant parmigiana and scaloppine al lemon.

### REATA    24 | 26 | 24 | $40

*Sundance Sq., 310 Houston St. (3rd St.), 817-336-1009; www.reata.net*

◪ It may be "billed as cowboy cuisine, but cowboys never ate so well" as they do at this Southwestern "reincarnation of an old favorite" Downtown, which may have "lost its view" in the move to new digs "but not its style" ("lots of Western memorabilia, but done with decorum"); since "they put enough on the plate for two ranch hands", go with a "big appetite", or just kick back with a longneck and appetizers in the "rooftop dining area."

### Rough Creek Lodge    ▽ 28 | 27 | 25 | $53

*County Rd. 2013 (US 67 S., 9 mi. south of Glen Rose), Glen Rose,*
*254-918-2550; www.roughcreek.com*

■ Corporate titans and world-class marksmen are typical patrons at this Glen Rose retreat where chef Gerard Thompson prepares "amazing" New American fare (particularly game) that's served by a precision team in a "truly unique setting" with an outside patio "overlooking a lake" and an elegant ranch-style room with a soaring fireplace; it's a "long drive" out there (about 50 miles from Ft. Worth), so "if you can, stay the night" in the lodge.

### SAINT-EMILION ⧅    27 | 24 | 27 | $46

*3617 W. Seventh St. (Montgomery St.), 817-737-2781*

■ The "crème de la crème" of French dining in town is Bernard Tronche's Cultural District "cottage" "hideaway" where you'll "feel like you've been transported" to an "intimate" "country farmhouse" in Provence as "timely" servers deliver "divine" food and "superb wines" from a list that's strong on Bordeaux; in sum, it's a "leisurely" "escape for a few hours" and an "ideal spot for a romantic tryst."

**Silver Fox Steakhouse** 🗷   24 | 23 | 24 | $51 |
*1651 S. University Dr. (I-30), 817-332-9060*
*1235 William D. Tate Ave. (W. Dallas Rd.), Grapevine, 817-329-6995*
■ Two pros who know how to spawn successful mega concepts have taken a pair of erstwhile diners and converted them into "clubby", "old-line steakhouses" where the "comfort-food sides" are included in the price of the "solid entrees"; filled with a photo gallery of luminaries, this "well-managed" duo in the University Area and Grapevine also has an "impressive" wine selection.

**TEXAS DE BRAZIL**   23 | 22 | 23 | $46 |
*101 N. Houston St. (Weatherford St.), 817-882-9500;*
*www.texasdebrazil.com*
■ While "not as well known as the competition", this "dark", "cool"-looking Brazilian churrascaria chainster is a "place to take out-of-town guests" ("you'll never have to feed them again" during their stay) for "lots of" "well-seasoned" meat (of "fine quality", especially "for the money") served on "big skewers" by a "very accommodating staff"; as befits examples of this genre, an "excellent salad bar" is also available.

# Honolulu

## TOP 10 FOOD RANKING

| | Restaurant | Cuisine |
|---|---|---|
| **28** | Alan Wong's | Hawaii Regional |
| **27** | La Mer | New French |
| | Hoku's | Pacific Rim |
| | 3660 on the Rise | Pacific Rim |
| **26** | Roy's | Hawaii Regional |
| | Chef Mavro | New French/Hawaii Regional |
| | Ruth's Chris | Steakhouse |
| **25** | Mekong Thai | Thai |
| | Hy's | Steakhouse |
| | L'Uraku | Japanese |

## ADDITIONAL NOTEWORTHY PLACES

| | |
|---|---|
| Bali by the Sea | Pacific Rim |
| Diamond Head Grill | Hawaii Regional |
| Golden Dragon | Chinese |
| Indigo | Asian/Eclectic |
| Longhi's | Italian/Med. |
| Orchids | American/Seafood |
| Padovani's | French/Med. |
| Pineapple Room | Hawaii Regional |
| Sansei | Pacific Rim |
| Side Street Inn | Hawaiian |

| F | D | S | C |
|---|---|---|---|

**ALAN WONG'S**                                 28 | 21 | 25 | $57
*McCully Ct., 1857 S. King St. (bet. Hauoli & Pumehana Sts.), 808-949-2526; www.alanwongs.com*
■ Voted Most Popular and No. 1 for Food in Honolulu, this "favorite" "hidden" on the edge of Ala Moana "never disappoints and always impresses" thanks to "heaven-in-your-mouth" Hawaii Regional cuisine featuring a "wonderful blend of ingredients" ("try Da Bag" or the "flavorful signature ginger-crusted onaga") prepared by "inventive Alan Wong", the "masterful" chef-owner; with such "sumptuous" fare and "seamless service", "who cares" about the "tight quarters and constant din"?

**Bali by the Sea** ⓈⒷ                          24 | 27 | 24 | $61
*Hilton Hawaiian Vlg., 2005 Kalia Rd. (Ala Moana Blvd.), 808-941-2254; www.hiltonhawaiianvillage.com*
■ A "romantic" "special-occasion place", this "Beauty by the Sea" in "the huge Hilton Hawaiian Village complex" boasts an "elegant" open-air dining room with "alluring views" of Waikiki Beach, "excellent" Pacific Rim cuisine and "friendly" service from an "efficient" staff; a few call it "overpriced" and "touristy", but most sum it up as "outstanding"; N.B. the Food score does not reflect the post-*Survey* arrival of chef Roberto Los Baños.

### Chef Mavro　　　　　　　　26　23　26　$64
*1969 S. King St. (McCully St.), 808-944-4714; www.chefmavro.com*
◪ The "fantastic flavors" of "island ingredients" are "perfectly blended" with "Provençal" "culinary style" into "impressive" and "delicious" New French–Hawaii Regional cuisine by a "first-rate" chef, the "mavrolous" George Mavrothalassitis himself, at this "beautiful" and "relaxing" venue on the edge of Ala Moana, then "wonderfully paired" with "amazing wines" and proffered by "attentive", "informed" servers who "pamper you"; a vocal minority grumbles about "tiny", "overpriced portions", but most "wish they could afford it more often."

### Diamond Head Grill　　　　24　25　23　$51
*W Hotel, 2885 Kalakaua Ave. (Diamond Head), 808-922-3734; www.diamondheadgrill.com*
◪ The "hip", "upwardly mobile" "all-dressed-up crowd" flocks to this "stylishly Zen" Hawaii Regional eatery "in the W Hotel" (on the edge of Waikiki) that's known for "innovative" and "fantastic" dishes served by a "knowledgeable", "accommodating" staff; still, some complain it's "expensive" and "too noisy" thanks to the "trendy bar", while lamenting that there's "no ocean view"; N.B. the Food rating may not reflect the post-*Survey* arrival of chef Todd Wells and his introduction of a new menu.

### Golden Dragon　　　　　　24　25　22　$43
*Hilton Hawaiian Vlg., 2005 Kalia Rd. (Ala Moana Blvd.), 808-946-5336; www.hiltonhawaiianvillage.com*
■ "This dragon isn't laggin'" say surveyors "satisfied in every respect" with this "upscale" "fine-dining" Chinese "favorite", a bastion of "tranquility amid the bustle of the Hilton Hawaiian Village"; chef Steve Chiang's "delicious", "authentic Cantonese and Szechuan cuisine", as well as "innovative dishes" like the signature "lobster curry with fried haupia coconut pudding (a must-have)", are coupled with "impeccable" service and an "elegant", "luxurious" setting with "great views", making for "a really nice evening" "from the first cup of tea to the last fortune cookie."

### HOKU'S　　　　　　　　　　27　26　26　$54
*Kahala Mandarin Oriental Hotel, 5000 Kahala Ave. (off of Kealaolu Ave.), 808-739-8760*
■ Located in the Kahala Mandarin Oriental hotel, this "top-of-the-line" eatery (whose name means 'star' in Hawaiian) shines thanks to "creative" chef Wayne Hirabayashi's "exquisitely prepared and presented" Pacific Rim cuisine, "fantastic" service and a "prime location" "by the sea" ("request a window table" for the "breathtaking view" of a "secluded beach"); it's a "dream place" of "understated elegance" that's "worth the splurge" and "the drive", as the "parking lot strewn with Ferraris, Mercedes Benzes and Lexuses" attests.

### Hy's Steak House　　　　　25　23　25　$55
*Waikiki Park Heights Hotel, 2440 Kuhio Ave. (Uluniu Ave.), 808-922-5555; www.hyshawaii.com*
■ "A Waikiki institution", this "old-fashioned steakhouse" is "a must for the beef lover" according to fans of its "fabulous steaks" and "delicious prime rib", not to mention its "pleasant, attentive staff" and their "showmanship" in the "tableside preparation of salads and desserts" such as "to-die-for cherries jubilee", or its

"traditionally elegant" setting, which "reminds some of an English castle library"; though the "modern"-minded lament the "dated decor and menu", purists predict it will remain "a mainstay for years" to come.

### Indigo ⌧                                         22 | 22 | 19 | $37
*1121 Nuuanu Ave. (Hotel St.), 808-521-2900; www.indigo-hawaii.com*
■ A "wonderful blend of East and West" awaits at this "exotic" Asian-Eclectic "in the middle of Chinatown" ("convenient to the Hawaii Theatre" Center), where chef Glenn Chu's "interesting menu" "delights", the "fantastic lunch buffet" offers "value for the money" and the "great bar" makes "the meanest martinis in town"; nature enthusiasts suggest you "ask for a table outside" in the "romantic", "tropical" setting of its "beautiful patio"; P.S. though "parking is a nightmare", "valet [service] is available."

### LA MER                                          27 | 28 | 27 | $74
*Halekulani Hotel, 2199 Kalia Rd. (Lewers St.), 808-923-2311;*
*www.halekulani.com*
■ "Feel like royalty" at this "romantic", "idyllic restaurant" in the Halekulani Hotel just steps from the "waves lapping" at Waikiki Beach, where "inventive" chef Yves Garnier's "flawless" New French cuisine "with an island twist" combined with "an extensive (if expensive) wine list", "exquisitely" "superb service" from an "attentive-but-not-intrusive" staff and "beautiful sunsets over the Pacific" creates a "feast for all the senses"; such "elegance does not come cheap", so "bring your platinum card" to this "special-occasion place."

### Longhi's                                        – | – | – | E
*Ala Moana Shopping Ctr., 1450 Alamoana Blvd. (Atkinson Dr.),*
*808-947-9899*
Opened by Carol Longhi O'Leary and brother Peter Longhi, this Italian-Med family affair (an outpost of the popular Maui-based mini-chain founded in 1976 by their father, chef Bob Longhi) is now helmed by yet another sibling, Charlie Longhi; located in the Ala Moana Shopping Center, its swank, open-air setting features the clan's famous cooking, along with romantic sunset ocean views; N.B. a lower-priced lunch menu makes it a must for foodies.

### L'Uraku                                         25 | 22 | 23 | $42
*Uraku Tower, 1341 Kapiolani Blvd. (Piikoi St.), 808-955-0552;*
*www.luraku.com*
■ From the "imaginative and spectacular" food to the "friendly, quick service" and "chic", "creative decor" featuring "colorful umbrellas" "hanging from the ceiling", this "real find" "off the beaten path" near Ala Moana "pleasantly surprises"; the menu "fuses Eastern and Western flavors" "with a Hawaiian touch" for a "unique take on Japanese" cuisine, and "don't miss the Weekender Lunch, a four-course gourmet meal for $16"; N.B. the Food rating may not reflect the post-*Survey* departure of chef Hiroshi Fukui.

### Mekong Thai                                      25 | 15 | 18 | $21
*1295 S. Beretania St. (bet. Keeaumoku & Piikoi Sts.), 808-591-8842*
*1726 S. King St. (McCully St.), 808-941-6184*
■ Though they may have "less flash" than some competitors, these twin Ala Moana eateries attract "in-the-know people" who "enjoy" their "authentic", "flavorful Thai cuisine", which is not only "high quality" but dished out at "non-tourist prices" that make it

a "great bargain"; sure, the "seating is tight" and the "decor could be improved", but "you come for the food", especially the "yummy tom yum" soup, "great satays" and the "not-to-be-missed" Evil Jungle Prince, a famous creation of founding chef Keo Samanikone.

## Orchids     25 | 26 | 25 | $50 |

*Halekulani Hotel, 2199 Kalia Rd. (Lewers St.), 808-923-2311; www.halekulani.com*

■ "Bravo! bravo!" boom bloom boosters bowled over by this "magical" and "romantic" venue at the Halekulani Hotel, "right on the beach in Waikiki", who say its "to-die-for views" coupled with "creative" American fare (including "fabulous seafood and beef selections" and "killer homemade pastries") and "impeccable service" make it a "favorite" for "special occasions", a "must for Sunday brunch" and a top "choice when taking out mainland visitors"; it's a bit "pricey", but fans say it's "worth every penny."

## Padovani's Restaurant & Wine Bar     24 | 21 | 22 | $58 |

*Doubletree Alana Hotel, 1956 Ala Moana Blvd. (Kalakaua Ave.), 808-946-3456*

☑ "Bursting with flavor", the "outstanding" and "refined French"-Med cuisine of "imaginative" chef Philippe Padovani (ex La Mer) draws devotees to this "nice, romantic" spot in the Doubletree Alana Hotel, as does the "stand-out service" and "sensational wine list" "a mile long" (with more than 70 by-the-glass pours); despite these attributes, dissenters are "disappointed" that it's "a little off the beaten path from Waikiki's main strip" and aren't impressed with some "stuffy" staffers.

## Pineapple Room     24 | 20 | 21 | $37 |

*Macy's, Ala Moana Shopping Ctr., 1450 Ala Moana Blvd. (Atkinson Dr.), 808-945-6573; www.alanwongs.com*

■ "Hidden" in an "odd location for an upscale" eatery – an "airy and comfortable room" "inside Macy's", within the "busy" Ala Moana Shopping Center – "innovative" owner "Alan Wong's second triumph" is hailed as "almost as good as" "his namesake restaurant", offering his signature style of "cutting-edge Hawaii [Regional] cuisine" at more "casual prices" but with the same "warm, friendly, attentive" service, making this "aloha experience" a "must-stop for all visiting foodies."

## ROY'S     26 | 21 | 24 | $48 |

*6600 Kalanianaole Hwy. (Keahole St.), 808-396-7697; www.roysrestaurant.com*

■ "Overlooking Maunalua Bay" in "peaceful Hawaii Kai", this "original" "flagship" "is still the best" location of "legendary" chef-owner Roy Yamaguchi's "classy" international "empire", and just "keeps getting better" thanks to his "consistently excellent" Hawaii Regional cuisine – including "mouthwatering fresh fish" dishes and "excellent chocolate soufflé" – plus "outstanding service" and "lovely sunsets"; since the "din and clatter" from the "open kitchen" can make the "crowded" "upstairs dining room too noisy", regulars recommend the "quieter downstairs" area.

## Ruth's Chris Steak House     26 | 21 | 23 | $53 |

*Restaurant Row, 500 Ala Moana Blvd. (bet. Punchbowl & South Sts.), 808-599-3860; www.ruthschris.com*

■ Carnivores clamor for this Restaurant Row chain outpost, "a chip off the ol' block" that's "absolutely" "as good as it gets in

Hawaii for top-quality steaks", with "huge portions" ("no stinginess here") of "scrumptious" meat so "juicy" and "tender" "you can cut it with a fork and skip the knife", sided with their "signature creamed spinach", a "delightful wine list" and "first-rate service" from an "incredibly attentive staff"; though some are worried about the "cholesterol level" and "eye-popping prices", most agree it's "*extra* extraordinarily wonderful."

### Sansei Seafood Restaurant & Sushi Bar　　24 │ 17 │ 19 │ $39 │

*Restaurant Row, 500 Ala Moana Blvd. (South St.), 808-536-6286; www.sanseihawaii.com*

■ Following the success of his Maui original, "inventive" chef-owner Dave 'D.K.' Kodama opened this Restaurant Row sibling similarly specializing in "contemporary" Pacific Rim fare; with a "mind-boggling" "menu that's so big it can take all night to read", "there's surely something to please every palate", and though his "creative flair" results in some "nontraditional" selections that might "make a purist cringe", those who "love" an "interesting twist" appreciate the "unique" take of his "original combos"; P.S. "check out the early-bird specials."

### Side Street Inn　　24 │ 7 │ 15 │ $21 │

*1225 Hopaka St. (Piikoi St.), 808-591-0253*

■ Though some say it's "more a bar than a restaurant", this "unpretentious" Ala Moana "hole-in-the-wall" is "known for" "simple", "out-of-this-world" Hawaiian "comfort food" at "bargain prices" and is "especially" "popular for its" "delicious" "fried pork chops", "the house specialty", as well as "very good blackened ahi" and "surprising chicken katsu"; an "always-busy favorite" of "in-the-know" "local folks", it's also "frequented by" some of "Hawaii's greatest chefs", who "can be found" "hanging out" and "feasting" "when off duty."

### 3660 ON THE RISE　　27 │ 20 │ 23 │ $46 │

*3660 Waialae Ave. (Wilhelmina Rise), 808-737-1177; www.3660.com*

■ "The best of Hawaii's cutting-edge Pacific Rim cuisine" awaits at this "hidden" "find in Kaimuki", a "quiet neighborhood" "away from the hubbub of Waikiki", where a "wizard" of a "creative chef"-owner, Russell Siu, "rises to the occasion" with "fresh, inspiring" specialties ("try the ahi katsu", "the best around") accompanied by a "great wine list" and offered with "pampering service" from an "accommodating staff"; P.S. "save room for" the "wonderful", "decadent desserts", such as the "truly *ono* Mile-High Waialae Pie" or the "No. 1 bread pudding in the known universe."

# Houston

## TOP 20 FOOD RANKING

| Restaurant | Cuisine |
| --- | --- |
| *28* Mark's | New American |
| Chez Nous | French |
| *27* Pappas Bros. | Steakhouse |
| *26* Cafe Annie | Southwestern |
| Indika | Indian |
| Quattro | New American/Italian |
| Da Marco | Italian |
| Brennan's | French/Creole |
| Churrascos | South American/Steakhouse |
| *25* Ashiana | Indian |
| Damian's Cucina Italiana | Italian |
| Ruth's Chris | Steakhouse |
| Aries | New American |
| Tony's | Continental |
| Américas | South American |
| Simposio | Northern Italian |
| Capital Grille | Steakhouse |
| Goode Co. Texas BBQ | Barbecue |
| Kubo's | Japanese |
| *24* Artista | New American |

## ADDITIONAL NOTEWORTHY PLACES

| | |
| --- | --- |
| Azuma | Japanese |
| benjy's | New American |
| Charivari | European |
| Daily Review Café | New American |
| Fleming's Prime | Steakhouse |
| Fogo de Chão | Brazilian/Steakhouse |
| Goode Co. Texas Seafood | Seafood |
| Hugo's | Mexican |
| La Griglia | Italian |
| La Mora Cucina Toscana | Northern Italian |
| Lankford Grocery | Burgers |
| Mockingbird Bistro | New American |
| Pesce | Seafood |
| Rainbow Lodge | Gulf Coast |
| Ruggles | New American |
| 17 | New American |
| Shade | Eclectic/New American |
| t'afia | Mediterranean |
| Tony Mandola's | Cajun/Italian |
| Zula | New American |

### AMÉRICAS 🏠                          25 | 26 | 22 | $40
*The Pavilion, 1800 Post Oak Blvd. (bet. San Felipe St. &*
*Westheimer Rd.), 713-961-1492; www.cordua.com*
■ The South American menu at Michael Cordua's Galleria-area
"crown jewel" has much in common with its "less pricey cousin,
Churrascos" (including the "mouthwatering" steaks), but this is
the "place to take out-of-town guests for the wow factor" of its
"amazing decor" (like a "tree house in the middle" of a "rainforest
on acid"); other attributes include "superior service" and "solid
seafood" options (the "corn-crusted snapper is a must").

### Aries 🏠                             25 | 21 | 23 | $54
*4315 Montrose Blvd. (Richmond Ave.), 713-526-4404;*
*www.ariesrestaurant.com*
■ For four years now, Scott Tycer's Montrose hot spot has won over
Houston "foodies" with an "adventurous" New American menu
featuring "exotic combinations of ingredients and cooking styles"
and a "unique wine list"; his "clever and creative kitchen" produces
"food that entrances", including "seafood so good" fans feel the
place "should have been called Pisces", and though the "well-
mannered" staff is "often busy", service "doesn't suffer for it."

### Artista                             24 | 26 | 21 | $42
*Hobby Ctr. for the Performing Arts, 800 Bagby St. (Walker St.),*
*713-278-4782; www.churrascos.com*
■ Set in Downtown's Hobby Center, this new venue has been
"well-received" thanks to its "dramatic decor" and "intriguing"
New American menu "that lets you pick and choose among meats,
accompaniments and sauces" (don't miss the "crunchy, smoky
crawfish taquito appetizer"); looky-loos like to "sit on the balcony
for great people-watching" and a "marvelous view of Downtown",
while theatergoers appreciate the "quick", "outstanding" service
"that doesn't leave you nervous you're going to miss the first act."

### Ashiana                             25 | 20 | 22 | $29
*12610 Briar Forest Dr. (Dairy Ashford Rd.), 281-679-5555; www.ashiana.cc*
■ The "very good (but not very expensive) lunch buffet" at this
"upscale" Memorial Indian spot "gives the novice the opportunity
to try something new in a posh environment", but subcontinental
sophisticates savor its "more formal dinners" as "epic, sumptuous
dining events"; with a list boasting 450 labels, it's no wonder the
venue also hosts regular wine meals, featuring "new creations"
by "delightful chef-owner" Kiran Verma.

### Azuma                               23 | 23 | 18 | $33
*5600 Kirby Dr. (Nottingham St.), 713-432-9649; www.azumajapanese.com*
◪ This Japanese spot near the Rice Village is "the place to go" for
"hyper-fresh, delicious raw fish", "inventive rolls" and "authentic"
robata dishes cooked over an open-fire grill; don't miss "their
specialty, the hot-rock beef" (Kobe steak that "you cook" yourself
"on what looks like a heated pet rock"); while the atmosphere
within the "Asian-chic interior" is "fun", some surveyors complain
that "the service lags behind the food."

### benjy's                             24 | 20 | 21 | $33
*Rice Vlg., 2424 Dunstan St. (Kelvin Dr.), 713-522-7602; www.benjys.com*
■ Owner Benjy Levit keeps his Rice Village New American the "hip
and happening spot for Houston's trendy set" with "wonderful"

cuisine ("out-of-this-world salads", "stunning desserts") featuring Asian influences and "adventurous combinations of flavors"; "the only thing hotter" than the "modern", "minimalist decor" is the "attentive", "well-trained staff", and the "slick upstairs bar" and lounge "is a destination in itself"; P.S. "don't miss" the "fabulous Sunday brunch", which fans feel "is one of the best in Houston."

### BRENNAN'S OF HOUSTON | 26 | 25 | 26 | $49 |
*3300 Smith St. (Stuart St.), 713-522-9711;*
*www.brennanshouston.com*
■ With "French Quarter–inspired interiors", a "stunning" courtyard for "romantic alfresco dining" and a staff that "exemplifies Southern hospitality", this French-Creole "institution" in Midtown (cousin of the Big Easy's Commander's Palace) "brings the best of New Orleans to Houston"; go for the "wonderful jazz brunch" on Sunday, and "try the turtle soup" as well as the "classic bananas Foster", but "don't leave without your complimentary homemade praline"; N.B. jacket and tie requested.

### CAFE ANNIE Ⓢ | 26 | 25 | 26 | $56 |
*1728 Post Oak Blvd. (San Felipe St.), 713-840-1111;*
*www.cafeannie.com*
◪ The place that "put Southwestern food on the map", this "first-tier restaurant" known for its "unfussy elegance", "unmatched wine selection", and "consistently outstanding" and "innovative" cuisine is a "perennial" favorite in the Galleria area; popular with "the beautiful people and businessmen alike", it's "the best thing to come out of Houston since oil" say most surveyors; chef-owner Robert del Grande has created a separate, more casual menu for the new Bar Annie space.

### Capital Grille, The | 25 | 24 | 24 | $52 |
*5365 Westheimer Rd. (Yorktown St.), 713-623-4600;*
*www.thecapitalgrille.com*
■ "True carnivores" covet this "traditional steakhouse" – part of "a national chain, [but] without the chain feel" – for its "ab-fab" "dry-aged steaks" and servers who "go out of their way to make you feel special"; with a "lively bar scene" and a "men's-club"-meets-"library atmosphere", it's "great for entertaining clients as well as having fun with friends", though some sensitive snouts are "turned off" by the "cigar bar" and the "stench of smoke" that "permeates" "the dining room at times."

### Charivari Ⓢ | 24 | 19 | 23 | $39 |
*2521 Bagby St. (McGowen St.), 713-521-7231; www.charivarirest.com*
■ The "hands-on owner" and "European-trained chef" Johann Schuster along with Irmgard-Maria, "his wife, are charming hosts" and offer up "amazing Transylvanian" and "Bavarian-style food" at this "hidden gem in Midtown", where it feels "like dining in a four-star European hotel"; "the service is attentive and paced", and "you can actually hear the conversation"; P.S. "they go nuts when white asparagus is in season."

### CHEZ NOUS Ⓢ | 28 | 22 | 26 | $50 |
*217 S. Ave. G (Staitti St.), Humble, 281-446-6717;*
*www.cheznousfrenchrestaurant.com*
■ "Far off the beaten path" from Houston proper, this "charming" "treasure" set "in an old church" "hidden in downtown Humble" is a French "gastronomic oasis in the middle of a dining desert";

"for special occasions", foodies flock northward for its "fine cuisine" (including "excellent duck" and "sinful desserts" such as crème brûlée), not to mention "friendly, low-key service and quaint ambiance."

### CHURRASCOS ⚫ 26 | 21 | 23 | $36

*Shepherd Sq., 2055 Westheimer Rd. (S. Shepherd Dr.), 713-527-8300*
*9705 Westheimer Rd. (Gessner Rd.), 713-952-1988*
*www.churrascos.com*

■ Michael Cordua's duo of "comfortable, casual" South American steakhouses are known for "sublime churrasco steaks" served with "addictive chimichurri sauce"; but this is "not just another big-hunk-of-meat restaurant" – the "hefty portions" of "fabulous beef" come with an "unusual grilled veggie assortment" (plus "crispy plantain" chips to start), and be sure to save room for the "amazing *tres leches*" for dessert; N.B. the Decor rating may not reflect a post-*Survey* remodeling of the 9705 Westheimer location.

### Daily Review Café 23 | 16 | 20 | $29

*3412 W. Lamar St. (Dunlavy St.), 713-520-9217;*
*www.dailyreviewcafe.com*

■ "Hidden away on a River Oaks side street", this "stylish and clever" New American "gem" may be "hard to find", but "in-the-know" folks feel it's "worth the search" for its "creative", "ever-changing menu" of "chicken-pot-pie comfort food" "taken up a notch"; an "interesting wine list", "pretty patio" and "friendly staff" also help make it "a staple" for "brunch, lunch or a quiet dinner for two."

### Da Marco ⚫ 26 | 20 | 23 | $49

*1520 Westheimer Rd. (Mulberry St.), 713-807-8857*

■ "Excellent chef" and owner Marco Wiles "dares to differ" from the Italian restaurant formula at this "cozy" Montrose spot with "superb" cuisine "steeped in tradition (but always inventive)", plus a "good wine selection" and a "friendly staff" that "never rushes you"; the "romantic" and "charming interior space" "seems bathed in a golden glow", but the "pretty patio" might be better "if you have a hearing problem."

### Damian's Cucina Italiana ⚫ 25 | 21 | 25 | $41

*3011 Smith St. (Rosalie St.), 713-522-0439; www.damians.com*

■ Overflowing with "old-world charm", this "classic" "white-tablecloth" Midtown Italian is "the kind of place you'd expect Frank and Dean to roll into", and savoring "top-notch food" and "impeccable service" with the local Rat Pack may make you feel like a "Houston insider" ("something about the cozy interior makes people divulge their secrets"); P.S. its "close-to-Downtown" site makes it "great for a business luncheon or a pre-theater meal."

### Fleming's Prime Steakhouse & Wine Bar 24 | 23 | 23 | $52

*River Oaks Ctr., 2405 W. Alabama St. (Kirby Dr.), 713-520-5959;*
*www.flemingssteakhouse.com*

■ "A haunt of the Houston power-broker set", this "'in' place" (the River Oaks outlet of a national chain) with a "knowledgeable" staff is "giving [its competitors] a run for their money" thanks to "wonderful steaks" that are "crispy outside", "rare inside" and accompanied by "zillions of wines by the glass"; there's also a "hopping bar scene on the weekends" – and the "deafening noise" that goes with it.

### Fogo de Chão
24 | 20 | 24 | $48

*8250 Westheimer Rd. (Dunvale Rd.), 713-978-6500; www.fogodechao.com*

■ With a "dizzying flock" of "gaucho"-style waiters using "swords to slice a huge variety" of "tender", "tasty", "high-quality meats" "off of steaming skewers" and "right onto your plate" "till you beg them to stop", this "authentic Brazilian steakhouse" in the Galleria area is definitely a "carnivore's paradise"; the "impressive salad bar" "is also exceptional", but consider it "your enemy" if you want to "eat your money's worth" of "quite-good animal flesh."

### Goode Co. Texas BBQ
25 | 16 | 18 | $15

*8911 Katy Frwy. (Campbell Rd.), 713-464-1901*
*5109 Kirby Dr. (bet. Bissonnet St. & Westpark Dr.), 713-522-2530*
*www.goodecompany.com*

■ "Visitors and locals alike" love to "get their fingers dirty" at Jim Goode's pair of "funky Texana" BBQ smokehouses where the food is served "cafeteria style" but the "tender and meaty ribs", "first-class brisket", "homemade jalapeño cheese bread" and "killer pecan pie" are "worth every stand-in-line minute"; there's "limited indoor seating", but with an "icy cold beer" even "dining on the long picnic tables outside" seems like "heaven on earth."

### Goode Co. Texas Seafood
23 | 17 | 20 | $25

*10211 Katy Frwy./I-10 W. (Gessner Dr.), 713-464-7933*
*2621 Westpark Dr. (Kirby Dr.), 713-523-7154;*
*www.goodecompany.com*

■ Jim Goode's seafood "masterpieces" offer "a truly unique taste of the Gulf Coast" "served with a sparkle" ("don't miss" the "worth-a-special-journey campechana seafood cocktail" or the "perfect mesquite-grilled" fish); partially housed in an old "railroad boxcar", the Upper Kirby District branch has a "fun, funky" "down-home" atmosphere, while the Memorial address is a little more "uptown."

### Hugo's
22 | 22 | 19 | $35

*1602 Westheimer Rd. (Mandell St.), 713-524-7744*

◪ Chef-owner Hugo Ortega offers "an excellent, high-end, truly authentic experience" at his "lively" Montrose establishment that's "not your typical chips-and-salsa place" – instead, you'll find "out-of-this-world squash blossom appetizers", "meats with the flavor of Mexico", "great Spanish wines and powerful Grand Marnier margaritas" on the menu; still, those "underwhelmed" by certain "indifferent" staffers say the "somewhat lacking service" "could use some improvement."

### INDIKA ⬚
26 | 21 | 21 | $36

*12665 Memorial Dr. (Boheme Dr.), 713-984-1725; www.indikausa.com*

■ "East meets West" at this "upscale", "gourmet" two-year-old set in a "cozy house in Memorial"; "inspired chef" and owner Anita Jaisinghani "takes Indian to a new level" by using "Western influences" to create an "adventurous" menu of "inventive and delicious" dishes that are "pleasing to the eye and the palate"; needless to say, this is "not the same old saag panir."

### Kubo's
25 | 19 | 18 | $34

*2414 University Blvd. (Morningside Dr.), 713-528-7878;*
*www.kubos-sushi.com*

■ "Regular sushi eaters" claim this "comfortable and serene" Rice Village favorite serves the "freshest in the city", and with fish flown in from California daily then fashioned into "creative, large portions", they just might be right; some say the experience may be a little "highly priced", but considering the "vivacious service", "elegant, subdued decor" and "convenient location with lots of parking", most maintain it's "worth every penny."

### La Griglia 23 22 22 $37
*River Oaks Ctr., 2002 W. Gray St. (bet. McDuffie St. & Shephard Dr.), 713-526-4700*

■ This River Oaks Italian is a "fun favorite" for the "chichi crowd" thanks to "excellent food" and "bend-over-backward" service; with a "party atmosphere" and "lively bar crowd", it "can be a little noisy on weekends", but there's always "great people-watching" to "replace conversation" – or one can "try sitting on" the "quieter and more intimate patio" "for outdoor dining", "weather permitting"; the ratings may not reflect a post-*Survey* change in ownership.

### La Mora Cucina Toscana 🗷 24 22 23 $38
*912 Lovett Blvd. (Montrose Blvd.), 713-522-7412*

■ A "hideaway in the heart of the city", this Montrose Northern Italian is "one of Houston's best-kept secrets" for "authentic Tuscan fare" such as "*molto bene* risotto" and "outstanding gnocchi", not to mention a "superb wine list" and "knowledgeable", "attentive" servers; lovers laud the "cozy" "villalike" digs as perfect for a "romantic date" – and "especially charming at night."

### Lankford Grocery & Market ⌿ 24 10 17 $10
*88 Dennis St. (Boston St.), 713-522-9555*

■ What this Midtown "greasy spoon" in a "clean-but-curious" "old corner market" "lacks in decor, it more than makes up for" with truly "bad-ass burgers"; but that's not the only "reason for the lunchtime lines" – there are also "oniony beef enchiladas and to-die-for chicken-fried steak" some days (plus "incredible *migas*" for early-risers); P.S. two pieces of advice: "don't sass the cashier" and "watch out for the tilty floors."

### MARK'S AMERICAN CUISINE ◐ 28 25 26 $52
*1658 Westheimer Rd. (bet. Dunlavy & Ralph Sts.), 713-523-3800; www.marks1658.com*

■ Surveyors "sing hallelujah" for this "heavenly" Montrose venue in a "charming converted church building" blessed with "vaulted ceilings" and a "wine 'cellar' in the choir loft", voting it No. 1 for Food and Popularity among Houston restaurants; "innovative chef"-owner Mark Cox's "extraordinary New American fare" is supported by a "superb wine list" and served by a "knowledgeable" and "genuinely helpful staff", so followers gladly put up with "closely packed tables" and "nearly impossible reservations."

### Mockingbird Bistro 23 20 22 $40
*1985 Welch St. (bet. Hazard & McDuffie Sts.), 713-533-0200; www.mockingbirdbistro.com*

■ John Sheely's "crowded neighborhood hangout", "tucked away" in a residential area just south of the River Oaks Shopping Center, offers "simple but modern" New American "bistro fare" (you "gotta have the frites!") and a "very good and reasonably priced wine list" in a "quirky", "gothic" setting; regulars report the "enthusiastic" staff "always knows your name and favorite glass" of vino.

## PAPPAS BROS. STEAKHOUSE 🗷  27 | 24 | 25 | $54
*5839 Westheimer Rd. (Fountain View Dr.), 713-780-7352;*
*www.pappasbros.com*

■ When on "someone else's expense account", head to this "manly-man" Galleria-area steakhouse for "melt-in-your-mouth beef", "wonderful à la carte sides", "a wine list about as big as *War and Peace*", "desserts grandma wishes she could make" and a "clubby atmosphere" reminiscent of "an old-style New York dining room" complete with "cigar lounge" ("be careful if you're sensitive to smoke"); but don't come casual – "expect to see ladies in cocktail dresses and gentlemen in sport coats."

## Pesce 🗷  24 | 24 | 22 | $50
*3029 Kirby Dr. (W. Alabama St.), 713-522-4858*

■ "See and be seen" at this "glitzy" Upper Kirby District *mer*-fare "destination" that benefits from "electric atmosphere", a "nice bar scene", "first-class service" and a "great selection" of "excellently cooked and seasoned fish" dishes; "don't miss the seafood martini" or the "sublime Dover sole (when available)", "but first see your loan officer" as this "posh", "lovely place" can be "extremely pricey."

## Quattro  26 | 26 | 25 | $48
*Four Seasons Hotel, 1300 Lamar St. (Austin St.), 713-276-4700;*
*www.fourseasons.com*

■ The former site of the stuffy old Deville in Downtown's Four Seasons Hotel was "reincarnated" as this "sleek" and "chic" "cosmopolitan" three-year-old that's popular for "great power lunches", "excellent dinners" and "incredible Sunday brunches"; "awesome chef" Tim Keating's New American–Italian menu features the "freshest" and "finest ingredients" combined in "familiar" yet "creative" ways ("try the french fries with truffle oil", "an addiction unto themselves"), and "spectacular service" also keeps fans returning.

## Rainbow Lodge  23 | 27 | 23 | $45
*1 Birdsall St. (Memorial Dr.), 713-861-8666;*
*www.rainbow-lodge.com*

■ "A wilderness oasis" within the "concrete jungle", this "hunting lodge"–inspired Regional American on the edge of River Oaks offers "amazing game dishes", including "unusual entrees such as ostrich and wild boar"; the "romantic setting" features "beautiful grounds" for a stroll before dinner and "scenic views of the tree-lined bayou" during your meal, making it a "great place to take a date" or "pop the question" – "as long as she's a carnivore"; N.B. the Food rating may not reflect a post-*Survey* chef change.

## Ruggles  24 | 19 | 18 | $37
*Saks Fifth Avenue, The Galleria, 5115 Westheimer Rd.*
*(bet. Post Oak Blvd. & Sage Rd.), 713-963-8067*
*903 Westheimer Rd. (Montrose Blvd.), 713-524-3839* ◐

■ Of husband-and-wife team Bruce and Susan Molzan's pair of "great New American" grills, the original Montrose branch, an "institution", remains a "fun", "happening" place where "people-watching" and "huge portions" of "original" Southwestern-influenced cuisine add up to "loud" "crowds on weekends"; its more "sleek" and "chic" Galleria sibling is popular with "well-dressed" "beautiful people" for its "beautifully presented and perfectly prepared" French-accented fare, "prettier dining room" and "shorter wait."

### Ruth's Chris Steak House
25 | 19 | 23 | $50

*6213 Richmond Ave. (bet. Fountain View & Hillcroft Aves.), 713-789-2333*
*14135 Southwest Frwy./Hwy. 59 S. (bet. Sugar Creek &*
*Williams Trace Blvds.), Sugar Land, 281-491-9300*
*www.ruthschris.com*

☑ "Yes, it's a chain", note surveyors, but these "gold-standard" steakhouse sisters are "still gems" thanks to their "clubby", "quiet environments", "polite" and "welcoming" staffers and, most of all, "thick and juicy" cuts of "first-class" beef (committed carnivores claim that the "portly portions" of "butter-soaked steaks" are even "fit to tempt vegetarians"); still, if you're looking for "a more upscale and refined feel", most maintain "the newer Sugar Land location" edges out its Galleria sibling.

### 17
‒ | ‒ | ‒ | VE

*Sam Houston Hotel, 1117 Prairie St. (San Jacinto St.), 832-200-8888;*
*www.17food.com*

Housed in Downtown's historic Sam Houston Hotel, this newcomer attracts locals and visitors alike with chef Jeff Armstrong's New American cuisine, which is inventive but not frightening to foodies-in-training; a wine list of almost 300 bottles complements such signature dishes as the petite filet mignon with braised short ribs – and you can't leave without ordering the sinful chocolate s'mores cake with homemade marshmallows.

### Shade
‒ | ‒ | ‒ | E

*250 W. 19th St. (Rutland St.), 713-863-7500;*
*www.shadeheights.com*

Much-loved chef Claire Smith returns to Houston with her latest venture, this new venue located in the city's quaint Heights neighborhood; the contemporary, minimalist space designed by Ferenc Dreef is the perfect complement for her Eclectic–New American cuisine, which incorporates influences from across the globe; favorites such as wasabi-and-cucumber-encrusted grouper and chicken-fried pork medallions can be enjoyed inside or on the patio.

### Simposio ⌀
25 | 16 | 22 | $40

*5591 Richmond Ave. (Chimney Rock Rd.), 713-532-0550;*
*www.simposiorestaurant.com*

■ "Don't let the strip mall fool you" – the exterior "does not do justice to the kitchen" at this Galleria-area "Northern Italian gem", where "remarkable chef" and owner Alberto Baffoni creates "serious food", including a selection of "lovely pastas" and "fantastic osso buco" "to suck marrow for"; combine that with "proper service" and a "well-thought-out wine list" and you've got a "warm, satisfying dining experience" that transcends its "plain location."

### t'afia ⌀
‒ | ‒ | ‒ | E

*3701 Travis St. (bet. W. Alabama & Winbern Sts.), 713-524-6922;*
*www.tafia.com*

Already one of the booming lower Midtown district's biggest draws, this newcomer is helmed by chef-owner Monica Pope, who makes every effort to incorporate locally grown, organic ingredients into her coastal Mediterranean fare, turning out such memorable dishes as pistachio-crusted salmon; be warned, though, that one trip is not enough – the adventurous menu changes almost daily.

**Tony Mandola's Gulf Coast Kitchen**   23 | 18 | 22 | $32 |
*River Oaks Ctr., 1962 W. Gray St. (McDuffie St.), 713-528-3474; www.tonymandolas.com*
■ A "neighborhood favorite", this "casual, comfortable", "convivial Cajun-Italian" seafooder in River Oaks "inspires loyalty" with "incredibly fresh and beautifully prepared fish", "lovely oysters", "delicious crab" and "New Orleans–style po' boys" served by "attentive" and "knowledgeable" waiters who treat everyone like "a member of the extended Mandola family"; in short, it's a "real Gulf Coast experience."

**Tony's** ☒   25 | 23 | 25 | $64 |
*1801 Post Oak Blvd. (bet. San Felipe St. & Westheimer Rd.), 713-622-6778*
☑ "Hurray for Tony" Vallone – the man "knows how to run a restaurant" say fans of this Galleria-area Continental, a 40-year-old "Houston institution" that's still "the place to see celebrities and social climbers", especially in the "front room on weekends" (jacket required on Saturday nights); while some call it a "faded rose", "many older Houstonians" stand by the "classic" menu, the "exquisite details" like Versace plates and the "fawning", "over-the-top" service; N.B. at press time, a move is planned for early 2005.

**Zula** ☒   23 | 25 | 21 | $42 |
*705 Main St. (Capitol St.), 713-227-7052; www.zulahouston.com*
■ This "fashionable" New American is home to chef Lance Fegan, whose "creative, well-executed menu" of "flashy food" includes "absolutely fantastic crab cakes and river trout"; "consistently excellent service", "spectacular" "Las Vegas"–style decor and a crowd that sometimes includes "local professional athletes" combine to give this "upscale place" "the cool factor."

# Kansas City

## TOP 10 FOOD RANKING

| Restaurant | Cuisine |
|---|---|
| **27** Bluestem | New American |
| **26** Stroud's | American |
| Oklahoma Joe's | Barbecue |
| Le Fou Frog | French Bistro |
| American Rest. | New American |
| Fiorella's Jack Stack | Barbecue |
| Tatsu's | French |
| Grille on Broadway | New American |
| Starker's Reserve | New American |
| Danny Edwards' | Barbecue |

## ADDITIONAL NOTEWORTHY PLACES

| | |
|---|---|
| André's Confiserie Suisse | Swiss |
| Café Sebastienne | New American |
| d'Bronx | Pizza/Deli |
| 40 Sardines | New American |
| Grand St. Cafe | Eclectic |
| Lidia's | Northern Italian |
| McCormick & Schmick's | Seafood |
| Pachamama's | Eclectic |
| Plaza III | Steakhouse |
| zin | New American |

| F | D | S | C |
|---|---|---|---|

**AMERICAN RESTAURANT** ☒    26 | 25 | 27 | $52
*Crown Ctr., 200 E. 25th St. (Grand Ave.), 816-545-8000;*
*www.theamericanrestaurantkc.com*
■ With "superb service" and "magnificent" city views, this
"showpiece" at Hallmark's Crown Center is a "KC institution" and a
"favorite of professionals and gourmet diners alike" – especially
now that "imaginative" toque Celina Tio has "invigorated" the
New American menu ("lots of game") to go with the "excellent"
1,500-label wine list; "you feel grand gliding down the staircase"
into the "cathedrallike" dining room, though more than a few snipe
the "'80s decor" needs a "major face-lift"; P.S. the $21 "three-
course prix fixe lunch is a steal."

**André's Confiserie Suisse** ☒    24 | 19 | 23 | $16
*5018 Main St. (bet. 50th & 51st Sts.), 816-561-3440*
*4929 W. 119th St., Overland Park, KS, 913-498-3440*
*www.andreschocolates.com*
■ "Much closer than Zurich", the Country Club Plaza's "charming",
"authentic" 50-year-old "chalet"-style Swiss "confectionary" –
also the city's honorary consulate – proffers "retro food and
ambiance" that's "so out it's in"; "helpful, courteous" "European
ladies in cute lace aprons" serve $12 prix fixe lunches ("daily quiche

and two specials" plus "delectable" desserts) and afternoon tea –
though sugar babies urge "go for the chocolate and skip the rest";
N.B. the two-year-old Overland Park branch is convenient to
Kansas' suburban office parks.

### BLUESTEM    | 27 | 23 | 23 | $41 |

*900 Westport Rd. (Roanoke Rd.), 816-561-1101*

■ Voted KC's No. 1 for Food, this "sophisticated" New American
newcomer named after a variety of prairie grass offers grazers an
"eclectic, adventurous menu" that "balances the flavors" of "local
seasonal items" to "sublime" effect; the "artful" "presentation is
candy for the eyes" – as housemade desserts are for the mouth –
and a "mature crowd" also enjoys the "simple" "urban comfort" of
the "intimate" Westport space; what with it being so "expensive",
however, habitués hope it will soon get over its "growing pains."

### Café Sebastienne    | 25 | 25 | 23 | $31 |

*Kemper Museum of Contemporary Art, 4420 Warwick Blvd. (45th St.),*
*816-561-7740; www.kemperart.org*

■ At this "striking" yet "serene" "urban escape", an "airy",
mural-bedecked venue at the Kemper Museum of Contemporary
Art near the Country Club Plaza, "outstanding" chef Jennifer
Maloney pleases palates with a palette of "fresh, local, seasonal
and creative" New American cuisine (the "food they probably
serve in heaven"); patrons praise "relaxed" servers too, while
pointing out to prodigious partiers that "nighttime hours are limited"
(Friday–Saturday only, till 9:30 PM).

### Danny Edwards' Famous    | 26 | 9 | 17 | $14 |
### Kansas City Barbecue 🍽

*(fka Little Jake's Eat It & Beat It)*
*1227 Grand Blvd. (E. 13th St.), 816-283-0880*

■ "Don't dress up" for lunch at second-generation pitmeister
Danny Edwards' "funky", "git-down" "dump of a place", but do be
prepared to eat; this Downtown "hole-in-the-wall" serves smoky
specialties that are "among the best 'cue in the rib capital of the
world" ("awesome burnt ends", "moist and flavorful beef" "so good
I could not stop licking my fingers after the meal"); factor in a
"friendly staff" and "price-is-right" tabs and it's obvious why BBQ
buffs "wish they were open more"; N.B. kitchen closes at 2:30 PM.

### d'Bronx 🍽    | 25 | 14 | 16 | $12 |

*3904 Bell St. (39th St.), 816-531-0550*

■ "A slice of the Big Apple in the heart of Cowtown", this fave in
the 39th Street area draws "customers from all over" for "deli
sandwiches so big and real they could fool a lifelong New Yorker"
and the "best damn pizza in KC" ("thick-loaded and delicious");
"nobody seems to mind" the "rustic", "no-frills" setting, with its
"relaxed atmosphere", but those who give a Bronx cheer to the
"long lines and noise" may prefer the take-out outpost at Crown
Center; P.S. "the only beer here is root beer."

### FIORELLA'S JACK STACK    | 26 | 22 | 22 | $22 |

*101 W. 22nd St. (Wyandotte St.), 816-472-7427; www.fiorellas.com*
*13441 Holmes Rd. (135th St.), 816-942-9141; www.fiorellas.com*
*9520 Metcalf Ave. (95th St.), Overland Park, KS, 913-385-7427;*
*www.jackstack.com*

■ "Who says that authentic BBQ has to come from a greasy
joint with Formica tables?" ask aficionados of this "high-toned"

trio where the "posh" interiors perplex pit purists ("'cue with white linen napkins?") even as the "yuppie" chow proves downright "addictive": "fork-tender brisket", "decadent burnt ends", "succulent lamb" and the city's "best sides" ("heavenly cheesy corn", "fabulous" baked beans); everyone agrees "it's worth the wait" – and what with the no-reservations policy, "wait you will."

### 40 Sardines
| 24 | 21 | 22 | $40 |

*11942 Roe Ave. (W. 119th St.), Leawood, KS, 913-451-1040; www.40sardines.com*

■ "Enterprising" "husband-wife chef team" Michael Smith and Debbie Gold (ex American) "wow" "epicurean adventurers" at their "refreshing" two-year-old New American in suburban Leawood, whipping up "subtle", "imaginative and flavorful meals" ("influences from Cajun to Asian") and offering a "budget-friendly list of great $20 wines" ("amazing pairings") with the assistance of "engaging and thoughtful servers"; the "industrial but not hip" room, decorated in blues and greens, can be "abominably noisy when crowded" but reviewers report that recent changes "have improved acoustics dramatically."

### GRAND ST. CAFE
| 24 | 22 | 24 | $32 |

*Country Club Plaza, 4740 Grand St. (47th St.), 816-561-8000; www.eatpbj.com*

☑ Featuring "everything from burgers to steak and seafood" (the signature double-cut pork chop is "worthy of a crown") ferried hither and yon by "friendly" and "efficient" folks, this "upscale", "upbeat" Eclectic eatery near the Plaza remains a "lively" "lunch venue for business or pleasure" and a "classic standby" for dinner; "try to sit outside" on the "best patio in town" suggest sound-sensitive surveyors who blame "hard surfaces" for indoor "noise", while others wonder "is the decor getting tired – or does it just seem that way because we go there so often?"

### Grille on Broadway ⊠
| 26 | 20 | 24 | $33 |

*3605 Broadway (Valentine Rd.), 816-531-0700*

☑ "Bringing new meaning to 'cozy'", this "tiny" (40-seat) Midtowner with a "kitchen the size of a phone booth" turns out "delicious, imaginative and memorable" New American fare, especially "terrific fresh fish" ("choice" BBQ oysters, "sublime" sea bass); partisans also praise "experienced and polite" staffers whose "efficiency" helps make this "well-kept secret" the "ultimate great date place" – though naturally claustrophobes complain that it's "cramped."

### LE FOU FROG
| 26 | 19 | 22 | $38 |

*400 E. Fifth St. (Oak St.), 816-474-6060; www.lefoufrog.com*

☑ Francophiles are *fou* for this "little bit of Paris" in the River Market area, a "charming", "funky" bistro where chef-owner Mano Rafael serves up "Midwestern portions" of Gallic *gastronomie* (steak au poivre, steamed mussels) plus "unusual" entrees like elk and ostrich; meanwhile, a "skillful", "knowledgeable" staff helps the con*fou*sed peruse chalkboard menus that change daily and "one of KC's finest wine lists" – so though foes fret about the "gritty" neighborhood, "tough-to-find" location and "elbow-to-elbow seating", most maintain the "wonderful meal" is "well worth it all."

### LIDIA'S　　　　　24　27　23　$33
*101 W. 22nd St. (Baltimore Ave.), 816-221-3722; www.lidiasitaly.com*
☑ TV chef and NYC culinary matriarch Lidia Bastianich is the force behind this "chic, stylish" and "spectacular" showplace, a "rehabbed" "brick station house" (note the "breathtaking" Dale Chihuly chandelier) in the "revitalizing" Crossroads arts district; *amici* assert the "delicious" Northern Italian eats (e.g. the $25 prix fixe pasta trio) "sometimes achieve the sublime" and "value-priced" vinos are a boon for the "wine-challenged"; "disappointed" dissenters declare the place "has lost some of its spark", citing "uneven service" and "hit-or-miss" food.

### MCCORMICK & SCHMICK'S　　　25　25　23　$36
*448 W. 47th St. (Pennsylvania Ave.), 816-531-6800;*
*www.mccormickandschmicks.com*
■ "Seafood lovers" stranded "1,000 miles from an ocean" are "delighted" by the "staggering array" of "exceptional" fin fare at this Country Club Plaza chainster, voted the area's Most Popular restaurant; a "happening place" for "movers and shakers" at lunch and "lively fun" after work ("top-notch" $1.95 "happy-hour eats"), this "yuppie" magnet provides "prompt service" and a "pleasant ambiance", with a "beautiful stained-glass rotunda" and "patio overlooking the Plaza"; even if curmudgeons carp it can be "noisy", "packed" and "pricey for KC", hooked habitués harrumph it's "worth every friggin' dollar."

### OKLAHOMA JOE'S
### BARBECUE & CATERING ⑤　　　26　9　16　$12
*Shamrock Gas Station, 3002 W. 47th Ave. (Mission Rd.),*
*Kansas City, KS, 913-722-3366; www.oklahomajoesbbq.com*
■ "Winners of umpteen contests", the "smoked-arts" practitioners at this Roeland Park fave now have lipsmackers queueing up for their "moist", "tender, lean" KC-style meats with "heavenly sauce", "great short-ends" and "addictive" fries seasoned to perfection", plus the signature "fabulous" North Carolina pulled pork; located "inside a gas station", the joint gets "points" for "down-and-dirty" "authenticity", too, though fastidious folks feel the "Decor score could be a negative number", and fuss there's "limited seating" for the "unlimited line" of folks waiting to fill up.

### Pachamama's　　　25　22　21　$35
*2161 Quail Creek Dr. (22nd St.), Lawrence, KS, 785-841-0990;*
*www.pachamamas.com*
☑ Located in Lawrence, 40 miles from KC, this "delightful" Eclectic has excited explorers exclaiming "you never know what will show up on the menu" – chef-owner Ken Baker's "creative seasonal" slates are likely to include "Midwestern staples" as well as "unique entrees with amazing flavor combos"; "thoughtful" servers help visitors find "value-priced" vinos on the "impressive list" as aesthetes appreciate the "country-club-meets-chic-nouveau" interiors and "peaceful" golf-course vistas; nevertheless, some are left unimpressed by this "expensive" "West Coast wanna-be."

### PLAZA III THE STEAKHOUSE　　　25　21　25　$43
*Country Club Plaza, 4749 Pennsylvania Ave. (Ward Pkwy.),*
*816-753-0000; www.plazaiiisteakhouse.com*
☑ "Great beef and this establishment both prove some things do get better with aging", laud loyalists of this "old-line" "mainstay"

on the Country Club Plaza; it's an "earthy", "dark-wood" den where "any CEO would feel comfortable" thanks to "perfect" porterhouses, "delish steak soup", "salads you can identify", a "fabulous" 350-label cellar and the ministrations of an "elegant, charming staff"; still, some longtimers lament this "tired" place may now be "past its prime"; P.S. the bar downstairs offers "access to the full menu" plus "outstanding" live jazz four nights a week.

### Starker's Reserve Ⓢ                 26  24  25  $45
*Country Club Plaza, 201 W. 47th St. (Wyandotte St.), 816-753-3565; www.starkersreserve.com*

■ "Often overlooked" and "underpatronized", this second-story, "top-notch" New American on the Country Club Plaza is an "exquisite" "treasure", swoon smitten surveyors who savor the "feeling of exclusivity" inside the "romantic", "casual French" room while "looking out on the activity" below; owner "Cliff Bath's attention to detail" comes through in "outstanding food" and an "incomparable" cellar of more than 1,500 wines, and a "wonderful staff" that's "unobtrusive but available" helps make "special occasions" celebrated here "elegant, intimate" and "memorable."

### STROUD'S                           26  14  22  $19
*1015 E. 85th St. (Troost Ave.), 816-333-2132*
*5410 NE Oak Ridge Dr. (Vivion Rd.), 816-454-9600*
*www.stroudsrestaurants.com*

■ "Legendary fried chicken" served with "otherworldly cream gravy", "extraordinary cinnamon rolls" and other Traditional American favorites "worth traveling for" are the draw at these "living memorials" to "grandma's farm cookin'"; the South KC original, dating from 1933, is a "warped" yet "homey" "roadhouse" ("a wonderful dump"), while the larger 19th-century homestead north of the river offers "country atmosphere", antique furniture and a live piano player; staffers are "very friendly", which helps keep patrons' spirits up during the "horrific waits"; N.B. no reservations.

### Tatsu's                            26  19  24  $37
*4603 W. 90th St. (Roe Ave.), Prairie Village, KS, 913-383-9801; www.tatsus.com*

☑ "Consistency, thy name is Tatsu", declare denizens of this Prairie Village "perennial" who note that its menu "changes very slowly – thank God"; chef-owner Tatsu Arai continues to assemble "old-style" "haute" "French cuisine of the first order" ("poached fish done perfectly", "out-of-this-world scallops", "outstanding Grand Marnier soufflé") in his "civilized", "discreet", "genteel" restaurant, assisted by an "exemplary" staff; however, cutting-edge types crack the "place and its clientele have aged together" and claim the "outdated" decor is in "dire need of a face-lift."

### zin Ⓢ                              25  22  24  $40
*1900 Main St. (19th St.), 816-527-0120; www.zinkc.com*

■ Located in the "blossoming" Crossroads arts district, this "sexy", stripped-down New American with a "cool urban feel" "attracts the cultured crowd", especially on "First Fridays when the galleries are open late"; hipsters hoover up "innovative", "gorgeous" and "delicious" seasonal specialties (not to mention a "worth-it" $60 tasting menu) and appreciate the "charming", "attentive" staffers' "impeccable advice" about the "excellent wine list", though a few fogeys cluck it's too "trendy with a capital T."

# Las Vegas

## TOP 20 FOOD RANKING

| Restaurant | Cuisine |
|---|---|
| **28** Nobu | Japanese |
| Renoir | New French |
| **27** Picasso | New French |
| Malibu Chan's | Pacific Rim/Asian Fusion |
| Le Cirque | New French |
| Rosemary's | New American |
| Michael Mina | Seafood |
| Bradley Ogden | New American |
| Lotus of Siam* | Thai |
| Prime | Steakhouse |
| **26** Andre's | French |
| NOBHILL | Californian |
| Delmonico | Steakhouse |
| Del Frisco's | Steakhouse |
| Roy's | Hawaii Regional |
| Mayflower Cuisinier | Chinese/French |
| Sterling Brunch | New American |
| Michael's | Continental |
| Steak House | Steakhouse |
| Shintaro | Japanese |

## ADDITIONAL NOTEWORTHY PLACES

| | |
|---|---|
| Alizé | New French |
| Aureole | New American |
| Bellagio Buffet | Eclectic |
| Bouchon | French Bistro |
| Commander's Palace | Cajun-Creole |
| Craftsteak | Steakhouse |
| Eiffel Tower | French |
| Emeril's New Orleans | Cajun-Creole/Seafood |
| Firefly | Spanish/Tapas |
| Gaetano's | Northern Italian |
| Hugo's Cellar | Continental |
| Medici Café | Mediterranean |
| N9ne | Steakhouse |
| Osteria del Circo | Northern Italian |
| Pamplemousse | French |
| Piero's Trattoria | Northern Italian |
| Pullman Grille | Steakhouse |
| Seablue | Seafood |
| 3950 | Continental |
| Valentino | Northern Italian |

---

* Indicates a tie with restaurant above

### Alizé　　　　　　　　　25 | 28 | 25 | $64

*Palms Casino Hotel, 4321 W. Flamingo Rd. (Arville St.), 702-942-7777;*
*www.alizelv.com*

■ Dine on a "decadent meal in the sky" at "great" chef-proprietor
Andre Rochat's "romantic", "fancy-schmancy" New French
flaunting the city's "best view of the Strip" "through floor-to-
ceiling glass on three sides" "56 stories up" and to the west atop
the Palms, one of "Vegas' hippest resorts"; don't neglect the
foreground, though, as when the "discreet, professional staff"
sets down the flowered plates and "removes the silver lids in
unison – ta-da!" – they reveal "truly superb" culinary treasures.

### Andre's　　　　　　　　26 | 25 | 26 | $61

*Monte Carlo Resort & Casino, 3770 Las Vegas Blvd. S. (bet. Harmon &*
*Tropicana Aves.), 702-798-7151*
*401 S. Sixth St. (bet. Bridger & Clark Aves.), 702-385-5016 🏵*
*www.andrelv.com*

■ Francophilic followers of "hometown celebrity chef" Andre
Rochat's "tooooo romantic" eateries (the "original", a "cozy"
"French-countryside auberge" transported to Downtown, and its
sibling, a "peaceful respite" "a world away" from, and yet within,
the Monte Carlo casino) "would eat here every night"; "prepare
to be pampered" with "superb" fare ferried by "attentive, well-
informed, entertaining" servers at this "Vegas tradition."

### AUREOLE　　　　　　　25 | 27 | 24 | $69

*Mandalay Bay Hotel, 3950 Las Vegas Blvd. S. (Hacienda Ave.),*
*702-632-7401; www.charliepalmer.com*

☑ It's 'bottoms up' at Mandalay Bay's oenophilic outpost of Charlie
Palmer's "happening" NYC New American where sipping at the
bar is "excellent" "when sitting beneath" the cable-hoisted
"goddesses" of the grape "flying" up the many-thousand-bottle
"tower of power", the centerpiece of the "stunning interior"; "the
best food that too much money can buy" "wows crowds" of
"glitterati", but while the "sommeliers are helpful" in navigating
the "cool computerized wine list", the rest of the "snotty" staff
"needs to cork its attitude."

### BELLAGIO BUFFET　　　　24 | 19 | 19 | $29

*Bellagio Hotel, 3600 Las Vegas Blvd. S. (Flamingo Rd.), 702-693-7111;*
*www.bellagio.com*

■ Next to a royal flush, the best spread at the Bellagio is this
Eclectic "buffet for people who would otherwise not be caught
dead at one"; an "embarrassment of riches" including "orgasmic"
Kobe beef (holidays only), "mountains of excellent king crab
legs" (at dinner) and "bottomless" bubbly (during the weekend
brunches), this "opulent" "feast" might be "higher priced" than
other "smorgasbords", but "never has quality matched quantity
like this", particularly if you're cruising past the "long wait" with
a "comp for the pass line."

### Bouchon　　　　　　　　– | – | – | E

*3355 S. Las Vegas Blvd. (Sands Ave.), 702-414-6200;*
*www.bouchonbistro.com*

Foodies are flocking to this notable newcomer, a French bistro by
renowned restaurateur Thomas Keller (of Napa Valley's French
Laundry fame) done on the larger-than-life scale of The Venetian's
Venezia Tower; breakfasts boast such classics as coddled eggs

with toasted brioche, while dinners feature favorites including steak frites, roasted chicken and boudin noir, all created by chef de cuisine Mark Hopper and offered within Adam Tihany's Francophile-friendly interior (complete with pewter bar) or on the patio overlooking the pool; N.B. lunch is not served.

### Bradley Ogden
27 25 26 $72

*Caesars Palace, 3570 Las Vegas Blvd. S. (Flamingo Rd.), 702-731-7110; www.caesars.com*

■ Connoisseurs come to Caesars Palace not to bury chef Bradley Ogden but to praise him for his "extravagant, outstanding" New American cuisine featuring "superb" organic dishes such as a "foodie-heaven" "Maytag blue cheese soufflé", presented with "serious china and linens" by a "warm", "engaging" staff; "farm-fresh doesn't come cheap" though, so you'd "better win big or you'll leave hungry."

### Commander's Palace
25 23 25 $55

*Desert Passage at Aladdin, 3663 Las Vegas Blvd. S. (Harmon Ave.), 702-892-8272; www.commanderspalace.com*

■ The Aladdin's "worthy offspring of the great New Orleans" Brennan family Cajun-Creole institution is "a bastion of civilization in a sea of sweatpants and spandex"; amid "gorgeous" "reminders of the Vieux Carre", "out-of-this-world" pecan-encrusted fish and "bread pudding made to order" "from heaven" are ferried by a "knowledgeable staff" with "graciousness and charm"; "while it ain't the original – what in Vegas is?" – it's still "tons" of "top-drawer" "fun", especially during the "transporting jazz brunch."

### Craftsteak
24 23 23 $68

*MGM Grand Hotel, 3799 Las Vegas Blvd. S. (Tropicana Ave.), 702-891-7318; www.mgmgrand.com*

■ "Craft your own meal" at this "gorgeous" "high roller", a surf 'n' turfer in the MGM from Manhattan chef Tom Colicchio, whose menu is a virtual "primer on artisanal and organic foods" ("incredible vegetables", "moo-velous" beef from "grass-fed" cattle), which allows guests to "graze on so many" "pure", "unique flavors"; the "family-style" feasting means the "fun" just "gets better the larger your group" is, but be sure to leave any folks who "don't like to serve themselves" back in the hotel room.

### Del Frisco's Double Eagle Steak House
26 23 24 $63

*3925 Paradise Rd. (Corporate Dr.), 702-796-0063; www.delfriscos.com*

■ "Attentive servers treat everyone like a whale" (not the marine mammal but, in Vegas parlance, a high roller), and what does such a big spender eat for an "elegant break from the tables"? – "nothing but savory steak", "juicy, delicious" and "perfectly done" with "fabulous" sides, "fantastic" wines and "hot, messy bread brought right away" at this "excellent", "high-end" beef palace east of the Strip, where a Wednesday–Saturday pianist adds "polish" to the "white lines, heavy wood and cigar bar" of the "clubby" environs.

### Delmonico
26 24 25 $63

*Venetian Hotel, 3355 Las Vegas Blvd. S. (bet. Flamingo & Spring Mountain Rds.), 702-414-3737; www.emerils.com*

■ Food Network chef "Emeril [Lagasse] knows how to keep it real" at his "modern and uncluttered" Venetian "meat lover's dream", where he "kicks steaks up a notch", making it so tender that "you don't need a knife"; an "(almost overly) attentive wait staff" ensures a "special experience", delivering the "spicy, juicy", "decadent comfort foods" via their "signature synchronized service"; in short, "your wallet and cardiologist will be mad, but your stomach will thank you."

### Eiffel Tower                    22  26  22  $69
*Paris Las Vegas, 3655 Las Vegas Blvd. S.*
*(bet. Flamingo Rd. & Harmon Ave.), 702-948-6937;*
*www.eiffeltowerrestaurant.com*
☑ "Look down your nose at the people on the Strip" from this "half-size re-creation" of the Parisian landmark where the "fabulous view of the Bellagio fountains" complements a "marvelous" French menu and "reserve wines" "similar" to those found "in Toulouse and Cannes"; still, coin-counting connoisseurs complain that "the bill is as high as the elevator takes you" and claim the "food is phony as the tower", with all-too-authentic servers who "treat you like you just parked your mobile home" outside.

### EMERIL'S NEW ORLEANS          24  19  22  $51
### FISH HOUSE
*MGM Grand Hotel, 3799 Las Vegas Blvd. S. (Tropicana Ave.),*
*702-891-7374; www.emerils.com*
☑ Bam-fans swear "you can almost smell the Mississippi" at this "fantastic fish house" in the MGM Grand, a "charming N'Awlins bistro" where "ragin' Cajun" and Creole are presented by Lagasse's "smart" servers; the joint's "packed to the gills" with "tourists" so "you gotta like noise", though the "underenthused" implies that "Emeril needs to go back in the kitchen and out of the limelight."

### Firefly ●                       –  –  –  M
*3900 Paradise Rd. (bet. Flamingo Rd. & Twain Ave.), 702-369-3971;*
*www.fireflylv.com*
Tapas-style dining finally takes flight in this buffet-heavy town with this bright, new Spaniard, a late-night, indoor-outdoor nosh spot just east of the Strip near Restaurant Row that's helmed by chef John Simmons; flit through tastes from artichoke toasts and mango babyback ribs to cured tuna and Parmesan frites while getting lit on a pitcher of the housemade sangria.

### Gaetano's                       24  22  22  $35
*10271 S. Eastern Ave. (Siena Heights Dr.), Henderson, 702-361-1661;*
*www.gaetanoslv.com*
■ Rory and Gaetano Palmeri are "owners who care about their customers", keeping their "personal attention" "on premises" "to ensure your dining experience" at their "warm", "wonderful" Northern Italian newcomer in Green Valley; with "delicious" menu items like "incredible gnocchi and butternut squash ravioli", 10 to 15 "tempting specials" per night and those "pleasant" proprietors prompting you to eat, "no one goes hungry here."

### Hugo's Cellar                   25  21  24  $49
*Four Queens Casino Hotel, 202 Fremont St. (Casino Center Blvd.),*
*702-385-4011; www.fourqueens.com*
☑ "When you want to impress someone", step "down the stairs to the class [act] of Downtown", this "delightfully retro" Continental "Rat Pack"-er with "romantic ambiance"; "the staff will pamper you from start to finish" with "tableside salad tossed" "to your

specifications", "plentiful" steak and lobster, a "top-shelf wine list" and "a long-stemmed rose" for female guests; and if modernists mutter the act seems "tired", faithful "cellar dwellers" counter it's "dated, but aging gracefully."

### LE CIRQUE
27 | 27 | 26 | $78

*Bellagio Hotel, 3600 Las Vegas Blvd. S. (Flamingo Rd.), 702-693-8100; www.bellagio.com*

☑ Move over Cirque du Soleil – "the best circus in town" is this "powerhouse of elegance and gastronomic pleasure" by "real pros" Sirio Maccioni and family; "it's like you're eating under the big top", with "flamboyant" "fabric" tenting high above "decor as rich as" the "luxurious" New French dishes "from heaven" coupled with "first-class" wines; "you don't have much privacy" at the "crowded" tables, and the staff is "about as uptight as it gets", but this jacket-and-tie "spectacular" is still "worth the splurge."

### Lotus of Siam
27 | 10 | 21 | $21

*Commercial Ctr., 953 E. Sahara Ave. (bet. Maryland Pkwy. & Paradise Rd.), 702-735-3033*

■ "As soon as the first bite enters your mouth", you'll sigh "wonderful, wonderful, wonderful" over the "plentiful" portions of "flavorful" Southern and "ethereal" Northern Thai cuisine at this "hole-in-the-wall" "jewel" east of the Strip; "put decor and location aside" and savor "addictive, delicious" "whole sizzling catfish" and "fabulous mango and sticky rice" complemented by an "excellent list of German wines" – plus you'll pay "ridiculously low prices."

### MALIBU CHAN'S ●☒
27 | 21 | 23 | $31

*W. Sahara Promenade, 8125 W. Sahara Ave. (bet. Buffalo Dr. & Cimarron Rd.), 702-312-4267; www.malibuchans.com*

■ For an "innovative" "menu of Pacific Rim"–"Asian fusion" fare, including the "best squid appetizer in Vegas" and "mouthwatering" sushi, complemented by the "delicious banana Chan dessert", visit this "great local joint" on the West Side; with "early-birds" landing for "excellent", "special-value" entrees and the "beautiful people" sighing "it's all about the tapas, baby" at the 10 PM–2 AM "reverse happy hour", this "absolutely fabulous" "joint" is "worth the drive" anytime.

### Mayflower Cuisinier ☒
26 | 20 | 23 | $34

*Sahara Pavilion, 4750 W. Sahara Ave. (Decatur Blvd.), 702-870-8432; www.mayflowercuisinier.com*

■ Set sail for the west-of-Strip Sahara Pavilion shopping center, and "you won't feel your time was wasted" when you land at this "delightful", "high-class", "creative Chinese-French fusion" "gem", a "longtime favorite of locals" that's "not your run-of-the-mill" Asian; you'll get "hooked on" the "beautiful presentation" and "great flavors" of "interesting dishes" including "wonderful appetizers", "Hong Kong chow mein filled with scallops, chicken, etc." and "Mongolian beef that can be cut with a fork" – no wonder fans feel it's a "great place to discover."

### Medici Café
▽ 23 | 25 | 24 | $34

*Ritz-Carlton, Lake Las Vegas, 1610 Lake Las Vegas Pkwy. (Grand Mediterra Blvd.), Henderson, 702-567-4700; www.ritz-carlton.com*

■ Only a few have managed the "getaway" to Henderson where this "relaxing", "outstanding" Mediterranean offers "creative", "well-presented" dishes in an "impressive" setting overlooking serene Lake Las Vegas; the "friendly" service is as "graceful" and "attentive" as "you would expect from the Ritz", and in-the-know aficionados advise you to hold back for "phenomenal desserts" such as the "wonderful" apple torte.

### MICHAEL MINA
27 | 25 | 25 | $67

(fka Aqua)

*Bellagio Hotel, 3600 Las Vegas Blvd. S. (Flamingo Rd.), 702-693-7111; www.bellagio.com*

■ "Stunning attention to detail" is the hallmark of this "swimmingly wonderful" Bellagio "beauty" of a seafooder; chef Michael Mina brings "delish" fish to "the middle of the desert", offering "high rollers" "exquisite" ocean items ("especially a lobster pot pie that's "all it's cracked up to be") and an "outstanding tasting menu"; service is "like a ballet", as waiters move "gracefully" through the "posh", "romantic" room, making for an "upscale experience" that is "worth the home equity loan."

### Michael's
26 | 22 | 26 | $76

*Barbary Coast Hotel & Casino, 3595 Las Vegas Blvd. S. (Flamingo Rd.), 702-737-7111; www.barbarycoastcasino.com*

■ It might be "hard to believe that this long-running gourmet room is still better than most of the new designer" haunts, but this "venerable" Barbary Coast "institution" "is out of this world" for "classy" Continental cuisine; slip into an "old-time red booth" amid "romantic" decor "right out of Bugsy's days", nibble at the "special pre-meal crudité" and peruse the "throwback" "ladies' menu" sans those "silly prices" as your "high-rolling" date treats you to signature Dover sole served by a staff that "treats you like royalty."

### N9ne Steakhouse ●
▽ 27 | 24 | 22 | $67

*Palms Casino Hotel, 4321 W. Flamingo Rd. (Arville St.), 702-933-9900; www.n9negroup.com*

■ "Superb" "steaks that melt in your mouth" coupled with "bold", "beautiful" sides are only half the attraction of this "chic" "meat market" west of the Strip that's "perfect for meeting gorgeous girls and handsome hunks"; from the "center champagne and caviar bar" to the "sterno" where you "cook your own marshmallows before you put them on chocolate-covered graham crackers", "celebs" are toasting all over the "ultrahip", "high-end" space.

### Nobhill
26 | 25 | 25 | $63

*MGM Grand Hotel, 3799 Las Vegas Blvd. S. (Tropicana Ave.), 702-891-1111; www.mgmgrand.com*

■ Good thing the atmosphere is so "serene" because you're in for vertigo over chef Michael Mina's "knock-your-socks-off", "roll-your-eyes-to-the-back-of-your-head good" San Francisco cuisine; made from organic ingredients, the "addictive" dishes come in "exquisite variety" and include "sublime lobster pot pie", while service is "professional and polished" amid the "stylin'" "California" "minimalist decor" featuring "glass-enclosed" booths where you can cry "wow!" without bothering your neighbors.

### NOBU
28 | 23 | 24 | $69

*Hard Rock Hotel & Casino, 4455 Paradise Rd. (bet. Flamingo Rd. & Harmon Ave.), 702-693-5090; www.nobumatsuhisa.com*

■ "Whether hot or cold", chef Nobu Matsuhisa's "excellent" offerings are "so beautiful you hate to eat them", but do because the "master chef/showman's" "trendy" east-of-Strip Japanese is rated No. 1 for Food among Las Vegas restaurants; "crowded" with the "young and hip" having "noisy" "fun" over "magnificent" raw fish and other "mind-blowingly" "artful" creations, it's "not a great place for the rookie", and you need to "bring your yen for incredible yang", but "its reputation precedes it", and it does "live up to the hype."

**Osteria del Circo**  25 | 26 | 24 | $59 |

*Bellagio Hotel, 3600 Las Vegas Blvd. S. (Flamingo Rd.), 702-693-8150; www.bellagio.com*

☑ Le Cirque's "ringmasters", the Maccionis, move down the midway for this "epicurean" sideshow of Tuscan "delights" at the Bellagio; the "formal" staff "elegantly" juggles "exquisitely prepared" plates and "fantastic wines" in the "chic, playful" "fantasy room", a "noisy", "non-stuffy" place that has barkers bellowing "run, don't walk, in your Manolo Blahniks" for a "memorable experience"; still, others opine that the "ridiculously priced", "overhyped" fare takes "second" billing to the "awesome view of the water show."

**Pamplemousse**  25 | 21 | 26 | $50 |

*400 E. Sahara Ave. (bet. Joe W. Brown Dr. & Paradise Rd.), 702-733-2066; www.pamplemousserestaurant.com*

■ "Old-time Vegas is brought to life" at chef Georges LaForge's "quaint" east-of-Strip French that has "never lost its magic", in part due to the incantatory powers of "impeccable" servers who "recite the menu every night", describing the "excellent, garlicky escargot" and rack of lamb with pistachio crust while you "pick at" "the huge basket of crudité" brought gratis to table; "romantics" rate it "perfect" for "a great meal with someone you love."

**PICASSO**  27 | 29 | 27 | $91 |

*Bellagio Hotel, 3600 Las Vegas Blvd. S. (Flamingo Rd.), 702-693-7223; www.bellagio.com*

■ "If you had a choice for your last meal on earth", the Bellagio's "fancy", Spanish-influenced New French offers just the "sensual experience to savor" in your final moments; garnering Most Popular status among Las Vegas restaurants, this prix fixe "theater" is home to "genius" Julian Serrano, whose "artfully crafted" and "exquisitely served" dishes match the mastery of the "walls of Picassos"; it may be "ridiculously expensive", but this "ridiculously over-the-top" experience is also "ridiculously good."

**Piero's Trattoria**  ∇ 20 | 19 | 21 | $36 |

*Hughes Ctr., 325 Hughes Center Dr. (Flamingo Rd.), 702-892-9955; www.pierostrattoria.com*

☑ Evan Glusman has followed in the legendary footsteps of his father, restaurateur Freddy Glusman, with this casual sister spot serving some "excellent" Northern Italian dishes east of the Strip; its Tuscan bean soup, panini, pasta and pizza are "better for lunch than dinner", making for a power-players' midday choice, while the stylish bar is "another place to see old friends."

**Prime**  27 | 27 | 26 | $72 |

*Bellagio Hotel, 3600 Las Vegas Blvd. S. (Flamingo Rd.), 702-693-7111; www.bellagio.com*

■ "What all steakhouses hope they grow up to be", this "classic, classy" chophouse in the Bellagio is a "carnivore's delight" courtesy of chef-partner Jean-Georges Vongerichten's "signature panache", where "rich, rich, rich" refers to the "sumptuous" decor and the "brilliant" beef, "perfectly prepared" following "fabulous appetizers", paired with "unforgettable" sides and settled with "great martinis"; the "beautiful fountain views" and "knowledgeable", "gracious service" are themselves "worth the hefty prices."

### Pullman Grille
23 | 22 | 21 | $40

*Main Street Station Hotel, 200 N. Main St. (Ogden Ave.), 702-387-1896; www.boydgaming.com*

■ Trainspotters in search of "excellent steaks" will find this cattle car "off the beaten track" (in Downtown's Main Street Station Hotel) "relaxing", with a "great ambiance" in a dining room "beautifully decorated" with "massive wood accents" and "priceless antiques", plus "Louisa May Alcott's railroad" cabin serving as an "interesting" cocktail-and-cigar lounge; "excellent everything" includes "reliable" Black Angus beef, seafood and poultry portered by a "superb" staff.

### RENOIR ⊠
28 | 28 | 28 | $93

*Mirage Hotel, 3400 Las Vegas Blvd. S. (Spring Mountain Rd.), 702-791-7353; www.themirage.com*

■ "Having dinner with a Renoir poised over your partner's head is an experience you'll not soon forget", particularly when it happens to be accompanied by the "flawless" New French fare of chef Alessandro Stratta whose "masterpieces among masterpieces" would "convert the most Neanderthal diner" in a "quiet" room that "belies the chaos just outside the door" at the Mirage; the "exceptional" staff "guides you through unfamiliar territory" with "genuine interest"; N.B. no smoking.

### Rosemary's
27 | 21 | 25 | $53

*W. Sahara Promenade, 8125 W. Sahara Ave. (bet. Buffalo Dr. & Cimarron Rd.), 702-869-2251; www.rosemarysrestaurant.com*

■ "Locals love" "former Emeril protégé" Michael Jordan and his wife Wendy's "wonderful and creative" French-influenced New American on the West Side; the couple cooks up "musts" like BBQ shrimp with Maytag blue cheese, as well as "terrific prix fixe" multicourse meals, enticing with "spectacular food in a lovely, unpretentious setting" that's "definitely worth the cab ride" to their "strip-mall" location.

### Roy's
26 | 24 | 25 | $47

*620 E. Flamingo Rd. (Palos Verdes St.), 702-691-2053*
*8701 W. Charleston Blvd. (bet. Durango Dr. & Rampart Blvd.), 702-838-3620*
*www.roysrestaurant.com*

■ "Chef Roy Yamaguchi is the Wolfgang" Puck of the Islands, overseeing these East-of-Strip and West Side "fine-dining" favorites that feature "creative, colorful" Hawaii Regional cooking and a vibe as "comfortably unpretentious" as a "honeymoon in Kauai"; "even though they're part of a chain", they'll "send your taste buds to heaven" with dishes that "delight all the senses" – from the "sticky, flavorful" ribs to the "incredible fish" fare (such as "wonderful" blackened ahi) to the "oozing chocolate soufflé" that'll leave you "raving."

### Seablue
| – | – | – | E |

*MGM Grand Hotel, 3799 Las Vegas Blvd. S. (Tropicana Ave.),*
*702-891-3486; www.mgmgrand.com*

Set in the reworked Strip room formerly held by Neyla, chef Michael Mina's new seafood spot is already a hot spot for celeb watching, including all those Mr. Limpets in the cylindrical aquarium; stone waterwalls and a central raw bar add to the panache of a place where ocean offerings winged in daily are charred on an open wood-fired grill, with some finished in a Moroccan clay oven; the tapas-style menu encourages something that's rare in this high-rolling town: sharing.

### Shintaro
| 26 | 25 | 22 | $59 |

*Bellagio Hotel, 3600 Las Vegas Blvd. S. (Flamingo Rd.), 702-693-7111;*
*www.bellagio.com*

■ "Whether you're at" the sushi bar backed by a "colorful jellyfish tank", at "the hibachi tables" or in the "dining room with a view of the Bellagio water displays", you can always expect a feast for your eyes" and "your mouth" at this "superb Japanese" triple threat; "after a hard day of gambling", the "luxurious surroundings" are "wonderfully relaxing" for "unwinding" with plates of "toro like butter" and "tender" Kobe beef, or with the chef's "amazing" tasting menu, though some suggest that "overpricing" makes it strictly the "rich man's Benihana."

### Steak House
| 26 | 21 | 23 | $44 |

*Circus Circus Hotel, 2880 Las Vegas Blvd. S. (Riviera Blvd.),*
*702-794-3767; www.circuscircus.com*

■ "Cattle prodders" say "fight your way through the sea of parents and sticky, screaming children" in the lobby to get to this "surprisingly good steakhouse" with a fine Sunday brunch in the "most unlikely setting", the "not-so-classy" Circus Circus; as you might expect, there's "a nice bit of theatrics to the meal" that's juggled out of the "open kitchen" into a room "crowded" with "locals" scarfing down "huge" slabs, "brilliantly prepared" and offered at "reasonable prices" that make them some of the "best deals in Vegas, baby."

### Sterling Brunch
| 26 | 20 | 23 | $60 |

*Bally's Las Vegas Hotel, 3645 Las Vegas Blvd. S. (bet. Flamingo Rd. &*
*Tropicana Ave.), 702-739-4111; www.ballys.com*

■ "A little bit of heaven in Sin City", Bally's "luxurious" New American brunch lets you "gorge on unlimited" "delicacies such as lobster, caviar, rack of lamb" and "bottomless glasses of fine French champagne", all before 2:30 PM on a Sunday; overseen by "a perfect, old-school" maitre d', it's the "only" spread "where you don't have to fight your way through" "using your fork as a defensive weapon", and the "orgasmic" offerings make it just about the "finest" morning meal "in the United States."

### 3950
| 23 | 24 | 23 | $55 |

*Mandalay Bay Hotel, 3950 Las Vegas Blvd. S. (Hacienda Ave.),*
*702-632-7414; www.mandalaybay.com*

☑ "Excellent" bisque and steaks might be "traditional classics", but they're "finely prepared" with "creative flair" to match the "colorful", "hi-tech room" at this Continental at Mandalay Bay, and the "attentive service" is just as "snappy" as the "modern" decor; however, you pay by the decibel at the "pricey" place:

"trying really hard to be trendy" with music cranked "too loud", it's "crawling with tourists" and a "dressed-to-thrill" "young crowd" that can be "quite noisy."

**Valentino Las Vegas** 24 | 22 | 23 | $66

*Venetian Hotel, 3355 Las Vegas Blvd. S. (bet. Flamingo & Spring Mountain Rds.), 702-414-3000; www.welovewine.com*
☑ Scale the heights of the "*alta cucina*" for a "culinary adventure" courtesy of Luciano Pellegrini, an "Italian-born chef with the right attitude", at this "classy" Venetian cousin of "maestro" Piero Selvaggio's Santa Monica original offering "remarkable" Northern dishes and "a wine list envied by Bacchus himself" proffered by a "smooth" staff in a newly enlarged, "elegant" room; still, some call the cuisine "not up to the standards in CA" and "not worth the money", suggesting you try a less "pricey" lunch at their grill.

# Long Island

## TOP 20 FOOD RANKING

| Restaurant | Cuisine |
| --- | --- |
| **28** Mill River Inn | New American/Eclectic |
| **27** Kotobuki | Japanese |
| Peter Luger | Steakhouse |
| Mirko's | Eclectic |
| **26** Mirabelle | French |
| La Plage | Eclectic |
| La Piccola Liguria | Northern Italian |
| Louis XVI | New French |
| Da Ugo | Italian |
| Polo | New American |
| Dario | Northern Italian |
| Barney's | New American/French |
| Piccolo | Italian/New American |
| Panama Hatties | New American |
| Le Soir | French |
| Siam Lotus* | Thai |
| Kitchen a Bistro | French |
| **25** Tellers Chophouse | Steakhouse/Seafood |
| Dave's Grill | Continental/Seafood |
| Stone Creek Inn | French/Mediterranean |

## ADDITIONAL NOTEWORTHY PLACES

| | |
| --- | --- |
| American Hotel | French/American |
| Barolo | Continental/Italian |
| Bryant & Cooper | Steakhouse/Seafood |
| Cheesecake Factory | American |
| Chez Noëlle | New French |
| Collins & Main | New American/Eclectic |
| Coolfish | New American |
| Giulio Cesare | Italian |
| Harvest on Fort Pond | Northern Italian/Med. |
| Jimmy Hay's | Steakhouse |
| La Pace | Northern Italian |
| L'Endroit | French |
| Nick & Toni's | Mediterranean |
| Palm Court | Continental/New American |
| Pasta Pasta | Italian |
| Plaza Cafe | New American |
| Rialto | Northern Italian |
| Robert's | Italian |
| 1770 House | Continental |
| Solé | Italian |

---

\* Indicates a tie with restaurant above

### American Hotel

24 | 24 | 21 | $56

*The American Hotel, Main St. (bet. Bay & Washington Sts.), Sag Harbor, 631-725-3535; www.theamericanhotel.com*

■ This "Hamptons landmark", a "romantic" destination in a historic, "wonderful old hotel" in Sag Harbor, is "tried and true"; the "outstanding" Classic French–American cuisine (with sushi and caviar available) is "serious grown-up food" with a "brilliant wine list" to match, and although the servers have been known to exhibit "attitude", they're generally "attentive" and "professional"; the "marvelous" setting provides "paradise" on the porch in summer and is made "cozy" by a fireplace in winter; N.B. now serving lunch too.

### Barney's

26 | 23 | 25 | $57

*315 Buckram Rd. (Bayville Rd.), Locust Valley, 516-671-6300; www.barneyslocustvalley.com*

■ A "mainstay in Locust Valley", this "distinctive", "cozy country spot" is home to a "bold and inventive" chef who's "not afraid to experiment", making for "sophisticated" New American–French cuisine that's accompanied by an "outstanding wine list"; the experience is "enhanced by the warm decor" of its "quaint" rooms (especially "with the fireplace going"), not to mention the "lovely service" of its even "warmer staff"; N.B. "special prix fixe dinners" are offered early evenings Sunday–Friday.

### Barolo ⑤

24 | 21 | 23 | $47

*1197 Walt Whitman Rd. (bet. Old Country & Sweet Hollow Rds.), Melville, 631-421-3750*

■ "Worth a trip from almost anywhere on Long Island", this "little-known hidden gem" in Melville delivers "top-drawer", "creative Continental dishes with Italian flair" that display "occasional touches of brilliance"; believers cry "bravo" to the "impeccable" staff overseen by an "owner who makes sure everything is just right", and the "lovely", "elegant" interior is conducive to "quiet conversation"; it may be "pricey", but it's still a "fine choice for a special meal."

### BRYANT & COOPER STEAKHOUSE

25 | 19 | 21 | $54

*2 Middle Neck Rd. (Northern Blvd.), Roslyn, 516-627-7270*

■ "Thick, buttery" steaks, "out-of-this-world seafood and chops" and "wonderful sides", all washed down by "fine red wines", have champions chomping at the bit for this Roslyn beef bastion beloved by the "country-club" set; complaints include a "noisy" ambiance and "long waits, even with reservations", but the "attractive" setting, "knowledgeable" staff and, of course, "mega" meat make it one of the "best of its kind on Long Island."

### CHEESECAKE FACTORY ◑

19 | 18 | 16 | $26

*Mall at the Source, 1504 Old Country Rd. (Merrick Ave.), Westbury, 516-222-5500; www.thecheesecakefactory.com*

■ "There's something for everyone" on the "novel"-sized menu at this Westbury chain link, and "everything is good" according to the hungry hordes who descend for "mammoth portions" of American fare including "mountains of salad" and "massive sandwiches", all "scrumptious" and well priced; the weary warn "pitch a tent" for the "ridiculous waits", but admit the "high-quality" food is "worth it"; P.S. "no matter how full you are, be sure to have the cheesecake."

### Chez Noëlle ☒　　　　　25　17　22　$51
*34 Willowdale Ave. (S. Bayles Ave.), Port Washington, 516-883-3191*
■ This "culinary" "gem in a strange, lost Port Washington location" has been turning out "fabulous", "consistently solid" and "high-quality" New French cuisine (including "delicious desserts") for more than 20 years; devotees call it an "unpretentious", "romantic spot" with a "wonderful owner" and "warm service" and talk up the "unbeatable" $25 prix fixe offered every night but Saturday.

### Collins & Main ☒　　　　　24　23　23　$47
*100 Old S. Main St. (Collins Ave.), Sayville, 631-563-0805;*
*www.collinsandmain.com*
■ The "fab owners" and "concerned" staff "go above and beyond" to ensure a "wonderful" and "unrushed" evening at this "snazzy" Sayville restaurant/lounge; "sophisticated", "superb" New American–Eclectic "dishes are presented as works of art" and "excite the taste buds" as well, and the "lovely", "upscale" decor makes it "great for special occasions"; P.S. live music on weekends is a "delight."

### COOLFISH　　　　　25　22　21　$48
*North Shore Atrium, 6800 Jericho Tpke. (Michael Dr.), Syosset,*
*516-921-3250; www.tomschaudel.com*
■ "Tom Schaudel has the golden touch" assert admirers of this New American in Syosset that reels in schools of "fashionable", "cool" customers trolling for "fabulous", "superb", "inspired" eats served in a "contemporary" setting in an unlikely location (the back of an office building); true, some critics carp about "attitude" from the staff, but most report a "delightful experience."

### Dario ☒　　　　　26　18　24　$51
*13 N. Village Ave. (bet. Merrick Rd. & Sunrise Hwy.), Rockville Centre,*
*516-255-0535*
■ "Excellent" pastas, the "freshest fish", the "best veal chops" and other "wonderfully prepared" dishes "amaze" *amici* of this "incomparable", "upscale" Northern Italian in Rockville Centre; its "big-time old-world charm" makes it an "impressive date place", and the "European"-style "service is fantastic"; one caveat: it's "small", so vets advise "make reservations at your christening."

### Da Ugo ☒　　　　　26　19　24　$47
*509 Merrick Rd. (Long Beach Rd.), Rockville Centre, 516-764-1900*
■ A "perennial favorite" for "extraordinary" Italian cuisine ("exquisite specials"), this Rockville Centre "special-occasion place" is "the real thing"; the "small", "softly lit" room is "elegant" (if a bit "crowded"), the "wonderful owner will do anything to please" and the "exceptional" staff provides "personal service"; enthusiasts exude that it's "worth the moola."

### Dave's Grill　　　　　25　16　20　$46
*468 W. Lake Dr. (bet. Flamingo Ave. & Soundview Dr.), Montauk,*
*631-668-9190; www.davesgrill.com*
■ "If you're in Montauk, do whatever it takes" to get into this "small" Continental seafooder offering fin fare so "amazing" they "can get away with" a "crazy" same-day reservation policy; the "wonderful fish", "excellent" preparations and "fab" signature chocolate bag dessert "add up to a winner" dinner, and the "unusually professional staff" "obviously cares a great deal";

while the interior's "comfortable and cozy", "sitting outside by the docks is even more special"; N.B. open seasonally only.

**Giulio Cesare Ristorante** ⊠  24 | 17 | 22 | $46
*18 Ellison Ave. (Old Country Rd.), Westbury, 516-334-2982*
■ "One of the best, year after year" vow votaries of this "authentic", "old-fashioned" Italian that's been a Westbury "favorite" since 1972; "Giulio and Cesare never fail to deliver" "fabulous food", including "excellent pastas" and what advocates vote the "best veal chop ever", and the service is "first-rate"; a few insist "it's time to redecorate" but agree that the "regulars won't let them close long enough to do the work"; P.S. "reservations are a must."

**Harvest on Fort Pond**  25 | 21 | 21 | $45
*11 S. Emery St. (Rte. 27), Montauk, 631-668-5574; www.harvest2000.com*
■ Happy campers dock their boats then harvest "huge portions" of "wonderful, tasty and innovative" Northern Italian–Med dishes ("best bruschetta ever") at this "great" family-style stalwart in Montauk; "beautiful views across Fort Pond" and a "charming garden" for dining add to its appeal, but its "popularity" means it's "hard to get reservations in season."

**Jimmy Hay's**  25 | 18 | 23 | $46
*4310 Austin Blvd. (Kingston Blvd.), Island Park, 516-432-5155*
■ "The only place for filet mignon" maintain meatheads who marvel at this "homey", "excellent" Island Park steakhouse that's also celebrated for "outstanding porterhouses", "good seafood", "incredible onion rings" and "efficient, pleasant" service; critics who make hay of the decor may now sing a different tune thanks to a post-*Survey* renovation; N.B. reservations are taken only for parties of six or more.

**Kitchen a Bistro** ⊅  26 | 8 | 18 | $33
*532 N. Country Rd. (Lake Ave.), St. James, 631-862-0151*
■ "If you're looking for ambiance, look elsewhere"; gleeful gastronomes are oblivious to the "tiny", "crowded" setting of this St. James "hideaway" as they savor "sophisticated", "innovative" and "fantastic" French food at "rock-bottom prices" (a BYO policy "brings costs down" even more); "nobody does fish better than chef Eric [Lomando]", who continues to produce the same daily changing "top-flight" fare that put this "fabulous place" on the map in the first place; N.B. make reservations for weekend seatings "way in advance."

**KOTOBUKI**  27 | 17 | 19 | $33
*377 Nesconset Hwy. (Rte. 111), Hauppauge, 631-360-3969*
*86 Deer Park Ave. (Main St.), Babylon, 631-321-8387*
■ "Perfection on a plate" has wasabi worshipers "waiting forever" for the "sublime sushi" served at these "treasures" in Babylon and Hauppauge; the "best Japanese, raw or cooked" includes sashimi "so fresh you're tempted to look for the hook", and even if the "contemporary" interior is "crowded" with "eager throngs" on weekends, it's "worth it" for the "outrageous", "creative" cuisine.

**La Pace**  25 | 22 | 24 | $51
*51 Cedar Swamp Rd. (2nd St.), Glen Cove, 516-671-2970*
■ "One need only taste the fare to see why" this "old-fashioned charmer" has been around for a quarter-century; "delicious" Northern Italian dishes paired with an "incredible wine list that

includes hard-to-come-by vintages" "enchant" an "older crowd" getting "cozy" "by the fire"; "pampering" from a "caring and visible owner" and his "experienced staff" have diners feeling as if they've "come home", though the place "could use an update."

### La Piccola Liguria 26 19 25 $51
*47 Shore Rd. (bet. Mill Pond & Old Shore Rds.), Port Washington, 516-767-6490*

■ It's "worth a trip from anywhere on the Island" to this tiny Port Washington destination for the "creative", "amazing", "authentic Northern Italian cuisine" that's served "with great panache" by an "impressive" crew that can recite a list of "seemingly hundreds of wonderful specials"; though the "decor won't win any awards", the atmosphere's "warm", and for many connoisseurs "it doesn't get any better than this."

### La Plage 26 18 23 $50
*131 Creek Rd. (Sound Rd.), Wading River, 631-744-9200; www.laplagerestaurant.com*

■ "If you can find this out-of-the-way place", it's "worth the expedition" for "extraordinary Eclectic cuisine" presented in a "charming, romantic", small space near a "windy beach" in "sleepy" Wading River; the "innovative", "beautifully prepared dishes" are "appropriately geared toward fish", infused with "subtle flavors" and served by a "superior" staff; adoring admirers acclaim it as comparable to the best Hamptons eateries, sans "noise and pretension."

### L'Endroit ⊠ 24 23 24 $58
*290 Glen Cove Rd. (Park Dr.), East Hills, 516-621-6630*

⬛ "Sophisticated, delicious Classic French" specialties in an "elegant", "romantic" room "combined with attentive service" ensure this East Hills vet is "always a treat"; a few pout the staff's "pompous" and the setting's "fusty", but more sigh it's a "gorgeous", "special place to celebrate"; P.S. the "soufflé is just a little ramekin of heaven."

### Le Soir 26 19 22 $42
*825 Montauk Hwy. (Bayport Ave.), Bayport, 631-472-9090*

■ Devotees declare they're "never disappointed" by this "find on the South Shore" in Bayport that dishes up "delicious", "authentic" Classic French fare; though "small", the interior imparts an "outstanding" "country-inn" feel that contributes to a "memorable" experience, and the "professional" service that "never rushes you" makes it a piece of *gâteau*; when you factor in "great-value" specials Sunday and Tuesday–Thursday, it's no wonder supporters say "*c'est magnifique!*"

### Louis XVI 26 29 25 $71
*600 S. Ocean Ave. (Masket Dock), Patchogue, 631-654-8970; www.louisxvi.org*

■ Loyal subjects are "transported to another time and place" at this waterfront "palace in Patchogue" with fluted columns and crystal chandeliers creating "surroundings fit for royalty"; "if you're willing to pay Paris prices" (choose from prix fixe or tasting menus) for "top-of-the-line" New French cuisine, then "dress to the nines" and enjoy an "extravagant" evening complete with "artful, delicious" fare, "a staff that could not be more accommodating" and a "fabulous view."

### MILL RIVER INN
28 | 22 | 26 | $64

*160 Mill River Rd. (bet. Lexington Ave. & Oyster Bay-Glen Cove Rd.), Oyster Bay, 516-922-7768*

■ Still No. 1 for Food on Long Island, this "remote jewel" in Oyster Bay continues to wow with "imaginative", "exquisite" New American–Eclectic dishes courtesy of chef Nick Molfetta; located in a "little cinderblock building", the "surprisingly" "quaint", "intimate and romantic" interior is warmed by a fireplace, and the staff's "gracious" and "caring"; though it's certainly "pricey", the "exceptional experience" makes "the high cost of a meal here seem like a bargain."

### MIRABELLE
26 | 22 | 25 | $65

*404 N. Country Rd. (Edgewood Ave.), St. James, 631-584-5999; www.restaurantmirabelle.com*

■ "Get ready for an explosion of taste" "deserving of all the accolades" that this "worthy" St. James "jewel" has received over the past 20 years; "Guy Reuge's take on French fare is awesome", with "creative", "outstanding", "flawlessly executed" fare; "marvelous", "unstuffy" service and a "serene" setting in a "quaint" converted house also elicit bravos, and though the prices may "blow your mind", the "food's so delicious you won't care" (and the Tuesday–Friday "prix fixe is a fantastic bargain").

### MIRKO'S
27 | 23 | 24 | $60

*Water Mill Sq., 670 Montauk Hwy. (bet. Old Mill & Station Rds.), Water Mill, 631-726-4444; www.mirkos.com*

■ Overflowing with "power brokers", this "understated little gem" in Water Mill Square treats diners to "superb", "consistent" Eclectic cuisine in an "intimate", "serene haven" indoors or alfresco on the "comfortable terrace" in summer; a "welcoming, warm" atmosphere is created by chef-owner Mirko Zagar and his "charming" wife, Eileen, as well as the "caring" staff, so surveyors say if "you're lucky enough to get a table", you're in for a "memorable experience."

### Nick & Toni's
24 | 20 | 22 | $56

*136 N. Main St. (bet. Cedar St.), East Hampton, 631-324-3550*

■ "Forget the hype – when you're looking for delicious food", this East Hampton Mediterranean "is the place", as the "brilliant chef" offers "excellent", "adventurous" dishes along with "sublime" wood-oven pizzas accompanied by "lovely wines"; its "pretty" interior and garden are also "great for stargazing" (though "even non-celebs get good service"), so "if you can get a reservation, grab it" and remember that it "truly sparkles in the off-season."

### Palm Court at the Carltun
24 | 27 | 24 | $56

*Eisenhower Park (Merrick Ave.), East Meadow, 516-542-0700; www.carltun.com*

■ Fascinated foodies feel as though they're in a "fairy tale" at this "fancy-schmancy" Continental–New American in the midst of Eisenhower Park in East Meadow, where "elegant surroundings" and "first-class", "white-glove" service contribute to a "delightful" dinner; the "wonderful", "creative" food and "marvelous" wine list make it "excellent for a special occasion", but only if you're willing to "splurge" or use the "corporate card"; N.B. at press time, a significant renovation is underway, including a new space for private parties.

### Panama Hatties
26 | 24 | 23 | $69

*Post Plaza, 872 E. Jericho Tpke./Rte. 25 (2 mi. east of Rte. 110), Huntington Station, 631-351-1727; www.panamahatties.com*

■ Executive chef (and now owner) Matthew Hisiger is a "true culinary artist, combining flavors as a painter would colors on canvas" say gushing groupies of the "world-class" cuisine served at this New American in Huntington Station; "you'll forget you're in a strip mall" thanks to the "gorgeous" interior, and though service can be "pretentious", it's "impeccable"; the set-price dinner is "high", but most "don't mind mortgaging the house" for such a "stupendous" experience (at press time, plans are underway to add an à la carte menu); N.B. the change of proprietors is not necessarily reflected in the above scores.

### Pasta Pasta
25 | 19 | 21 | $36

*234 E. Main St. (Main St.), Port Jefferson, 631-331-5335; www.pastapasta.net*

■ Despite a name that "evokes a chain", this "nouveau Italian trattoria" is "the place to eat in Port Jeff" insist epicures who've sampled its "imaginative", "consistently wonderful", "cooked to perfection" offerings that extend beyond "awesome pasta"; the "casual but elegant" setting and "attentive yet unrushed" service add to the "charm", and though a few quibble over "cramped quarters", more insist the "tiny" space adds to the "intimacy."

### PETER LUGER ⊅
27 | 16 | 21 | $57

*255 Northern Blvd. (Tain Dr.), Great Neck, 516-487-8800; www.peterluger.com*

■ "All hail the king of steaks" proclaim patrons who've pronounced this Great Neck meatery "the pinnacle of carnivorous indulgence" and Long Island's Most Popular restaurant as well; "Fred Flintstone would be satisfied with the size" of the "simply amazing", "juicy, buttery" cuts, and though it "may be pricey", most maintain the chops are "worth every cent" (not to mention "the lunch deals are a steal"); P.S. "remember, it's cash only" unless you "have a Peter Luger credit card" or use your debit card.

### Piccolo
26 | 20 | 24 | $52

*Southdown Shopping Ctr., 215 Wall St. (bet. Mill Ln. & Southdown Rd.), Huntington, 631-424-5592*

■ Cineastes compare this Huntington "favorite" to a film with a "top director and great cast on a crowded set"; the array of Italian–New American cuisine is "fantastic" and the "delicious, daring" specials are matched by an "extensive wine list"; the "knowledgeable servers" are "superb", and the "romantic" ambiance is supported by a "wonderful jazz piano player" and a "sophisticated bar", so it's no surprise that box office is boffo.

### Plaza Cafe
25 | 23 | 24 | $53

*61 Hill St. (bet. 1st Neck & Windmill Lns.), Southampton, 631-283-9323; www.plazacafe.us*

■ "Fish is Doug Gulija's forte, and he's creating some of the most innovative" dishes around ("great seafood shepherd's pie") accompanied by a "fabulous" all-USA wine list at this "hard-to-find" Southampton New American; the "small", "civilized" setting is made warm by a fireplace and "elegant" by cathedral ceilings, and the service is "congenial" and "excellent"; N.B. oenophiles can check out the quarterly vintner dinners.

### Polo
| 26 | 26 | 25 | $57 |

*Garden City Hotel, 45 Seventh St. (Franklin Ave.), Garden City, 516-877-9353; www.gchotel.com*
■ Remodeling has rendered the setting of this "deluxe" "treat" in the Garden City Hotel even more "beautiful", "elegant" and "romantic"; meanwhile, the "creative", "incredible" New American cuisine, "great wine list" and "attentive", "professional" staff contribute to the "not-to-be-missed experience", and even though it's "oh-so-pricey", it's "worth it" for a "celebration"; P.S. the "popular" Sunday brunch is "one of a kind."

### Rialto
| 25 | 19 | 23 | $49 |

*588 Westbury Ave. (bet. Glen Cove Rd. & Post Ave.), Carle Place, 516-997-5283*
■ "Awesome", "melt-in-your-mouth entrees" served at this "consistently excellent" Northern Italian "jewel" await admirers willing to seek out its "hidden" location in Carle Place; the "attractive", "homelike setting" and "personable" hosts who treat guests "like part of the family" create a "top-notch" dining ambiance as well, for an interlude that's "warm from beginning to end"; N.B. no jeans or sneakers.

### Robert's
| 25 | 23 | 23 | $56 |

*755 Montauk Hwy. (Water Mill traffic light), Water Mill, 631-726-7171*
■ This "charmer" in Water Mill with "warm country" accents like hand-hewn beams and a fireplace provides a "low-key" but "romantic" and "sophisticated" environment for "outstanding" Italian dishes prepared with "finesse" ("heavenly" pasta with truffles) and "excellent wines"; owner Robert Durkin is a "true personality", the staff's "professional" and though you may see "celebrities", the "real star is the food."

### 1770 House Restaurant & Inn, The
| 25 | 24 | 23 | $60 |

*1770 House, 143 Main St. (Dayton Ln.), East Hampton, 631-324-1770; www.1770house.com*
■ Chef Kevin Penner can "really showcase his talents" in this "beautiful", "completely renovated" "rising star" in a historic East Hampton inn; he creates "delicious" and "intellectual" Continental cuisine that's presented by "attentive, professional" servers to an "old-money crowd"; it all adds up to a "romantic", "even haunting experience", and if some find the prix fixe options too "expensive", there's the newer, more casual Tavern downstairs.

### Siam Lotus Thai
| 26 | 15 | 23 | $32 |

*1664 Union Blvd. (bet. 4th & Park Aves.), Bay Shore, 631-968-8196*
■ "No contest" declare devotees who deem this "jewel" the "best Thai on Long Island" worth "a detour on the way to the ferry" in Bay Shore; it's as "big as a minute", but the "pretty" digs are "immaculate" and the fare's "fresh", "excellent" and "elegant", with "wonderful specials"; add "attentive" "service with a smile" and manageable prices, and you'll see why lotus eaters exclaim "this is the place!"

### Solé
| 25 | 15 | 19 | $31 |

*2752 Oceanside Rd. (Merle Ave.), Oceanside, 516-764-3218*
■ "Finally, a restaurant in Oceanside that's worth the wait in line" rave "dazzled" diners about this "innovative" Italian "find" that deserves "kudos for offering marvelous food at reasonable prices"

that's served by an "excellent" staff; even if it's "ridiculously hard to get a table on weekends", sage surveyors predict "you'll be back"; P.S. "every bottle of wine on the nice list is $20."

### Stone Creek Inn                25 | 22 | 23 | $51
*405 Montauk Hwy. (bet. Carter Ln. & Wedgewood Harbor), East Quogue, 631-653-6770; www.stonecreekinn.com*
■ The inn crowd acclaims this "outstanding" East Quogue French-Med for its "beautiful" dining rooms, "attentive" but "unobtrusive service" and "superb", "creative" cuisine matched by a "first-rate wine list"; a few throw stones at the "din" that arises when it's crowded, but more report a "satisfying experience" that's enhanced by one of the "best prix fixe deals on Long Island"; N.B. call for off-season hours.

### Tellers American Chophouse      25 | 26 | 23 | $57
*605 Main St. (Rte. 111), Islip, 631-277-7070; www.tellerschophouse.com*
■ A "cool converted bank" with "high ceilings, beautiful photos and a dark-wood bar" is drawing interest in Islip in its current incarnation as a "shrine to meat"; also accounting for the attraction are "jumbo portions" of "incredible steaks and seafood", all "cooked to perfection", accompanied by "outstanding wines" cellared in a former "walk-in safe" as well as "wonderful service"; it's certainly "pricey", but "worth it" for such "unbelievable dining."

# Los Angeles

## TOP 20 FOOD RANKING

| Restaurant | Cuisine |
|---|---|
| 28 Sushi Nozawa | Japanese |
| Matsuhisa | Japanese |
| Water Grill | Seafood |
| Mélisse | French/New American |
| 27 Saddle Peak Lodge | New American |
| Angelini Osteria | Italian |
| Joe's | Californian/New French |
| Sushi Sasabune | Japanese |
| Spago | Californian |
| Katsu-ya | Japanese |
| Derek's | New American/Calif. |
| Mastro's | Steakhouse |
| Takao | Japanese |
| Patina | Californian/French |
| La Cachette | French |
| Shiro | Californian/Asian |
| 26 Brent's Deli | Deli |
| Bastide | French/Provençal |
| Campanile | Californian/Med. |
| Belvedere, The | New American |

## ADDITIONAL NOTEWORTHY PLACES

| | |
|---|---|
| A.O.C. | Californian/Med. |
| Bel-Air Hotel | Californian/French |
| Bistro 45 | Californian/French |
| Café Bizou | Californian/French |
| Capo | Italian |
| Chaya Brasserie | Asian/Eclectic |
| Chinois on Main | Eurasian |
| Christine | Californian/Med. |
| Depot | Eclectic |
| Grace | New American |
| Grill on the Alley | American |
| JiRaffe | Californian |
| Josie | New American |
| L'Orangerie | French |
| Mimosa | French |
| Mori Sushi | Japanese |
| Nobu Malibu | Japanese |
| Palm, The | Steakhouse |
| Sona | New French |
| Valentino | Italian |

### Angelini Osteria　　　　　　　27 | 17 | 22 | $44 |

*7313 Beverly Blvd. (Poinsettia Pl.), 323-297-0070*

■ "Sublime" Italian fare supplied by "true maestro" Gino Angelini
has the "Hollywood hordes" stampeding this LA "knockout" where
the "perfectly prepared" offerings "allow impeccable ingredients
to shine", making even the "most familiar dishes" like the "best
branzino" seem revelatory; the "personable" staff "imported" from
The Boot makes "excellent wine suggestions", and though the
"matchbox-size" room's "cramped" and the din "deafening", the
"food keeps you coming back."

### A.O.C.　　　　　　　　　　　26 | 23 | 23 | $48 |

*8022 W. Third St. (Laurel Ave.), 323-653-6359; www.aocwinebar.com*

■ "Glorious", "imaginative" tapas with French, Cal and Med
influences, a "stellar" selection of wines by the glass or carafe, an
"excellent" charcuterie bar – no wonder this "groundbreaking"
Third Street sophomore from Suzanne Goin and Caroline Styne has
"been anointed the place to be" by "celebrities", "hipsters" and
"foodies alike"; the "sleek", "beautiful" decor by Barbara Barry
and "charming", "knowledgeable" staff enhance the "satisfying
experience", and though one's "wallet will be slimmer" as a result,
that's "A.O.K." by admirers.

### Bastide ☒　　　　　　　　　　26 | 26 | 27 | $101 |

*8475 Melrose Pl. (La Cienega Blvd.), West Hollywood, 323-651-5950*

☑ Though the departure of chef Alain Giraud may not be reflected in
the Food score, this "magical" West Hollywood bastion is saluted
for "sublime" Provençal fare offered in "brilliant" tasting menus
paired with "exceptional wines" as well as "incomparable",
"sweet" service; Andrée Putman's "divine", "elegant" interior
and the "dreamy" patio are equally "memorable", and though
"getting a reservation is a bit like Steve Martin going to L'Idiot"
in *LA Story* and it's all "terribly expensive", devotees declare it's
"worth every 100-dollar bill."

### Bel-Air Hotel　　　　　　　　26 | 28 | 27 | $64 |

*Bel-Air Hotel, 701 Stone Canyon Rd. (Sunset Blvd.), Bel Air, 310-472-1211;
www.hotelbelair.com*

■ Supplying a "civil oasis in Gomorrah", this "ultimate romantic
hideaway" in the Bel-Air Hotel is renowned for its "gorgeous",
"blue-blood" decor and "breathtaking" grounds replete with
"soothing swans" sailing by; "beautifully presented", "superb"
Cal-French fare and "fine wines" are "perfectly" served by the
"top-notch" staff, and though it's "pricey", it's "unbeatable for
any occasion", especially if you reserve the private Table One;
N.B. jacket required during fall and winter.

### Belvedere, The　　　　　　　26 | 27 | 27 | $65 |

*The Peninsula Beverly Hills, 9882 Little Santa Monica Blvd.
(Wilshire Blvd.), Beverly Hills, 310-788-2306; www.peninsula.com*

■ "If you see stars missing in the sky, they're here" at this "epitome
of perfection" inside the "opulent" Peninsula Beverly Hills, where
the ambiance is "peaceful unless you run into CAA people" from
next door; it's a "wonderful place" to "dress up" and dine on "great"
chef Bill Bracken's "spectacular", "innovative" New American
cuisine "impeccably" served by an "attitude"-free staff "with
eyes in the backs of their heads"; naturally, it's "pricey", but it's
"impressive" "when something special is in order."

### Bistro 45
26 | 23 | 24 | $50

*45 S. Mentor Ave. (bet. Colorado Blvd. & Green St.), Pasadena, 626-795-2478; www.bistro45.com*

■ "Perfect for a special occasion", this Pasadena "favorite" is "consistently fine, year in and year out", offering "sensational", "inventive" Cal-French fare, "heavenly desserts" and "excellent" wines; "consummate proprietor" Robert Simon oversees the "impeccable", "old-world" service, and whether you dine in the "stunningly romantic" room or on the "pleasant patio", you're "ensured an unforgettable" (if "high-priced") experience.

### Brent's Deli & Restaurant
26 | 13 | 20 | $17

*19565 Parthenia St. (bet. Corbin & Shirely Aves.), Northridge, 818-886-5679; www.brentsdeli.com*

■ Even if Westsiders hate to admit it, the "best deli in LA hands down" graces an SF Valley mini-mall where "gluttonous portions" of "Jewish soul food" including "heavenly pastrami" and "football-size éclairs" await "rejoicing ex–East Coasters"; though it's "too popular for its own good and yours", the "expert staff turns tables without rushing you."

### CAFÉ BIZOU
23 | 19 | 21 | $29

*91 N. Raymond Ave. (Holly St.), Pasadena, 626-792-9923*
*Water Gdn., 2450 Colorado Ave. (26th St.), Santa Monica, 310-582-8203*
*14016 Ventura Blvd. (bet. Costello & Murietta Aves.), Sherman Oaks, 818-788-3536*
*www.cafebizou.com*

■ A "frugal gourmet's dream" come true and the Most Popular among LA-area restaurants, these Cal-French triplets are "always a treat" with "consistently delicious" food from an "appealing" menu and an "incredible" $2 corkage fee (as well as an "unbelievably low-priced" roster of wines); the "professional", "excellent" service and "romantic", "pleasant surroundings" also elicit kisses, and even when "mobbed on weekends", these bistros "live up to their great reputation."

### CAMPANILE
26 | 24 | 24 | $50

*624 S. La Brea Ave. (bet. 6th St. & Wilshire Blvd.), 323-938-1447; www.campanilerestaurant.com*

■ "Grilled-cheese Thursday nights are a religious experience" at this "institution" where Mark Peel's "sophisticated", "always-delicious" Cal-Med fare is "still exciting and flawless after all these years"; the "beautiful", "comfortable" interior is located in an "old Charlie Chaplin haunt" and features a "romantic" patio, the service is "outstanding", and though it all comes at a "serious cost", it "never disappoints"; P.S. you can pick up its "legendary" bread at next-door sibling La Brea Bakery.

### Capo ⊠
26 | 23 | 22 | $72

*1810 Ocean Ave. (Pico Blvd.), Santa Monica, 310-394-5550; www.foodcowest.com*

◪ "Forgo private school for your kids to experience the heirloom tomato salad, truffled pasta and perfectly grilled meats" from "artistic chef" Bruce Marder, whose "superb" Italian cuisine uses the "highest quality" ingredients and is supported by "fine wines" at this Santa Monica "Shangri-la"; the "warm", "beautiful" decor replete with wood-burning fireplace and "top-notch" service are also "treats", but the "criminally" high prices and the fact that you "need a capo to get your reservation on time" have some muttering "never" again.

### Chaya Brasserie
24 | 23 | 21 | $44 |

*8741 Alden Dr. (bet. Beverly Blvd. & 3rd St.), West Hollywood, 310-859-8833; www.thechaya.com*

■ "Still hip after all these years", this 20-year-old Asian-Eclectic next to Cedars is "still at the top of the list" for "reliably excellent" fare from "great sushi" to the "best lobster ravioli", as well as "wonderful martinis" and "amazing" desserts; the "dramatic" decor's "smashing", the crowd "young", "thin" and "beautiful", the staff's "helpful" and if the "high energy" results in "ear-splitting noise levels", it "doesn't stop the food from tasting good."

### Chinois on Main
26 | 20 | 22 | $55 |

*2709 Main St. (bet. Ashland Ave. & Ocean Park Blvd.), Santa Monica, 310-392-9025; www.wolfgangpuck.com*

☑ "In the beginning, there was the to-die-for crispy catfish" at Wolfgang Puck's Santa Monica mainstay, and after more than 20 years, the "heavenly" Eurasian cuisine is still "wonderful", with a "changing menu that keeps it interesting"; the service is "excellent" ("long reign manager Bella" Lantsman) and the room's "lovely", though the "painfully crowded" quarters and "excruciating" din mar the experience for some; still, the "tried-and-true formula" keeps fans returning for a "fix" and feeling it's "worth the splurge."

### Christine
25 | 19 | 24 | $37 |

*Hillside Village, 24530 Hawthorne Blvd. (Via Valmonte), Torrance, 310-373-1952; www.restaurantchristine.com*

■ "Genius" chef Christine Brown "continues to reinvent herself" at this Torrance mini-mall "South Bay jewel" with her "tantalizing", "excellent" and often "exotic" Cal-Med fare; "unequaled", "knowledgeable" service and a "charming" interior featuring a balcony help create a "consistently enjoyable experience"; P.S. the "tasting menu paired with wines is too good for words."

### Depot, The ☒
24 | 22 | 23 | $35 |

*1250 Cabrillo Ave. (Torrance Blvd.), Torrance, 310-787-7501; www.depotrestaurant.com*

■ "Personable" chef-owner "Michael Shafer is the king" at this "excellent" Eclectic located in a "historic" Old Torrance train terminal, where the "innovative", "superb" offerings, many with "Asian flair", supply "something for everyone" ("indulge in the silken mac 'n' cheese" and "delicious" homemade ice cream); the "wonderful" space and "enthusiastic" service ensure its "popularity" with the "automotive corporate-lunch crowd", and if a few are steamed that it's "pricey for the area", more maintain it's the "best in the South Bay."

### Derek's ☒
27 | 23 | 25 | $53 |

*181 E. Glenarm Ave. (Marengo Ave.), Pasadena, 626-799-5252; www.dereks.com*

■ "Once you get over" the Pasadena strip-mall location, you'll enjoy being "treated" to a "gastronomic adventure" comprising "incredible" New American–Cal fare created by a "perfectionist" kitchen, as well as "wonderful wines"; "master restaurateur" Derek Dickenson and his "superb" staff display "encyclopedic knowledge", and the "romantic", "comfortable" room provides an "adult dining experience" at this "worth-the-hype" "treasure."

### Grace
25 | 25 | 24 | $56

*7360 Beverly Blvd. (Fuller Ave.), 323-934-4400; www.gracerestaurant.net*

■ "Veteran chef and local hero Neal Fraser" earns accolades for his "amazing" New American cuisine including "tasty, unusual" game selections at this "fantastic" sophomore; the wines are equally "imaginative", the "sophisticated", "lovely" Michael Berman–designed space has "no obvious Siberia" and the "top-notch" staff is "knowledgeable"; though it's "undoubtedly a scene" and decidedly "pricey", devotees declare "may it grace LA for years to come"; P.S. leave room for the "divine jelly doughnuts."

### Grill on the Alley, The
24 | 20 | 24 | $50

(aka The Grill)

*9560 Dayton Way (Wilshire Blvd.), Beverly Hills, 310-276-0615; www.thegrill.com*

■ "The perfect two-martini lunch spot" may be this Beverly Hills "institution" where even after 20 years the "buzz is great" thanks to "fine American cuisine" including "must-try Caesar salad", the "best filet on the Westside" and "drinks that pack a punch"; "polished", "snappy" service and a "clubby" environment make it a "serious power scene" for the "entertainment" "elite" who can well afford the "expensive" tabs.

### JiRaffe
26 | 22 | 23 | $48

*502 Santa Monica Blvd. (5th St.), Santa Monica, 310-917-6671; www.jifferrestaurant.com*

■ "Perfect for a special occasion, like Tuesday night", chef-"impresario" Raphael Lunetta's Californian located just down from the Third Street Promenade proffers "fine dining sans attitude"; the "outstanding", "simply elegant" food and "swoon"-worthy specials are served by a "solicitous", "informed and charming" staff; factoring in the "chic", bi-level setting leads supporters to stick their necks out and name it "one of the few that can compete with the big boys in NY."

### Joe's
27 | 21 | 23 | $46

*1023 Abbot Kinney Blvd. (bet. Main St. & Westminster Ave.), Venice, 310-399-5811; www.joesrestaurant.com*

■ "Wizard" chef Joe Miller is "always innovative" and his Cal–New French cuisine is "always delicious" at this "winner" where locals take guests "to impress them with the Venice lifestyle"; the "astute" staff "takes care of you" as you dine in the "cool", "upscale" interior or "gorgeous" patio with a "gurgling fountain", and even if it's "pricey", it's considered a "superb bargain for the quality" of the offerings (and has "one of the best lunch deals in town").

### Josie Restaurant
26 | 23 | 24 | $54

*2424 Pico Blvd. (25th St.), Santa Monica, 310-581-9888; www.josierestaurant.com*

■ "Chef Josie Le Balch doesn't miss a beat" at this "wonderful treasure" on the southeastern edge of Santa Monica where the "adventurous" French-accented New American cuisine is "elegant" and "delicious", featuring "delicately" prepared game dishes; "impressive wines", "fantastic", even "witty" service and the "lovely" "upscale lodge setting with wood-burning fireplace" create a "fabulous experience" that's "worth the thousands of pennies" you'll spend.

### Katsu-ya
27 | 14 | 20 | $37 |

*11680 Ventura Blvd. (Colfax Ave.), Studio City, 818-985-6976*

■ "As confirmed by the hordes lining up at 5:30 PM", this "small" mini-mall Japanese in Studio City supplies what the "obsessed" consider "some of the best sushi of all time", using "unbelievably fresh fish", as well as "amazing, creative specials"; "even with reservations", you should "be prepared to wait", but it's "entirely worth it", and in-the-know surveyers suggest you "leave yourself at the chef's mercy" for a "heavenly omakase" that's a "great deal."

### La Cachette
27 | 25 | 26 | $56 |

*10506 Santa Monica Blvd. (bet. Beverly Glen Blvd. & Overland Ave.), Century City, 310-470-4992; www.lacachetterestaurant.com*

■ "One of the prettiest places in town", this "civilized little" Century City "hideaway" serves "simply divine" and, most significantly, not overly "rich" *cuisine française*; it's a "throwback to more traditional, elegant dining" in a room with "enough space between the tables to carry on a conversation" and a "serious, knowledgeable" staff, prompting patriots to add "who says we don't love the French?"

### L'Orangerie
26 | 27 | 25 | $83 |

*903 N. La Cienega Blvd. (Willoughby Ave.), West Hollywood, 310-652-9770; www.lorangerie.com*

■ West Hollywood's "grande dame of French cuisine still dazzles" despite chef turnovers and the fact that there's "nothing trendy or fusion about it"; indeed, its "exquisite" food, including "must-have" soufflés, "incredibly attentive" service and "extravagant château"-like setting could put Versailles to shame and has jacket-wearing courtiers coveting "more generous expense accounts" (there's a "hefty fee" for this "heaven on earth").

### Mastro's Steakhouse
27 | 23 | 24 | $62 |

*246 N. Cañon Dr. (bet. Clifton & Dayton Ways), Beverly Hills, 310-888-8782; www.mastrossteakhouse.com*

■ Every day's a "power day" at this Beverly Hills chophouse whose "signature bone-in filets" are "still sizzling when you dig in" with sides and desserts that are equally "delectable"; the more sedate downstairs is suitable for "conversation", but upstairs has "all the action" and a piano bar, plus "good star-watching" that "gives you something to talk about" and makes "you wish you were a West Coast Soprano" or at least had their "big wallets."

### MATSUHISA
28 | 16 | 23 | $68 |

*129 N. La Cienega Blvd. (bet. Clifton Way & Wilshire Blvd.), Beverly Hills, 310-659-9639; www.nobumatsuhisa.com*

■ The "granddaddy" of Nobu Matsuhisa's worldwide empire, this Beverly Hills "shrine to the raw and rare" still "blows minds" with its "fascinating" sushi plus "outstanding" hot dishes like the black cod with miso that'll "make you faint"; a "lackluster" interior contradicts the "self-confidence" found in the staff and on the bill (which "you'll think is in yen"), but most recommend going for broke with the omakase menu to taste "the best of everything."

### MÉLISSE
28 | 25 | 26 | $74 |

*1104 Wilshire Blvd. (11th St.), Santa Monica, 310-395-0881; www.melisse.com*

■ Treat "your senses to an incredible adventure" rivaling premier "Paris dining" at "exacting" chef-owner Josiah Citrin's "special-occasion" French–New American in Santa Monica that's known for its "wonderful cheese course" and tasting menu representing "gluttony at its best"; recently redecorated with contemporary touches, the room "refreshes tired spirits" and has "stools to place your purse on", which is fitting since a meal here makes impending "penury a pleasant prospect."

### Mimosa 🅢                22 | 18 | 21 | $39

*8009 Beverly Blvd. (bet. N. Edinburgh & N. Laurel Aves.), 323-655-8895; www.mimosarestaurant.com*

■ Some suspect there "must be a French *maman* back in the kitchen" of this Fairfax District bistro, but they're mistaken as it's chef-owner Jean-Pierre Bosc who whips up the "excellent steak frites", "wonderful bouillabaisse" and a "take on mac 'n' cheese that brings new life to the concept"; *en plus,* there's a "friendly" staff, a "secret back patio for groups" and overall "good quality for the price."

### Mori Sushi 🅢                25 | 19 | 20 | $61

*11500 W. Pico Blvd. (Gateway Blvd.), West LA, 310-479-3939*

■ West LA "sushi lovers" fantasize that "fish are waiting in line to be the next creation" of "master" Mori Onodera, a "perfectionist" who dazzles with "hyper-elegant", "bite-size" cuts presented on his handcrafted "art"-like ceramic dishes; service is alternately described as "knowledgeable" and "arrogant", but most deem the portions "delicate for the price."

### Nobu Malibu                26 | 20 | 21 | $61

*3835 Cross Creek Rd. (PCH), Malibu, 310-317-9140; www.nobumatsuhisa.com*

■ "You can wear sweatpants and still not feel under-dressed", but make sure your terry cloth is designer-labeled because you're in for "star-watching galore" while dining on "high-end", "fascinating" and utterly "phenomenal" sushi and other Peruvian-accented Japanese "delicacies" at Matsuhisa's Malibu outpost; whether you "eat on the patio" or in the "clinically white room", you'll be rubbing elbows with "hipsters" and "rockers" who aren't deterred by the "*trop cher*" tabs.

### Palm, The                23 | 19 | 22 | $54

*1100 S. Flower St. (11th St.), 213-763-4600*
*9001 Santa Monica Blvd. (bet. Doheny Dr. & Robertson Blvd.), West Hollywood, 310-550-8811*
*www.thepalm.com*

☑ "Sinatra food at its best" is the calling card at this "holy" chain with branches Downtown near Staples and in West Hollywood; "stiff drinks", "superb steaks", the "biggest lobsters you've ever seen", "surprising" Italian dishes and "incredible" sides are served by a "seasoned", "professional" staff in a "clubby setting"; even if naysayers knock it as "too noisy" and "overpriced", its pack proclaims "you can never go wrong."

### Patina                27 | 25 | 25 | $70

*141 S. Grand Ave. (2nd St.), 213-972-3331; www.patinagroup.com*

■ Moving from Melrose to the "glorious" Disney Hall Downtown has done nothing to diminish the luster of this "true foodie experience" courtesy of Joachim Splichal, whose "imaginative" Cal-French menu offers "wow after wow", with "top-quality ingredients" making for "ecstasy-inducing" dishes complemented by "impeccable wines"; the "flawless" service is like a "well-choreographed ballet", and the "ultramodern" Hagy Belzberg–designed space is "dazzling" but "relaxing"; though the "gold-standard" cuisine requires "gold-bullion" payment, it's "worth it" for "one of the country's top dining" destinations.

### SADDLE PEAK LODGE　　　　　27 | 28 | 26 | $56 |
*419 Cold Canyon Rd. (Piuma Rd.), Calabasas, 818-222-3888;*
*www.saddlepeaklodge.com*
■ "High wood-beam ceilings", "hunting trophies on the walls"
and "large fireplaces" distinguish this Calabasas "destination"
that supplies a "welcome change from the stark, modern decor of
top LA" restaurants, and the "exotic" New American fare from
"genius chef Warren Schwartz" spotlighting "outstanding" game
dishes is equally "memorable"; the "pampering" but "unobtrusive"
service contributes to the peak experience, and though it's "pricey"
and "off the beaten path", it's "perfect for a special occasion."

### Shiro　　　　　　　　　　　　27 | 16 | 23 | $42 |
*1505 Mission St. (Fair Oaks Ave.), South Pasadena, 626-799-4774;*
*www.restaurantshiro.com*
■ Long the top-rated restaurant in South Pasadena, this "local
spot with world-class food" uses "only the finest ingredients"
to create "memorable" Cal-Asian fare with an emphasis on
"outstanding seafood", including its signature fried catfish in
ponzu sauce that's "still a wow"; though the space is "small", the
ambiance is "convivial" and the service is "friendly", and the food's
"quality never misses."

### Sona　　　　　　　　　　　　26 | 22 | 25 | $72 |
*401 N. La Cienega Blvd. (bet. Beverly Blvd. & Melrose Ave.),*
*West Hollywood, 310-659-7708; www.sonarestaurant.com*
■ "Intellectually challenging" and ultimately "exquisite" and
"delicately balanced" New French fare with global influences
creates a "symphony in your mouth" at this "mind-blowing"
destination in West Hollywood, where chef-owner David Myers
is the "conductor" and his wife and pastry wizard, Michelle,
"should be sainted"; the "ravishing Zen" decor is "serene", the
"pampering" service is "amazing", and even if the "prices are
exorbitant, it's worth every penny"; P.S. the "tasting menus are
the star" with "great wine pairings."

### SPAGO　　　　　　　　　　　27 | 25 | 25 | $65 |
*176 N. Cañon Dr. (Wilshire Blvd.), Beverly Hills, 310-385-0880;*
*www.wolfgangpuck.com*
■ The "star in LA's culinary crown", Wolfgang Puck's Beverly Hills
"benchmark" is "still hot after all these years" thanks to "brilliant"
chef Lee Hefter, who's "continually reinventing" Californian cuisine
using Austrian and "Asian influences" to create "dazzling" dishes
as well as the "signature pizzas"; Sherry Yard's desserts are
"sinful", the "movie star"–bedecked space is "beautiful", the
service is "exemplary" and "maestro" Wolfie "defies physics" by
"making an appearance the night you happen to be there"; even
though the tabs are "high", it "lives up to the hype."

### SUSHI NOZAWA Ø　　　　　　28 | 7 | 16 | $52 |
*11288 Ventura Blvd. (Main St.), Studio City, 818-508-7017*
■ Rated No. 1 for Food among LA-area restaurants, this now-
"legendary" Studio City Japanese serves "sweet", "succulent"

sushi and sashimi bursting with the "most delicate flavors ever to have emerged from the ocean"; acolytes gladly "bow" before "master" Kazunori Nozawa and "adhere to the mantras" ("no soy", "one piece, one bite" and "trust the chef") for the "euphoric sensation" of eating his "perfect" fish, and even "celebs" endure "perpetual waits" for the privilege of "worshiping" in the "no-nonsense" setting; N.B. closed weekends.

### Sushi Sasabune 🗷
27 | 8 | 17 | $53

*11300 Nebraska Ave. (Sawtelle Blvd.), West LA, 310-268-8380*

■ "Nozawa's worthy offshoot" subscribes to the same "'trust-me' philosophy" to "wonderful" effect in West LA, and even if it's "not for control freaks", it's a sushi "purist's" "idea of heaven" with "amaaazing", "incredibly fresh" fish served over "warm, sweet rice"; the "divey decor" and "put-you-in-the-poorhouse" prices notwithstanding, it's "one of those experiences you just have to have", so "sit down, shut up and enjoy" — and "don't criticize the food or you may be banned for life"; N.B. closed weekends.

### Takao
27 | 13 | 21 | $46

*11656 San Vicente Blvd. (bet. Barrington & Darlington Aves.), Brentwood, 310-207-8636*

■ Chef Takao Izumida (ex Matsuhisa) leaves loyalists "speechless every time" with his "artful", "ethereal", "scrumptious" sushi made with "sea creatures you've never heard of" and "fantastic cooked" Japanese dishes served by a "charming staff" at this Brentwood "nirvana"; a few contend the "cramped" room's "awfully stark at these prices", but regulars retort "when you're this good with fish, you don't need to pay attention to the surroundings"; P.S. the "delightful bento lunches are a bargain."

### Valentino 🗷
26 | 23 | 26 | $64

*3115 Pico Blvd. (bet. 31st & 32nd Sts.), Santa Monica, 310-829-4313; www.welovewine.com*

■ "*In vino veritas*" intone oenophiles about the "encyclopedic" wine list that's paired with "refined", "wonderfully prepared" Italian cuisine at this "always-special" Santa Monica stalwart; "personalized", "attentive" service and a "romantic" setting that's "great for small, intimate events" add up to an "experience beyond compare", even if some feel the decor "could use an update", and though it's "very expensive", fans insist it's "worth every darn penny."

### WATER GRILL
28 | 24 | 26 | $57

*544 S. Grand Ave. (bet. 5th & 6th Sts.), 213-891-0900; www.watergrill.com*

■ Despite the departure of longtime executive chef Michael Cimarusti, this "superb" seafooder in Downtown is an "absolute must" for finatics, serving "fresh, artfully prepared" aquatic fare, a "raw bar bursting with shellfish" and a "dream of a wine list"; "professional" service and a "low-key", "wood-paneled" room with "comfortable, relaxing" seating create a "clubby" atmosphere, and while the pisces are "pricey", for many this "shrine to the sea" represents "power dining at its best"; N.B. the Food rating may not reflect the post-*Survey* chef change.

# Miami

## TOP 20 FOOD RANKING

| Restaurant | Cuisine |
|---|---|
| **28** Chef Allen's | New World |
| Shibui | Japanese |
| Nobu Miami Beach | Japanese |
| **27** Norman's | New World |
| Tropical Chinese | Chinese |
| **26** Joe's Stone Crab | Seafood |
| Cacao | Nuevo Latino |
| Osteria del Teatro | Northern Italian |
| Ortanique on the Mile | Caribbean |
| Romeo's Cafe | Northern Italian |
| Mark's South Beach | Floribbean |
| Azul | New French/Caribbean |
| Capital Grille | Steakhouse |
| Pascal's on Ponce | New French |
| Francesco | Peruvian/Seafood |
| Pit Bar-B-Q | Barbecue |
| **25** Matsuri | Japanese |
| Toni's Sushi Bar | Japanese |
| Café Ragazzi | Italian |
| Miss Saigon Bistro | Vietnamese |

## ADDITIONAL NOTEWORTHY PLACES

| | |
|---|---|
| Acqua | Northern Italian |
| AltaMar | Seafood |
| Blue Door | New French |
| Carmen The Restaurant | Nuevo Latino |
| Casa Juancho | Spanish/Tapas |
| Casa Tua | Northern Italian |
| Cheesecake Factory | American |
| Chispa | Nuevo Latino |
| Escopazzo | Italian |
| Forge, The | Continental/Steakhouse |
| Garcia's | Seafood |
| Graziano's Parrilla | Argentinean |
| La Dorada | Spanish/Med. |
| Mundo | New World |
| Nemo | New American |
| Pacific Time | Pan-Asian |
| Prime 112 | Steakhouse/Seafood |
| Roger's | American |
| Versailles | Cuban |
| Wish | New American |

### Acqua
— | — | — | VE

*Four Seasons, 1435 Brickell Ave. (bet. SE 14th Ln. & 14th Terr.),*
*305-358-3535; www.fourseasons.com*

Quality and quietude pervade this ultra-luxurious Northern Italian on the seventh floor of Downtown Miami's elegant, new Four Seasons, where an oasis of a dining room abuts a lush patio overlooking pools and foliage; prices are as breathtaking as the 80-ft. waterfall at the hotel's entrance, but a steady flow of monied regulars and visiting dignitaries, who start the evening sipping from the extensive wine list at the outdoor Bahía bar, don't seem to mind.

### AltaMar
23 | 15 | 23 | $36

*1223 Lincoln Rd. (Alton Rd.), Miami Beach, 305-532-3061*

■ "Gracious" chef-owner Claudio Giordano "keeps tabs on everything" at this SoBe "gem" tucked away from the "zoo that is Lincoln Road proper"; the Med-inspired seafood and pastas are "fresh" and "fantastic", the staff's "super" and the prices are quite "reasonable" according to the local "condo crew" and moviegoing regulars; however, some say occasionally "rushed" service in the "small" setting mars the experience.

### Azul ☒
26 | 27 | 25 | $63

*Mandarin Oriental Hotel, 500 Brickell Key Dr. (8th St.), 305-913-8358;*
*www.mandarinoriental.com*

☑ "Michelle Bernstein has raised the bar" with her "trailblazing" Asian-accented French-Caribbean cuisine served at the Mandarin Oriental Hotel on Brickell Key near Downtown; the "tremendous views", "sleek", "elegant room", "accomplished" service and "serious wine list" also reap raves, but the "haunting" dishes and "exquisite presentations" elicit "bravas"; however, the unimpressed cite "overrated" offerings and "sky-high prices."

### BLUE DOOR ●
24 | 27 | 21 | $62

*Delano Hotel, 1685 Collins Ave. (17th St.), Miami Beach, 305-674-6400;*
*www.chinagrillmgt.com*

☑ "Ian Schrager's Philippe Starck–designed" "fantasy island" in the "amazing" Delano Hotel epitomizes the "South Beach mystique", with its "Cocteau-like surreal setting" and terrace "overlooking a pool that melts into the turquoise ocean"; "beautiful people" "love" the "sublime" Brazilian-influenced New French fare from chef Claude Troisgros, but lament that the "prices are as jaw-dropping as the decor."

### Cacao ☒
26 | 26 | 24 | $44

*141 Giralda Ave. (bet. Galiano St. & Ponce de Leon Blvd.), Coral Gables,*
*305-445-1001; www.cacaorestaurant.com*

■ A "chocoholic's wonderland", this "impressive", "must-try" Nuevo Latino in the Gables offers "original", "spectacular" and "delectable" dishes, many using cacao, from "creative chef" Edgar Leal, as well as "exemplary" desserts and "outstanding wines"; the "fantastic" (and, at press time, soon-to-be-expanded) interior and "excellent" service help make this "one of the best places" on Restaurant Row.

### Café Ragazzi
25 | 14 | 25 | $33

*9500 Harding Ave. (95th St.), Surfside, 305-866-4495*

■ Cafe society swarms this "teeny", family-owned Surfside Italian, where the inevitable "long waits" "on the sidewalk" for a table are "eased by a complimentary glass of wine"; it's "worth a trip" for the "exceptional", "authentic" cuisine, especially grandma's homemade pasta, and it doesn't hurt that the "charming" owner and "flirty" waiters make everyone "feel gorgeous"; N.B. construction that's expected to double capacity should ease the squeeze by the end of 2004.

### Capital Grille, The    26 | 25 | 25 | $54

*444 Brickell Ave. (SE 5th St.), 305-374-4500; www.thecapitalgrille.com*
■ "An 'in' place for Miami power brokers", this "solid" Downtown steakhouse chain link is the "best place to close the deal" proclaim potentates who praise "wonderful", "CEO"-worthy service and the "beautiful" "wood, brass and glass"–filled decor; starting with the house cocktail ("great pineapple-infused vodka") and proceeding to "top-quality" beef and seafood accompanied by "terrific sides", it provides a "marvelous" experience; the only lament: "I wish my banker would let me eat here every day."

### Carmen The Restaurant    25 | 22 | 23 | $42

*David William Hotel, 700 Biltmore Way (Cardena St.), Coral Gables, 305-913-1944; www.carmentherestaurant.com*
■ "Carmen Gonzalez is back and better than ever" at her Nuevo Latino "surprise" within Coral Gables' David William Hotel; the "diminutive chef" "delivers big flavors" with "excellent" cuisine that's "creative but not wild", the setting's "elegant", the service is "impeccable" and wallet-watchers sing arias of love about the "reasonable prices"; P.S. it's a "great neighborhood bar" too.

### Casa Juancho ◐    22 | 22 | 20 | $38

*2436 SW Eighth St. (bet. SW 24th & 25th Sts.), 305-642-2452; www.casajuancho.com*
■ You'll "forget about Calle Ocho" once you walk into this chapter of "earthy Hemingwayesque Spain" with an "old Madrid" vibe in Little Havana; "excellent tapas", "huge portions" of "delicious", Ernestly "authentic" entrees and an "extensive" Iberian wine list are prelude to a "party", with guitar-playing troubadours providing a "lively" evening.

### Casa Tua ⊠    22 | 29 | 21 | $70

*Casa Tua, 1700 James Ave. (bet. Collins & Washington Aves.), Miami Beach, 305-673-1010; www.casatualifestyle.com*
☑ "Savvy sophisticates and furtive celebs" agree this "ravishing", "romantic" South Beach "newcomer" tucked into a "beautifully restored home" and its "enchanted garden" are "divine"; what's more, the Northern Italian fare is "sublime" and service can be "charming", but critics caution "you have to rob a bank to pay for it all"; P.S. loyalists laud the "large community table" next to the kitchen for a "little mingling while you eat."

### CHEESECAKE FACTORY ◐    20 | 19 | 18 | $25

*Aventura Mall, 19501 Biscayne Blvd. (NE 195th St.), Aventura, 305-792-9696*
*CocoWalk, 3015 Grand Ave. (Virginia St.), Coconut Grove, 305-447-9898*
*Dadeland Mall, 7497 N. Kendall Dr. (88th St.), Kendall, 305-665-5400*
*www.thecheesecakefactory.com*
☑ With its fabled "menu longer than the latest Harry Potter" and portions large enough "to serve an entire canasta" group, these "dependable" chain links attract "masses" who "line up" for

"good" American fare and "dynamite desserts"; sure, they're "noisy" and the lines can be "prohibitively long", but the staff's "quick and efficient" and the "well-done corporate formula" is "great for the kids."

**CHEF ALLEN'S**　　　　　　　　28 | 23 | 26 | $60
*19088 NE 29th Ave. (bet. 191st St. & 28th Ave.), Aventura, 305-935-2900; www.chefallens.com*

■ "Not just a meal, but an amazing experience", this "bastion of culinary excellence" in Aventura is once again Miami's No. 1 for Food, thanks to the "artistry" of chef-owner Allen Susser, whose New World cuisine is "extraordinary", "exciting" and "delicious", and complemented by "excellent wines"; the staff is "impeccable" and "intelligent" and, with monthly art exhibits, the "atmosphere's great", making it "worth a return trip."

**Chispa ●**　　　　　　　　– | – | – | E
*225 Altara Ave. (Ponce de Leon Blvd.), Coral Gables, 305-648-2600; www.chisparestaurant.com*

One of the original Mango Kings, Robbin Haas (most recently of Baleen), has resurfaced at this stunning Nuevo Latino in Coral Gables where lively decor featuring orange beaded lamps, wood and leather accents and colorful floor tiles accord with the place's name ("spark" in Spanish); large portions of dishes such as imaginative seviche and daily paellas are eminently shareable.

**Escopazzo ●**　　　　　　　25 | 21 | 24 | $51
*1311 Washington Ave. (bet. 13th & 14th Sts.), Miami Beach, 305-674-9450; www.escopazzo.com*

■ "You'd be crazy not to eat" at this "delightful little corner of Italy hidden" in SoBe; the "superior" rotating offerings ("excellent risottos") are "memorable" as are "outstanding wines", and the "incredibly romantic" room comes "complete with fountain"; "gracious" owners Pino and Giancarla Bodoni and their staff clearly "love what they do", and if this eatery's "a bit pricey", it "never fails to impress."

**Forge, The**　　　　　　　　24 | 25 | 24 | $61
*432 Arthur Godfrey Rd. (Royal Palm Ave.), Miami Beach, 305-538-8533; www.theforge.com*

☑ "Still a classic for a romantic evening" for nearly the past four decades, this "charming" Miami Beach "institution" keeps forging ahead with its "outstanding" Continental steakhouse fare, "excellent" wine list comprising 300,000 bottles, "top-notch service" and "opulent" (some say "bordello"-like) decor; protesters say the "prices will give you a heart attack before the beef does", however, and lament it's "lost its luster"; N.B. the just-added party room and courtyard might add new shine to the atmosphere during private affairs.

**Francesco ⊠**　　　　　　　26 | 15 | 22 | $36
*325 Alcazar Ave. (bet. Le Jeune Rd. & Salzedo St.), Coral Gables, 305-446-1600; www.francescorestaurant.com*

■ "As close to Lima as you'll get" in Coral Gables, this Peruvian seafooder offers a "unique" opportunity to sample "excellent", "inventive" dishes as well as "superb" seviche and other "well-priced" dishes; the service is "attentive" but not "obsequious", and though the tables are a bit "crowded, it's worth it to experience" the "excellent" fin fare and new wine list.

### Garcia's
22 | 12 | 17 | $21

*398 NW North River Dr. (NW 5th St. Bridge), 305-375-0765*

■ It may be "tricky to find" and "hard to park" at this "funky" "local treasure" on the shores of the Miami River skirting Downtown, but "it's worth it" to "feast" on the "best fish sandwiches in town" as well as "cheap" but "sophisticated" seafood; its "overcrowded" digs are affectionately deemed a "dump", but "natives" know there's a "nice patio" that's perfect for "long Friday lunches."

### Graziano's Parrilla Argentina
24 | 19 | 20 | $41

*9227 SW 40th St./Bird Rd. (92nd Ave.), Westchester, 305-225-0008; www.parrilla.com*

■ What started as "a hole-in-the-wall" is now Miami's "best Argentinean", and this "impressive", "popular" Westchester *parrillada* (grill) has had to expand to accommodate the hungry carnivores who stampede for "excellent" steaks and "great" sweetbreads complemented by an "extensive" selection of "reasonably priced" wines; repentant regulars warn you'll have to "go to confession" if you indulge in the dulce de leche crêpes.

### JOE'S STONE CRAB
26 | 19 | 22 | $54

*11 Washington Ave. (1st St.), Miami Beach, 305-673-0365; www.joesstonecrab.com*

☑ "Go early" to this "forever classic" nonagenarian South Beacher, Miami's Most Popular, because "getting seated is like winning the lottery"; once inside, however, you'll "devour" the "best" crustaceans "on the planet" (in season, when the joint is open mid-October–mid-May) and "heavenly" sides in an "old-school" setting; cognoscenti counsel "avoid the ridiculous waits" by getting takeout next door – either way, don't forget to "leave room for the Key lime pie."

### La Dorada ❶
24 | 19 | 22 | $53

*177 Giralda Ave. (Ponce de Leon Blvd.), Coral Gables, 305-446-2002*

☑ Afishionados affirm this "upscale" Coral Gables "Madrid-style" Mediterranean offers "one of the best experiences" around thanks to "excellent" seafood that's "flown in daily from Spain (in first class, judging from the prices)" as well as the "delightful" "old-world" waiters; opponents object it's "overrated", but perhaps they haven't sampled the "amazing salt-baked fish."

### Mark's South Beach
26 | 21 | 23 | $58

*Nash Hotel, 1120 Collins Ave. (bet. 11th & 12th Sts.), Miami Beach, 305-604-9050; www.chefmark.com*

■ "When form meets substance, magic happens", most Mark-edly when "celebrity chef"-owner Militello is manning the stoves, and this "chic", "contemporary" SoBe "gem" in the Nash Hotel "never fails" to "amaze" with "refined yet robust" Floribbean fare that "satisfies the most discriminating palate"; the "penthouse"-caliber cuisine, "fantastic" service and an alternative alfresco space "by the pool" divert attention from the "dark downstairs" digs.

### Matsuri
25 | 13 | 20 | $29

*5759 Bird Rd. (Red Rd.), West Miami, 305-663-1615*

■ The sushi queue swears by the "fresh, fresh, fresh" and "reasonably priced" fin fare at this West Miami "little dive", where a "loyal Japanese clientele" along with "Gloria Estefan" go for "the real thing"; despite the "crowded" digs that "could use an upgrade", partisans praise "great original dishes" as well as what may be the "best rolls in town."

### Miss Saigon Bistro
25 | 14 | 23 | $25

*148 Giralda Ave. (Ponce de Leon Blvd.), Coral Gables, 305-446-8006*
*9503 S. Dixie Hwy. (bet. Kendall Blvd. & Hwy. 104), Pinecrest,*
*305-661-2911*
*www.misssaigonbistro.com*

☑ "Vietnamese food is hard to come by in Miami", which makes pho-natics especially grateful for this "authentic", family-owned "little storefront" in the Gables; "outstanding" noodles and other "distinctive", "delicious" dishes at "reasonable prices" as well as "wonderful" service mean "long lines", but it's "worth the wait"; N.B. the Pinecrest location opened post-*Survey*.

### Mundo
– | – | – | E

*Village of Merrick Park Mall, 325 San Lorenzo Ave. (Salzedo St.),*
*Coral Gables, 305-442-6787; www.normans.com*

With more than 10,000 sq. ft. and 300-plus seats, there is nothing small about this world, after all; a handsome newcomer to the competitive Coral Gables scene, it's the more casual cousin to Norman Van Aken's eponymous eatery, offering a selection of global fare (naturally), everything from hot-pressed sandwiches to cool seviche to Key lime crème brûlée; there's a take-out market and bakery to boot.

### Nemo ◑
25 | 22 | 21 | $50

*100 Collins Ave. (1st St.), Miami Beach, 305-532-4550;*
*www.nemorestaurant.com*

■ Finding this "sophisticated" "favorite" "off the beaten path" in South Beach is "well worth the trip" say schools of supporters who swoon over the "superb raw bar", "inventive" New American fare, "heavenly Sunday brunch" and "orgasmic" desserts; the interior's "beautiful", the courtyard "in the winter months is especially divine" and the staff's "pleasantly professional"; though a few pout that "prices are creeping up", more maintain the "great people-watching" alone makes it a "must-go."

### NOBU MIAMI BEACH ◑
28 | 22 | 22 | $68

*The Shore Club, 1901 Collins Ave. (20th St.), Miami Beach,*
*305-695-3232; www.noburestaurants.com*

■ "Celebrities" and "glam, skinny" types jam Nobu Matsuhisa's South Beach branch in the Shore Club and pronounce it "as good as the NYC" flagship, serving the "ultimate sushi and sashimi" and "exceptional" Peruvian-accented Japanese dishes like "excellent miso cod" (albeit at "outrageous" prices); the "swanky", "nouveau *Miami Vice*" digs set the stage for a "lively" scene, "service is superior" and though it only accepts reservations for parties of six or more, you can wait in the popular bar.

### NORMAN'S ⊠
27 | 25 | 26 | $63

*21 Almeria Ave. (Douglas Rd.), Coral Gables, 305-446-6767;*
*www.normans.com*

■ "From start to finish", a meal at chef-owner Norman Van Aken's "treasure" is "perfection incarnate"; the "wowed" avow "it's worth a drive from anywhere" to this "grand" Coral Gables "gastronomic nirvana" for "amazing", "adventurous" New World cuisine, as well as "suave", "attentive" service and a "romantic" setting; sure, it's "expensive", but "worth it" for "quintessential Florida fine dining."

## Ortanique on the Mile   26 | 23 | 23 | $48

*278 Miracle Mile (Le Jeune Rd.), Coral Gables, 305-446-7710;*
*www.cindyhutsoncuisine.com*

■ Caribbean cuisine "doesn't get any better" than at this "jewel of Miracle Mile" in Coral Gables, where chef-owner Cindy Hutson turns out "inspired", "exquisite" (if "a bit pricey") fare using island spices that "make your taste buds sing" and a bit of French-Asian flair; the majority maintains the "festive", tropical atmosphere with its "funky" decor and "enthusiastic" servers make for a "lively" evening, though a few fume the "tables are too close together" for "dinner conversation."

## Osteria del Teatro 🗷   26 | 15 | 24 | $50

*1443 Washington Ave. (Española Way), Miami Beach, 305-538-7850*

■ "They know what they're doing" at this "top-of-the-line" SoBe "standby" that still does boffo box office thanks to its "creative", "habit-forming" handmade pastas and other "delicious" Northern Italian specials; owner/maitre d' Dino Perola provides a "warm welcome" and ensures the "quality never wavers", and though the setting's rather "so-so", "super service" and that "incredible" food keep it "popular."

## Pacific Time   25 | 20 | 22 | $54

*915 Lincoln Rd. (bet. Jefferson & Michigan Aves.), Miami Beach,*
*305-534-5979; www.pacifictime.biz*

☑ "This Pan-Asian trendsetter" is now firmly entrenched as a "classic" thanks to chef-owner Jonathan Eismann's "unusual" but "consistent" cuisine ("memorable seafood") and a "dizzying wine list" that lure both "locals" and imported "pretty people"; the SoBe setting's "beautiful" and staff "professional", so even though prices are "shocking" and clock-watchers warn "its time has come and gone", more retort "it gets better every year."

## Pascal's on Ponce 🗷   26 | 19 | 24 | $47

*2611 Ponce de Leon Blvd. (bet. Almeria & Valencia Aves.), Coral Gables,*
*305-444-2024; www.pascalmiami.com*

☑ "Exactly what a restaurant should be" report frontliners of this "outstanding" New French in Coral Gables where "each dish is an essay in perfection" overseen by chef Pascal Oudin and his wife, Ann-Louise, as well as an "impeccable" staff "committed to providing a fantastic experience"; complaints of "small portions" and "tight" quarters notwithstanding, most maintain it offers a "*magnifique*" meal at moderate prices; P.S. "don't miss out on the soufflé" and do have a drink at the new bar.

## Pit Bar-B-Q, The   26 | 8 | 14 | $13

*16400 SW Eighth St. (Krome Ave.), 305-226-2272*

☑ Sure, it's a "little hole-in-the-wall near the Everglades" with "no air-conditioning" and "bench seating", but BBQ junkies believe this thirtysomething veteran turns out the "best in South Florida"; the "feast" includes "wonderful pork", ribs, frogs' legs and "light, fluffy fry biscuits with honey", and even though it's a "long drive" for a pit stop, acolytes aver "it's worth it."

## Prime 112   – | – | – | VE

*112 Ocean Dr. (1st St.), Miami Beach, 305-532-8112; www.prime112.com*
The name refers not only to the fine steak coming out of this swank surf 'n' turfer's kitchen but also to its primo SoFi (south of Fifth)

locale on South Beach – and both explain why this latest venture from Myles Chefetz (Big Pink, Nemo, Shoji) is a runaway hit; celebs and socialites stop in for dry-aged beef, just-caught fish and stellar desserts plus an impressive wine list, but be advised you might have to mortgage your own choice real estate to pay the tab.

### Roger's                                         – | – | – | M
*1601 79th St. Cswy. (Bay Dr.), North Bay Village, 305-866-7111; www.rogersrestaurant.com*
Locals and tourists have hopped aboard this Traditional American newcomer owned by an amateur pilot in North Bay Village because it's the kind of place that Miami has long lacked: a moderately priced, waterside eatery with a bayside terrace, lively bar scene and good, basic fare for a top-flight casual night out.

### Romeo's Cafe ⊠                          26 | 20 | 26 | $62
*2257 SW 22nd St./Coral Way (bet. 22nd & 23rd Aves.), 305-859-2228; www.romeoscafe.com*
■ "Charming" chef-owner Romeo Majano "customizes your dining experience" at this "tiny" Coral Way Northern Italian, where six "fabulous", "nightly changing" prix fixe courses ("no written menu") are "tailored to your taste" and "prepared to perfection"; "romantic atmosphere" and "personal" but "unobtrusive" service transform an "expensive" proposition into a "worthwhile splurge"; P.S. "book in advance" for the weekend seatings.

### SHIBUI ●                                     28 | 21 | 24 | $31
*10141 SW 72nd St. (102nd Ave.), Kendall, 305-274-5578; www.shibuimiami.com*
■ There may be a "zillion places" offering sushi in Miami, but this moderately priced family-owned "gem" in Kendall has been a "sentimental favorite" for over 20 years, and with reason – the "quality" fare's "fresh", "imaginative" and "consistent" and the service is "excellent"; vets advise reserving to avoid a "long wait", and add the upstairs tatami rooms are "great for dates."

### Toni's Sushi Bar ●                         25 | 19 | 20 | $34
*1208 Washington Ave. (12th St.), Miami Beach, 305-673-9368*
■ Though the SoBe "scene has changed over the last decade", this "fabulous" sushi "oasis" has remained true to the owners' ideals, serving "splendid", "100 percent fresh" fish and "other wonderful Japanese delicacies" at "moderate prices"; the "beautiful people" and other "locals go once a week", and suggest that the bead-curtained "sunken tables" create "romantic" spots for rendezvous.

### TROPICAL CHINESE                      27 | 19 | 22 | $30
*Tropical Park Plaza, 7991 SW 40th St./Bird Rd. (SW 79th Ave.), Westchester, 305-262-7576; www.tropical-chinese.com*
■ Despite its "unassuming" Westchester strip-mall locale, this "landmark" transports devotees to Hong Kong via "succulent", "delicate" and "delightful" dumplings (served during daily dim sum lunches) and "unusual", "upscale Chinese" dishes; it's "fun to watch the kitchen behind a glass wall", the staff's "friendly" and though it can get "crowded", it remains a "locals' favorite."

### Versailles ●                                21 | 14 | 18 | $20
*3555 SW Eighth St. (SW 35th Ave.), 305-444-0240*
■ You certainly get the "feel of Little Havana" at the "gold standard of Calle Ocho" where "Miami's Latin power brokers" sip "killer"

cafecitos and eat "arguably the best Cuban food anywhere"; there may be "a long wait for a table" in the "raucous", "kitschy" room and it "helps to speak Spanish" (though "gringos are welcome"), but prices are "reasonable" and it's still the "place to be seen."

**Wish** 24 | 25 | 21 | $56
*Hotel of South Beach, 801 Collins Ave. (8th St.), Miami Beach, 305-674-9474; www.wishrestaurant.com*
■ The menu at this "quiet oasis in swinging South Beach" designed by Todd Oldham may have been transformed since the departure of their star chef but it remains an "ethereal" place for "romantic" sorts who come for New American cuisine with Asian touches in a stunning setting featuring a "magical garden"; sure, some wish it were less "pricey" and that service were "less slow", but more find it "leaves nothing to be desired."

# Milwaukee

## TOP 10 FOOD RANKING

| Restaurant | Cuisine |
|---|---|
| **29** Sanford | New American |
| Watermark | Seafood |
| **27** Dream Dance | New American |
| Ristorante Bartolotta | Northern Italian |
| **26** Immigrant Room/Winery | Eclectic |
| Heaven City | New American |
| Three Brothers | Serbian |
| Eddie Martini's | Steakhouse |
| Riversite, The | American |
| **25** Coquette Cafe | French Bistro |

## ADDITIONAL NOTEWORTHY PLACES

| | |
|---|---|
| Bacchus | New American |
| Dancing Ganesha | Indian |
| Jackson Grill | Steakhouse |
| Lake Park Bistro | French Bistro |
| Maggiano's | Southern Italian |
| Moceans | Seafood |
| Osteria del Mondo | Northern Italian |
| P.F. Chang's | Chinese |
| River Lane Inn | Seafood |
| Singha Thai | Thai |

| F | D | S | C |
|---|---|---|---|
| – | – | – | E |

### Bacchus ⊠
*Cudahy Towers, 925 E. Wells St. (Prospect Ave.), 414-765-1166;
www.bacchusmke.com*
Joe Bartolotta (Lake Park Bistro, Ristorante Bartolotta) breathes
new life into the Downtown space that once housed the red-walled,
French-postered Boulevard Inn, transforming it into a big-city
New American with a cream-colored palette and brown-leather
banquettes and booths; chef Brandon Wolff (ex Dream Dance)
mans the high-profile kitchen, turning out trademarks such as his
venison Rossini and oven-roasted halibut, which are served by a
confident, knowledgeable staff.

### Coquette Cafe ⊠

| 25 | 22 | 23 | $33 |
|---|---|---|---|

*316 N. Milwaukee St. (St. Paul Ave.), 414-291-2655;
www.coquettecafe.com*
■ "Tucked away" in the "trendy" Third Ward, this "charming bistro"
(the "more casual" and "affordable" French "little sister" of award-
winning toque Sandy D'Amato's "renowned Sanford") features chef
de cuisine Andrew Schneider's "homey" yet "nuanced" fare (folks
"love" the "excellent hanger steak") "served with a Midwestern
lack of pretension"; P.S. proximity to a plethora of play purveyors
makes it a "great" "place for pre- or post-theater dining."

### Dancing Ganesha
| 22 | 20 | 20 | $27 |

*1692-94 N. Van Buren St. (Brady St.), 414-220-0202;*
*www.dancingganesha.com*

■ When you "want something a little different from your standard Indian restaurant", drop in to this "inventive" East Side seven-year-old that "puts a unique twist on" subcontinental fare via a "creative menu" marked by "deep, rich flavors"; perhaps it's "not the most authentic", but most say it's "a sure bet", especially if you "venture to order the edgier" offerings – "they'll make you dance!"

### DREAM DANCE ⬧
| 27 | 23 | 26 | $53 |

*Potawatomi Bingo Casino, 1721 W. Canal St. (16th St.),*
*414-847-7883; www.paysbig.com*

◪ "Hidden away" in Downtown's Potawatomi Bingo Casino is this "classy" "special-occasion" venue, a "little pot of dining gold" featuring a "fantastic", "innovative [New] American" menu that "showcases local specialties" and is "superbly served" by "outstanding" staffers who go "above and beyond"; still, it's "not a dream for" those who "can't get past" its "incongruous setting" "upstairs" from a "smoke-filled" "gambling hall"; P.S. the Food rating may not reflect the fact that former executive "chef Brandon Wolff moved on."

### EDDIE MARTINI'S
| 26 | 24 | 26 | $51 |

*8612 Watertown Plank Rd. (84th St.), 414-771-6680*

■ Diners "take a step back in time" ("think Humphrey Bogart") at this "always-crowded", "clubby" steakhouse, a West Side "favorite" for "mouthwatering" meat and "delicious seafood"; "personable" "team" "servers in white coats" "make you feel like a favorite customer", though the flip side, standoffish sorts say, is that service "can get overdone" – and you'd better "plan on spending a boatload of money."

### Heaven City
| 26 | 25 | 23 | $40 |

*S91 W27850 National Ave./Hwy. ES (Edgewood Ave.), Mukwonago,*
*262-363-5191; www.heavencity.com*

■ "Knowing the history of this" "romantic", "worth-a-drive" venue set "in an old house" "hidden away" in Mukwonago "is half the fun"; reportedly a "former" "gangster hideout", "religious retreat and house of ill repute" (at different times), it's now a "fun, funky place" where "always-creative" New American dinners, including "many theme nights" (folks "love May Mushroom Madness"), are served in "a maze of small, romantic rooms"; no wonder fans feel it's a little slice of "heaven in Cheeseland."

### IMMIGRANT ROOM & WINERY, THE ⬧
| 26 | 26 | 27 | $60 |

*American Club, 419 Highland Dr. (School St.), Kohler, 920-457-8888;*
*www.destinationkohler.com*

■ "Top-notch service", "superb food" and "an incredible setting" inside Kohler's American Club Resort have diners immigrating from far and wide to this "ultimate" Eclectic, a "wonderful" (albeit "pricey") place that leaves "every one of your senses satisfied"; its "lovely", "old European-style" dining room is "a treat for a special occasion" or to signal "a spectacular end to a day on the golf course or at the spa"; P.S. the separate Winery Bar offers "unique appetizers" and "outstanding wines", plus "their cheese selection is the best" around.

### Jackson Grill ⌧　　　　▽ 28 | 18 | 23 | $35 |
*3736 W. Mitchell St. (38th St.), 414-384-7384*

■ "The word is out" on this "tiny" South Side steakhouse that's "reminiscent of a supper club from the past"; owner Jimmy Jackson, son of noted late Milwaukee restaurateur Ray, serves a "small but incredible menu" ("excellent steaks", "to-die-for" specials), but be sure to "come early" – since its opening in 2003, the "retreat" has grown into a "busy" "neighborhood place."

### LAKE PARK BISTRO　　　　25 | 26 | 24 | $45 |
*Lake Park Pavilion, 3133 E. Newberry Blvd. (Lake Park Rd.), 414-962-6300; www.lakeparkbistro.com*

■ With this East Side "French jewel", Joe Bartolotta "has created a masterpiece" inside a "perfect setting": Frederick Law Olmsted–designed Lake Park ("romantics" recommend "ask for a table by the window with a view of Lake Michigan"); adoring eaters exclaim "Seine-sational!" about the "top-shelf", "consistently wonderful" "classic and modern bistro fare", but even die-hard devotees deride the "unacceptable noise level."

### MAGGIANO'S LITTLE ITALY　　　20 | 18 | 19 | $28 |
*Mayfair Mall, 2500 N. Mayfair Rd. (W. North Ave.), 414-978-1000; www.maggianos.com*

☑ Big appetites are appeased at this West Side outpost of a chain of "great family-style places" that's "still going strong" with its "abundant" "red-sauce" Southern "Italian comfort-food" concept and "vibrant atmosphere" ("a touch old Italy, a touch Rat Pack"); still, the jaded jot that "it's not worth the wait" to tolerate what they find to be "forgettable food", merely "competent service" and "overcrowded" conditions.

### Moceans ⌧　　　　　　– | – | – | E |
*747 N. Broadway (bet. Mason St. & Wisconsin Ave.), 414-272-7470; www.moceans.com*

Bringing energy and spunk to the formerly staid dining digs of the now-defunct Grenadier's, this new Downtown seafood hot spot is the domain of chefs Karla Fischer (late of River Lane Inn) and Eric Vollman, who take a minimalist approach in preparing large portions of fresh seafood such as hash brown–crusted halibut; there's also a raw oyster selection ranging from Bluepoints to Belons, and the white linen–topped tables are patrolled by poised tag-team servers.

### Osteria del Mondo　　　　25 | 23 | 23 | $43 |
*1028 E. Juneau Ave. (N. Astor St.), 414-291-3770; www.osteria.com*

■ "Take someone you want to impress" to chef-owner Marc Bianchini's "elegant", "special-date" place, a "nice surprise for Downtown Milwaukee" that satisfied supporters say shines like a "supernova" (though, unlike that short-lived celestial phenomenon, it has lasted for 10 years); with its "authentic" Northern Italian cuisine, "good wine selection" and "charming", "comfortable" front patio, it "stacks up against any other for quality", even if the "crowds and critics tend to overlook" it.

### P.F. CHANG'S CHINA BISTRO　　20 | 19 | 18 | $26 |
*Mayfair Mall, 2500 N. Mayfair Rd. (W. North Ave.), 414-607-1029; www.pfchangs.com*

☑ Champions of this "Chinese chain" gang branch on the West Side cheer it as a "consistent", "good choice" for "great", "upscale"

"Americanized food" ("everyone loves the lettuce wraps") in a "fun", "noisy and crowded" atmosphere that's staffed by "upbeat servers"; at two years of age, it's a "welcome addition" that's "still relatively new", and some critics contend it "needs to get a better grounding" and "could stand some fine tuning" vis-à-vis service.

### RISTORANTE BARTOLOTTA   27 | 23 | 23 | $41
*7616 W. State St. (Harwood Ave.), 414-771-7910;*
*www.bartolottaristorante.com*
■ "Anything [restaurateur Joe] Bartolotta touches is great", so it's no surprise followers brave a "high noise level" and tables practically "on top of each other" just to get a piece of his longest-running endeavor, this 11-year-old West Side "favorite" where "dreamy" Northern Italian fare and "gracious service" find a "rustic", "comfortable" yet "classy" home; remember, though, that "reservations are a must", since "crowds" of "smiling people" mean it's "still hard to get into after all these years."

### River Lane Inn ⬛   24 | 17 | 21 | $35
*4313 W. River Ln. (Brown Deer Rd.), 414-354-1995*
☑ "Wonderful opportunities to try" "great seafood" (including some Cajun-Creole specialties such as the "best blackened fish around") abound at this "off-the-beaten-path" North Shore spot, the casual counterpart to Jim Marks' The Riversite; "popular with locals", it's a "fantastic place" that fans feel is "like an old friend or a favorite sweater", though a few naysayers negate the menus as "a little tired."

### Riversite, The ⬛   26 | 25 | 24 | $43
*11120 N. Cedarburg Rd. (Mequon Rd.), Mequon, 262-242-6050*
■ "A beautiful view of the Milwaukee River", "exceptional wines" and the skills of "creative" chef Tom Peschong keep this "reliable", "upscale" North Shore American on its audience's A-list; "superbly hospitable" owner Jim Marks is often "present and will guide you through the myriad choices" of "extraordinary appetizers", "exquisitely prepared game" dishes and "excellent seafood"; P.S. the "nice setting" is "especially lovely when the snow flies."

### SANFORD ⬛   29 | 26 | 29 | $66
*1547 N. Jackson St. (Pleasant St.), 414-276-9608;*
*www.sanfordrestaurant.com*
■ "If I only had one meal left, I would have it here" attest acolytes "astounded" by this "intimate", "elegant" East Side New American mecca that "defines gourmet in Milwaukee", setting "the standard" by scoring top honors for Food among Milwaukee restaurants; "genius" co-owner and "chef Sanford D'Amato never fails to amaze with his spectacular cooking" from an "adventurous menu", and the "fantastic" staff provides "outstanding service", making this "true culinary experience" "worth the splurge"; P.S. "don't miss" the "wonderful tasting menus" that "change seasonally."

### Singha Thai   25 | 16 | 19 | $19
*2237 S. 108th St. (Lincoln Ave.), 414-541-1234; www.singhathai.com*
■ Though "any of the curries are great", fans of this "awesome" West Side Thai know to "go to the back page" of its "expansive menu" "for house specialties", including Singha beef, charcoal chicken, crispy shrimp and spicy noodles; "don't expect to be wowed" by "its typical strip-mall" location, "but at least you aren't paying for frills."

### Three Brothers ⊄     26 | 17 | 22 | $27
*2414 S. St. Clair (Russell Ave.), 414-481-7530*
■ Owners Branko and Patricia Radicevic "treat you like family the minute you walk in the door" of their "one-of-a-kind" Serbian set in an old South Side Schlitz tavern that oozes "simple", "old-world charm"; ranging from "well-dressed businessmen to everyday anarchists", the "crowd" "spends hours" at this "authentic" "fixture" sampling the likes of burek, chicken paprikash and goulash – all foods that "warm your heart."

### WATERMARK SEAFOOD ⊠     29 | 24 | 24 | $42
*1716 N. Arlington Pl. (Brady St.), 414-278-8464*
■ Summer 2003 witnessed the debut of this "underwater treasure", a "chic" yet "comfortable" East Side spot with "instant-classic" potential thanks to chef-owner and "seafood magician" Mark Weber (Lake Park Bistro's former top toque), whose daily changing menu of "simple, subtle, perfect" dishes showcases "fresh" fin fare; even if certain staffers seem "a bit challenged", it's still "a fantastic addition to the Milwaukee scene."

# Minneapolis/St. Paul

## TOP 10 FOOD RANKING

| Restaurant | Cuisine |
|---|---|
| **28** Bayport Cookery | New American |
| La Belle Vie | Med./New French |
| **27** Goodfellow's | New American |
| D'Amico Cucina | Northern Italian |
| Vincent | French Bistro |
| Manny's | Steakhouse |
| Levain* | New American |
| Alma | New American |
| **26** Oceanaire | Seafood |
| Lucia's | New American |

## ADDITIONAL NOTEWORTHY PLACES

| | |
|---|---|
| Bakery on Grand | French Bistro |
| Heartland | Regional American |
| Kincaid's | Steakhouse/Seafood |
| Origami | Japanese |
| Punch Neapolitan | Pizza |
| Ristorante Luci | Italian |
| Solera | Spanish |
| St. Paul Grill | American |
| True Thai | Thai |
| Zander Cafe | New American |

| F | D | S | C |
|---|---|---|---|

### Alma
27 | 21 | 24 | $39

*528 University Ave. SE (6th Ave.), Minneapolis, 612-379-4909;
www.restaurantalma.com*

■ "A treasure", this Dinkytown "destination" "near the University"
of Minnesota is "always packed" thanks to a "constantly changing
menu" of "astonishingly good" New American fare "meticulously
prepared" by "creative chef" Alex Roberts, who is "dedicated
to fresh local ingredients" and "sustainable" agriculture; the
"spruced-up storefront" space is "beautiful" yet "homey", and
the "attentive" staff provides "welcoming service", making it
"a class act all the way" – though some sigh "if [only] it were
a little cheaper."

### Bakery on Grand
25 | 15 | 20 | $32

*3804 Grand Ave. S. (38th St.), Minneapolis, 612-822-8260*

■ "Much more than a bakery", this "bustling" South Minneapolis
storefront with owner and "majordomo Doug [Anderson] at the
helm" is "simultaneously a neighborhood restaurant and a
destination for the entire metro area" thanks to "inventive",
"hearty [French] bistro" fare; the "spartan setting" may be a bit

---

* Indicates a tie with restaurant above

"bare-bones", but the staff is "unpretentious" and the "prices are reasonable", especially for the "excellent lunch" and "Sunday night prix fixe special."

### BAYPORT COOKERY    28  20  25  $51
*328 Fifth Ave. N. (Rte. 95), Bayport, 651-430-1066; www.bayportcookery.com*
■ "A pleasant 30-minute drive from Downtown" through the "beauty of the St. Croix [River] area", this "small storefront" spot (rated No. 1 for Food among Minneapolis–St. Paul area restaurants) "wows" with "amazing" New American fare offered via "ever-changing, imaginative" "five-course" prix fixe meals or a new à la carte menu; a recent remodeling has rendered it an even more "lovely place for a romantic dinner", so "get reservations well in advance"; P.S. "the springtime morel festival is not to be missed."

### D'AMICO CUCINA ☒    27  25  27  $52
*Butler Sq., 100 N. Sixth St. (2nd Ave.), Minneapolis, 612-338-2401; www.damico.com*
■ With "top-flight, creative [Northern] Italian cuisine" and a "superb wine list", this "fancy standby" in the Warehouse District is "a can't-miss choice" "for special nights out", and "still the one to beat for entertaining clients" ("try the unparalleled and inventive tasting menu"); the "Tuscan" "atmosphere is soothing", "the mood is formal but not uptight" and the "attentive staff" "spoils you rotten" – but be sure to "bring a well-stuffed wallet."

### GOODFELLOW'S ☒    27  25  26  $54
*City Ctr., 40 S. Seventh St. (bet. Hennepin & Nicollet Aves.), Minneapolis, 612-332-4800; www.goodfellowsrestaurant.com*
■ "The queen of the classics", this "Downtown institution" receives "bravos" for its "beautiful presentations" of "amazing" New American fare and "wonderful wine list", as well as the "spectacular decor" of its "art deco landmark" setting; some "knock the prices" as "not 'Minnesota nice'", but "superb", "personal service" eases the pain for most; P.S. the Food rating may not reflect the mid-*Survey* arrival of "new chef" Jason Robinson.

### Heartland ☒    25  21  23  $45
*1806 St. Clair Ave. (S. Fairview Ave.), St. Paul, 651-699-3536; www.heartlandrestaurant.com*
■ "Minnesota cuisine is no longer an oxymoron" thanks to this Groveland "neighborhood jewel", "home" of "gifted chef" Lenny Russo, whose "mission" is fashioning "fresh Midwestern ingredients", "locally produced", into Regional American "food worthy of a national reputation"; a few critics complain that the "skimpy portions" are "not cheap", but more maintain that additional pluses such as "a strong wine list" and a "comfortable" "Prairie School interior" make the experience "worth it."

### KINCAID'S    23  22  23  $41
*380 St. Peter St. (6th St.), St. Paul, 651-602-9000*
*8400 Normandale Lake Blvd. (84th St.), Bloomington, 952-921-2255*
*www.kincaids.com*
☑ Fans of this "suburban steak-and-fish joint" and its younger "Downtown St. Paul" spin-off say that each is "the place" in their respective locales for "special occasions", "dinner with a date" or "a business lunch" thanks to "traditional", "elegant" food "with service to match", not to mention some of the "best patio dining

around"; some detractors may detect a "chain-ish sensibility pervading" their "formulaic menu" ("ho-hum") and "uninteresting settings", but more maintain they're "a cut above their peer group."

### LA BELLE VIE
28 | 24 | 27 | $51

*312 S. Main St. (Nelson Alley.), Stillwater, 651-430-3545;*
*www.labellevie.us*

■ "There's not a bad choice on" the "imaginative Med"–New "French menu" at this "chef-owned" Stillwater venue where partners Tim McKee and Josh Thoma's "care and attention is evident in the ingredient selection and preparation"; similarly, the "service is impeccable" and the "lovely wine list is well chosen and fairly priced", making the "experience worth every nickel"; P.S. at press time, a "move to Downtown Minneapolis'" soon-to-debut Chambers Hotel is planned for May 2005.

### Levain ⌧
27 | 17 | 22 | $50

*4762 Chicago Ave. (48th St.), Minneapolis, 612-823-7111;*
*www.restaurantlevain.com*

⌧ Hidden in "out-of-the-way" South Minneapolis, this New American yearling can be nearly "impossible to spot", so look for the "little red door" behind which awaits "fabulous new chef Steven Brown's" "trendy NY restaurant–style food (with NY prices)" complemented by an "exemplary wine list"; some decry the "noisy, noisy, noisy" atmosphere and quip that the fare's "as amazing as the decor is sparse", but most suggest you "do not miss" this "rare find."

### Lucia's
26 | 20 | 24 | $35

*1432 W. 31st St. (Hennepin Ave.), Minneapolis, 612-825-1572;*
*www.lucias.com*

■ A "pioneer of nouvelle Minnesota cooking", this "upscale neighborhood joint" "in the heart of Uptown" is "always a treat", offering a "small", "balanced" and "frequently changing menu" of New American food made from "fresh, locally produced" provender "cooked in creative ways" by chef-owner Lucia Watson; the "simple", "intimate environment" is further enhanced by a "friendly staff" making "excellent service" look "effortless"; P.S. check out her "good wine bar" next door, too.

### MANNY'S STEAKHOUSE
27 | 20 | 25 | $53

*Hyatt Regency, 1300 Nicollet Mall (Grant St.), Minneapolis,*
*612-339-9900; www.mannyssteakhouse.com*

■ "Still the benchmark" for local chophouses, this "meat eaters' nirvana" in Downtown's Hyatt Regency boasts an "accomplished staff" that serves "perfectly prepared, Flintstone-sized steaks" to a "fairly formal, business-oriented" crowd; some suggest the "old boys' club" decor is "a bit too male" ("women eat steak too!"), but most "satisfied carnivores" suggest you "save your pennies and appetite – you'll need both"; P.S. with its "photographs of past guests", "the bar is definitely the place to sit for ambiance."

### OCEANAIRE SEAFOOD ROOM
26 | 23 | 25 | $51

*Hyatt Regency, 1300 Nicollet Mall (Grant St.), Minneapolis,*
*612-333-2277; www.theoceanaire.com*

■ The "fish is flown in fresh" at this "special-occasion" "seafood palace" in Downtown's Hyatt Regency, a "loud, crowded" outpost of a national chain that's the Most Popular restaurant "in the landlocked Minneapolis"–St. Paul area; the kitchen "doesn't miss a beat" in orchestrating an "amazing fish adventure" ("the old standbys are better than you remember, but try their more creative fare – it's excellent"), and the "elegant, attentive" service befits the "swank", "'30s-style" room reminiscent of a "grand ocean liner."

### Origami
26 | 18 | 20 | $35

*Ridgedale Mall, 12305 Wayzata Blvd. (Ridgedale Dr.), Minnetonka, 952-746-3398*
*30 N. First St. (1st Ave.), Minneapolis, 612-333-8430* ⊠
*www.origamirestaurant.com*

☑ "Others may be cheaper, but nobody is fresher" than this "classy Japanese restaurant" in the "quiet Warehouse district", where it's "easy to binge on the fine, inventive" "raw-fish" fare ("the guys behind the bar really know how to take care of you"), not to mention the "nice selection" of "great cooked food"; the new suburban branch splits surveyors, with some saying it "misses the mark" and others opining it serves "suburban sushi worth eating."

### Punch Neapolitan Pizza
24 | 15 | 18 | $16

*3226 W. Lake St. (Excelsior Blvd.), Minneapolis, 612-929-0006*
*704 Cleveland Ave. S. (Highland Pkwy.), St. Paul, 651-696-1066* ⊠
*8353 Crystal View Rd. (Prairie Center Dr.), Eden Prairie, 952-943-9557*

■ Even "on a cold night, it's worth the long wait standing outside" these "popular" purveyors that are many a Minnesotan's "personal favorite" for "close-to-perfect", "authentic Neapolitan" pies that "redefine what pizza can be"; "reasonable prices" (including a "value wine list"), "timely, friendly service" and "consistently high quality" at all branches also contribute to their "institution" status – though die-hard devotees declare that "the original Highland Park location is the tops."

### Ristorante Luci ⊠
26 | 17 | 24 | $34

*470 Cleveland Ave. S. (Randolph Ave.), St. Paul, 651-699-8258;*
*www.ristoranteluci.com*

■ "Fine", "authentic Italian" fare "like your mamma would have cooked if she were a native" of The Boot is the forte of this "crowded but cozy" "neighborhood restaurant" in Highland Park, where "superb meals" that would be "a bargain at twice the price" are offered "in a pretension-free atmosphere"; P.S. it can be "hard to get a reservation", so regulars recommend you call "two weeks in advance – the food is worth" the extra effort.

### Solera
24 | 24 | 21 | $39

*900 Hennepin Ave. (9th St.), Minneapolis, 612-338-0062;*
*www.solera-restaurant.com*

☑ "Colorful Gaudí-inspired decor" that's "sensual without being overwrought" evokes "sunny Spain" at this "new favorite" Downtown ("from the La Belle Vie folks") that "tantalizes" with "an unending list of tasty tapas" "made for sharing" and ferried by a "friendly, helpful" staff; it's not every "epicurean's dream come true", though, with some wondering "what all the hype's about" and warning that those "teeny-tiny" dishes "quickly add up, pricewise"; nevertheless, "the rooftop terrace is all the rage."

### St. Paul Grill
24 | 24 | 24 | $43

*St. Paul Hotel, 350 Market St. (5th St.), St. Paul, 651-224-7455;*
*www.stpaulgrill.com*

■ "Grand dining in a grand room of a grand hotel" sums up the appeal of this "grande dame" in Downtown St. Paul that "continues to impress" with its "classy", "clubby atmosphere", "gorgeous mirrored bar" and "wonderful view of Rice Park"; it's where the "old-money" crowd meets for "true power lunches" and "excellent pre-theater" dinners of "well-done Traditional American" fare "graciously served" – no wonder well-wishers willingly "spend too much, eat too much and always adore it."

**True Thai** 🗷                           25 | 13 | 19 | $21 |
*2627 Franklin Ave. E. (27th Ave.), Minneapolis, 612-375-9942;*
*www.truethairestaurant.com*
■ "As the name states, true Thai" is on the "truly interesting menu" at this "gem" in an "offbeat" South Minneapolis location, where seekers of "authentic" Siamese find "true bliss" ("every bite's a treat"); true, the "hole-in-the-wall" decor is a bit "bare-bones", but the "first-class" kitchen "will do special requests" and offers "spiciness choices" that allow you to have it "as hot as you like", prompting pleased patrons to proclaim the place truly "Thai-namite!"

**VINCENT** 🗷                           27 | 23 | 24 | $48 |
*1100 Nicollet Mall (11th St.), Minneapolis, 612-630-1189;*
*www.vincentrestaurant.com*
■ "A welcome oasis", this Downtown "chef-owned gem" is helmed by "imaginative", "charismatic" toque Vincent Françoual, who "sincerely cares what his clients think" and garners *beaucoup de "mercies"* from them for giving his "high-end French bistro" fare a "Contemporary" American interpretation then pairing it with a "thoughtful wine list"; the "top-notch staff" and "elegant, minimal decor" with "hardwoods, high ceilings and loads of windows" for "people-watching on Nicollet Mall" "complete the package"; P.S. "try the chef's table" in the kitchen.

**Zander Cafe**                           25 | 18 | 22 | $35 |
*525 Selby Ave. (bet. Kent & Mackubin Sts.), St. Paul, 651-222-5224*
■ "Thank goodness for a great neighborhood place we can afford" – so say Selby sorts smitten with this "warm and friendly" "jewel", the "signature restaurant" of chef-owner Alexander "Zander" Dixon ("the Zorro of gastronomy"), who dishes up a "creative, inventive" New American menu; the "smart and casual staff", "a wine list to boggle the mind" and "live jazz some nights" are additional attributes that will "keep you coming back" to its "funky, hip" "storefront setting."

# New Jersey

## TOP 20 FOOD RANKING

| | Restaurant | Cuisine |
|---|---|---|
| **28** | Ryland Inn | New French |
| **27** | Nicholas | New American |
| | DeLorenzo's | Pizza |
| | Cafe Panache | Eclectic |
| | Whispers | New American |
| | Scalini Fedeli | Northern Italian |
| | Union Park | New American |
| | Origin | French/Thai |
| | Saddle River Inn | French/New American |
| | Daniel's on B'way | New American |
| | Serenäde | New French |
| | Washington Inn | American |
| **26** | Bernards Inn | New American |
| | Joe & Maggie's* | New American |
| | Cafe Matisse | Eclectic |
| | Jocelyne's | French |
| | Giumarello's | Northern Italian |
| | Stage House | New French |
| | Siri's | Thai/French |
| | Ritz | Seafood |

## ADDITIONAL NOTEWORTHY PLACES

| Restaurant | Cuisine |
|---|---|
| Amanda's | New American |
| Bay Point Prime | Steakhouse |
| Blue Point Grill | Seafood |
| Cucharamama | South American |
| Dining Room | New American |
| Doris & Ed's | Seafood |
| Ebbitt Room | New American |
| Fascino | Italian |
| 410 Bank St. | Creole/Caribbean |
| Frog and the Peach | New American |
| Highlawn Pavilion | New American |
| K.O.B.E. | Japanese |
| La Campagne | French |
| Latour | French/American |
| Rat's | New French |
| River Palm Terrace | Steakhouse |
| Robongi | Japanese |
| Savaradio | Eclectic |
| Waters Edge | New American |
| Zafra | Nuevo Latino |

*  Indicates a tie with restaurant above

### AMANDA'S
25 | 24 | 23 | $41

*908 Washington St. (bet. 9th & 10th Sts.), Hoboken, 201-798-0101;*
*www.amandasrestaurant.com*

■ "Enjoyable in every way", this "romantic", "elegant" "charmer"
set in a "beautiful brownstone" is "Hoboken's finest" "fine-
dining restaurant", "transporting" devotees with "delicious New
American food", a "stellar wine list", "lovely ambiance" and
"world-class service" (it's "well worth" the "difficult" "search for
parking"); P.S. "don't miss" the "great early-bird special" "served
Monday through Saturday" – "at $25 for three courses", this "prix
fixe dinner for two is a bargain."

### Bay Point Prime
– | – | – | VE

*1805 Ocean Ave. (Rte. 35), Point Pleasant Beach, 732-295-5400*
City-style steak comes to the Shore at this clean-lined, light-wood
BYO newcomer from the Garden State's granddaddy of top toques,
Dennis Foy, and his newest protégé chef, Kevin Pomplun (ex
Ryland Inn); though the porterhouse and prime sirloin burger rule,
respondents also rave about the multi-tiered shellfish platter,
groovy iceberg-lettuce salad and spud-licious lineup of sides.

### Bernards Inn, The ⊠
26 | 26 | 26 | $55

*27 Mine Brook Rd. (Quimby Ln.), Bernardsville, 908-766-0002;*
*www.bernardsinn.com*

■ Set in "a phenomenal inn that's truly found its niche", this
"exquisite" New American takes "romance to the utmost level"
with "superb cuisine", "top-class service" from an "informed
staff" and a "classy" "setting epitomizing Bernardsville"; factor
in an "unpretentious" sommelier proffering a "wine book, not a
list", and you'll see why it's a true "special-occasion" "destination";
N.B. the Food rating may not reflect the post-*Survey* departure of
former co-owner and chef Edward Stone and arrival of toque
Corey Heyer (ex Nicholas).

### Blue Point Grill
25 | 15 | 21 | $33

*258 Nassau St. (Pine St.), Princeton, 609-921-1211;*
*www.bluepointgrill.com*

■ "The menu is an A-to-Z of what thrives under the sea" at this
Princeton seafooder BYO that "sets the standard" for "solid,
basic" preparations of "pristine, blessedly *au naturel* fish"; the
"extremely knowledgeable staff" "recommends" dishes to "suit
your tastes" and "helps" you select from the many "different kinds
of (raw) oysters on any given day."

### Cafe Matisse
26 | 25 | 24 | $60

*167 Park Ave. (bet. E. Park Pl. & Highland Cross), Rutherford,*
*201-935-2995; www.cafematisse.com*

■ "Paint the town red" at this "wonderful" BYO set in a "drop-dead
gorgeous" "renovated firehouse" in Rutherford where it's "tough
to get a reservation" thanks to the "artful" "fusion of flavors" in its
Eclectic dishes, which are "prepared by a master" then "elegantly
presented and served"; "a bonus is the wine store out front, where
you can pick up" *vin* "without ultra-marked-up prices."

### CAFE PANACHE ⊠
27 | 19 | 24 | $52

*130 E. Main St. (Rte. 17), Ramsey, 201-934-0030*

■ It's not so "unbelievable that a restaurant of NYC caliber is in
Ramsey" when you consider that "innovative chef" and owner

"Kevin [Kohler] is always raising the bar" at this BYO, "growing some of the herbs and vegetables" he uses to "deliver inventive", "spectacular New French"-, Italian- and Asian-influenced Eclectic fare that's "outstandingly served in a warm setting"; N.B. the Decor score may not reflect a post-*Survey* renovation.

**Cucharamama**   – | – | – | E
*233 Clinton St. (bet. 2nd & 3rd Sts.), Hoboken, 201-420-1700*
Warmed by a wood-burning oven that yields everything from breads to empanadas, this upscale, artfully chic South American helmed by chef, anthropologist and cookbook author Maricel Presilla is Hoboken's biggest hit since Zafra, her casual sister spot in the mile-square city; do dress for her successful reproductions of rustic Latin cuisines, and expect a wine-and-spirits list that keeps pace with the pure-bred chow.

**Daniel's on Broadway**   27 | 26 | 24 | $54
*416 S. Broadway (4th Ave.), West Cape May, 609-898-8770;*
*www.danielscapemay.com*
■ For "a top-notch dining experience", this "elegant" BYO in West Cape May from "meticulous" chef-owner Harry Gleason "never disappoints", "providing a wonderfully prepared menu" of New American fare emphasizing "outstanding, innovative seafood" in a "charming, old renovated house" (parts of which date to the 1700s); with "several small dining areas" that "give an intimate feel", it's "a lovely setting for a romantic, special night."

**DELORENZO'S TOMATO PIES** ∅   27 | 8 | 14 | $14
*530 Hudson St. (bet. Mott & Swann Sts.), Trenton, 609-695-9534*
■ "Fourth-generation addicts" of the "gold standard of thin-crust pizzas" would gladly "stand in the rain, snow, sleet or burning sun" on "lines that stretch all the way to Napoli" just to get into "this hole-in-the-wall" "Trenton landmark" and savor the "consistent perfection" of its "crisp, nutty" pies, "judiciously sauced and cheesed"; "come with clean hands and an empty bladder", though, as "there are no restrooms."

**Dining Room, The** ⊠   26 | 26 | 27 | $69
*Hilton at Short Hills, 41 JFK Pkwy. (Rte. 24), Short Hills, 973-379-0100;*
*www.hiltonshorthills.com*
■ "Just steps from The Mall at Short Hills", this "elegant, upscale" Hilton New American is "the ultimate" say surveyors who suggest you "sink into a plush" "upholstered banquette", be "soothed" by the "serenading harpist" (weekends only) and learn "how royalty eats"; you'll be "paying high prices", but "for this caliber of food", "presentation and service", it's "worth it"; N.B. the Food rating may not reflect the post-*Survey* arrival of chef Robert Trainor, who has added à la carte options to the formerly prix fixe–only menu.

**Doris & Ed's**   25 | 18 | 22 | $54
*348 Shore Dr. (Waterwitch Ave.), Highlands, 732-872-1565;*
*www.dorisandeds.com*
■ "A classic that has stayed in touch with the times", this Highlands "Shore standard" for "super seafood" sports a two-part 'Yesterday/Today' American menu; purists "love the old side's" "excellent traditional" standbys, whereas young turks tout "the virtues of the inventive side's" "gourmet" specials; "seasoned service", a "fabled wine list" and a "comfortable" setting round out its appeal.

### Ebbitt Room, The
26 │ 25 │ 23 │ $53

*Virginia Hotel, 25 Jackson St. (bet. Beach Dr. & Carpenter Ln.),*
*Cape May, 609-884-5700; www.virginiahotel.com*

■ "Outstanding" "on all counts", this "classy" "favorite" is "now a
tradition in Cape May" for "beautifully prepared" New American
cuisine "delightfully served" by a "friendly, knowledgeable staff"
within the "charming", "romantic setting" of a "small boutique
hotel" that makes many feel as though they've "been transplanted
to the Old South"; all told, "it's a pleasure to spend money" for a
"delicious dining experience" of such "pure elegance."

### Fascino 🖾
– │ – │ – │ VE

*331 Bloomfield Ave. (bet. Grove & Willow Sts.), Montclair, 973-233-0350;*
*www.fascinorestaurant.com*

This progressive, warm-toned new Italian BYO in Montclair is
shepherded by the DePersio family, with son/chef Ryan as the
culinary force in the *cucina,* creating the likes of Sicilian-braised
lamb shanks and bronzino with gremolata risotto cake; mom/
pastry chef Cynthia ends things sweetly with delicious desserts
such as pistachio-praline bread pudding.

### 410 Bank Street
26 │ 20 │ 23 │ $47

*410 Bank St. (bet. Broad St. & Lafayette Ave.), Cape May, 609-884-2127*

■ Set in a "small house surrounded by lush green plants", this
"favorite" "Jersey Shore standout" is a "must-stop" "when you're
in Cape May"; in fact, some "travel miles for chef" Henry Sing
Cheng's "superb menu" of "phenomenal" Creole-Caribbean fare;
"stunning crowds" can mean "long waits" at this BYO, and the
"cramped quarters put the 'din' in dinner", but those who "can get
in" insist the "exquisite food makes" all that "seem to not matter."

### Frog and the Peach, The
25 │ 22 │ 23 │ $54

*29 Dennis St. (Hiram Sq.), New Brunswick, 732-846-3216;*
*www.frogandpeach.com*

■ "Impress all the people who say New Jersey is the pits" by taking
them to this "granddaddy of the New American restaurant in the
Garden State"; devotees declare its "consistently innovative"
and "delicious" cuisine is "definitely the best thing to happen to
New Brunswick", and the "solicitous" staff ensures it'll be "perfect
for your first date or to pop the big question."

### Giumarello's 🖾
26 │ 24 │ 22 │ $46

*329 Haddon Ave. (bet. Cuthbert Blvd. & Kings Hwy.), Westmont,*
*856-858-9400; www.giumarellos.com*

■ "Perfect for a romantic dinner", this "excellent" Northern Italian
is a place where the "menu is clearly in the hands of indisputable
culinary professionals" whose "breathtaking presentation" is
matched by an "impeccable" staff with "to-die-for timing"; add in
"warm decor" and a "relaxing, elegant ambiance" and you have a
"rare dining experience" that's "one of the richest in South Jersey."

### Highlawn Pavilion
23 │ 28 │ 23 │ $55

*Eagle Rock Reservation (Prospect Ave.), West Orange, 973-731-3463;*
*www.highlawn.com*

■ "That view, those entrees, those desserts" – all have enthusiasts
enraptured with this "pricey" "mountaintop aerie" in West Orange;
"ask for a window table" "so you can enjoy" the "spectacular"
sight of the "unbelievable NYC skyline" "twinkling in the distance"

as your "palate is delighted" by "delicious" New American fare; "high-class all the way", it's "the place to go with your love."

**Jocelyne's** 26 | 20 | 23 | $46
*168 Maplewood Ave. (Baker St.), Maplewood, 973-763-4460;*
*www.jocelynesrestaurant.com*
■ "Jocelyne Althoiz's warm welcome is a harbinger of wonderful things to come" at this "small French storefront" in Maplewood that could "pose as an inn" in Provence; "authentic", "exquisite" fare "served sans Gallic scorn" prompts patrons to proclaim "if it were in NYC, you couldn't get in", but be forewarned this "tiny" BYO seats just 38, so "it can be difficult to secure a reservation."

**Joe & Maggie's Bistro** 26 | 20 | 22 | $45
*591 Broadway (bet. Bath & Norwood Aves.), Long Branch, 732-571-8848;*
*www.joeandmaggiesbistro.com*
■ "Long Branch is perking up", but this "succulent and superior" New American "preceded the perk-up" and reigns in the city by the sea; "year in and year out", it offers "consistently great food" with "out-of-this-world flavor in every dish", not to mention "gracious service" and a "romantic, intimate atmosphere"; no wonder folks "often detour to eat here" "when down the Shore."

**K.O.B.E.** – | – | – | E
*The Commons at Holmdel, 2132 Rte. 35 S. (Laurel St.), Holmdel,*
*732-275-0025; www.kobecuisine.com*
Subtle and sophisticated, Holmdel's citified Japanese BYO offers celebratory style with bone-colored banquettes set off by dark-wood appointments and soft-hued accents; those going fishing will find Bahamas Rolls and shrimp sashimi as well as the classic *snomono* (a seafood and cucumber dish) and halibut poached in sweet sake (but none of the namesake beef).

**La Campagne** 26 | 23 | 25 | $50
*312 Kresson Rd. (bet. Brace & Marlkress Rds.), Cherry Hill, 856-429-7647;*
*www.lacampagne.com*
■ "Bring your favorite Burgundy" to this "fabulous" Cherry Hill BYO whose "outstanding" "seasonal" French cuisine, "quaint" "old farmhouse setting" and "friendly" service (the staff seeks "to satisfy, yet is never underfoot") have diners declaring it a "true delight" tantamount to a Gallic "mini-vacation"; a plus in warm weather is the "delightful" patio.

**Latour** 26 | 20 | 23 | $49
*6 E. Ridgewood Ave. (Broad St.), Ridgewood, 201-445-5056*
■ "One of Ridgewood's stars", this "wonderfully quaint" French-American "hard by the railroad tracks" is where "charming" chef-owner Michael Latour works "his magic", "attending to every detail" and ensuring that the "fabulous", "traditional" dishes (like his signature beef Wellington) are just about "as good as it gets"; dollar-watchers recommend the "fantastic bargain" of a prix fixe (five courses for $39.50 Tuesday–Thursday); P.S. "bring that special bottle", because it's BYO.

**NICHOLAS** 27 | 24 | 28 | VE
*160 Hwy. 35 S. (bet. Navesink River Rd. & Pine St.), Middletown,*
*732-345-9977; www.restaurantnicholas.com*
■ The "crème de la crème" of Monmouth County, this "swanky" Middletown venue offers a "true awakening of the senses"

courtesy of "incredible" New American prix fixe menus, a "fascinating wine list" and an "outstanding staff"; "the young couple who own the place", Melissa and Nicholas Harary, ensure their "special-occasion dining" destination is "magical" "in every way", so be "prepared for a hefty check"; N.B. the Food rating may not reflect the post-*Survey* departure of chef de cuisine Corey Heyer.

### Origin   27 | 18 | 19 | $32

*25 Division St. (Main St.), Somerville, 908-685-1344; www.originthai.com*

☑ "Thai marries French and we eat happily ever after" is how enthusiasts sum up the "superb blending" of cuisines on the "unusual menu" at this "small-side-street" BYO that makes folks "finally feel like Somerville has a scene"; in fact, some say the "only problem" is that the sometimes "brusque staffers" "pack you in like sardines" then "rush to turn over the tables"; P.S. "call ahead."

### Rat's   25 | 29 | 23 | $64

*Grounds for Sculpture, 16 Fairgrounds Rd. (Sculptor's Way), Hamilton, 609-584-7800; www.ratsrestaurant.org*

■ An "unbelievable" "fantasy for adults", this "magical" New French is nestled within a "whimsical" reproduction of "Monet's Giverny" village surrounded by the "dramatic artwork" of "J. Seward Johnson's beautiful Grounds for Sculpture" in Hamilton; "fresh ingredients", including "produce from [the owner's] organic farm", "make every course flavorful", while "attentive service" adds to the "quality dining experience"; P.S. "free entry" to the park comes with your meal.

### Ritz Seafood   26 | 18 | 20 | $32

*910 Haddonfield-Berlin Rd. (White Horse Rd.), Voorhees, 856-566-6650*

■ "A place to go again and again", this Voorhees BYO "does an exquisite job with seafood" in a "tranquil atmosphere" complete with a pond and waterfalls; you'll feel "transported to some location in Asia" reviewers report, since the "unique assortment of fish" offered and its "commendable presentation" overcome "packed-tight" seating; P.S. there's an "infinite variety of incredible teas", as well as prix fixe options Tuesday–Thursday.

### RIVER PALM TERRACE   24 | 18 | 20 | $51

*1416 River Rd. (Palisade Terr.), Edgewater, 201-224-2013*
*41-11 Rte. 4 W. (bet. Paramus & Saddle River Rds.), Fair Lawn, 201-703-3500*
*209 Ramapo Valley Rd. (Rtes. 17 & 202), Mahwah, 201-529-1111*
*www.riverpalm.com*

■ "Rigorous consistency" in the kitchen yields "well-prepared", "fantastic dry-aged steaks" (including an "awesome porterhouse") served by a "polite, efficient staff" at this trio of "completely unpretentious" North Jersey steakhouses that many beef eaters say are "as good as the more famous names"; some "love the Fair Lawn location", others say "the one in Mahwah is the nicest", though for many the recently renovated "original in Edgewater is still best."

### Robongi   26 | 16 | 22 | $23

*520 Washington St. (bet. 5th & 6th Sts.), Hoboken, 201-222-8388*

■ This Hoboken Japanese is the darling of those who claim it's a "cut above the sushi bars opening on every corner" for its "great selection of rolls and appetizers" that include a "wide" assortment of "fresh house specials"; the fact that it's "BYO is definitely a bonus" (making it "cheaper than local competitors"), as is the "accommodating staff."

### RYLAND INN, THE
28 | 27 | 27 | VE

*Rte. 22 W. (Rte. 523), Whitehouse, 908-534-4011; www.therylandinn.com*
■ Ranked No. 1 for Food among New Jersey restaurants, this dinner-only New French "standard"-bearer under the aegis of "superbly gifted" chef Craig Shelton offers "world-class", "spectacular" tasting menus (which can be paired with "fabulous wines") that leave "all sensory neurons firing like the Fourth of July"; the "beautiful", "romantic" 200-plus-year-old farmhouse setting in Whitehouse with grounds that feature an organic kitchen garden is "worth the journey" alone, and the "exquisite", "informed" service further adds to the near-"perfect dining experience"; N.B. reservations required for the dining room.

### SADDLE RIVER INN ⌧
27 | 25 | 25 | $57

*2 Barnstable Ct. (bet. E. Allendale Ave. & W. Saddle River Rd.), Saddle River, 201-825-4016; www.saddleriverinn.com*
■ "Getting a reservation" at this "northern NJ delight" housed "in a restored barn" in Saddle River can be as tough as "applying to college", but boosters insist its "divine", "well-presented" French–New American cuisine, "attentive", "unobtrusive" service and "warm", "charming", "rustic" setting make it "well worth the monthlong wait"; a few wish the "haughty" staff would "chill" a bit, but it's still a "first-rate experience", and though it's "pricey", "BYO keeps the cost down" a little.

### Savaradio ⇗
26 | 16 | 20 | $40

*5223 Ventnor Ave. (Little Rock Ave.), Ventnor, 609-823-2110*
■ A "special place" that's many "locals' favorite spot", this "cozy" Ventnor BYO is home to "innovative" chef-owner Lisa Savage, who "blasts you into the culinary stratosphere where few kitchens dare to go" with her "fantastic" Eclectic cuisine that's "executed with skill and care"; "easy prices" and "friendly" service are additional reasons that it's so "hard to get a reservation."

### SCALINI FEDELI ⌧
27 | 24 | 24 | $63

*63 Main St. (Parrot Mill Rd.), Chatham, 973-701-9200; www.scalinifedeli.com*
■ A "classic in all senses", this "sublime" Chatham Northern Italian (voted Most Popular among New Jersey restaurants) represents "what dining out's all about" with a seasonal menu of "masterful creations" served in the "splendor" of an "elegant" space by an "attentive" staff; in fact, most would "beg, borrow or steal" for a "fantasy evening" at this "jewel" – if they can "get a reservation."

### Serenäde
27 | 24 | 26 | $64

*6 Roosevelt Ave. (Main St.), Chatham, 973-701-0303; www.restaurantserenade.com*
■ An "ode" to "casual elegance", this Chatham spot is one of "the top special-occasion restaurants in the state" thanks to chef-owner James Laird's "flawless" New French cuisine (including "perfect" tasting menus matched with unusual wines", as well as some more well-known), "professional", "personable" service and "romantic", "elegant" decor; though a "meal costs more like a symphony than a song", pros promise a "satisfied glow" after an "ideal evening."

### Siri's Thai French Cuisine
26 | 22 | 25 | $37

*2117 Rte. 70 W. (bet. Haddonfield Rd. & Sayer Ave.), Cherry Hill, 856-663-6781; www.siris-nj.com*

■ "There must be angels in the kitchen" preparing "exotic, exquisite" Thai and French dishes that "delight your senses" at this "dependably outstanding" Cherry Hill "BYO bargain" where "gracious", "grown-up" service and a "beautiful setting" help make it an "all-time favorite dining adventure" for many; though it's located in an "unattractive strip mall", "once you're inside, you will be transported to paradise", a feeling enhanced by a no-cell-phone policy.

### Stage House Restaurant & Wine Bar
26 | 23 | 24 | $60

*366 Park Ave. (Front St.), Scotch Plains, 908-322-4224; www.stagehouseinn.com*

■ The plaudits pour in for the "outstanding" "gastronomic experience" that awaits at this Scotch Plains venue, where "little-known wines are artfully matched" with "exquisitely prepared" New French dishes and served in a "romantic Colonial inn" "with fireplaces in every room"; partisans admit it's "pricey" but willingly hand over the platinum card "for a celebration" or "special occasion"; N.B. the Food rating may not reflect the post-*Survey* departure of toque David Drake and promotion of former sous-chef Michael Clampffer.

### Union Park
27 | 26 | 27 | $48

*Hotel Macomber, 727 Beach Ave. (Howard St.), Cape May, 609-884-8811; www.unionparkdining.com*

■ It's got "class with a capital C" assert admiring acolytes of this "beautiful" yet "understated" New American BYO venue ensconced within the Hotel Macomber that many consider "the best place to eat in Cape May"; sure, it's a bit "pricey", but for truly "elegant dining" on "impeccably prepared", "knockout" fare brought to table by an "attentive" pro staff, connoisseurs concur "it hits the mark."

### Washington Inn
27 | 26 | 26 | $52

*801 Washington St. (Jefferson St.), Cape May, 609-884-5697; www.washingtoninn.com*

■ "Feel like royalty" at this "romantic oasis in Cape May" that's "a class act in all areas", from the "delicious, imaginative" American cuisine, backed by a "fabulous" 800-label wine list, to the "almost-flawless" "Victorian setting" to the "meticulous" staff providing "the type of service every Shore-goer wishes for"; while it's considered "beautiful" any time of year, yuletide mavens maintain it's a "must-see at Christmas."

### Waters Edge
26 | 21 | 23 | $49

*1317 Beach Dr. (Pittsburgh Ave.), Cape May, 609-884-1717; www.watersedgerestaurant.com*

■ Set astride the dunes and the waves, this "casual" yet ambitious Cape May New American "cools you in summer with its view of the Atlantic" and "warms you in winter with its glowing fireplace"; as if that weren't enough, its "creative" dishes featuring unusual "ingredient combinations" are "superbly executed" and well complemented by an "exceptional wine list", and the "caring, hands-on management" works hard to ensure that every diner's "expectations are surpassed."

## WHISPERS

27 | 24 | 26 | $47

*Hewitt Wellington Hotel, 200 Monmouth Ave. (2nd Ave.), Spring Lake, 732-974-9755; www.whispersrestaurant.com*

■ Spring Lake's "absolute culinary wonderland" is this "haute" New American with a kitchen helmed by new executive chef Scott Giordano (ex Saddle River Inn) and housed in "a delightful Victorian hotel", whose "truly refined", "creative" cuisine provides an "excellent escape from humdrum seafood and steaks"; the "hushed", "intimate" dining room is manned by a "quietly accomplished" staff exhibiting an "impeccable eye for detail"; P.S. "at these prices, thank goodness it's BYO."

## Zafra

25 | 20 | 18 | $27

*301 Willow Ave. (3rd St.), Hoboken, 201-610-9801*

■ Cuba-born culinary scholar Maricel Presilla is the force behind this "little" BYO "burst of culture" in Hoboken, where foodies are "blown away by the chef's combination" of "fabulous" Nuevo Latino tastes; add in an "extremely friendly" staff that's willing to "educate" diners about the menu, and it's no wonder most happily brave long "waits" to gain access to its "cheery", "brightly colored" space; P.S. bring a bottle of your "preferred wine" and they'll turn it into sangria.

# New Orleans

## TOP 20 FOOD RANKING

| Restaurant | Cuisine |
|---|---|
| **27** Peristyle | French/Contemp. Louisiana |
| Bayona | New American |
| Jacques-Imo's | Creole/Soul Food |
| Dick and Jenny's | Creole/French |
| Brigtsen's | Contemp. Louisiana |
| Gabrielle | Creole/Contemp. Louisiana |
| New Orleans Grill | Continental |
| Upperline | Creole |
| **26** Sal & Judy's | Italian/Creole |
| Stella!* | New American |
| Uglesich's | Cajun-Creole |
| Mosca's | Italian |
| August | New French |
| NOLA | Contemp. Louisiana/Creole |
| Commander's Palace | Creole |
| Irene's Cuisine | Italian |
| Dakota, The | New American |
| La Provence* | French |
| K-Paul's | Cajun |
| Crabby Jack's | Seafood/Po' Boys |

## ADDITIONAL NOTEWORTHY PLACES

| | |
|---|---|
| Antoine's | Creole/French |
| Arnaud's | Creole/Seafood |
| Brennan's | Creole/French |
| Clancy's | Creole |
| Eleven 79 | Italian/Creole |
| Emeril's | Contemp. Louisiana |
| Galatoire's | Creole |
| Gautreau's | New French/New American |
| Herbsaint | New American/New French |
| Kim Son | Asian |
| La Petite Grocery | Contemp. Louisiana/French |
| Martinique Bistro | French/Seafood |
| Mr. B's Bistro | Contemp. Louisiana |
| Muriel's | Creole |
| Nine Roses | Chinese/Vietnamese |
| Pelican Club | New American |
| René Bistrot | French Bistro |
| Rib Room | Continental/Steakhouse |
| Riomar | Spanish/Seafood |
| Ruth's Chris | Steakhouse |

---

\* Indicates a tie with restaurant above

### Antoine's ⊠
| 22 | 24 | 23 | $52 |

*713 St. Louis St. (bet. Bourbon & Royal Sts.), 504-581-4422; www.antoines.com*

☑ The birthplace of oysters Rockefeller, this antebellum Creole-French in the Vieux Carré is to many "New Orleans history epitomized", a "charming, picturesque" "old-world" "bastion" "dripping with tradition" and featuring "tuxedo-clad" servers, "elegant food" and an "elaborate wine list"; critics counter that "time is taking its toll", complaining of "dated" decor, "hurried" service (unless "your waiter knows you") and "heavily sauced" cuisine; in any event, "you'll empty your wallet filling your stomach"; N.B. jacket required.

### Arnaud's
| 24 | 24 | 24 | $50 |

*813 Bienville Ave. (bet. Bourbon & Dauphine Sts.), 504-523-5433; www.arnauds.com*

☑ A "welcome oasis from hectic Bourbon Street", this "legendary" "sentimental favorite" in the French Quarter has habitués hailing its "delectable" Creole seafood and the "alert, attentive" servers who ply their trays in "spacious dining rooms" with tall ceilings and leaded-glass windows or in the bistro where a Dixieland trio "swings" ("we were dancing in our chairs"); disgruntled doubters dissent, saying "perhaps its time has passed" now that this "overpriced" "classic has gone so touristy."

### August ⊠
| 26 | 27 | 25 | $54 |

*301 Tchoupitoulas St. (Gravier St.), 504-299-9777; www.restaurantaugust.com*

■ "Ambitious" chef John Besh may be the "hottest talent in New Orleans", cry cognoscenti who commend his "exquisite", "imaginative but not too precious" New French cuisine, "served with precision" by "polite", "polished" staffers – which may be why this "divine" CBDer with exposed-brick walls and crystal chandeliers is becoming a "destination unto itself"; however, petite portions leave some people peckish, which can be "hard to swallow when you're paying that much"; N.B. there's a five-course prix fixe dinner for $75.

### BAYONA ⊠
| 27 | 25 | 25 | $49 |

*430 Dauphine St. (bet. Conti & St. Louis Sts.), 504-525-4455; www.bayona.com*

■ "Connoisseurs of fine food and wine" say chef Susan Spicer's French Quarter "flagship" "merits its accolades"; the "superlative" New American cuisine is "impeccably prepared", and inside the "old Creole cottage" with its "picturesque" patio the "gracious" staff fosters an "intimate", "relaxing" atmosphere – it's "worth calling way ahead" for a reservation, since "it'd be a bargain at twice the cost."

### BRENNAN'S
| 23 | 24 | 23 | $49 |

*417 Royal St. (bet. Conti & St. Louis Sts.), 504-525-9711; www.brennansneworleans.com*

☑ "Brunch has become an art form" – and a "splurge" – at this Creole–Classic French "institution", the "epitome of everything New Orleans", with "sublime food" (including "knee-weakening" bananas Foster), "amiable", "attentive" servers and a "labyrinth" of "genteel" rooms ("explore – you'll need the exercise"); seen-it-alls shrug, though, that it's "famous for being famous", calling it "too high-priced, too crowded, too touristy"; N.B. a partial redo may outdate the above Decor score.

### BRIGTSEN'S ⧄
| 27 | 22 | 26 | $45 |

*723 Dante St. (Maple St.), 504-861-7610; www.brigtsens.com*

■ "King" Frank Brigtsen still "rules" with a "deft hand" over his "tiny kitchen" in Riverbend, creating "rooted-in-tradition yet" "innovative" Contemporary Louisiana cuisine that's so "dazzling" his subjects "want to lick their plates clean" ("rabbit tenderloin makes my heart hop"); regulars report the staff's "Old South graciousness" renders this "super-quaint" cottage "truly homey"; N.B. reservations a must; closed Mondays.

### Clancy's ⧄
| 26 | 20 | 24 | $41 |

*6100 Annunciation St. (Webster St.), 504-895-1111*

■ For "all the Creole without the tourists", "well-heeled Uptown locals" congregate at this "lively", "*très* clubby" "hangout" "in a residential neighborhood" (so "hidden" "you need a secret decoder ring to find it"); the draw is "consistent", "inspired" "New Orleans haute cuisine" (especially the "mouthwatering" oyster-and-Brie appetizer) served by a "sarcastic" yet "friendly" staff – some, however, complain the scene can be so "noisy" and "crowded" "you can't hear yourself eat."

### COMMANDER'S PALACE
| 26 | 26 | 26 | $54 |

*1403 Washington Ave. (Coliseum St.), 504-899-8221;*
*www.commanderspalace.com*

■ NO's Most Popular yet again, this Garden District "celebration place" is considered by many the "unrivaled crown jewel" in the Crescent City's culinary coronet, preserving the "essence of New Orleans" in "stellar" "haute Creole cuisine" (Sunday's jazz brunch is "phenomenal"); a "near-psychic" staff and "venerable", "truly romantic" surroundings convince most that this "classic" still "deserves its reputation" – though a few fret that the "granddaddy" has "lost a step."

### Crabby Jack's ⧄
| 26 | 8 | 15 | $13 |

*428 Jefferson Hwy. (Knox Rd.), Jefferson, 504-833-2722*

◪ A lunch-only "sibling of Jacques-Imo's", this unassuming Jefferson sandwich shop serves up "divine", "awesome po' boys" "piled high" with "slow-roasted duck", rabbit and "the plumpest, most delicious oysters ever", plus "specials that are a bargain at twice the price"; "limited seating" means "there's always a line", and once you get inside the "decor is sparse", but "who cares?" – you can always "call for takeout."

### Dakota, The ⧄
| 26 | 21 | 24 | $40 |

*629 N. Hwy. 190 (¼ mi. north of I-12), Covington, 985-892-3712;*
*www.restaurantcuvee.com*

■ It may be far to go north to The Dakota, but devotees really dig this Covington "gem" for its "fresh and innovative" yet "unpretentious" New American cuisine (including a crabmeat-and-Brie soup that "can't be beat"), extensive wine list, "attentive" servers and "warm and inviting ambiance."

### DICK AND JENNY'S ⧄
| 27 | 21 | 23 | $34 |

*4501 Tchoupitoulas St. (Jena St.), 504-894-9880*

■ "Phenomenal" Creole-French cuisine at "tremendous bargain" prices entices local epicures to "revel in pure deliciousness" at this "unpretentious" Uptown "cottage" where "gracious" service, a "congenial" "at-home" vibe and tables that are "unbelievably close together" combine to conjure "a dinner-party feel"; "thanks to the new expansion" the "long-but-worth-it" "waits have dwindled" but the no-reservations policy endures, so you'll want to "get there early" or "phone ahead."

### Eleven 79 ⊠

25 | 21 | 22 | $45

*1179 Annunciation St. (Erato St.), 504-299-1179*

■ "Fabulous veal", "rich, garlicky" pastas and other "expensive-but-worth-it" Italian-Creole specialties attract an "older crowd" to this "renovated old cottage" "under the bridge" in the Warehouse District, where the cypress-accented decor creates an "intimate", "masculine" atmosphere and the "accommodating" servers "can be a lot of fun"; given the "small" space, though, "it's hard to get in" – if not "one of the toughest tables in town."

### EMERIL'S

25 | 23 | 24 | $55

*800 Tchoupitoulas St. (Julia St.), 504-528-9393; www.emerils.com*

☑ "Don't hate it because of Emeril's overexposure", urge Lagasse loyalists who assert that his Warehouse District "flagship" still serves up "stellar" Contemporary Louisiana cuisine that's "exquisitely presented" by a "coordinated" contingent of "eager waiters"; the recently revamped, rawly modern room has a "trendy" feel, though "with no sound insulation" it can get "objectionably noisy", and given "max-out-the-credit-card" prices, many maintain the celeb chef owes "more attention to his namesake restaurant."

### Gabrielle ⊠

27 | 18 | 23 | $44

*3201 Esplanade Ave. (Ponce de Leon St.), 504-948-6233; www.gabriellerestaurant.com*

■ "Every bite a delight", sing supporters who serenade chef-owner Greg Sonnier's "distinctive", "delectable" Creole–Contemporary Louisiana "haute cuisine", which inspires them to "keep driving" till they get to the "cozy", "charming" triangular building in Faubourg St. John; a "friendly" ambiance and "unobtrusive" service help make the "tight quarters" more palatable but claustrophobes still "wish the tables were spread out more."

### GALATOIRE'S

26 | 23 | 25 | $48

*209 Bourbon St. (Iberville St.), 504-525-2021; www.galatoires.com*

■ Perhaps the only restaurant "where the waiters are more important than the chef", this beloved "epicenter" of haute Creole cuisine in the French Quarter is "the defining New Orleans dining experience", with "reliable renditions of old favorites" from an extensive menu that "never changes", "understated" yet "inviting decor" and "genuine" "old-style service and charm"; the renovated, reservable second floor is quieter, but locals say you "gotta sit downstairs", "especially on Fridays" for "long martini lunches and gossip"; N.B. closed Mondays.

### Gautreau's ⊠

26 | 23 | 24 | $45

*1728 Soniat St. (Danneel St.), 504-899-7397; www.gautreaus.net*

■ A "culinary jewel box" with a "Paris bistro feel", this "tiny" Uptowner in a converted antique drugstore is so "charming" it has "locals trying to keep it a secret"; surveyors savor chef Mathias Wolf's "superb" New French–New American cuisine (especially "wonderful appetizers") and call the "lovely" atmosphere and "polished" service "perfect for a date" "when you really like her."

## Herbsaint ⊠     25 | 20 | 22 | $40

*701 St. Charles Ave. (Girod St.), 504-524-4114; www.herbsaint.com*
■ Serial restaurateur Susan Spicer (Bayona) and chef Donald Link have concocted an "adventurous" New American–French menu of "fabulous appetizers", "small plates" and "novel twists" on "Southern-favorite" entrees for this "lovely neighborhood bistro" on the edge of the Warehouse District; it's a "mix of NY and NO" with a "chic", "minimalist" interior and "well-trained, personable" staff that has out-of-towners wishing they could "dine here every week."

## Irene's Cuisine     26 | 20 | 22 | $37

*539 St. Philip St. (Chartres St.), 504-529-8811*
■ "Folks are waking up to this Italian sleeper" "tucked away" in the French Quarter, perhaps because of "wafting" aromas "you can smell a block away" that reveal the "succulent", "authentic" specialties to be had in this "dark, cozy", "romantic" refuge, administered by an "attentive but not suffocating" staff; even so, given the no-reservations policy, habitués hate to rate since the wait's already too great.

## JACQUES-IMO'S CAFE ⊠     27 | 20 | 21 | $30

*8324 Oak St. (S. Carrollton Ave.), 504-861-0886; www.jacquesimoscafe.com*
■ "Definitely now *on* the beaten track", this "whimsical" Carrollton "joint" has become a "true foodie destination"; even locals still "wait here like they are being led to the Promised Land" for a chance to eat Jacques Leonardi's "sensational" Creole–soul food; "upbeat servers" help sustain the "ordered chaos" in the "rustic", colorful dining rooms while the "amiable" chef-owner "roams" "in his shorts"; N.B. reservations for five or more accepted.

## Kim Son ⊠     22 | 10 | 16 | $18

*349 Whitney Ave. (Westbank Expwy.), Gretna, 504-366-2489*
◪ Connoisseurs "stick to the Vietnamese" vittles when they cross the bridge to this unassuming Gretna Asian for "super" spring rolls, "filling" soups and "fantastic" salt-baked crustacean specialties; it's "cheap and fast" but they take "no reservations" so "you may have to wait a bit"; N.B. closed in July.

## K-Paul's Louisiana Kitchen ⊠     26 | 20 | 23 | $45

*416 Chartres St. (bet. Conti & St. Louis Sts.), 504-524-7394; www.kpauls.com*
◪ Expect a line of tourists outside this "culinary shrine" to "genius of taste" Paul Prudhomme; it's a "homey" French Quarter "institution" where you can "stuff yourself" with "robust" Cajun classics like "out-of-this-world jambalaya", "fantastic duck" and "blackened fish, of course", served "with panache and personality" by "the same professional waiters year after year"; even leery locals admit that after a quarter of a century "it has found its rhythm", but prices are now "laughably high"; N.B. reservations now accepted for all dining areas.

## La Petite Grocery ⊠     – | – | – | E

*4238 Magazine St. (General Pershing St.), 504-8913377*
The newest venture from chef Anton Schulte (ex Peristyle and Clancy's) is this renovated Uptown corner store (c. 1890), now a charming vintage-style cafe; wife Diane greets the foodies who

flock here to dine on the maestro's Contemporary Louisiana–French bistro fare (which focuses on regional ingredients) and imbibe from a select list of Gallic wines ($15 corkage fee if you BYO).

**La Provence**  26  24  22  $45

*25020 Hwy. 190 (bet. Lacombe & Mandeville), Lacombe, 985-626-7662; www.laprovencerestaurant.com*

■ Food that's "first class but never pretentious" is the province of this "always-a-treat" Gallic, where super-chef Chris Kerageorgiou and his talented staff proffer "pâté instead of bread and butter", "excellent" Sunday brunch and "generous" three-course prix fixe dinners; the "charming" Lacombe auberge with "fireplaces ablaze" is a literally "warm", "welcoming" venue that feels like a "true bit of French countryside right here in rural Louisiana."

**Martinique Bistro**  25  22  22  $36

*5908 Magazine St. (bet. Eleonore & State Sts.), 504-891-8495*

☑ One of the "best-kept secrets in town", this Uptown bistro remains a "longtime" favorite of locals seduced by its "stand-out" "Caribbean-influenced" Gallic seafood; indoors the atmosphere is "intimate", like being in a "small French village", but dining in the "magical" courtyard "under the stars" "on a balmy evening" feels downright "enchanted"; breaking the spell, however, is "spotty", sometimes snaillike service; N.B. the above Food score may not reflect a post-*Survey* chef change.

**Mosca's**  ☒⊘  26  10  18  $36

*4137 Hwy. 90 W. (bet. Butler Dr. & Live Oak Blvd.), Avondale, 504-436-9942*

☑ When hunting down this hard-to-find Italian "out on the highway" in Avondale, "go with a group" "that's not afraid of garlic", since its enormous "family-style servings" of "piquant", "luscious" seafood are "meant to be shared" – but "don't look" around, "just eat", because this "rustic" "joint" has "worn" wooden floors and "decor as basic as it comes"; even so, "it's not cheap", so "bring lots of cash"; N.B. closed in August.

**Mr. B's Bistro**  24  22  23  $40

*201 Royal St. (Iberville St.), 504-523-2078; www.mrbsbistro.com*

■ "The place to B" for "tourists and natives" alike, this "lively" and "crowded", "wood-paneled" bistro "reliably" proffers an "upscale" yet "unpretentious" Contemporary Louisiana menu, served by "friendly" teams who "handle" the "huge numbers" "admirably"; relatively "moderate prices" for the Quarter and a Sunday jazz brunch that "rocks the house" have more than a few calling this Brennan family offshoot a "stellar performer."

**Muriel's**  21  24  21  $38

*Jackson Sq., 801 Chartres St. (St. Ann St.), 504-568-1885; www.muriels.com*

■ Executive chef Erik Veney's "classic" yet "contemporary Creole" "food will revive the most jaded gourmand" gush the spellbound surveyors who haunt this historic haven on a "stunningly beautiful corner of Jackson Square"; after a meal in the "gorgeous dining rooms" "appointed with antiques" or on the wraparound balcony upstairs, visitors can settle into the "magical" séance lounge, a study in "exoticism" done up with "red tapestry and comfy sofas."

### New Orleans Grill
27 | 28 | 27 | $63

(fka Grill Room, The)

*Windsor Court Hotel, 300 Gravier St. (bet. S. Peters & Tchoupitoulas Sts.), 504-522-1992; www.windsorcourthotel.com*

■ When the already-elegant Grill Room was recently renamed the New Orleans Grill it also unveiled a million-dollar renovation, cementing its status as a "sumptuous" CBD hotel "oasis"; meanwhile, chef Jonathan Wright, Britain's "culinary gift to the city", is still wowing high-end foodies with his "exquisite" Louisiana-influenced Continental cuisine, presented by a "superb" staff; expect a "magical night", surveyors say – "for that price it should be."

### Nine Roses
24 | 16 | 17 | $18

*1100 Stephen St. (Westbank Expwy.), Gretna, 504-366-7665*

■ This "friendly", "family" West Bank "can't miss" is a "great choice" since it "aims to please" with a "huge menu" of "excellent" Chinese and Vietnamese fare ("great pho", "wonderful" hot and sour shrimp soup, "outstanding" low-fat meats, fish and vegetarian dishes); when you want to "sample a lot" of the "authentic" eats, "go with a big group or do takeout."

### NOLA
26 | 23 | 24 | $48

*534 St. Louis St. (bet. Chartres & Decatur Sts.), 504-522-6652; www.emerils.com*

◪ "Bam!-tastic" boom boosters blown away by the "sassy" Contemporary Louisiana–Creole "creations" and "top-notch service" at this "casual", "terrific two-story" "hot spot" in the French Quarter; sure, it's "packed with Emeril worshipers" but the "mouthwatering eats" make it "worth putting up with the hustle and bustle"; "it should be called Noise, not NOLA" opine opponents, who are also deterred by "overzealous" servers and "tourist prices" and gripe "things ain't been the same since" the "legendary chef" "done got fame."

### Pelican Club
25 | 24 | 23 | $47

*312 Exchange Pl. (Bienville Ave.), 504-523-1504; www.pelicanclub.com*

◪ Though "still sort of undiscovered" by visitors, this "consistently winning" New American is "packed with local faces" tucking into its "enticing", "unique blend of Asian and Creole cuisines" proffered by "prompt, superb" servers in an "elegant room"; alas, the "bustling bistro atmosphere" can get "too noisy", so wise owls advise dining at dusk to enjoy what some term "the best early-bird meal in the Quarter."

### PERISTYLE ⊠
27 | 24 | 26 | $52

*1041 Dumaine St. (N. Rampart St.), 504-593-9535*

■ "Ambrosia" is how adoring admirers acclaim the "amazing" French–Contemporary Louisiana cuisine from this culinary champ, which was voted No. 1 for Food in New Orleans once again; set "on the fringe of the Quarter", the "bistro-esque" scene (with "sublime" "vintage bar") bustles with "cordial", "unobtrusive" servers; true, the "small" size makes it "tough to get a reservation – but it's worth fighting for"; N.B. following chef/co-owner Anne Kearney's post-*Survey* departure, new proprietor Tom Wolfe (Wolfe's of New Orleans) has stepped up to supervise the stove.

### René Bistrot    25 | 23 | 23 | $40
*Renaissance Pere Marquette Hotel, 817 Common St. (Barrone St.),
504-412-2580; www.renebistrot.com*
■ "In a word – superb" say succinct supporters of this "stylish"
"surprise" situated in the Renaissance Pere Marquette Hotel; the
"outstanding" French bistro fare is "creative yet unpretentious",
thanks to "magical" chef René Bajeaux, and the wine list is
"dazzling"; a "chic" but "comfortable" setting, "excellent service"
and "great-value" prix fixe lunch and dinner are other reasons
this CBD destination is such a "delightful getaway."

### Rib Room    25 | 24 | 24 | $50
*Omni Royal Orleans, 621 St. Louis St. (bet. Chartres & Royal Sts.),
504-529-7046*
■ A "see-and-be-seen spot in the Quarter", this veteran Continental
chophouse in the Omni Royal Orleans serves "magnificent" prime
rib, "stellar" steaks and "creative seasonal offerings" along with
"big, cold martinis" in a "lovely", "old-world" setting that epitomizes
"Southern elegance"; an "open rotisserie that allows you to watch
the chef", a crew of "professional" servers and "great people-
watching" ("especially at lunchtime") make this "safe port" a
perennial "favorite"; N.B. renovations are underway at press
time; until they are complete, guests will dine in the lounge.

### RioMar ☒    24 | 18 | 21 | $32
*800 S. Peters St. (Julia St.), 504-525-3474;
www.riomarseafood.com*
■ Some of the "most creative seafood in town" is served at this
"wonderful" piscatorium in the Warehouse District where the
"adventurous" dishes have strong Spanish and Latin accents,
including a "great assortment of seviche" and "divine serrano-
wrapped tuna" washed down by "excellent", "affordable" wines;
the staff's "friendly" and the setting's "casual", and even if it gets
a bit "noisy" at times, that may be because "chef-owner Adolfo
Garcia makes the fish positively sing."

### Ruth's Chris Steak House    26 | 21 | 23 | $48
*711 N. Broad Ave. (Orleans Ave.), 504-486-0810
3633 Veterans Memorial Blvd. (Hessmer Ave.), Metairie,
504-888-3600
www.ruthschris.com*
■ "Nothing beats eating in the original" Broad Avenue flagship that
spawned the "legendary" steakhouse chain, though the Metairie
branch offers the same "generous" portions of "always-perfect"
beef, "excellent" sides and "wonderful wines"; both spots lure
"local politicians" and "power" brokers, but the "superb staff"
treats "everyone like a VIP", and even though prices are decidedly
"high", most agree it's "worth it."

### Sal & Judy's    26 | 20 | 23 | $34
*27491 Hwy. 190 (14th St.), Lacombe, 985-882-9443*
■ Hungry pilgrims to the North Shore seek Sal-vation at this
"superior" Italian, saying it's definitely "worth the ride" to Lacombe
for "amazing", "more-than-you-can-finish" "Sicilian-type" Creole
fare in an "intimate setting"; "they make you feel like one of the
family" once you get in, but to reserve a place among the "inner
circle of regulars", "plan on calling two to three weeks ahead";
N.B. closed Monday–Tuesday.

## Stella! 26 22 24 $48

*Hôtel Provincial, 1032 Chartres St. (bet. St. Philip St. & Ursuline Ave.), 504-587-0091; www.restaurantstella.com*

■ Chef-owner Scott Boswell "puts it all together" with his "imaginative" slate of "superb" New American "fusion comfort food" at this "civilized, cute" charmer "set back from the craziness of the Quarter" that "tourists miss completely" and locals love for its "warmth, intimacy" and sophistication ("not a picture of Marlon Brando in sight"); a "professional yet friendly" staff provides "excellent service", and though high prices make a few people blanch, most simply shout "stellar!"; N.B. closed Tuesdays.

## Uglesich's ⊠⤢ 26 9 16 $22

*1238 Baronne St. (Erato St.), 504-523-8571; www.uglesichs.com*

■ "Please don't retire this year, Anthony", beseech acolytes who adore Mr. U's 80-year-old lunch-only "culinary mecca", a Garden District "monument to New Orleans eating" where the "sublime" "renditions of Cajun-Creole staples" "beat the pants off" the competition; disciples "dream of being spoon-fed shrimp Uggie 24 hours a day" and "would fight Mike Tyson for the BBQ oysters", which is why "limos" regularly "pull up outside" this "ramshackle", "decrepit" seafooder and the wait is "mind-numbing."

## Upperline 27 24 25 $42

*1413 Upperline St. (bet. Prytania St. & St. Charles Ave.), 504-891-9822; www.upperline.com*

■ "Magnificent" meals that "consistently" "delight" surveyors ("legendary fried green tomatoes with shrimp remoulade sauce", duck that "will forever spoil you") are the bottom line at this Uptown Creole "showplace", a historic building (1877) and the "best salon in town" thanks to "effervescent" owner JoAnn Clevenger, her "captivating" collection of vintage New Orleans art and a "pampering" staff; the combination creates an "atmosphere conducive to unwinding" – and the "nice prices" don't hurt; P.S. "try their theme menus."

# New York City

## TOP 25 FOOD RANKING

| Restaurant | Cuisine |
|---|---|
| **28** Le Bernardin | French/Seafood |
| Bouley | New French |
| Daniel | New French |
| Gramercy Tavern | New American |
| Sushi Yasuda | Japanese |
| Nobu, Next Door | Japanese |
| Nobu | Japanese |
| **27** Jean Georges | New French |
| Peter Luger | Steakhouse |
| Alain Ducasse | French |
| Gotham Bar & Grill | New American |
| Danube | Austrian |
| Il Mulino | Italian |
| Tasting Room | New American |
| Veritas | New American |
| Café Boulud | French |
| Aureole | New American |
| Sushi of Gari | Japanese |
| Chanterelle | French |
| Trattoria L'incontro | Italian |
| Pearl Oyster Bar | Seafood |
| Union Square Cafe | New American |
| Babbo | Italian |
| Scalini Fedeli | Northern Italian |
| Aquagrill | Seafood |

## ADDITIONAL NOTEWORTHY PLACES

| | |
|---|---|
| Asiate | French/Japanese |
| Balthazar | French Bistro |
| Bayard's | French/American |
| Blue Water Grill | Seafood |
| Café des Artistes | French |
| Carnegie Deli | Deli |
| Craft | New American |
| davidburke & donatella | New American |
| Eleven Madison Park | New American |
| Fiamma Osteria | Italian |
| L'Impero | Italian |
| Masa | Japanese |
| Matsuri | Japanese |
| Megu | Japanese |
| Milos | Greek/Seafood |
| Montrachet | French |
| Ouest | New American |
| per se | New American/French |
| Picholine | French/Med. |
| River Cafe | New American |
| Shun Lee Palace | Chinese |
| Smith & Wollensky | Steakhouse |
| Spice Market | Thai/Malaysian |
| Tavern on the Green | American |
| 21 Club | American |

### Alain Ducasse 🖾　　27 | 27 | 28 | $191
*Essex House, 155 W. 58th St. (bet. 6th & 7th Aves.), 212-265-7300;*
*www.alain-ducasse.com*
■ Now that Masa is officially NYC's most expensive restaurant, the prices at Alain Ducasse's "sybaritic" Central Park South showplace may seem "almost reasonable" considering what you get in return: "sumptuous" French creations from executive chef Christian Delouvrier, a "pomp-and-circumstance" setting, meticulous but "unpretentious service" and a "table that's yours for the night"; so "pretend you're Bill Gates" and trade a few shares for a "once-in-a-lifetime" indulgence in "pure hedonism."

### Aquagrill　　27 | 20 | 23 | $53
*210 Spring St. (6th Ave.), 212-274-0505; www.aquagrill.com*
■ As "happening" as ever, this SoHo seafooder thrills diners with "fresher-than-fresh" fish and oysters shucked at its "awesome raw bar"; the "consistent" kitchen and "spot-on" service draw a deep-pocketed crowd to the "tight", "always-packed" quarters.

### Asiate　　22 | 27 | 23 | $79
*Mandarin Oriental Hotel, 80 Columbus Circle, 35th fl. (60th St.), 212-805-8881; www.mandarinoriental.com/newyork/*
☑ "Drop-dead views of Central Park" highlight this "dramatic" new Japanese-French aerie in the Mandarin Oriental Hotel, where chef Nori Sugie's "complex", "delectable" cuisine is framed by "soaring" "walls of windows"; for some, it's the "cutting edge" of "luxurious dining", for others it's "a bit unfocused" "considering the price tag", but optimists say "wait till this baby matures."

### Aureole 🖾　　27 | 26 | 26 | $79
*34 E. 61st St. (bet. Madison & Park Aves.), 212-319-1660;*
*www.charliepalmer.com*
■ A "perennial" "wow", Charlie Palmer's "classically elegant" East Side townhouse offers chef Dante Boccuzzi's "celestial" New American fare, including some "showstopping desserts"; "meticulous service" caps the "idyllic experience", but "bring your entire paycheck" or opt for the "late-lunch bargain" to "savor the moment."

### Babbo ◑　　27 | 23 | 24 | $68
*110 Waverly Pl. (bet. MacDougal St. & 6th Ave.), 212-777-0303;*
*www.babbonyc.com*
■ The Mario Batali–Joe Bastianich team makes "culinary dreams come true" at their Village Italian "*paradiso*" where "life-altering" dishes in "perfect harmony" come with "A+" wines and "savvy", "spot-on" service; the "classy" carriage-house setting hums with "high energy", but you may wear out your "speed dial and luck" trying to score a "nigh impossible" reservation.

### Balthazar ◑　　23 | 23 | 19 | $50
*80 Spring St. (bet. B'way & Crosby St.), 212-965-1414;*
*www.balthazarny.com*
■ A "great show" that's "always in fashion", this "snazzy", "real-deal" SoHo French brasserie is a "classic" for "knockout" food (e.g. *plateau de fruits de mer,* steak frites) and "efficient" service in an authentic room abuzz with wanna-bes, used-to-bes and really ares; despite "tight" seating and the "inevitable out-of-towners", the addicted deem it a "forever-fabulous" "Paris fix."

### Bayard's ⌧　　　　23　24　24　$60
*1 Hanover Sq. (bet. Pearl & Stone Sts.), 212-514-9454; www.bayards.com*
■ "Step back into a classier time" at this ultra-"civilized" Financial District French-American triplex offering Eberhard Müller's "inspired" seasonal cuisine and a "magnificent", "blue-blood" setting in the circa-1851 India House; "white-glove service" and an "incredible wine list" are naturals in this "very adult" milieu, so only the "hard-to-find" location and the fact that it's a private club at lunch explain why this star is so little known; P.S. with handsome rooms of all sizes, it's a great place to give a party.

### BLUE WATER GRILL ●　　　　24　22　21　$49
*31 Union Sq. W. (16th St.), 212-675-9500; www.brguestrestaurants.com*
■ A "sophisticated", "metropolitan attitude" and "briny-fresh seafood" keep the trade brisk at Steve Hanson's "boisterous" Union Square "institution" that's still as "trendy" as ever ("long live *Sex and the City*!"); set in a restored, "beautiful old bank", it features "cool" jazz downstairs, "table terrace" seating outside and "always-smiling service" throughout its white-marble quarters.

### BOULEY ●　　　　28　26　26　$84
*120 W. Broadway (Duane St.), 212-964-2525;*
*www.bouleyrestaurants.com*
■ "Food god" David Bouley is back, playing at the top of his game at his "extraordinary" TriBeCa flagship; "everything clicks" here, from the "wonderful aroma of apples" at the entrance to the "gorgeous vaulted space", "standard-setting" service and "preposterously good", "beautifully presented" New French cuisine; of course, all this "luxury doesn't come cheap" – with the exception of the $35 prix fixe lunch.

### Café Boulud　　　　27　23　25　$74
*Surrey Hotel, 20 E. 76th St. (bet. 5th & Madison Aves.), 212-772-2600;*
*www.danielnyc.com*
■ A "less formal but no less superb" version of Daniel Boulud's eponymous flagship, this East Side French is "exquisite in every way", from its "savvy seasonal menu" to the "crisp" service and "sophisticated", "jubilant" mood; ok, you'll probably "drop a bundle", but what else would you expect for "near-perfect dining"?

### Café des Artistes ●　　　　22　26　23　$65
*1 W. 67th St. (bet. Columbus Ave. & CPW), 212-877-3500;*
*www.cafenyc.com*
■ "Romance is very much alive" at George and Jenifer Lang's West Side "aphrodisiac of a restaurant" thanks to a "ravishing" setting complete with lovely Howard Christy Chandler murals and "flowers everywhere"; add in "efficient service" and "excellent" if "costly" French food, and it's just the place to "charm your new love or rekindle an old one."

### Carnegie Deli ●⌀　　　　20　8　12　$24
*854 Seventh Ave. (55th St.), 212-757-2245; www.carnegiedeli.com*
◪ "Not for the small of stomach", this Midtown deli is famed for corned beef and pastrami "sandwiches so big they defy logic" served by "grumpy waiters" who "function as entertainment" for an audience that's half "tourists", half *Broadway Danny Rose* types; besides, it's a "quintessential NY experience" for its "stuff-of-legends cheesecake" alone.

### Chanterelle ⊠　　　　　27　26　27　VE
*2 Harrison St. (Hudson St.), 212-966-6960; www.chanterellenyc.com*
■ The "epitome of perfect dining", David and Karen Waltuck's
"enchanting" TriBeCa haute French "lives up to its lofty reputation"
with "phenomenal" cuisine, "service so flawless you won't even
notice it" and a "spacious, gracious" setting enhanced by "well-
spaced tables" and "gorgeous floral arrangements"; for the
price-conscious, the $38 prix fixe lunch is possibly the "best deal
on the planet."

### Craft　　　　　26　25　24　$67
*43 E. 19th St. (bet. B'way & Park Ave. S.), 212-780-0880*
■ "Settling in for the long run", Tom Colicchio's handsome Flatiron
New American invites those entering its "coolly minimalist"
quarters to "build their own menu" by selecting from a roster
of "superb", "deceptively simple" dishes; even though some
surveyors prefer the chef to assemble the meal and question the
"pay-for-each-ingredient approach", most diners consider this
a "home run."

### DANIEL ⊠　　　　　28　28　27　$102
*60 E. 65th St. (bet. Madison & Park Aves.), 212-288-0033;*
*www.danielnyc.com*
■ There's "true joie de vivre in the air" at Daniel Boulud's East
Side flagship, a "crème de la crème" experience where the
"sumptuous" New French cooking is the "stuff of dreams", the
wine list "vast", the service "flawless" and the flower-festooned
room "opulent to say the least"; in sum, it's the "ultimate special-
occasion restaurant", and as for the price, it's "still cheaper than
a midsize car."

### Danube ●▶⊠　　　　　27　28　26　$84
*30 Hudson St. (bet. Duane & Reade Sts.), 212-791-3771;*
*www.thedanube.net*
■ You can "step back in time" via the "surreal" world of "Klimt
paintings" at David Bouley's TriBeCa Viennese "epicurean
delight"; the "gilded" setting recalls a "countess' salon", the
French-inflected food offers a "platonic ideal of Austrian cuisine"
and the "impeccable" staff treats all like "royalty"; still, you may
need to bring the royal jewelry to settle the bill; P.S. the "Wiener
schnitzel is compulsory."

### davidburke & donatella　　　　　25　24　22　$72
*133 E. 61st St. (bet. Lexington & Park Aves.), 212-813-2121;*
*www.dbdrestaurant.com*
▧ "Imaginative" chef David Burke "strikes gold" at this "very
hot" East Side New American offering "witty" "amusement park
rides on a plate", finished off by "fabulous" desserts; its "*Bonfire of
the Vanities*" crowd feels at home with the "precise" service,
"stylish" rooms and hostess-with-the-mostess Donatella
Arpaia (Bellini), despite the "too-noisy", "tight" setup and zip
code–appropriate tabs.

### Eleven Madison Park　　　　　26　26　25　$62
*11 Madison Ave. (24th St.), 212-889-0905; www.elevenmadisonpark.com*
■ "Exciting and so classy", this "Danny Meyer triumph" on
Madison Park has "contemporary charisma" to burn thanks to
chef Kerry Heffernan's "impeccable" New American cuisine, an

"excellent wine list" and "terrific", "charm-school" service; a "grand, swanky" space with "sky-high ceilings" caps this "stand-out" experience that's worth every penny.

### Fiamma Osteria
24 | 24 | 23 | $61

*206 Spring St. (bet. 6th Ave. & Sullivan St.), 212-653-0100; www.brguestrestaurants.com*

■ Steve Hanson's "top-shelf" SoHo "knockout" has "flair" to spare, from its handsome triplex setting to the "inspired" Italian cooking, "polished" service and "spectacular wine list"; sure, you'll need "deep pockets" to afford this "class act", but its "well-heeled" following is "blown away" and "begging for more."

### GOTHAM BAR & GRILL
27 | 25 | 25 | $67

*12 E. 12th St. (bet. 5th Ave. & University Pl.), 212-620-4020; www.gothambarandgrill.com*

■ This "modern NY classic" has provided some 20 years of "high-end" Village dining and still stands tall in surveyors' esteem: chef Alfred Portale's "towering" New American creations continue to "tantalize", the "soaring-ceilinged" setting remains casually "glamorous" and service is "top-notch"; if prices also induce vertigo, a sure cure is the $25 bargain lunch.

### GRAMERCY TAVERN
28 | 26 | 27 | $72

*42 E. 20th St. (bet. B'way & Park Ave. S.), 212-477-0777; www.gramercytavern.com*

■ The "definition of fine dining" for many NYers, Danny Meyer's Flatiron New American – ranked No. 1 for Popularity among NYC restaurants – "exceeds expectations" on all fronts, from chef Tom Colicchio's "masterful" food to the "rustic" yet "luxuriant" decor and "beautifully choreographed", genuinely "warm" service; plan to book way ahead, and if you're price-conscious, try the less costly, but equally lovely, drop-in front tavern.

### Il Mulino ☒
27 | 17 | 23 | $77

*86 W. Third St. (bet. Sullivan & Thompson Sts.), 212-673-3783; www.ilmulinonewyork.com*

■ "Don't you have a higher rating?" ask fans of this 25-year-old Village Italian; for the "few lucky souls" with "fast redial fingers" who manage to snag a nearly "impossible" reservation, it's a "fabulously executed", "garlic"-laden "food orgy" replete with "incredible" black-tie service and "empty-the-bank-account" tabs.

### Jean Georges ☒
27 | 26 | 26 | $93

*Trump Int'l Hotel, 1 Central Park W. (bet. 60th & 61st Sts.), 212-299-3900; www.jean-georges.com*

■ "You'll never look at food in the same way" after a meal at Jean-Georges Vongerichten's "transcendent" Columbus Circle New French where the "stop-you-in-your-tracks" offerings are "fork-droppingly good"; add in "flawless" service and Adam Tihany's "sophisticated", "contemporary" design and the "high" tariffs are understandable – though you can bypass them via the "amazing-value" $20 prix fixe lunch offered in the "less formal Nougatine Room" and on the terrace.

### LE BERNARDIN ☒
28 | 27 | 27 | $95

*155 W. 51st St. (bet. 6th & 7th Aves.), 212-554-1515; www.le-bernardin.com*

■ "It simply doesn't get any better" for "transcendent seafood" than at Maguy LeCoze's Midtown French "dream" (ranked No. 1

for Food among NYC restaurants) where "spectacular" chef Eric Ripert's "beyond-sublime" cuisine "continues to astound" supplicants, while a "formal" pro staff serves with "seemingly effortless perfection" in "hushed", "elegant" quarters; such "incredible dining experiences" are sure to "sweep you off your feet" – as may the "price tag to match."

### L'Impero ⊠　　26 24 23 $67
*45 Tudor City Pl. (bet. 42nd & 43rd Sts.), 212-599-5045;*
*www.limpero.com*
■ "Civilized" and "chic", this "upscale" Italian "tucked away" in Tudor City ranks among the "best in town" thanks to "magician"-chef Scott Conant's "innovative" cuisine abetted by "superb" wines; also factoring into the meals "to remember" are the pleasingly "minimalist" decor and a staff that makes you "feel cosseted and special"; it's "definitely not cheap", but the "brilliant" prix fixe is an "excellent value."

### Masa ⊠　　▽ 28 25 26 $366
*Time Warner Ctr., 10 Columbus Circle, 4th fl. (60th St. at B'way),*
*212-823-9800*
■ Having closed his famed Ginza Sushi-Ko in order to open this "transporting", "Zen-like" Japanese in the Time Warner Center, LA sushi king Masayoshi Takayama is now producing "sublime" kaiseki-style dinners of a caliber never before seen in NYC; his tasting menus come with equally "stunning price tags" ($300 "before drink"), but given such "unmatched" quality, early visitors conclude "believe it or not, it's worth it."

### Matsuri ❶　　23 27 20 $53
*Maritime Hotel, 369 W. 16th St. (9th Ave.), 212-243-6400*
■ Further evidencing how hot West Chelsea has become, this "spectacular", "cavernous", "lantern"-filled space "under the Maritime Hotel" sports "star-sightings galore" as well as lots of could-bes; both the ambiance and chef Tadashi Ono's food dazzle diners, so the "only problem is getting a table"; N.B. be careful not to wash your hands in the urinal or sit in the sink.

### Megu ❶　　23 28 23 $93
*62 Thomas St. (bet. Church St. & W. B'way), 212-964-7777;*
*www.megunyc.com*
■ Bring megu-bucks to this TriBeCa Japanese newcomer occupying an "over-the-top" "Hollywood-meets-Tokyo" space, where everything from the "fabulous Buddha ice sculpture" to the "$25 edamame" contributes to the "pure drama" of the experience; as for the food, those who can focus on it report "exquisite, inventive" dishes that may "awaken taste buds you never knew existed."

### Milos, Estiatorio ❶　　25 23 22 $67
*125 W. 55th St. (bet. 6th & 7th Aves.), 212-245-7400; www.milos.ca*
◪ The "granddaddy of Greek estiatorios" is this modern Midtown "seafood temple" where you choose the "freshest imaginable" fish from a "crushed-ice display" and "pay by the weight" to have it "simply" and "beautifully" prepared; unless you order the affordable appetizers, the prices will be as "high" as the "quality" of the catch, but most report "it's worth it", especially since dining in this "airy", Aegean-inspired eatery always feels like a "summer vacation."

### Montrachet ⊠    25 | 18 | 23 | $67
*239 W. Broadway (bet. Walker & White Sts.), 212-219-2777;*
*www.myriadrestaurantgroup.com*

☑ "Still a winner" when stacked against TriBeCa's "new-school" eateries, Drew Nieporent's "civilized" "French classic" continues to "wow" with its "phenomenal" cuisine, "outstanding" wine list and "top-notch" service; as for the decor, it's undergoing a gradual redo at press time; P.S. the Friday-only $20 prix fixe lunch is "one of the best steals in NY."

### Nobu    28 | 23 | 24 | $76
*105 Hudson St. (Franklin St.), 212-219-0500;*
*www.myriadrestaurantgroup.com*

■ "The gold standard" for "dazzling" Peruvian-accented Japanese "fusion" cuisine and "celebrity whiplash" is this "transcendent" TriBeCa "perennial favorite" where the "A+" experiences are deemed "worth" the "ridiculous" tabs and "monthlong wait" for a reservation; cash-carefree cognoscenti say "omakase is the way to go" – just "sit back" and let the "top-notch" staff "take care of everything"; N.B. a new location near Carnegie Hall is scheduled to open in 2005.

### Nobu, Next Door ●⊠    28 | 22 | 22 | $63
*105 Hudson St. (bet. Franklin & N. Moore Sts.), 212-334-4445;*
*www.myriadrestaurantgroup.com*

■ "Next door, but no step down" is this "no-reservations" chip off the old block that's "lots easier to get into", so long as you don't mind waiting in line; it serves "basically the same" "sublime" Peruvian-accented Japanese cuisine as the mother ship, but is a bit "cheaper"; P.S. the "new take-out service is addictive."

### Ouest    25 | 23 | 23 | $58
*2315 Broadway (bet. 83rd & 84th Sts.), 212-580-8700;*
*www.ouestny.com*

■ Chef Tom Valenti's New American comfort cuisine "wows even the most jaded palate" at this "emerging institution" on the Upper West Side that's become something of a "living room" for the neighborhood's famous and "well-to-do"; the attractive, "clubby", banquette-filled space is matched by "impeccable" service and a "superb" wine list – now "if it were only easier to get a table."

### Pearl Oyster Bar ⊠    27 | 14 | 19 | $39
*18 Cornelia St. (bet. Bleecker & W. 4th Sts.), 212-691-8211;*
*www.pearloysterbar.com*

■ The "seats added" in a recent expansion "help", but this still guppy-size Village seafood "shack" remains "packed" to the gills with "happy-as-a-clam" fin-fare fanciers feasting on Rebecca Charles' "amazingly fresh", "New England–style" eats, including the "best lobster roll this side of Wiscasset"; "personable" staffers and reasonable tabs are more reasons that you must "get there early" or get in line.

### per se    ▽ 29 | 29 | 29 | $166
*Time Warner Ctr., 10 Columbus Circle, 4th fl. (60th St. at B'way),*
*212-823-9335*

■ The chosen few who've gained entry to Thomas Keller's new Columbus Circle sanctum report that it's "as good as its hype" and might even turn out to be NYC's best restaurant; "phenomenal"

New American–French tasting menus, a "simply elegant" setting by Adam Tihany, "beautiful" views and "top-notch" service add up to an "unforgettable" "event", so "put your phone on redial" and take out the "second mortgage" – it's "a must."

### Peter Luger Steak House ⌿　　　27 | 14 | 19 | $63
*178 Broadway (Driggs Ave.), Brooklyn, 718-387-7400;*
*www.peterluger.com*
■ "No way, no how" does steak get better than at Williamsburg's "peerless" "porterhouse palace"; it may look like a "bare-bones" "beer hall", but this "champ" chophouse is a "holy shrine" for carnivores who say "menus are for wimps" – those "gruff" waiters "know what you want and it moos"; remember to "hit the cash machine" before and "have your arteries cleaned" afterwards.

### Picholine　　　26 | 23 | 25 | $77
*35 W. 64th St. (bet. B'way & CPW), 212-724-8585*
■ All the makings for "a meal to remember" are in place at Terrance Brennan's "classy" Lincoln Center French-Med, a "best bet" pre-concert and "marvelous" anytime thanks to "inventive" food, "finely tuned service" and "elegant" decor, not to mention "phenomenal" *fromage* feasts orchestrated by cheese wiz Max McCalman; expect an unreservedly "rich experience", right down to the bill.

### River Cafe　　　25 | 28 | 25 | $76
*1 Water St. (bet. Furman & Old Fulton Sts.), Brooklyn, 718-522-5200;*
*www.rivercafe.com*
■ It's "the view" that keeps "romantics" swooning at Buzzy O'Keeffe's "swanky" New American tucked under the Brooklyn Bridge, though the "wonderful", "beautifully presented" cuisine and "stellar" service are nearly as "spectacular"; in short, it's "the best date [place] in the city", and while the prix fixe–only dining here is quite "expensive", the enamored enthuse it's "worth every penny."

### Scalini Fedeli ⌧　　　27 | 26 | 25 | $76
*165 Duane St. (bet. Greenwich & Hudson Sts.), 212-528-0400;*
*www.scalinifedeli.com*
■ "Invent a special occasion if you have to" but by all means go to this "superlative" TriBeCa Northern Italian that's "in the middle of nowhere" but well "worth the trek"; its "divine" cuisine is matched by "romantic, gorgeous" quarters and "impeccable" "formal" service, so no one's too surprised that tabs run "high."

### Shun Lee Palace ●　　　25 | 21 | 23 | $51
*155 E. 55th St. (bet. Lexington & 3rd Aves.), 212-371-8844*
■ "After all these years", Michael Tong's East Side Chinese "grande dame" is still "spoiling" patrons with "superb" "upscale" cuisine ("absolutely the best above Canal Street") and "gracious" service; a minority calls its "calm", "classy" setting "dated", but for most, experiences here are a "real treat."

### Smith & Wollensky ●　　　23 | 17 | 20 | $60
*797 Third Ave. (49th St.), 212-753-1530;*
*www.smithandwollensky.com*
■ Make "no bones about it" – this "noisy", "male-oriented" Midtown "meat palace" is "top-cow" for carnivores, thanks to its "fantastic hunks o' beef" and "kick-ass wine list"; there's also

a handsome steakhouse look to the crowded environs, with gruff waiters who complete the scene.

**Spice Market** ◐   23 | 27 | 20 | $54
*403 W. 13th St. (9th Ave.), 212-675-2322*
■ "Keep the new concepts coming" urge followers of star chef Jean-Georges Vongerichten, who's opened this "stunning" instant "hit" in the Meatpacking District; a "knockout for both the tongue and the eyes", it serves "fantastic", "glamorized" Thai-Malay "street food" in a "lavish" Jacques Garcia–designed duplex "wonderland" "chock-full of stars" and other "beautiful" types.

**Sushi of Gari**   27 | 11 | 18 | $57
*402 E. 78th St. (bet. 1st & York Aves.), 212-517-5340*
■ "Omakase-lovers" "make a reservation" and undertake the "trip to the East Side hinterlands" to let "genius" chef Gari "spoil their taste buds" with his "creative", "truly amazing" sushi; surveyors have little to say about the "average"-at-best decor, and as for prices, some feel "lucky not to live closer" because they'd "be broke by now."

**SUSHI YASUDA** ☒   28 | 23 | 24 | $72
*204 E. 43rd St. (bet. 2nd & 3rd Aves.), 212-972-1001;*
*www.sushiyasuda.com*
■ "Sit at the sushi bar and tell them to bring whatever" pleases the chef and you'll be "blown away" by the "buttery", "right-off-the-boat" cuts at Naomichi Yasuda's East 40s Japanese "temple of piscatory worship"; the "gracious, attentive" and "knowledgeable" staff and "crisp, clean", "tranquil" surroundings further enhance the "top-notch", top-dollar experience.

**Tasting Room** ☒   27 | 17 | 25 | $56
*72 E. First St. (bet. 1st & 2nd Aves.), 212-358-7831*
■ "Smart folks share" so they can "sample everything" on Colin Alevras' "magnificent" market-driven menu at this East Village New American whose "closet-size" quarters (just 25 seats) provide an excuse "to sit close" to your tasting partner; add a "tremendous" "all-American wine list" and "solicitous" service and it's clear why cost is no object at this up-and-comer.

**Tavern on the Green**   14 | 24 | 17 | $58
*Central Park W. (bet. 66th & 67th Sts.), 212-873-3200;*
*www.tavernonthegreen.com*
▨ The "quintessential place to celebrate" anything is this "over-the-top" Central Park American whose "fairyland" Crystal Room and huge garden area are the "must-see" backdrops for everything from "tourist"-jammed brunches to "surreal" holiday meals; sure, "you can find better food elsewhere", but few can conjure up the same "magic" or create a more festive party.

**Trattoria L'incontro**   27 | 18 | 23 | $43
*21-76 31st St. (Ditmars Blvd.), Queens, 718-721-3532;*
*www.trattorialincontro.com*
■ "Reason enough to move to Astoria", this "incredible" Italian features chef Rocco Sacramone playing at the "top of his game", creating "exceptional" cuisine (with a "tremendous" list of daily specials) as a "personable staff" keeps the "hubbub" in control; it's "not fancy", but cooking "doesn't get much better" – especially for the price; N.B. an adjacent wine bar is in the works at press time.

**21 Club** 🛇     21 | 22 | 23 | $63 |
*21 W. 52nd St. (bet. 5th & 6th Aves.), 212-582-7200; www.21club.com*
■ "Still vital" as Midtown's "power-rating barometer", this seriously pricey "jacket-and-tie" "icon" preserves its "old glory" thanks to a "rock-solid" American menu, which is matched by the "first-rate" staff's "professional aplomb"; as a "deal-making" locus dating to "speakeasy times", its downstairs bar/dining room has "cachet" that "never fails to impress"; P.S. check out its "classy" private party rooms and "legendary wine cellar."

**UNION SQUARE CAFE**     27 | 23 | 26 | $61 |
*21 E. 16th St. (bet. 5th Ave. & Union Sq. W.), 212-243-4020*
■ An "enduring" "all-star", Danny Meyer's "benchmark" New American off Union Square "has the magic" to elicit "wall-to-wall smiles" – credit goes to chef Michael Romano's "exhilarating", "soul-satisfying" cuisine, "seamless service" from "the smartest staff" going and a "genteel" but "not-too-formal" ambiance; while you'll "thank your lucky stars" when you land a "coveted reservation", those who "can't wait" "can always sit at the bar" for a "primo" bite.

**Veritas**     27 | 22 | 25 | $79 |
*43 E. 20th St. (bet. B'way & Park Ave. S.), 212-353-3700;*
*www.veritas-nyc.com*
■ The truly "phenomenal" wine list ("as thick as *War and Peace*") at this "top-class" Flatiron New American meets its match in chef Scott Bryan's "sumptuous" prix fixe menu; at $68 it may seem "costly", but the "expert" service and "intimate", "understated" room help make every meal a "special event."

# Orange County, CA

## TOP 10 FOOD RANKING

| Restaurant | Cuisine |
|---|---|
| **28** Picayo | French |
| **27** Ramos House Cafe | American |
| Aubergine | Californian/French |
| Studio | Californian/French |
| Basilic | French/Swiss |
| Pascal | French |
| **26** Pinot Provence | French |
| Golden Truffle | French/Caribbean |
| Pavilion | Californian/Med. |
| Ruth's Chris | Steakhouse |

## ADDITIONAL NOTEWORTHY PLACES

| | |
|---|---|
| Cheesecake Factory | American |
| Hobbit, The | French/Continental |
| Houston's | American |
| Il Fornaio | Italian |
| Mirabeau | French |
| Mr. Stox | New American/Continental |
| Napa Rose | Californian |
| P.F. Chang's | Chinese |
| Sage | New American |
| Zov's Bistro | Mediterranean |

| F | D | S | C |
|---|---|---|---|

### AUBERGINE
27 | 24 | 25 | $81

*508 29th St. (Newport Blvd.), Newport Beach, 949-723-4150*
☑ Once "offering only prix fixe menus", this "elegant" Californian-French now features à la carte selections of "absolutely amazing", "innovative" "food-as-entertainment" served within the "beautiful, serene setting" of "a tiny cottage" in Newport (it's "hard to find", so "call ahead for directions"); some decry the "microscopic portions" and "extravagant" prices with "attitude to match", but more enjoy "feeling like royalty."

### BASILIC ⌧
27 | 20 | 27 | $51

*217 Marine Ave. (Park Ave.), Newport Beach, 949-673-0570*
■ "So tiny you can miss it" if you're not careful, this "hidden gem" "on Balboa Island" is a "slightly quirky" bastion of French-"Swiss bliss" where visits begin with a "warm welcome" from "urbane chef-owner" Bernard Althaus; not only is the "classy cuisine" "extraordinary", but the "exceptional service" "adds to the complete dining experience."

### CHEESECAKE FACTORY
20 | 18 | 18 | $24

*Irvine Spectrum Ctr., 71 Fortune Dr. (Pacifica St.), Irvine, 949-788-9998*
*42 The Shops at Mission Viejo (I-5), Mission Viejo, 949-364-6200*
(continued)

(continued)

## CHEESECAKE FACTORY

*Fashion Island, 1141 Newport Center Dr. (Santa Barbara Dr.),*
*Newport Beach, 949-720-8333*
*www.thecheesecakefactory.com*

☑ "You could eat here every night for a year and not duplicate" a dish declare devotees of these American chain outposts where "huge portions" ensure "leftovers" and "no one's complaining" as the food's "delicious" and desserts "decadent"; sure, the waits are "horrific" and the service "erratic" (though "pleasant"), but the "dependable" fare and "excellent value" contribute to an "enjoyable experience" overall.

### Golden Truffle, The ⊠    26 | 15 | 23 | $44

*1767 Newport Blvd. (bet. 17th & 18th Sts.), Costa Mesa, 949-645-9858*

■ "You never know what he will dream up" say swooning fans of "creative-genius" chef-owner Alan Greeley, whose "exciting" French-Caribbean *carte du jour* "always surprises with new dishes"; even though the "drab" strip-mall site and "unassuming interior" provide "nothing-special" ambiance, it's a "great find" for diners who like to "experiment"; P.S. grape lovers should enjoy the "interesting list of lesser-known but excellent wines."

### Hobbit, The    26 | 24 | 26 | $69

*2932 E. Chapman Ave. (Malena St.), Orange, 714-997-1972;*
*www.hobbitrestaurant.com*

■ For a "full evening out", enjoy the "outstanding prix fixe" dinner at this "special-occasion" French-Continental in a "lovely old Spanish house" in Orange; "don't fill up on the hors d'oeuvres" served with "champagne in the wine cellar", as they're "followed by a delicious six-course meal upstairs" (with a "wonderful intermission" during which "pampered" guests "tour the kitchen and meet the chef"); all told, it's "a truly exceptional experience."

## HOUSTON'S    21 | 20 | 19 | $29

*Park Pl., 2991 Michelson Dr. (Jamboree Rd.), Irvine, 949-833-0977;*
*www.houstons.com*

■ "You can't go wrong" at this "consistent" chain for "adults" where the "addictive", "varied" American dishes include a "not-to-be-missed" spinach dip, "tender, top-notch" ribs and "excellent gourmet burgers" ferried by a "terrific" staff; the decor features "clubby leather booths" and the "dim" "lighting makes anyone look good", and even though it's "crazy busy" (resulting in "long waits"), loyalists laud it as a "formula that works."

## IL FORNAIO ⊠    20 | 19 | 18 | $31

*Lakeshore Tower, 18051 Von Karman Ave. (bet. Main St. &*
*Michelson Dr.), Irvine, 949-261-1444; www.ilfornaio.com*

■ With "wonderful" pastas, pizzas and "great bread" from a wood-burning oven (the name means 'the baker'), it's "hard to believe it's a chain", but this "upscale" trattoria "maintains high standards"; monthly changing menus "add variety", the "casual" setting is "lovely" and best of all, the experience "won't break the bank."

### Mirabeau ●    ▽ 25 | 21 | 20 | $37

*17 Monarch Bay Plaza (Crown Valley Pkwy.), Monarch Beach,*
*949-234-1679; www.mirabeaubistro.com*

■ For a "slice of Paris in Monarch Beach", "brave a shopping-center parking lot filled with deluxe sedans" then duck into the "warm bistro setting" of this "cozy little French charmer" where a "limited menu" of "authentic" "classics" is matched by a "balanced wine list"; "if weather permits, dine outside" for a "view of the Pacific"; P.S. it's "a great place for a late date."

### Mr. Stox ◐ 25 | 22 | 25 | $46
*1105 E. Katella Ave. (bet. Lewis St. & State College Blvd.), Anaheim, 714-634-2994; www.mrstox.com*

■ Dubbed "Mr. Reliable", this "high-end" "longtime" "favorite" in Anaheim features "first-class" New American–Continental feasts ("succulent" steaks, "the best crab cakes"), a "gargantuan wine list" "with some bargains" and "gracious", "impeccable" hospitality; "richly decorated" and boasting "private booths", it has a "quiet atmosphere" that's "ideal" for "serious business meals or a romantic evening out"; P.S. "take home" some of the "imaginatively prepared breads."

### Napa Rose 26 | 25 | 25 | VE
*Grand Californian Hotel, 1600 S. Disneyland Dr. (Katella Ave.), Anaheim, 714-300-7170*

■ Though "you'd never expect a world-class restaurant in Disneyland", this "unbelievably excellent" "surprise" "in the Grand Californian Hotel" delivers a "thrillingly top-notch food experience" thanks to "inventive" "master chef" Andrew Sutton's "wonderful" Californian cuisine (with "dishes as adventurous as nearby Space Mountain"); GM-sommelier Michael Jordan provides "genius recommendations", and the "meticulously trained staff" is "attentive" but "never cloying"; P.S. "the regularly changing vintner's menu" is "truly a gourmand's delight."

### Pascal ⊠ 27 | 21 | 24 | $57
*1000 N. Bristol St. (Jamboree Rd.), Newport Beach, 949-752-0107; www.pascalnewportbeach.com*

◪ "You'll think you're in France", so "stellar" is the experience at this "classic country-French" "institution" in Newport Beach, where chef-owner Pascal Olhats' "tried-and-true" Provençal cooking is "impeccably served" by a "professional, friendly" staff in a "romantic" setting with "beautiful" "flowers throughout"; a few fault the "odd location" and say "the place could use a freshening up", but most maintain it's "still among SoCal's best"; P.S. "don't forget the *épicerie* next door."

### Pavilion 26 | 26 | 26 | $59
*Four Seasons Hotel, 690 Newport Center Dr. (Santa Cruz Dr.), Newport Beach, 949-760-4920; www.fourseasons.com*

■ It's "almost perfect" gush groupies of this "great hotel dining" venue in the "upscale" Four Seasons near the Fashion Island mall, where "star-quality" Cal-Med cuisine is "artfully presented" by an "attentive staff" amid "impressive", "luxe decor" and "old-money ambiance" (and at "fairly reasonable prices given the location"); sure, it's "not a trendy hangout", but for "quiet", "extraordinary" repasts befitting "special celebrations", many maintain "you can't do better" than this "superb experience."

### P.F. CHANG'S CHINA BISTRO 20 | 20 | 19 | $25
*Irvine Spectrum Ctr., 61 Fortune Dr. (Irvine Center Dr.), Irvine, 949-453-1211*
*800 The Shops at Mission Viejo (Crown Valley Pkwy.), Mission Viejo, 949-364-6661*

(continued)

(continued)
### P.F. CHANG'S CHINA BISTRO
*1145 Newport Center Dr. (Santa Barbara Dr.), Newport Beach,*
*949-759-9007*
*www.pfchangs.com*
■ It may be a chain, but this "upscale" Chinese "crowd-pleaser" offers "excellent" (if "inauthentic") food served by an "attentive" staff in "beautiful surroundings"; it's so "big and loud" you won't "feel bad about taking the kids along", and the "tasty drinks make for a Zenful experience."

### PICAYO
28 | 20 | 25 | $47

*610 N. PCH (Boat Canyon Dr.), Laguna Beach, 949-497-5051;*
*www.picayorestaurant.com*
■ Offering a taste of the "sunny south of France", this "North Laguna haven" is rated No. 1 for Food in OC on the strength of its "superb Mediterranean"-inspired French fare from chef-partner Laurent Brazier, whose kitchen "emphasizes flavors and freshness"; its location off a "Von's parking lot" detracts for some, but the "professional staff" is "attentive" and the "small space" is "warm, inviting" and "casual", yet "elegant enough for special evenings."

### Pinot Provence
26 | 25 | 24 | $53

*The Westin South Coast Plaza Hotel, 686 Anton Blvd. (Bristol St.),*
*Costa Mesa, 714-444-5900; www.patinagroup.com*
■ "Don't tell LA, but OC has the best Pinot of all" avow vaunters of this "super" Patina Group outpost in the lobby of The Westin South Coast Plaza Hotel, a French "favorite" for "pre-theater dining", "power dinners" or "dessert after the show"; "amazingly talented chef Florent Marneau" delivers "lovely, sophisticated" dishes, including "imaginative specials", in a "beautiful room with a real south-of-France feel", leading fans to hail it as "head and shoulders above the competition."

### RAMOS HOUSE CAFE
27 | 20 | 21 | $28

*31752 Los Rios St. (Ramos St.), San Juan Capistrano, 949-443-1342;*
*www.ramoshouse.com*
■ Devotees delight in chef-owner John Humphries' "one-of-a-kind", "funky patio restaurant" in San Juan Capistrano's "rustic" historic district, where "the Amtrak rumbles by" as daytime diners laze over "haute morning chow" and "amazing", "imaginative American" lunches "with a Southern accent"; it may be "pricey for what you get", but it "brims with bucolic charm" and the "owner's relaxing, welcoming vibe", making it "an escape from OC without leaving OC."

### RUTH'S CHRIS STEAK HOUSE
26 | 21 | 24 | $52

*2961 Michaelson Dr. (Carlson Ave.), Irvine, 949-252-8848;*
*www.ruthschris.com*
■ A "temple of cholesterol" or "low-carb heaven" depending on your diet deity, this "superb" steakhouse chain link attracts acolytes with its "sizzling" signature dish ("butter on steak is as good as you'd imagine"), "awesome sides" and "incredible wines"; disciples further declare that the "superior" service "surpasses" that of the competition, and the "plush" interior is praised for its "well-spaced tables"; though the "à la carte menu style can get pricey", it's "worth it" for such "gold-standard" fare.

### Sage
24 │ 20 │ 22 │ $38

*Eastbluff Shopping Ctr., 2531 Eastbluff Dr. (Vista del Sol),*
*Newport Beach, 949-718-9650; www.sagerestaurant.com*
■ Inland Newport's "hidden treasure" in a "nondescript strip mall" has "great local buzz" as a "foodie's delight" thanks to chef-owner Rich Mead's "sophisticated", "inspired" New American fare with "a little comfort thrown in"; the "simple" main room is often "crowded and noisy", so sage surveyors request the "lovely" "patio made for a secret rendezvous"; it's no wonder regulars "can't wait for the second location to open" near the coast very shortly.

### STUDIO
27 │ 27 │ 26 │ $78

*Montage Resort & Spa, 30801 S. PCH (Montage Dr.), Laguna Beach,*
*949-715-6420; www.montagelagunabeach.com*
■ The "shining star of the OC Riviera", this "sublime" yearling in Laguna's Montage Resort showcases chef James Boyce, who turns out "creative", "fabulously presented" Cal-French fare that's "off the charts" and matched by "great wines"; the "beautiful Arts and Crafts" dining room affords "drop-dead views of the Pacific", the staff has "ESP" and even if it's a "high-price-tag experience", it's still the "hottest ticket in town" if "you can get a reservation."

### Zov's Bistro
25 │ 19 │ 22 │ $35

*Enderle Ctr., 17440 E. 17th St. (Yorba St.), Tustin, 714-838-8855;*
*www.zovs.com*
■ Perhaps the "most dedicated chef in OC" is Zov Karamardian, who's "rewarded by a full house for lunch and dinner" at her "popular" Med "mecca" where the "inventive", "delicious" dishes include "wonderful lamb" and "excellent seafood" followed by "fantastic", "small works of art" from her "first-rate" bakery/cafe next door; "sophisticated service", a "divine" patio and "good-value" tabs are other reasons surveyors say "the place has it all."

# Orlando

## TOP 20 FOOD RANKING

| | Restaurant | Cuisine |
|---|---|---|
| **27** | Le Coq au Vin | French |
| | Victoria & Albert's | American |
| | Chatham's Place | Continental |
| | Del Frisco's | Steakhouse |
| **26** | Manuel's on the 28th | New American |
| | California Grill | Californian |
| | Flying Fish Café | New American/Seafood |
| | Emeril's Orlando | Creole |
| **25** | Maison & Jardin | Continental |
| | Christini's* | Northern Italian |
| | Roy's | Hawaii Regional |
| | K | Eclectic |
| | Morton's | Steakhouse |
| | Jiko | African |
| | Little Saigon | Vietnamese |
| | Palm | Steakhouse |
| | Thai House | Thai |
| **24** | Ruth's Chris | Steakhouse |
| | Arthur's 27 | Continental |
| | Antonio's La Fiamma | Italian |

## ADDITIONAL NOTEWORTHY PLACES

| Restaurant | Cuisine |
|---|---|
| Anaelle & Hugo | European/American |
| Boma | African |
| Café de France | French |
| Charley's | Steakhouse |
| Cheesecake Factory | American |
| Chef Justin's | Floribbean |
| Citricos | New American |
| Dux | New American |
| Emeril's Tchoup Chop | Asian/Polynesian |
| Enzo's on the Lake | Italian |
| Harvey's Bistro | European/New American |
| Hue - A Restaurant | Asian/New American |
| Le Cellier | Steakhouse |
| McCormick & Schmick's | Seafood |
| MoonFish | Seafood/Steakhouse |
| Norman's | New World |
| Primo | Italian |
| Seasons 52 | Eclectic |
| Vito's Chop House | Steakhouse |
| Wolfgang Puck Café | Californian |

---

\* Indicates a tie with restaurant above

### Anaelle & Hugo    – | – | – | M
*The Fountains, 7533 W. Sand Lake Rd. (Dr. Phillips Blvd.), 407-996-9292;*
*www.anaelleandhugo.com*
Everything from sculptural plates to Sunday jazz to the vivid colors
that accent the mahogany dining room conveys the arty attitude
of this Euro-American bistro, where chef/co-owner Francis Metais
composes dramatic dishes from ingredients new to Orlando
(salsify, red rice, porcini oil); meanwhile, commerce-conscious
customers will appreciate the reasonable prices.

### Antonio's La Fiamma 🔣    24 | 21 | 24 | $37
*611 S. Orlando Ave. (Maitland Ave.), Maitland, 407-645-1035;*
*www.antoniosonline.com*
■ "Delicious, authentic Italian food and handsome waiters" entice
diners to this Maitland mainstay "overlooking a nearby lake"; with
"elegant" service and a "superior wine list", it all adds up to a
"delightful setting" that's "comfortable" and "romantic" – though
sometimes "noisy": you can "hear the chefs yell at the waiters
through the open kitchen door."

### Arthur's 27 🔣    24 | 25 | 25 | $62
*Wyndham Palace Resort & Spa, 1900 Buena Vista Dr., 27th fl. (Rte. 535),*
*Lake Buena Vista, 407-827-3450; www.wyndham.com/palaceresort*
☑ "Go for an 8 PM dinner and catch the Disney fireworks" from
this 27th-floor "special-event place" at Lake Buena Vista's
Wyndham Palace; partisans praise the "excellent" Continental
meals, an "expansive" wine list and service that's "second to
none", while detractors conclude it's "coasting on its reputation";
still, all agree you'll end up with "a big bill" unless you order from
the prix fixe menu; N.B. closed Sunday–Tuesday.

### Boma    24 | 24 | 23 | $31
*Disney's Animal Kingdom Lodge, 2901 Osceola Pkwy. (Sherbert Rd.),*
*Lake Buena Vista, 407-938-4722; www.disneyworld.com*
■ "Remember not to eat anything the entire day" before heading to
Disney's "safari" smorgasbord, where everything has an "African
twist": the environment includes a thatched roof and has an "open
marketplace feel", and those with "adventurous palates" can
explore an "awesome diversity of food" that's "as wild as the
Animal Kingdom residents", including the signature Zebra Dome
dessert ("do not leave without having one"); given the "world-class
flavors", fans note, the price is "remarkably low."

### Café de France 🔣    23 | 18 | 23 | $44
*526 S. Park Ave. (Sherbanks Ave.), Winter Park, 407-647-1869;*
*www.lecafedefrance.com*
☑ Patrons of this Winter Park sidewalk bistro laud its "fabulous
French dishes", including pâtés that "should not be missed"; though
the decor is "basic", the "quaint atmosphere" is "quiet", and the
"friendly" staff is "always willing to suggest wines"; in short, most
conclude, you get "great food in a mediocre place at high prices."

### CALIFORNIA GRILL    26 | 25 | 24 | $45
*Disney's Contemporary Resort, 4600 N. World Dr., Lake Buena Vista,*
*407-824-1576; www.disneyworld.com*
■ This hotel Californian, tied with Emeril's Orlando as the Orlando
area's Most Popular restaurant, is "no Mickey Mouse" joint, say
smitten surveyors; local hotshot John State serves up "delectable"

fare ("great" pork tenderloin) that "sensuously melts in your mouth"; "enthusiastic" staffers "really know the menu" and 31 on-site sommeliers oversee 100 by-the-glass offerings; views of the Magic Kingdom's nightly fireworks are "spectacular" but can give rise to a "boisterous" atmosphere (some respondents feel like they're "sitting in a nursery school").

### Charley's Steak House　　24 │ 19 │ 22 │ $47
*2901 Parkway Blvd. (Space Coast Pkwy.), Kissimmee, 407-239-1270*
*8255 International Dr. (Sand Lake Rd.), 407-363-0228*
*6107 S. Orange Blossom Trail (bet. W. Lancaster & Oak Ridge Rds.), 407-851-7130*
*www.charleyssteakhouse.com*
■ Everyone knows that the "wood fire"–grilled hunks of aged prime beef at this carnivore's-delight chainlet "melt in your mouth", but it's "quite a surprise" to also find "fantastic" shrimp, seared tuna and other "excellent" seafood on its "classic steakhouse" menu; just make a selection from the "excellent", 1,000-strong wine list, and prepare for a "mm-mm-good", "top-notch" experience.

### CHATHAM'S PLACE　　27 │ 19 │ 25 │ $49
*7575 Dr. Phillips Blvd. (Sand Lake Rd.), 407-345-2992; www.chathamsplace.com*
■ Seek and ye shall find this Dr. Phillips Continental, an "intimate and lovely" spot in a hidden "office building location" that loyalists like for its "perfection in flavors and offerings": signature dishes ("excellent" grouper) are "exceptional" and the staff is "anxious to please"; though the dining room is "private and quiet", some lament "decor that's still in the '90s"; N.B. guitar music nightly.

### CHEESECAKE FACTORY ❷　　21 │ 20 │ 19 │ $27
*Mall at Millenia, 4200 Conroy Rd. (I-4), 407-226-0333*
*Winter Park Village, 520 N. Orlando Ave. (Lee Rd.), Winter Park, 407-644-4220*
*www.cheesecakefactory.com*
☑ "Excess takes on new meaning" at the two local links of this "festive" American chain: for the "giant" menu, "you may require a bookmark", and each entree is a "mountain" of "reliably good" food; also outsized, though, is the "outrageous" wait for a table, and naysayers nix "noisy" crowds and say servers "sometimes disappear like Houdini"; "you won't leave hungry and you won't leave broke", but "the word 'factory' says it all."

### Chef Justin's Park Plaza Gardens　　23 │ 25 │ 23 │ $46
*Park Plaza Hotel, 319 Park Ave. S. (New England Ave.), Winter Park, 407-645-2475; www.parkplazagardens.com*
■ "Finally, it's back!" shout fans of this "venerable" Winter Park "bastion", insisting the fare (now Floribbean) has "gone way up since Justin Plank took over as chef"; a "dependable" staff helps you "dine in style", whether alfresco "out on Park Avenue" or in the "charming" "indoor courtyard" with "huge trees in the middle of the dining room", all making for "a little bit of heaven in the center of town"; N.B. the Decor rating may not reflect a post-*Survey* revamp.

### Christini's　　25 │ 20 │ 25 │ $55
*The Marketplace, 7600 Dr. Phillips Blvd. (Sand Lake Rd.), 407-345-8770; www.christinis.com*
☑ "Food doesn't get much better in Orlando", which may be why "special-occasion" celebrants, "out-of-towners" and those "on

expense accounts" shell out at this "enjoyably over-the-top", "sorta schmaltzy" Dr. Phillips Tuscan, where staffers "take the pressure off men by giving every woman a rose" as they seat patrons in a "cozy and romantic", "old-world" dining room; meanwhile, "prices require a short-term loan", complain ciao hounds, who gripe "come on, it's Italian – do they have to charge that much?"

### Citricos 24 | 24 | 24 | $44

*Disney's Grand Floridian Resort & Spa, 4401 Grand Floridian Way, Lake Buena Vista, 407-824-2712; www.disneyworld.com*

■ "Inspired food and incredible service" effervesce eaters about this New American "tucked into the Grand Floridian", where chef Gray Byrum's "culinary genius" gives rise to a "sophisticated menu" of "creative creations" ("fish that melts in the mouth", "fantastic desserts"); the "striking", "Manhattan-chic decor" impresses too, as does the "accommodating" staff's "individualized attention to detail"; "not yet fully discovered by the masses", this "foodie must" is "so good even the locals flock to Disney."

### DEL FRISCO'S 27 | 19 | 24 | $54
### DOUBLE EAGLE STEAK HOUSE ⊠

*729 Lee Rd. (I-4, exit 88), Winter Park, 407-645-4443; www.delfriscos.com*

■ "Steaks you'll remember all your life" and "lobster tails so huge they belong in a 1950s mutant movie" make this Winter Park beef barn a favorite shrine for "red-meat pilgrimages" – "especially if someone else is paying"; 500 wines and staffers that "never say no" add appeal to a scene so "crowded, noisy and masculine" "you expect Sinatra to walk in"; aesthetes murmur that the decor "needs revamping", but of course that "isn't what you go for."

### Dux ⊠ 23 | 22 | 22 | $53

*Peabody Orlando Hotel, 9801 International Dr. (W. Century Blvd.), 407-345-4550*

☑ "Who says hotel food can't be great?" ask admirers of this New American near the convention center, where the fare "(down to the great bread basket) is lovely" and the formal room is "exquisite" and "quiet"; detractors dismiss the jackets-recommended venue as "overpriced" and say it's "time to revitalize the concept"; P.S. arrive at 5 PM to watch the Peabody ducks "march on a red carpet through the lobby to their penthouse retreat."

### EMERIL'S RESTAURANT ORLANDO 26 | 22 | 24 | $53

*Universal Studios CityWalk, 6000 Universal Blvd. (Vineland Rd.), 407-224-2424; www.emerils.com*

☑ Lagasse lovers laud this hot Creole, tied with California Grill as Orlando's Most Popular restaurant, as "an oasis in a desert of dreck" (read: Universal's CityWalk), gushing "all superlatives apply": food that's "beyond outstanding", a "phenomenal wine list" (650 labels), "expertly choreographed" service and a "casual but classy" space – but plenty have reservations, so to speak, deploring the need to save a table "weeks ahead" for a "hectic", "touristy" "joint" that doesn't "justify the long wait and huge tab."

### Emeril's Tchoup Chop 24 | 28 | 23 | $48

*Royal Pacific Hotel & Resort, 6300 Hollywood Way (Universal Blvd.), 407-503-2467; www.emerils.com*

■ "Oh yeah, babe", croon swooning supporters of Emeril's Asian-Polynesian in Universal's Royal Pacific Hotel; they enthuse about its "innovative", "enchanted", "sexy", "South Seas–style" David

Rockwell decor (complete with waterfall and pond) as well as "delectable", "innovative" dishes and "impeccable" service; some say the strong start suggests the "master" "has done it again", while others caution that this two-year-old may still be "going through some growing pains."

### Enzo's On The Lake ☒ 24 21 22 $45
*1130 S. Hwy. 17-92 (Wildmere Ave.), Longwood, 407-834-9872; www.enzos.com*

■ "Don't go if you want a quick meal – this needs to be savored", note *amici* of this Longwood Italian with "amazing antipasto" and other "old-world favorites" like the signature Dover sole or sauce "to rival your nonna's", served by a "superb" staff in a "gorgeous" waterside setting; for an even livelier outing, they say, "come with 15 of your closest friends" or "get Enzo to sing"; result: "it gets pretty loud in there."

### FLYING FISH CAFÉ 26 24 23 $45
*Disney's BoardWalk Inn, 2101 N. Epcot Resorts Blvd. (Buena Vista Dr.), Lake Buena Vista, 407-939-2359; www.disneyworld.com*

■ "Top-of-the-(fishing)-line" seafood lures loyal locals as well as returning tourists to Disney's New American reef 'n' beefer, which garners kudos for finny fare that "tastes like it was caught a few moments before", "amazing" steaks and "*très fantastique*" bananas Napoleon; the "whimsical", "oceanic" decor draws raves, but many say it's even more fun to "watch the chefs fling flying fish" as you dine by the open kitchen, then stroll on a "romantic" boardwalk that's "nothing like New Jersey's – thank God!"

### Harvey's Bistro ☒ 22 21 22 $30
*Bank of America Bldg., 390 N. Orange Ave. (E. Livingston St.), 407-246-6560; www.harveysbistro.com*

■ In the middle of Downtown, this European-leaning New American is a "cozy bistro" with a "delightful pub atmosphere" and "reasonable prices"; it's perfect for a "power lunch" or "pre-theater dinner", thanks to "homestyle-mixed-with-haute-cuisine" entrees that are "not like mom's – they're better" – and the ministrations of a "sophisticated and helpful" staff, especially the "entertaining" Rocky; after dark, a "great bar scene" draws a "post-trial crowd of attorneys and businessmen."

### Hue - A Restaurant ◑ 23 24 20 $42
*629 E. Central Blvd. (Summerlin Ave.), 407-849-1800; www.huerestaurant.com*

■ "Where did all these beautiful people come from?" wonder wags about Thornton Park's "sassy", "trendy" Asian–New American, as much a "hipster" "meat market" ("wear black and bring your attitude") as it is a "solid" eatery with "creative", "avant-charred" comestibles; noting it's "noisy as hell" – especially on Thursday nights, when it's "the place to be" – regulars recommend "be seen on the outdoor corner patio" and warn there's "almost always a wait" owing to a limited reservations policy.

### Jiko – The Cooking Place 25 26 25 $45
*Disney's Animal Kingdom Lodge, 2901 Osceola Pkwy., Lake Buena Vista, 407-938-3000; www.disneyworld.com*

■ Out of Africa comes the inspiration for Disney's "rare gem of resort dining", an "exotic", "stunning venue" where chef Anette Grecchi Gray blends "food from many cultures" with sub-Saharan flavors "in joyous harmony" for entrees that will make you "close your eyes and sigh" – fare you can pair with dozens of "enjoyable" South African wines; furthermore, gratified grazers express heart-veldt appreciation for a "knowledgeable, enthusiastic" staff that "treats you like a friend."

**K** ☒    25 20 23 $39

*2401 Edgewater Dr. (Vassar St.), 407-872-2332*

■ K is special, say kibitzers keen on this College Park kitchen, who give chef-owner Kevin Fonzo's Eclectic "50-seat oasis" kudos for "delicious", "worldly" K rations (including "to-die-for" monthly wine dinners and killer chocolate lava cake, "the best dessert in town"), and say a "superb", "helpful" staff treats them like kin; the "arty" setting, with "cool paintings" that change monthly, is also A-ok; N.B. closed Sunday–Monday.

**Le Cellier Steakhouse**    23 21 23 $38

*Epcot, Canada Pavilion, Lake Buena Vista, 407-939-3463*

☑ "Who knew Canadian food was more than maple syrup and bacon?" tease visitors to this Epcot cellar; in fact, the cave draws raves for steaks "cooked to perfection" and "fish so good you can't stop eating", served by a "hardworking" staff within a "cozy", "dark" space (a "welcome respite" from "hot, flat Florida"); overall it's more do-right than dud, but a contingent of critics judges this meatery "a little small" and its menu "boooooring."

**LE COQ AU VIN**    27 20 25 $43

*4800 S. Orange Ave. (Holden Ave.), 407-851-6980*

■ Voted No. 1 for Food in the area, this South Orlando Classic French has plenty to crow about, declare diners who dote on its "rich", "sublime" dishes (including the namesake entree, which *coq* fiends call a "masterpiece", and "top-notch" soufflés); better yet, this "hidden treasure", located in a "modest" house in an offbeat area, has the "nicest servers in town" and "bargain" prices, making it "the perfect place to go if you want to avoid the tourist traps"; N.B. closed on Monday.

**Little Saigon**    25 11 19 $16

*1106 E. Colonial Dr. (Mills Ave.), 407-423-8539*

☑ The pho-one-one on this East Orlando Vietnamese, according to the few who have found it, is that its "straightforward fare" (i.e. "filling soups full of foreign flavors", "noodle dishes with every combination of meat and seafood") is "perfect when you only have a few bucks to spend" on "dinner before hitting the clubs"; consider "carpooling to avoid the dearth of parking" or, since it's "cramped and hurried" inside, takeout is a good bet.

**Maison & Jardin** ☒    25 24 26 $53

*430 S. Wymore Rd. (State Rd. 436), Altamonte Springs, 407-862-4410*

☑ "Lovingly known as the Mason Jar", this Continental stalwart in Altamonte Springs "costs a fortune, but it's so worth it" say steadfast supporters; chef Hans Spirig "thrills" a "Francophile crowd" with culinary classics like "to-die-for" beef Wellington, the wine cellar is home to 1,200 labels and the "gracious", "formally attired" staff "does everything right" – though trendier types tsk that it's a "stuffy", "tired old dame" and liken a meal here to "going to the country club with your grandparents"; N.B. closed Sunday–Monday.

## MANUEL'S ON THE 28TH ⌘    26 | 28 | 27 | $59

*Bank of America Bldg., 390 N. Orange Ave. (Colonial Dr.), 407-246-6580;*
*www.manuelsonthe28th.com*

■ The "big tab is justified" by the "million-dollar view": "huge windows" on the 28th floor showcase Orlando's "burgeoning Downtown", so "at sunset" or "when thunderstorms roll in, this is where you want to be" – especially given its "impeccable" staff, "phenomenal" New American entrees and desserts that are "works of art"; in all, romantics rhapsodize, it's "the perfect place to propose"; still, despite the panorama, a few claim Manny Garcia's showpiece "doesn't live up to expectations."

## McCormick & Schmick's    22 | 21 | 20 | $36

*Mall at Millenia, 4200 Conroy Rd. (Millenia Dr.), 407-226-6515;*
*www.mccormickandschmicks.com*

■ Finatics sing "hallelujah!" now that this upscale national chain has arrived at the Mall at Millenia, testifying they've "only had fresh seafood" like this "on Cape Cod and in Maine" and praising the "darn good oysters"; meanwhile, "nautical" decor and "friendly, professional" servers create a "clubbish atmosphere"; M&S "delivers value" at the bar too, say some, in the form of imported drafts and "recommended" $1.95 eats in early and late evening.

## MoonFish Restaurant    23 | 24 | 19 | $39

*Fountains Plaza, 7525 W. Sand Lake Rd. (International Dr.), 407-363-7262;*
*www.fishfusion.com*

◪ Proponents of this Dr. Phillips surf 'n' turfer moon about its elaborate interior, a "gorgeous" "palace" where restrooms have "spigots shaped like porpoises" and "videos of swimming fish" above the urinals; many also maintain the "food's as cool as the bathroom", including a "daring and rewarding" menu of "spicy swimmers" and an "extensive" array of 400 wines, but skeptics snipe this place has "nothing to really distinguish itself except the decor" and bewail "expense-account" prices.

## Morton's, The Steakhouse    25 | 20 | 23 | $57

*Marketplace, 7600 Dr. Phillips Blvd. (Sand Lake Rd.), 407-248-3485;*
*www.mortons.com*

◪ "Popular with the limo set", this Restaurant Row link of the chain of upscale beefmongers is "like every other", with "fabulous steak", "yummy" sides, "must-have" chocolate cake, a "knowledgeable staff" and a "big-city atmosphere"; detractors grumble that the "testosterone level is too high" and "you have to yell at your companions" to be heard, saying that the experience is "not worth the price", but supporters suggest you "have someone bring you and make sure they're loaded."

## Norman's    – | – | – | E

*Ritz-Carlton Orlando, Grande Lakes, 4012 Central Florida Pkwy.*
*(John Young Pkwy.), 407-393-4333; www.normans.com*

Gastronaut Norman Van Aken brings his trademark New World cookery to Central Florida audiences at this dinner-only yearling, conjuring up concoctions of Caribbean and Latin American foods (yuca, habaneros, plantains) accompanied by thematic cocktails like the signature Cozumelpolitan (made with cactus-pear sorbet); the dining room, a romantic, well-windowed space with an octagonal wine vault rising through the center, is Ritzy indeed; N.B. there's a five-course tasting menu for $75.

### Palm

| 25 | 21 | 24 | $56 |

*Hard Rock Hotel, 5800 Universal Blvd. (Vineland St.), 407-503-7256;*
*www.thepalm.com*

☑ Meat lovers give the Palm a hand, dubbing this "great installation of a New York original" in the Hard Rock Hotel at Universal a "first-class steakhouse" with "out-of-this-world" lobster and "gargantuan sides", an "excellent" choice "for taking customers if you want to close" a deal; disregarding the "cheerful and attentive" service and celebrity caricatures painted on the walls, however, dissatisfied dissenters deliver a thumbs-down, deeming the place merely "functional" – not to mention "noisy, noisy, noisy and overpriced."

### Primo

| – | – | – | E |

*JW Marriott Orlando, Grande Lakes, 4040 Central Florida Pkwy.*
*(John Young Pkwy.), 407-393-4444; www.primorestaurant.com*

Maine-based maestro Melissa Kelly now gladdens mouths down South at the upscale JW Marriott Orlando Grande Lakes; her organic, Italian-influenced menus include such specialties as pork saltimbocca and farm-raised lamb chops (plus decadent desserts designed by Kelly's husband/partner/pastry chef Price Kushner) along with an international array of some 200 wines; the roomy Tuscan-farmhouse environs also feature garden seating for up to 30 people.

### Roy's Orlando

| 25 | 23 | 24 | $48 |

*Plaza Venezia, 7760 W. Sand Lake Rd. (Dr. Phillips Blvd.), 407-352-4844;*
*www.roysrestaurant.com*

■ "So much for a jaded palate", lei people say of their meals at this Dr. Phillips outpost of Roy Yamaguchi's "pricey" Hawaii Regional chain: "inspired, almost over-the-top" seafood entrees and the signature "oozy chocolate soufflé" "with a molten lava center" wake up "weary taste buds"; meanwhile, an "attentive but not obtrusive" staff steers patrons through this Pacific passage amid an atmosphere that some call "lively" and others "loud."

### Ruth's Chris Steak House

| 24 | 22 | 23 | $53 |

*7501 W. Sand Lake Rd. (Turkey Lake Rd.), 407-226-3900*
*Winter Park Vlg., 610 N. Orlando Ave. (Webster Ave.), Winter Park,*
*407-622-2444*
*www.ruthschris.com*

☑ Whether you "hang out in the bar and eat solo" or "take a big group and get a private room", you can't help but have a "wonderful experience" at these Sand Lake and Winter Park links of the chophouse chain according to acolytes of the "huge martinis", "big, juicy steaks" and "to-die-for sides"; if a few wonder "what all the fuss is about" and reproach its "everything's-à-la-carte" approach ("too pricey"), the majority simply sings the praises of its "serious beef" whose "quality holds true."

### Seasons 52

| 23 | 25 | 23 | $36 |

*Plaza Venezia, 7700 W. Sand Lake Rd. (Dr. Phillips Blvd.), 407-354-5212;*
*www.seasons52.com*

☑ "It's like sin and forgiveness all in one" at this Eclectic from the former chef and manager of California Grill, with "craveworthy" entrees all "under 475 calories" and "almost guilt-free desserts" served in shot glasses; "warm wood" and "inviting textures" make this lakeside locale "one of Orlando's prettiest", and the "polite" staff "tries hard"; still, antagonists dislike what they call the "bland food", and the promise of low-cal luxury attracts so many weight-watchers you may have to "wait, wait, wait."

**Thai House** ◨  25 | 16 | 21 | $22
*2117 E. Colonial Dr. (N. Hillside Ave.), 407-898-0820*
■ The "spartan" decor at this "homey" East Colonial Thai "neighborhood favorite" is just "ok" (if not "dumpy"), but "this place is all about the food, and it is fantastic" agree adherents, urging readers to delve into "inexpensive" dishes that are "packed with flavor" with the assistance of "friendly" staffers who "encourage" visitors "to try something new."

**VICTORIA & ALBERT'S**  27 | 26 | 27 | $85
*Disney's Grand Floridian Resort & Spa, 4401 Grand Floridian Way, Lake Buena Vista, 407-939-7707; www.disney.com*
■ Ecstatic epicures "feel like well-fed royalty" at this formal American (jacket required) in the Magic Kingdom, where a gaslight-era "night of delights" includes a "maid-and-butler" duo who "anticipate every need", an "exquisite" six-course meal you can "embellish" with picks from the 700-label wine list and sometimes even a harpist; fans rave it's "worth the six-month wait" to sit at the chef's table for a personalized "plethora of delicacies"; though to a few the whole experience seems "slightly contrived", by consensus it's "the best splurge in Orlando."

**Vito's Chop House**  23 | 21 | 20 | $46
*8633 International Dr. (Austrian Row), 407-354-2467; www.vitoschophouse.com*
☑ "Perfectly aged" and "seasoned" chops "served just as you like them" plus a "staggering" wine list (950 entries) entice I-Drive conventioneers to this "Italian-influenced steakhouse" lauded for "lower-than-average prices", but beware of "pushy" servers and laissez-faire management "oriented toward the tourist."

**Wolfgang Puck Cafe**  22 | 20 | 19 | $34
*Downtown Disney West Side, 1482 E. Buena Vista Dr. (Hotel Plaza Blvd.), Lake Buena Vista, 407-938-9653; www.wolfgangpuck.com*
☑ It's "not quite Spago, but what is?" observe patrons of this Downtown Disney casual Californian; still, it offers "the best pizza this side of the Atlantic", "super-fresh sushi" and "eclectic yet safe" entrees; the decor is "cool" and "colorful", but be prepared for "slow" service – and "bring earplugs."

# Palm Beach

| F | D | S | C |
|---|---|---|---|

**Café Boulud** — | – | – | VE |

*Brazilian Court Hotel, 301 Australian Ave. (Hibiscus Ave.), 561-655-6060; www.danielnyc.com*

New York City super-chef Daniel Boulud's long-awaited Palm Beach outpost in the renovated Brazilian Court Hotel offers a menu reflecting that of the Manhattan original, with the maestro's signature mix of traditional and interpretive French dishes; samplers can savor the specialties in the sunny, Provence-inspired dining rooms or opt for the courtyard with fountain; acolytes are advised to book early for what's expected to be one of the hottest tickets in town during the season.

**Cafe Chardonnay** 25 | 21 | 22 | $48 |

*Garden Square Shoppes, 4533 PGA Blvd. (Military Trail), Palm Beach Gardens, 561-627-2662; www.cafechardonnay.com*

☑ A "time-tested favorite" in Palm Beach Gardens, this New American may prove to be the "classiest dining experience you'll ever have in a strip mall"; "outstanding", "artfully prepared" dishes including "incredible seafood" are paired with "fabulous wines", the staff is "happy to educate the customer" and an interior some previously found "drab" has been spiffed up; N.B. the renovation may outdate the above Decor score.

### CAFÉ L'EUROPE          26 | 27 | 25 | $67
*331 S. County Rd. (Brazilian Ave.), 561-655-4020; www.cafeleurope.com*
☑ The "killer" atmosphere at this "still-going-strong Palm Beach staple" "says 'you have arrived, dahling'", with "gorgeous" flowers and "beautiful people" ("see the wonders Botox has wrought") adorning the recently refreshed room; the "flawless" Continental cuisine is "marvelous" and the wine list is "extraordinary", so even though the service ranges from "pampering" to "pompous" and the offerings are "extremely expensive", vets advise "dress up", "break the bank and live the good life."

### CHEESECAKE FACTORY ❶          20 | 19 | 18 | $25
*5530 Glades Rd. (Butts Rd.), Boca Raton, 561-393-0344*
*CityPlace, 701 S. Rosemary Ave. (Okeechobee Blvd.), West Palm Beach, 561-802-3838*
*www.thecheesecakefactory.com*
☑ With its fabled "menu longer than the latest Harry Potter" and portions large enough "to serve an entire canasta" group, these "dependable" chain links attract "masses" who "line up" for "good" American fare and "dynamite desserts"; sure, they're "noisy" and the lines can be "prohibitively long", but the staff's "quick and efficient" and the "well-done corporate formula" is "great for the kids", which may be why these are the Palm Beach area's Most Popular eateries.

### CHEZ JEAN-PIERRE BISTRO ⌧          28 | 22 | 26 | $62
*132 N. County Rd. (bet. Sunrise & Sunset Aves.), 561-833-1171*
■ Fans "fly to Palm Beach just to eat" at this "premier" French "favorite of the old guard and NP (new people)" alike; the "exquisite yet unpretentious" preparations are "masterpieces" (the "best sea bass", "to-die-for sorbets"), and the "wonderful", "longtime" staff along with "charming" owners Jean-Pierre and Nicole Leverrier "make you feel at home"; the "lovely" setting with "zany" trompe l'oeil art completes the picture, and if it's all "a little overpriced", well, it's worth a "splurge."

### De la Tierra          21 | 27 | 19 | $46
*Sundy House Inn, 106 S. Swinton Ave. (Atlantic Ave.), Delray Beach, 561-272-5678; www.sundyhouse.com*
■ Tropical tastes are still tops at this "special-occasion" "must" in downtown Delray Beach's "spectacular" Sundy House; celeb chef Kevin Graham is now overseeing the "outstanding" menu, bringing Southwestern spice to the seasonal Floribbean cuisine with such additions as lobster quesadillas, two-flavor sunset bisque and design-your-own-salads, plus a tapas menu at the bar, all using homegrown produce; similarly freshened up are the appointments and entrance to the "delightful garden" rooms.

### Echo          24 | 24 | 21 | $50
*230A Sunrise Ave. (N. County Rd.), 561-802-4222;*
*www.echopalmbeach.com*
■ This "happening" Palm Beach Asian fusion showplace is "so chic" you'll "wonder whether you're hip enough to dine there"; the menu is a "brilliant broad brush" stroke of eastern offerings including "fresher-than-fresh sushi" and "the best Peking duck for miles" as well as "wonderful" drinks, all "beautifully presented" by a staff with "impressive knowledge" – just expect the experience to be "pricey"; N.B. delivery available.

### 11 MAPLE STREET                               28 │ 23 │ 24 │ $46

*3224 NE Maple Ave. (11th Ave.), Jensen Beach, 772-334-7714*

■ Its "low-key atmosphere" belies the "haute" New American cuisine served at this downtown Jensen Beach "charmer" that surveyors have voted No. 1 for Food in the Palm Beach area; chef-owner Mike Perrin uses the "freshest ingredients" to create "novel", "astonishing" dishes and his "gracious" wife, Margie, "greets you like an old friend"; the "delightful" "converted old house" alone is "worth the drive" for a "special date"; N.B. closed Mondays, Tuesdays and off-season Sundays.

### FOUR SEASONS – THE RESTAURANT   28 │ 28 │ 28 │ $68

*Four Seasons, 2800 S. Ocean Blvd. (Lake Ave.), 561-533-3750; www.fourseasons.com*

■ "A tribute to the talents" of "master" chef Hubert Des Marais, this "faultless" Four Seasons hotel New American "continues to amaze" with "phenomenal" fish and other "extraordinary" entrees using regional ingredients that are all a "joy to behold"; the "superior" staff is "there before you know you need something", and the setting, while "formal", is "luxurious", "beautiful" and graced with nightly live piano music; naturally, it's "expensive", but "perfect for special occasions."

### Kathy's Gazebo Cafe ⊠               25 │ 23 │ 23 │ $54

*4199 N. Federal Hwy. (Spanish River Rd.), Boca Raton, 561-395-6033; www.kathysgazebo.com*

☑ For more than 20 years, the Boca brigade has "dressed up" to dine at this "upscale", "traditional" Continental where the "top-notch" dishes are "prepared with care"; though the "beautiful" setting is "stuffy" to some, and the "skilled" staff can be "frosty" "if you're not a regular", cafe society decrees it "the greatest."

### KE-E GRILL                          25 │ 22 │ 22 │ $41

*17940 N. Military Trail (bet. Champion Ave. & Clint Moore Rd.), Boca Raton, 561-995-5044*
*14020 US 1 (Donald Ross Rd.), Juno Beach, 561-776-1167*

☑ These Palm Beach County seafooders offer "consistently superb" fin fare as well as steaks and "fantastic side dishes", all at a "great value"; the "attractive", "casual" environs with "tropical" decor and "smooth-as-silk" service help ameliorate the "long waits" (Juno takes no reservations but Boca books three weeks out).

### La Vieille Maison                   26 │ 28 │ 25 │ $63

*770 E. Palmetto Park Rd. (NE Olive Way), Boca Raton, 561-391-6701*

☑ Though it's added a new steakhouse menu to the mix, this Boca Raton "icon" remains "unwavering in its commitment to wonderful classic French cuisine", and devotees declare it "deserves its great reputation" for "fabulous" food, "exceptional wines" and "outstanding" staffers in a "gorgeous", multiroomed setting; even if *non*-sayers opine this old house is "past its prime" and deplore "snooty service", more maintain it's still "the gold standard."

### Le Mistral                          25 │ 19 │ 23 │ $47

*Northbeach Plaza, 12189 US 1 (PGA Blvd.), North Palm Beach, 561-622-3009*

■ This North Palm Beach "favorite" has Francophiles exclaiming "ooh-la-la" over the "consistently" "delicious" Gallic goodies presented in "charming" surroundings that feature "comfortable banquettes"; though "perfect for special occasions", it's also acclaimed for its "good summer prix fixe menu", so boosters advise "bring your hunger and ignore your cholesterol"; N.B. it's closed Sunday–Monday in summer.

### Little Moirs Food Shack 🗷    23 | 13 | 19 | $24
*103 US 1 (E. Indiantown Rd.), Jupiter, 561-741-3626;*
*www.littlemoirsfoodshack.com*

■ "From the looks and the name you'd expect a burger joint", but the specialty of this Jupiter "hole-in-the-wall" is "unbelievably fresh", "imaginative" seafood with "tropical flair", via a "chef sideshow in full view"; an enthusiastic crowd of "surfing and fishing" types apparently doesn't mind the "cramped" interior, "faux-island" decor and "lackadaisical" servers some grouse about; N.B. closed for dinner Sunday–Tuesday.

### Marcello's La Sirena    26 | 19 | 22 | $50
*6316 S. Dixie Hwy. (Forest Hill Blvd.), West Palm Beach, 561-585-3128;*
*www.lasirenaonline.com*

☑ "A little bit of Mulberry Street" "hidden" in West Palm Beach, this "excellent" "New York–style" Italian offers "delicious", "creative" cuisine using the "freshest ingredients" accompanied by "superb wines"; the "pleasant surroundings" create a "peaceful oasis" in an "out-of-the-way" location, and though the service can be "desultory" and the fare's "pricey", it remains a "longtime favorite"; N.B. closed July–August.

### NEW YORK PRIME    26 | 21 | 23 | $61
*2350 Executive Center Dr. NW (Glades Rd.), Boca Raton, 561-998-3881;*
*www.newyorkprime.com*

☑ "Yabba dabba Boca!" exclaim "devoted carnivores" before tucking into *Flintstones*-sized portions of "excellent" steaks, "amazing" seafood and "great salads and sides" at this "fabulous" "beef parlor"; the interior (including a lounge with live music) is "beautiful" and service "doting", but its status as the "ultimate power scene" has parvenus pouting it's almost "impossible to get a reservation" at this "pricey" place ("only steady customers are taken care of").

### Reef Grill    25 | 14 | 20 | $30
*12846 US 1 (Juno Isles Blvd.), Juno Beach, 561-624-9924*
*251 S. US 1 (Indiantown Rd.), Jupiter, 561-746-8857*

■ "Don't tell your friends" – these "local" "favorites" in Juno and Jupiter are "crowded enough", though regulars with reef madness don't mind the waits for "spectacular" fin fare from an "awesome menu" of "exciting", Caribbean-accented dishes; even if the "casual" settings border on "divey", the "excellent" wines (no cocktails) are served in "quality" Riedel stemware.

### RUTH'S CHRIS STEAK HOUSE    25 | 22 | 23 | $52
*661 US 1 (Lighthouse Dr.), North Palm Beach, 561-863-0660;*
*www.ruthschris.com*

■ Staunch members of this "elegant" chain's gang argue it serves the "best steak north of Argentina" ("signature" beef on "sizzling, butter-coated platters") and "great seafood" in "ample portions"; the "sophisticated, country club"–style scene and "experienced" staff who "treat customers like royalty" also please partisans, though a few ruthless sorts slam the "stiff prices."

### Spoto's Oyster Bar
24 | 18 | 21 | $34

*125 Datura St. (bet. N. Flagler Dr. & S. Narcissus Ave.), West Palm Beach, 561-835-1828*

■ "The real deal for shellfish lovers" is this "terrific" seafooder, the "hip, hot and happening" "place to be" in downtown West Palm Beach; connoisseurs won't clam up about the "wonderful raw bar" and "extensive menu" of "flavorful fish" and "irresistible pastas", all at a "great value" and served by "pros" in a "quaint", "casual" and "crowded" setting with sidewalk seating; N.B. Parrot Head alert: Jimmy Buffett's been known to stop by.

### 32 East
24 | 20 | 20 | $43

*32 E. Atlantic Ave. (bet. SE 1st & Swinton Aves.), Delray Beach, 561-276-7868; www.32east.com*

▨ Chef Nick Morfogen "just keeps getting better" at this "high-velocity" Delray Beach New American where the "impeccably prepared" cuisine is "urbane without being pretentious", the 250-bottle wine list is "incredible" and the staff "memorizes a new menu daily"; the "very W Hotel"–esque, newly spruced-up dining room features an open kitchen, and though it can therefore get "noisy", there's a "relaxing" space upstairs; some pout it's "a little pricey for Florida", but regulars retort "it never disappoints."

# Philadelphia

## TOP 20 FOOD RANKING

| Restaurant | Cuisine |
|---|---|
| **28** Fountain | New French/Continental |
| Le Bec-Fin | French |
| Le Bar Lyonnais | French Bistro |
| Django | Eclectic |
| Birchrunville Store | French/Italian |
| Lacroix/Rittenhouse | French |
| Vetri | Italian |
| **27** Gilmore's | French |
| Morimoto | Japanese |
| Buddakan | Asian Fusion |
| Bluefin | Japanese |
| La Bonne Auberge | French |
| Deux Cheminées | French |
| **26** Swann Lounge | New American/New French |
| Citrus | Eclectic |
| High St. Caffé | Cajun-Creole |
| Savona | French/Italian |
| ¡Pasión! | Nuevo Latino |
| Brasserie Perrier | New French |
| Mainland Inn | New American |

## ADDITIONAL NOTEWORTHY PLACES

| | |
|---|---|
| Alison at Blue Bell | New American |
| Blue Sage | Vegetarian |
| Carmine's Creole | Cajun-Creole |
| Dmitri's | Med./Seafood |
| Founders | New French |
| General Warren Inne | American |
| Jake's | New American |
| L'Angolo | Italian |
| Little Fish | Seafood |
| Meritage | European/Eclectic |
| Nan | New French/Thai |
| Ota-Ya | Japanese |
| Overtures | French/Med. |
| Peking | Chinese/Japanese |
| Pif | French Bistro |
| Prime Rib | Steakhouse |
| Shiao Lan Kung | Chinese |
| Susanna Foo | Chinese/New French |
| Totaro's | Eclectic |
| Washington Square | Eclectic |

### Alison at Blue Bell ⓈⱤ  25 | 15 | 21 | $42

*721 Skippack Pike (Penllyn-Blue Bell Pike), Blue Bell, 215-641-2660;*
*www.alisonatbluebell.com*

■ "Superbly done fish" by celebrated chef Alison Barshak attracts the Montgomery County "scene-and-heard" herd to this "minimalist" New American BYO, where they're tended by "knowledgeable" staffers "without an ounce of pretension"; though the "corporate-center" setting can be "as noisy and crowded as the cafeteria at Beverly Hills High" (a dubious bonus: "overhearing neighbors' conversations"), and a few fret Barshak "tries to get too cute with basics", most give thanks for this "suburban salvation."

### BIRCHRUNVILLE STORE CAFE ⓈⱤ  28 | 22 | 25 | $45

*1407 Hollow Rd. (Flowing Springs Rd.), Birchrunville, 610-827-9002;*
*www.birchrunvillestorecafe.com*

■ Francis Trzeciak lures city slickers out to the "bucolic" "wilds of Chester County" with his "superb", "classical yet innovative" "fusion of haute cuisine" from France and Italy that leaves "taste buds happy"; as a result, his "charming", "relaxed", cash-only BYO in a "converted country store" (circa 1792) is one of the highest-rated rooms outside the metropolis; you'll have to reserve a table "at least a month in advance" – so "don't go if you're in a hurry"; N.B. closed Sunday–Tuesday.

### Bluefin Ⓢ  27 | 15 | 23 | $32

*1017 Germantown Pike (Virginia Rd.), Plymouth Meeting, 610-277-3917;*
*www.allthatsushi.com*

■ "No superlative is excessive" for this "tiny", "quaint" Japanese BYO "sleeper" in a Plymouth Meeting mini-mall, where the "wonderful" sushi chef "builds a meal you could only dream of" from his 89 menu offerings; pick up a "six-pack of Kirin" or "your own sake", savants suggest, to round off an "unquestionably" "fabulous" meal; the place is a mere "hole-in-the-wall", however, so "do make reservations" to avoid "terrible waits on busy nights."

### Blue Sage Vegetarian Grille Ⓢ  26 | 13 | 22 | $24

*772 Second Street Pike (Street Rd.), Southampton, 215-942-8888;*
*www.bluesagegrille.com*

■ "Wow! who cares that it's vegetarian?" rhapsodize respondents about Mike and Holly Jackson's "friendly" Bucks County BYO; the "unassuming" "strip-mall location" may "not look like much", but the local "king of veggie fare" exhibits such "exceptional", "artful" takes on the green stuff ("like jazz improvisations" that "take you way out and eventually return to the melody") that even committed carnivores "swoon" and marvel that he "eschews tofu, seitan and mock-anything."

### Brasserie Perrier  26 | 24 | 24 | $52

*1619 Walnut St. (bet. 16th & 17th Sts.), 215-568-3000;*
*www.brasserieperrier.com*

■ "Even New Yorkers" venture south to "linger, dine, enjoy" (and "impress the in-laws") at Georges Perrier's "Le Bec-Fin lite" on Restaurant Row; chef-partner Chris Scarduzio's "phenomenal" New French cuisine pleases "discriminating palates", while aesthetes adore the "sexy, sumptuous" art deco–inspired dining room, where "cultured" staffers deliver "stellar" service without "pretense"; meanwhile, the "happening" lounge bursts with "personality, from clamor to glamour"; P.S. opt for the "$28 prix fixe three-course lunch" to have the BP "experience without selling your first-born."

**BUDDAKAN** | 27 | 27 | 23 | $49 |

*325 Chestnut St. (bet. 3rd & 4th Sts.), 215-574-9440*

■ "Believe the hype", avow disciples, who still swoon ("I died and went to a higher plane") over Stephen Starr's "ab fab", "über-cool" Old City Asian fusion "wonder", voted Philly's Most Popular; culinary connoisseurs "just don't get tired of" Scott Swiderski's "creative", "delicious" dishes, served in the shadow of a 10-ft. golden Buddha by "fast-paced" "young 'uns"; tabs can end up "a little on the completely outrageous side", so most pilgrims achieve true "serenity" only when "on an expense account."

**Carmine's Creole Cafe** | 25 | 13 | 20 | $32 |

*5 Brookline Blvd. (Darby Rd.), Havertown, 610-789-7255;*
*www.carminescreolecafe.com*

■ "Reservations are a must" "even on weeknights" at John Mims's "charming" but "always packed" Cajun-Creole BYO in Havertown; Philly folk even "leave the city" for his "fantastic" she-crab soup and "out-of-this-world" jambalaya that outdoes "95 percent of the places in New Orleans"; surroundings are still "informal" after a recent renovation incorporating a purple-and-gold Mardi Gras theme (which may not be reflected in the Decor score); N.B. credit cards now accepted.

**Citrus** 🅱🍴 | 26 | 14 | 21 | $30 |

*8136 Germantown Ave. (bet. Abington Ave. & Hartwell Ln.),*
*215-247-8188*

■ Vegetarians squash in to this "tiny", "quirky", earth-friendly Eclectic BYO in Chestnut Hill to relish its "amazing" cuisine ("incredible bananas Foster") for surprisingly few greenbacks; because of a no-res policy, however, "plan to wait" or "have a drink across the street and leave your cell number"; however, cynics and carnivores are soured on "pretentious" "political signs" that say "'you can't wear fur', yet they serve fish" (but not meat or poultry).

**Deux Cheminées** 🅱 | 27 | 27 | 26 | $76 |

*1221 Locust St. (bet. 12th & 13th Sts.), 215-790-0200;*
*www.deuxchem.com*

■ "Chef-owner Fritz Blank "continues to outdo himself" and "never ceases to amaze" with the "sublime" French cuisine in his "opulent" 1875 townhouse in Center City; cognoscenti count on a "perfect romantic meal" with "flawless execution" all around ("you'll hug" Blank "after dinner" – then ask to see his "cookbook collection"); the four-course prix fixe dinner is $85, but even if a "home-equity loan may be necessary", it's "worth every cent" to enjoy this "rare treat."

**DJANGO** | 28 | 19 | 25 | $41 |

*526 S. Fourth St. (South St.), 215-922-7151*

■ "Get your speed-dial ready 30 days in advance" if you plan to djingle Bryan Sikora and Aimee Olexy's "hard-to-get-into", 38-seat, Euro-style Eclectic BYO; despite its "understated storefront" setting off South Street, meteoric Food ratings testify to Sikora's "complex", "inventive combinations"; savants suggest "save room" for the "ambrosial cheese course" with Olexy's "commentary", just one aspect of the "expert service."

### Dmitri's
24 | 13 | 19 | $28

*2227 Pine St. (23rd St.), 215-985-3680*
*795 S. Third St. (Catharine St.), 215-625-0556* ⊅
■ Dmitri Chimes' "inexpensive" Med seafood sibs bear a family resemblance – "über-fresh", "no-frills", "top-notch plates" ("divine" grilled octopus), "frazzled" yet "efficient" servers who "deserve Olympic medals for gymnastics in cramped spaces" and "loud, loud, loud" acoustics – but the Queen Village original is a cash-only BYO "shoebox" where regulars cheerfully "wait in line before opening" so they can "sit in their neighbors' laps", while the slightly larger Fitler Square one takes cards and serves liquor.

### Founders
25 | 28 | 26 | $57

*Park Hyatt at the Bellevue, 200 S. Broad St. (Walnut St.), 215-790-2814*
■ "Nothing but top marks" for this "luxurious" New French "high atop the city" in the Park Hyatt at the Bellevue; an "old-money" crowd crows it's "the best value in town", with "top-of-the-line" prix fixes ($24 lunch, $38 pre-theater), a "smart" 500-label cellar and those "stunning", "panoramic" views; meanwhile, servers maintain a "tasteful" air whether you're marking a "special occasion", "taking in-laws to Sunday brunch" ($34.50 buffet) or rushing to get out by curtain time; N.B. chef David Wolf departed post-*Survey.*

### FOUNTAIN RESTAURANT
28 | 28 | 29 | $76

*Four Seasons Hotel, 1 Logan Sq. (bet. Benjamin Franklin Pkwy. & 18th St.), 215-963-1500; www.fourseasons.com*
■ Once again rated the city's No. 1 for Food, the Four Seasons' "always-superb" culinary "mecca" continues to be Philadelphia's favorite venue for "impressing the date or closing the deal"; maestro Martin Hamann's "heavenly" New French–Continental cuisine seems "impervious to the trends du jour"; "experienced" staffers demonstrate "brilliant attention to minuscule details", and the "elegant" room "glistens"; in all, reviewers rhapsodize, "what a grand experience" – of course "you do pay for such excellence"; N.B. jacket required.

### General Warren Inne ⊠
25 | 25 | 24 | $47

*General Warren Inne, Old Lancaster Hwy. (Warren Ave.), Malvern, 610-296-3637; www.generalwarren.com*
■ A Main Liners' "mainstay" in Malvern, this "subdued" Traditional American in a "comfortable old" Revolutionary-era (1745) house "takes you back in time" for "classic favorites" ("crab cakes dispatched from heaven") while "knowledgeable, professional" attendants "make you feel like a million bucks"; fresh-air folks "love the deck out back in spring."

### Gilmore's
27 | 23 | 26 | $51

*133 E. Gay St. (bet. Matlack & Walnut Sts.), West Chester, 610-431-2800; www.gilmoresrestaurant.com*
☑ "Why did Georges Perrier ever let this man leave?" puzzle foodies who find Le Bec-Fin alum Peter Gilmore's Classic French cuisine "as imaginative" as it is "spectacular" every time they celebrate "special occasions" at his "adorable" BYO in West Chester; "warm" staffers are "excellent" as well, though all report it's almost "impossible to get a reservation" due to the restaurant's 35-seat capacity (so "cramped" that you might "eat your neighbor's salad" and "so noisy that the chef probably couldn't hear our compliments").

### High Street Caffé
26 | 18 | 22 | $32

*322 S. High St. (Dean St.), West Chester, 610-696-7435;*
*www.highstreetcafe.com*

■ It might be "decorated like a New Orleans cathouse" ("very small and very purple", with big mirrors on the walls) but this "funky" Cajun-Creole BYO in West Chester has one of the area's most "creative" kitchens, conjuring up "spicy", "mystical creations" that will leave you "begging for more" ("don't order 'voodoo' anything without medication"); waiters are "so friendly you want to take them home", and the "noisy, delightfully young", Big Easy–esque vibe is enhanced by "swank jazz" on weekends.

### Jake's
26 | 21 | 24 | $51

*4365 Main St. (bet. Grape & Levering Sts.), 215-483-0444;*
*www.jakesrestaurant.com*

■ "You can never go wrong" at Bruce Cooper's "Manayunk mainstay", which still gets a "thumbs-up" for "consistently" "splendid" New American cuisine that makes you want to "lick the plates clean"; "charm to the max" and "stellar service" "take the worry out of entertaining for business or pleasure"; a mid-*Survey* redo bumped up the "minimalist" surroundings, but at busy times patrons are still "packed in like sardines", and parking remains a "royal pain."

### La Bonne Auberge
27 | 26 | 24 | $68

*Village 2 Apartment Complex, 1 Rittenhouse Circle (Mechanic St.), New Hope, 215-862-2462; www.bonneauberge.com*

☑ "Close your eyes and you are on the Continent" exclaim enthusiasts of this "intimate" Haute French; actually, it's located in a New Hope "condo complex", but still "worth the effort to find" for "special-occasion" dining, most maintain, due to Gerard Caronello's "fantastic" cooking and the "warm, attentive" service; some urge "eat before you go", though, because of "small" portions that don't justify "high prices"; N.B. open Thursday–Sunday for dinner only.

### LACROIX AT THE RITTENHOUSE
28 | 27 | 26 | $74

*Rittenhouse Hotel, 210 W. Rittenhouse Sq. (bet. Locust & Walnut Sts.), 215-790-2533; www.rittenhousehotel.com*

■ "Ooh-la-la!" gush gastronomes over Jean-Marie Lacroix's "sleek", formal Classic French "masterpiece" in the Rittenhouse Hotel; they love his "extraordinary concept": "scrumptious" "tasting menus" of three ($55), four ($65) or five ($75) small plates (lunch, a "foodie's bargain", is $24 for four courses); the "airy" "minimalist" design and view of the Square are "as conducive to a romantic dinner as to a power lunch", and a "congenial" staff "overlooks nothing"; it's "worth every dollar your platinum card is debited."

### L'Angolo
25 | 17 | 21 | $31

*1415 Porter St. (Broad St.), 215-389-4252*

■ "I wish it could stay a secret" sigh stalwarts smitten by Davide and Katheryn Faenza's "tiny, charming" BYO boîte, an "offbeat oasis" "not far from the stadiums" in South Philly; they cherish "authentic" Boot "basics" ("killer pasta") that will satisfy even "your picky Italian father", "amiable service" and comfy "amber-colored" environs "like a neighbor's living room"; "if you haven't been there yet, good luck getting a table", but when you do "you're going to be happy."

### LE BAR LYONNAIS ⊠
28 | 23 | 25 | $54

*1523 Walnut St. (bet. 15th & 16th Sts.), 215-567-1000;*
*www.lebecfin.com*

■ Beloved by the "Botox" crowd who "take someone they want to seduce", this "clubby" bistro/bar hidden in Le Bec-Fin's "glamorous cellar" is the "casual alternative" to the main room upstairs; bargain-hunters beam it's a way to "get a taste of Perrier" – LBF's "wonderful French fare" and "impeccable" service – at "half the price" ("one can go in jeans and leave with one's shirt"); still, some sing sadly, "smoke gets in your eyes."

### LE BEC-FIN ⊠
28 | 28 | 28 | $120

*1523 Walnut St. (bet. 15th & 16th Sts.), 215-567-1000;*
*www.lebecfin.com*

■ "To hell with carbs, fats and money" – Georges Perrier's oh-so-"elegant" Center City "institution" (a "magnificent dinosaur, thank God") is the "perfect splurge" during a "bull market"; his legions laud "*le best*" French cuisine ("every morsel a thrill" – plus a "Volkswagen-size dessert cart"), recently "toned-down" Victorian decor and a staff so "attentive" "you'll feel like a movie star"; in all, it's "better" and "cheaper than flying to Paris" – though with three-figure dinner prices, it's "not for the thin of wallet."

### Little Fish ⊅
25 | 11 | 21 | $31

*600 Catharine St. (6th St.), 215-413-3464*

■ "As crowded as a can of sardines" ("you can seat more people in your car"), John Tiplitz's "charming" "one-man" seafood BYO in Queen Village nevertheless does a whale of a job with "inspired" surf suppers and "unobtrusive" service; staffers "pay attention to you but also stay back" when not needed, and, hey, "if you have a question for the chef, he's right there"; P.S. the "small size means reservations are absolutely required."

### Mainland Inn
26 | 23 | 25 | $46

*17 Main St. (Wambold Rd.), Mainland, 215-256-8500*

■ "Business dinners", "birthdays" and other "special occasions" draw diners to this "consistent" "old friend", a "traditional" New American in central Montgomery County that's among the "best of the burbs"; a "stellar" menu, "elegant" atmosphere and staff that "bends over backwards and sideways" all make it popular with big spenders whose "Porsches, Mercedeses and BMWs" sit "lined up in the lot like steeds awaiting their riders."

### Meritage Philadelphia ⊠
– | – | – | VE

*500 S. 20th St. (Lombard St.), 215-985-1922;*
*www.meritagephiladelphia.com*

Veteran restaurateurs James Colabelli and Taylor Barneby not only run this *très élégant* Euro-Eclectic jewel box in Center City, but they also wait tables to assure perfection; the menu is stocked with modern twists on old-school faves and there's a 250-label wine list; N.B. it rhymes with heritage.

### Morimoto
27 | 27 | 25 | $74

*723 Chestnut St. (bet. 7th & 8th Sts.), 215-413-9070;*
*www.morimotorestaurant.com*

■ Nobu no more: this storefront near Washington Square from '*Iron Chef* Japanese' Masaharu Morimoto and Stephen Starr is a "transporting visual and culinary experience" not unlike a tongue-

"titillating" "*Star Trek* episode"; "sensual" "techno-funk" interiors attract "Philly's who's who" for "ambrosial" omakase ("omigodzi!"); service, while "skilled", seems to some "too rehearsed" and the meal will "cost you $2 per bite", but after tasting and judgment almost all agree the Food Network star "reigns supreme."

**Nan** ⊠      | 25 | 16 | 20 | $36 |

*4000 Chestnut St. (40th St.), 215-382-0818*

■ "This is why Philly is so fat", sigh satisfied surveyors who smile at Kamol Phutlek's "splendid" specialties, in which he deploys "French culinary techniques" and Thai "flavor combinations" with "fantastic" results; at his "casual", "relaxing" BYO in an "aesthetically challenged" slice of University City, service is "friendly" (if sometimes "abysmally slow"), and a renovation at press time is expected to address nan-descript, "one-step-up-from-a-luncheonette" decor.

**Ota-Ya**      | 26 | 17 | 22 | $33 |

*10 Cambridge Ln. (Sycamore St.), Newtown, 215-860-6814; www.ota-ya.com*

■ "Bring your copy of the *Tale of Genji*" and "all the sake you can drink" to this "genuine-article" Japanese in Newtown, which makes only a "few concessions to Western cuisine" (fortunately, "forks are available if needed"); you're sure to "recognize the regulars" eating "imaginative sushi" and "creative specials" ferried about the "low-key" room by "attitude"-free staffers.

**Overtures**      | 25 | 22 | 23 | $46 |

*609 E. Passyunk Ave. (bet. Bainbridge & South Sts.), 215-627-3455*

■ It "deserves a standing ovation" rhapsodize respondents who sing arias about this "charming" French-Med BYO "oasis" "off crazy South Street"; they savor the "*saveur*" of "elegant" fare "done very well every time" ("the midweek fixed-price menu may be the best bargain in the city"), a "courteous", "unpretentious" staff and "grand yet intimate" atmosphere ("you want romance, this is romance"); the only sour note is struck by those who wish the menu changed more often.

**¡Pasión!**      | 26 | 24 | 24 | $55 |

*211 S. 15th St. (bet. Locust & Walnut Sts.), 215-875-9895*

■ People are "passionate" about the "swimmingly delish" seviche and other "inventive", "flavorful" fare at Guillermo Pernot's "sexy", "highbrow" Nuevo Latino in Center City; sit in the airy, shuttered dining room to "feel like you're in the tropics" or at the "open kitchen's counter" to "watch the action"; even "novices" and "fish haters" can trust the "informative, helpful" staff, so "come with an adventurous palate" – and, if possible, "an expense account."

**Peking**      | 25 | 19 | 21 | $28 |

*Granite Run Mall, 1067 E. Baltimore Pike (Middletown Rd.), Media, 610-566-4110*

■ "The food is always a wow" at Margaret Kuo's high-class Asian, where "creative" Chinese and Japanese menus allow for "wonderful combinations" ("sushi followed by Peking duck") and "servers try to be as helpful as possible"; in short, "get over" the Granite Run Mall location – hey, it "saves a trip to Center City" – because this is not one of those "greasy" "red-and-gold" Delaware County joints.

### Pif
| 25 | 14 | 22 | $42 |

*Italian Mkt., 1009 S. Eighth St. (bet. Carpenter St. & Washington Ave.), 215-625-2923*

■ "Don't publish this!" beg fans of this "hard-to-get-into", BYO French bistro in "the heart of Italian South Philly"; David Ansill has a "delightful European touch" and "just enough attitude" when he "wanders" the "cramped" dining room "during meals", while staffers provide "personal" attention; even with "no-froufrou" environs and a "lack of scenesters", rising tabs suggest the owners have "priced themselves out of the area"; N.B. closed Tuesdays.

### Prime Rib
| 25 | 25 | 24 | $61 |

*Radisson Plaza Warwick Hotel, 1701 Locust St. (17th St.), 215-772-1701; www.theprimerib.com*

■ People primed for a *Flintstones*-size slab" of "tender, flavorful" beef can "step back in time" to this "Atkins heaven" in Center City's Warwick Hotel, a "luxe", "swanky" chain link "reminiscent of '40s supper clubs"; live piano music and a dress code (gentlemen must wear jackets) "make it even more special" and well-trained, tuxedoed attendants "set a high bar for service", though a few recalcitrant razzers rib it's "stodgy" and "starchy."

### Savona
| 26 | 26 | 25 | $64 |

*100 Old Gulph Rd. (Rte. 320), Gulph Mills, 610-520-1200; www.savonarestaurant.com*

■ You "feel like you've entered another world" at Dominique and Sabine Filoni's "exotic" and "lovely" Riviera-inspired Main Line Franco-Italian, where "high rollers" "rub elbows" over "sublime" cuisine (including "stand-out seafood" dishes) and a "fantastic wine list" thanks to "impeccable but not intrusive service" from a "knowledgeable staff"; given the "private-jet prices", though, it's a "splurge" best enjoyed on "someone else's tab."

### Shiao Lan Kung
| 25 | 8 | 17 | $20 |

*930 Race St. (bet. 9th & 10th Sts.), 215-928-0282*

■ "Never mind the decor – just try the salt-baked" shrimp ("utter perfection"), "excellent hot pots" or other "unusual items prepared sizzling and fresh" at this "no-frills" but "insanely great and authentic" Chinatown BYO packed with "many Chinese patrons"; its "friendly staff" "isn't flustered by crowds", fortunately, and it's open "after midnight" to "satiate late-night cravings."

### Susanna Foo
| 26 | 24 | 24 | $57 |

*1512 Walnut St. (bet. 15th & 16th Sts.), 215-545-2666; www.susannafoo.com*

☑ You'll be "smiling for hours after" dining at this "sophisticated" Asian-French "standout" on Restaurant Row, according to acolytes of "wonderful chef" and "innovator" Susanna Foo, who challenges patrons to "put aside all preconceptions about Chinese food" with "breathtaking" dishes that take many "to new heights of rapture"; still, Foo fighters find the "petite portions" "ridiculously small" ("you might need two entrees") and say it's best "if someone else pays."

### Swann Lounge ◗
| 26 | 27 | 27 | $50 |

*Four Seasons Hotel, 1 Logan Sq. (Benjamin Franklin Pkwy. & 18th St.), 215-963-1500; www.fourseasons.com*

■ "If you want the Fountain without the formality" (or "the cost"), this "other restaurant in the Four Seasons" will "wow" you with "great dining" amid more "casual" yet nevertheless "lovely" surroundings; count on "delicious" New American–New French cuisine and "unpretentiously superb" service from your vantage point "overlooking the beautiful [Benjamin Franklin] Parkway"; P.S. "the Sunday brunch is a little slice of heaven."

### Totaro's
25 13 20 $47

*729 E. Hector St. (bet. Righter & Walnut Sts.), Conshohocken, 610-828-9341*

■ "From the outside, you'd never guess" this "intimate" Italian-leaning Eclectic in a Conshohocken bar is thought to be "one of the best" in the region, but respondents rave "wait till you taste the food"; the kitchen consistently turns out "obscenely decadent" cuisine (including "interesting game" such as rabbit, buffalo and ostrich) "presented with panache" by a "cordial", "well-trained" staff; meanwhile, devotees debate whether decor is "overpriced or under-decorated."

### Vetri ⊠
28 23 27 $73

*1312 Spruce St. (bet. Broad & 13th Sts.), 215-732-3478*

■ "Leave your preconceptions about Italian food out on Spruce Street" and just "put yourself in Marc Vetri's hands"; at his "elegant" brownstone in Center City he'll put on an "astounding" "virtuoso display of creative cooking", while "personalized service" "anticipates your every need"; a few grumble that "the portions are teeny, the place too small and the bill too big", but it's still "easier to hit Powerball than to secure a reservation" here for Saturday night – and you may need the jackpot to cover the tab.

### Washington Square
– – – VE

*210 W. Washington Sq. (bet. Locust & St.James Sts.), 215-592-7787*

Stephen Starr has set up shop on long-overlooked Washington Square with this Eclectic featuring a menu assembled by NYC's culinary dynamo Marcus Samuelsson; global street food is the inspiration, but you won't find hot dogs or soft pretzels here – instead, you choose from small, medium and large plates (watermelon endive salad with serrano ham and goat cheese, jerk pork belly); diners enter through a dramatic, all-white garden created by Todd Oldham and proceed into three swank rooms designed by New York's Rockwell Group.

# Phoenix/Scottsdale

## TOP 10 FOOD RANKING

| Restaurant | Cuisine |
|---|---|
| **27** T. Cooks | Mediterranean |
| Michael's at the Citadel | New American |
| Pizzeria Bianco | Pizza |
| Mastro's | Steakhouse |
| **26** Mary Elaine's | New French |
| Marquesa | Mediterranean |
| Vincent Guerithault | New French/SW |
| **25** La Hacienda | Mexican |
| Convivo | New American/SW |
| Roy's | Hawaii Regional |

## ADDITIONAL NOTEWORTHY PLACES

| Christopher's Fermier | French Bistro |
|---|---|
| Cyclo | Vietnamese |
| Eddie V's Edgewater | Seafood |
| Houston's | American |
| Leccabaffi | Italian |
| Lon's at the Hermosa | New American/SW |
| P.F. Chang's | Chinese |
| Rancho Pinot Grill | New American |
| Roaring Fork | Western |
| Sassi | Southern Italian |

| F | D | S | C |
|---|---|---|---|

### Christopher's Fermier Bistro

| 24 | 21 | 22 | $43 |
|---|---|---|---|

*Biltmore Fashion Park, 2584 E. Camelback Rd. (N. 24th St.), Phoenix, 602-522-2344; www.fermier.com*

■ It's the "only real choice for Francophiles" insist devotees of this "informal" yet "refined" French brasserie known for its "off-the-charts" truffle-infused prime sirloin and "amazing wine list" (with some 100 selections available by the glass); chef-owner Christopher Gross, "one of the Valley's shining stars", keeps the mood "laid-back" while making sure that his "sumptuous" dishes are "served with verve"; P.S. it's a "great spot" to spend a "long, lazy Saturday afternoon" "after power shopping" at the Biltmore.

### Convivo ⌧

| 25 | 15 | 23 | $38 |
|---|---|---|---|

*Walgreens Shopping Ctr., 7000 N. 16th St. (E. Glendale Ave.), Phoenix, 602-997-7676*

■ "Glad it's in my neighborhood" cheer cultists who could happily eat Jeffrey Beeson's "fantastic" Southwestern-inspired New American cooking "every day"; though the "nondescript strip-mall" setting "leaves a lot to be desired", regulars don't mind, since the "friendly" chef "uses the freshest local ingredients possible" in his recently expanded and often-changing menu and presents his dishes in a most "imaginative way."

### Cyclo ⑤                                    – | – | – | I |
*1919 W. Chandler Blvd. (Dobson Rd.), Chandler, 480-963-4490;*
*www.go-cyclo.com*

Phoenix foodies flock to this charming, contemporary and often
crowded East Valley Vietnamese, where owner and menu designer
Justina Duong (who also painted the jungle mural) puts the
traditional dishes of her homeland in a modern context; she
serves up Southeast Asian standards (pho, crêpes, green-papaya
salad) as well as her own fusion flights of fancy (pork short ribs
with Thai basil, jasmine crème brûlée) – but no booze, so BYO.

### Eddie V's Edgewater Grille          25 | 24 | 21 | $43 |
*20715 N. Pima Rd. (E. Thompson Peak Pkwy.), Scottsdale,*
*480-538-8468; eddiev.com*

☑ The "superb" Gulf Coast seafood, "expertly prepared" and
"imaginatively" plated, reels in fin fanatics at this "sleek" North
Scottsdale two-year-old; though some say the service is "uneven",
admirers deem this "welcome addition" "promising" given the
"impeccable" cooking, "sophisticated", "inviting" surroundings
and live nightly entertainment (jazz, blues) in the lounge; P.S. you'll
"love the patio" overlooking the McDowell Mountains.

### HOUSTON'S                            21 | 19 | 20 | $27 |
*Camelback Esplanade, 2425 E. Camelback Rd. (24th St.), Phoenix,*
*602-957-9700*
*6113 N. Scottsdale Rd. (bet. E. Lincoln & E. McDonald Drs.),*
*Scottsdale, 480-922-7775*
*www.houstons.com*

☑ "Utterly consistent", these "safe bets" are an "excellent
value" for "solid" American standards (the "best spinach dip in
the universe", "yum-yum" soups and salads, "juicy burgers");
to avoid the "after-work crush" of "young professionals" at the
bar, insiders know to "go at off-hours" when the "team-server
approach" makes for a "well-oiled machine"; detractors, however,
dismiss what they call its "unremarkable" "chain food" and
complain about the "hurried" atmosphere.

### La Hacienda ⑤                         25 | 25 | 25 | $47 |
*Fairmont Scottsdale Princess, 7575 E. Princess Dr.*
*(bet. Pima & Scottsdale Rds.), Scottsdale, 480-585-4848;*
*www.fairmont.com/scottsdale*

■ There's "not a burrito in sight" at this "plush" and "relaxed"
"gourmet Mexican" tucked away at the Fairmont Scottsdale
Princess resort; instead, supporters cite "strolling mariachis",
"delicious margaritas" and signature roast suckling pig carved
tableside; although a few detractors declare that food and service
have "declined" of late, most maintain that this "romantic",
"traditional" spot is still the "cream of the crop."

### Leccabaffi                            25 | 18 | 21 | $44 |
*Mountain View Plaza, 9719 N. Hayden Rd. (E. Mountain View Rd.),*
*Scottsdale, 480-609-0429; www.leccabaffi.com*

☑ It's "like being in Italy" say diners devoted to this "authentic"
North Scottsdale trattoria where chef-owner Giovanni Scorzo
wanders all over The Boot, cooking up "great grilled antipasti",
"wonderful pastas" and "incredible" regional specialties; his
dishes are so "infused with rich flavors" that you'll be "licking
your mustache" (per the translation of its whimsical moniker), but

"disappointed" dissenters who deem it "overrated and overpriced" want to know "what's the big deal?"; N.B. closed Mondays.

**Lon's at the Hermosa**          25 | 27 | 23 | $49
*Hermosa Inn, 5532 N. Palo Cristi Rd. (E. Stanford Dr.), Paradise Valley, 602-955-7878; www.lons.com*

■ Once the "classic adobe" ranch house of cowboy artist Lon Megargee, this "secret hideaway in Paradise Valley" overlooking Camelback Mountain offers "romantic" meals in a "picturesque" interior of beehive fireplaces, rustic wood beams and vintage photos or on a "glorious" patio "under the stars"; inside or out, you get "incredible" Southwestern-accented New American cuisine with Central and South American influences; N.B. the Food rating may not reflect a post-*Survey* chef and menu change.

**Marquesa**          26 | 27 | 26 | $61
*Fairmont Scottsdale Princess, 7575 E. Princess Dr. (bet. Pima & N. Scottsdale Rds.), Scottsdale, 480-585-4848; www.fairmont.com/scottsdale*

■ "Absolutely beautiful", this "top-notch" North Scottsdale Mediterranean is a "foodie's delight", "from the imaginative appetizers" to the "exotic" entrees to the "fabulous desserts"; the "flawless" service means that guests are "treated like royalty", resulting in a "truly marvelous experience that makes any meal a special occasion"; of course it comes with a "big price tag", but "what's not to love" here?; P.S. its "amazing" Spanish market-style Sunday brunch, set outside in the courtyard, is "second to none."

**MARY ELAINE'S** ⌧          26 | 28 | 27 | $74
*The Phoenician, 6000 E. Camelback Rd. (N. 60th St.), Scottsdale, 480-423-2530; www.thephoenician.com*

■ "Bring your sweetheart" to this "gorgeous" room at The Phoenician for an "incredible dining experience" replete with "breathtaking views" of city lights and "exquisite" New French dishes "fit for a sultan (at prices to match)"; "doting" servers tend to the "tiniest details", even giving ladies "special footstools for their handbags" ("heaven forbid your Prada should touch the floor"); N.B. the Food rating may not reflect a post-*Survey* chef change; also, summer hours are limited, so call for availability.

**MASTRO'S STEAKHOUSE**          27 | 23 | 25 | $55
*La Miranda, 8852 E. Pinnacle Peak Rd. (Pima Rd.), Scottsdale, 480-585-9500; www.mastrossteakhouse.com*

■ Never mind that the "stylish lounge" at this "bold and brassy" chophouse in North Scottsdale is "populated by spaghetti-strapped young things" and "ancient swingers", because if you proceed to the "smartly decorated" dining room, you'll be treated to the "best steaks in town", accompanied by an impressive list of California wines and "martinis the size of fishbowls"; even if it's "noisy" and "pricey", the "people-watching is super" and you'll "love that doggy bag" tomorrow.

**MICHAEL'S AT THE CITADEL**          27 | 24 | 25 | $51
*The Citadel, 8700 E. Pinnacle Peak Rd. (Pima Rd.), Scottsdale, 480-515-2575; www.michaelsrestaurant.com*

■ Chef Michael DeMaria's New American menu, which begins with "artful tasting-spoon appetizers" and concludes with "inventive desserts", is just one reason admirers say it's "worth the drive to Pinnacle Peak"; also earning kudos are the "relaxing, elegant setting" enhanced by an indoor waterfall, as well as the "superb" staff and "knowledgeable sommelier"; P.S. Sunday brunch on the patio overlooking the garden is "a real treat"; N.B. closed Mondays.

### P.F. CHANG'S CHINA BISTRO           21 | 21 | 19 | $28 |
*Chandler Fashion Ctr., 3255 W. Chandler Blvd. (Rte. 101), Chandler, 480-899-0472*
*Scottsdale Fashion Sq., 7014 E. Camelback Rd. (bet. N. Goldwater Blvd. & N. Scottsdale Rd.), Scottsdale, 480-949-2610*
*Kierland Commons, 7132 E. Greenway Pkwy. (N. Scottsdale Rd.), Scottsdale, 480-367-2999*
*www.pfchangs.com*

☑ Perpetually packed, these local outposts of a national chain are collectively ranked the Most Popular restaurant in the Phoenix/ Scottsdale area thanks to devotees delighted with their "snazzy" Sino-style savories, especially "the best lettuce wraps ever"; though purists pan what they call "Americanized" results, most maintain this is "traditional Chinese food made even better"; P.S. those who hated the "long waits" will be pleased to learn that the "no-reservations" policy is no longer in force.

### PIZZERIA BIANCO                     27 | 20 | 21 | $22 |
*Heritage Sq., 623 E. Adams St. (7th St.), Phoenix, 602-258-8300*
■ Anointed "the patron saint of pizza" by legions of pie partisans, chef-owner Chris Bianco makes the "best wood-fired pizzas in town" – "hands down" – thanks to his relentless "focus" on "good, simple" ingredients and "attention to quality"; of course, this "historic" "little brick building Downtown is always busy", but the "freshness" of his handmade mozzarella alone makes it "well worth the wait"; besides, on weekend evenings patrons can "chill in his wine bar", Bar Bianco, next door.

### Rancho Pinot Grill 🕱                25 | 20 | 23 | $43 |
*Lincoln Vlg., 6208 N. Scottsdale Rd. (E. Lincoln Dr.), Scottsdale, 480-367-8030*
■ "Let's see, where to start?" muse regulars as they explain why this "local favorite", a "comfortable" "little gem", always exudes such "a good buzz"; first, Chrysa Kaufman's New American dishes are "awesome" (her "homey" signature fare includes Nonni's Sunday chicken – so "good" "you may never order anything else" here); then there's husband Tom's "top-flight" wine cellar, the "secluded setting" and the "most individualized" service; "bravo!"

### Roaring Fork                        25 | 21 | 23 | $40 |
*Finova Bldg., 4800 N. Scottsdale Rd. (Chaparral Rd.), Scottsdale, 480-947-0795; www.roaringfork.com*
■ "Charming" chef-owner Robert McGrath, a former Texan with a flair for cooking "hearty campfire food", rules the range at his bistro, which turns out Western cooking "with a true gourmet touch"; though many look forward to settling in at dinnertime over his pork porterhouse with a side of green-chile macaroni, others prefer to show up early for the "best happy hour in town", washing down their 'big-ass burger' with a huckleberry margarita; with "everyone having such a good time", expect "crowds" and "noise."

### ROY'S                               25 | 22 | 22 | $43 |
*J. W. Marriott Desert Ridge Resort & Spa, 5350 E. Marriott Drive (Deer Valley Rd. & Tatum Blvd.), Phoenix, 480-419-7697*

(continued)
**ROY'S**
*Scottsdale Seville, 7001 N. Scottsdale Rd. (E. Indian Bend Rd.),*
*Scottsdale, 480-905-1155*
*www.roysrestaurant.com*
☑ "Hip" and "energetic", these two "see-and-be-seen" outposts
of Roy Yamaguchi's Hawaii Regional dynasty "don't have that
chain feel" say loyalists who love the "must-have" potstickers,
"heavenly" chocolate soufflé and "everything in between"; while
a disgruntled few are put off by their "shopping center" locations
and "inconsistent" service, most are always ready to "sit outdoors"
on the patio and "imagine themselves on a tropical isle."

**Sassi** – – – M
*10455 E. Pinnacle Peak Pkwy. (Alma School Rd.), Scottsdale,*
*480-502-9095; www.sassi.biz*
Situated on six acres of North Scottsdale desert in the foothills of
Pinnacle Peak, this $10 million replica of an Italian estate boasts
fountains, trellises, vaulted ceilings, stone fireplaces and terra-
cotta tile; executive chef Wade Moises makes sure the kitchen
keeps up with its surroundings by concocting his own *salumi* as
part of an ambitious seasonal menu inspired by the rustic dishes
of Southern Italy (outstanding options include smoky lamb sausage
and fig-studded semifreddo).

**T. COOK'S** 27 28 26 $53
*Royal Palms Hotel & Casitas, 5200 E. Camelback Rd. (bet. N. Arcadia Dr. &*
*N. 56th St.), Phoenix, 602-808-0766; www.royalpalmshotel.com*
■ Nestled at the base of Camelback Mountain in a "charming",
"upscale resort" that still bears traces of the Spanish estate it
once was, this "gorgeous" "special-occasion" "destination" is
"the epitome of fine dining" in Phoenix and therefore No. 1 for
Food in the area; enthusiasts make it a point to "bring out-of-
town guests" here for the "whole package", which includes
"outstanding" Mediterranean cuisine, "classy but not stuffy"
service and a "cozy piano bar" redolent of "romance"; N.B. the
Food rating may not reflect a post-*Survey* chef change.

**Vincent Guerithault on Camelback** 26 21 24 $52
*3930 E. Camelback Rd. (N. 40th St.), Phoenix, 602-224-0225;*
*www.vincentsoncamelback.com*
☑ A "pioneer" in French-Southwestern "fusion", "delightful" chef-
owner Vincent Guerithault turns out "phantasmagorical" fare
that screams "special occasion" in every bite; long setting the
"standard" in Phoenix, his "romantic" refuge (recently redone to
make it reminiscent of a Provençal country inn) still provides a
"great dining experience", but doubters who find it "disappointing
after all the hype" feel it suffers from "missed details."

# Portland, OR

## TOP 10 FOOD RANKING

| Restaurant | Cuisine |
|---|---|
| **27** Genoa | Italian |
| Paley's Place | French/Pacific NW |
| Higgins | Pacific NW |
| Saburo's | Japanese |
| Heathman | French/Pacific NW |
| **26** Pho Van | Vietnamese |
| El Gaucho | Steakhouse/Continental |
| Castagna | French/Italian |
| Lemongrass | Thai |
| Caffe Mingo | Italian |

## ADDITIONAL NOTEWORTHY PLACES

| | |
|---|---|
| bluehour | New American/Med. |
| Caprial's Bistro | Pacific NW |
| clarklewis | New American/Pacific NW |
| Giorgio's | Italian |
| Jake's Famous Crawfish | Seafood |
| Joel Palmer House | Pacific NW |
| Lucy's Table | French/Italian |
| McCormick & Schmick's | Seafood |
| ¡Oba! | Nuevo Latino |
| Wildwood | Pacific NW |

| F | D | S | C |
|---|---|---|---|

### bluehour ☒
22 | 25 | 21 | $43

*Wieden & Kennedy Headquarters, 250 NW 13th Ave. (Everett St.), 503-226-3394; www.bluehouronline.com*

☑ With its "gorgeously chic setting", this "hip, hip, hip" "hot spot" in the "trendy Pearl District" offers "a bit of New York in Portland", where the smitten swoon for chef-partner Kenny Giambalvo's "creative menu" of New American–Med dishes such as "excellent scallops" wrapped in bacon and "to-die-for gnocchi with truffle sauce"; still, some are "underwhelmed" by the "sometimes inconsistent" kitchen and certain "snooty" staffers that seem like "supermodels who forgot to smile"; N.B. closed Sundays.

### Caffe Mingo
26 | 20 | 22 | $29

*807 NW 21st Ave. (Johnson St.), 503-226-4646*

☑ Despite "tables practically on top of each other", the "creative, rustic" *cucina* and "laid-back" servers ensure this "tiny" trattoria "beats out its fancier neighbors" on "Northwest's Italian Restaurant Row"; while the "no-reservations [policy for parties of fewer than six] can be a hassle", it's "worth the wait" – just "stand outside and enjoy a good glass of wine" or beer, soaking up the "cognoscenti cool" at the bar.

### Caprial's Bistro ⌷    26 | 20 | 23 | $36
*7015 SE Milwaukie Ave. (Bybee Blvd.), 503-236-6457; www.caprial.com*
■ The "PBS celebrity" chef's "zest is evident" in her often "Asian-inspired" "Pacific Northwest cuisine with zing", served by "attentive staffers" in this "light, airy" Westmoreland venue she co-owns with husband John "in a lovely neighborhood, with their cooking school nearby"; but it may be the "walls lined with wines" "at store prices" that prompt Pence-ive proponents to proclaim "Caprial, we love you!"

### Castagna/Cafe Castagna ⌷    26 | 21 | 24 | $43
*1752 SE Hawthorne Blvd. (18th Ave.), 503-231-7373*
☑ When seeking a "place to take food-loving friends", look no further than Ladd's Addition and this "elegant" eatery, acclaimed for its "consistently stunning" French-Italian fare created "with a loving eye on local sources" and dished by "super-efficient servers"; the sensitive sense an "aloof" "attitude" in the "high prices" and "stylish" if "sterile" decor, but no one minds that "you don't have to struggle with parking Downtown"; N.B. its Cafe next door offers casual bistro fare.

### clarklewis ⌷    – | – | – | E
*Eastbank Commerce Ctr., 1001 SE Water Ave. (bet. Taylor & Yamhill Sts.), 503-235-2294*
Bucking convention, this newcomer on the industrial East Side provides guests with flashlights for menu reading in its dim, cavernous dining area, and departure from the norm continues in the kitchen, where ever-inventive chef Morgan Brownlow creates rave-worthy New American–Pacific NW dishes (offered in three portion sizes), including homemade pastas, house-smoked meats and fried vegetables fairy-dusted with batter.

### El Gaucho ◑    26 | 22 | 26 | $51
*The Benson Hotel, 319 SW Broadway (bet. Oak & Stark Sts.), 503-227-8794; www.elgaucho.com*
☑ Carnivores crow over the "mouthwatering steaks" at this "barely lit", "trendy" Downtown "men's club" where business tycoons and pro athletes enjoy the "royal treatment", with everything from "live Latin guitars" to Continental "creations" "prepared tableside" with "retro" flair; of course, all this costs "obscene amounts of money", causing the cost-conscious to call it "El Gouge-o"; N.B. now serving lunch on weekdays.

### GENOA    27 | 21 | 27 | $71
*2832 SE Belmont St. (bet. 28th & 29th Aves.), 503-238-1464*
☑ "Be prepared to devote an entire evening to dining bliss" declare devotees of this "intimate", "elegant-but-unpretentious" "grande dame" on funky Belmont Street that's "expensive but worth saving for", given its "haute Italian" prix fixes "served dotingly by people" who "describe the courses like the parts of their lover's body"; even the "delighted" declare the digs "need updating", but when you're "perennially Portland's best" (No. 1 for Food), why worry?

### Giorgio's ⌷    24 | 23 | 24 | $36
*1131 NW Hoyt St. (12th St.), 503-221-1888*
■ "Beautiful presentation" and a "panoply of tastes" mark the "out-of-this-world" Italian fare prepared with French technique by chef

Michael Clancy at this "pearl in the Pearl" with tile floors, brocaded banquettes and a bar that's "right out of Rome"; "warm and personable" owner Giorgio Kawas and his "genial staff" "treat everyone like family" within the "intimate", "welcoming space."

### HEATHMAN      27 | 24 | 25 | $43

*The Heathman Hotel, 1001 SW Broadway (Salmon St.), 503-790-7752*
■ "Every plate is a masterpiece" in the "delicious marriage of French and healthy Pacific Northwest" fare in chef Philippe Boulot's hotel dining room, which also offers an "extensive wine list" and a beloved brunch presided over by a "stellar" staff; smack-dab in the center of the Cultural District's "sidewalk action", it's "a great place to take out-of-towners", whether for jazz and "Xmas-season high tea" in the "elegant" historic lobby or a light "before-show dinner" in the Marble Bar.

### HIGGINS RESTAURANT & BAR ◐      27 | 23 | 25 | $39

*1239 SW Broadway (Jefferson St.), 503-222-9070*
■ "Prof. [Greg] Higgins, I could have dined all night" – so sing supporters of the chef-owner's "dark, woody" Cultural District Downtowner dedicated to "distinctively Oregonian" (and often organic), seasonal "haute comfort food" served by an "exceedingly knowledgeable, well-trained staff"; however, "to keep the tab affordable", regulars recommend dining in the "cozy adjoining bar", a "respite for foodies in need of a beer" (there's "an amazing selection") and "a fabulous stop before or after the theater."

### JAKE'S FAMOUS CRAWFISH      24 | 21 | 23 | $35

*401 SW 12th Ave. (Stark St.), 503-226-1419;*
*www.jakesfamouscrawfish.com*
☑ "Nothing is more venerable" than this Downtown "institution", "still bustling and noisy" after 113 years with "nonstop tourist crowds" consuming "super-fresh fish" and "old-faithful" fare ("pan-fried oysters and local beers"), served by "waiters who are 'lifers'" amid "historic paintings" and "wood paneling" (wags wager the "decor hasn't changed since 1899 or so"); some salty dogs sniff it's "spendy", but they're swamped by satisfied sailors who proclaim it Portland's Most Popular.

### Joel Palmer House ⊠      25 | 23 | 23 | $44

*600 Ferry St. (6th St.), Dayton, 503-864-2995; www.joelpalmerhouse.com*
☑ "Everyone should make a pilgrimage" to this "beautiful" and "historic house" "in the heart of wine country", where Jack Czarnecki, "the nation's foremost mycologist/chef", "shares mushroom-hunting stories" and a "heavy" Northwest menu of "wonderful dishes" that feature fungi, including "fresh-picked black-and-white truffles", along with "outstanding Oregon Pinots"; despite occasionally "immature" service, most get happily high on this "shrine to 'shrooms in all their glory."

### Lemongrass ⊠≠      26 | 18 | 17 | $24

*1705 NE Couch St. (17th Ave.), 503-231-5780*
☑ It's "well worth the wait" that "will whet your appetite" at what Northeast natives call the "best Thai west of the Mississippi", where "the curries are fabulous" and the "perfectly balanced" "flavors of each dish are explosive"; just be aware that the kitchen crew really "means business when they say 'hot'" and members of the "shorthanded [staff] can be slow", as they navigate the "funky old house."

### Lucy's Table ☒  24 | 23 | 25 | $35
*704 NW 21st Ave. (NW Irving St.), 503-226-6126;*
*www.lucystable.com*
■ They all love Lucy, and not just for the "personal touch" of the "warm hosts" or the "chummy" staff that spreads a "contagious feeling" through the "cozy" Nob Hill haunt; almost as appealing are the "winning chances" the chef takes in combining the "deep, complex flavors" of the French and Italian countryside, including a signature goat cheese ravioli that's "a little slice of heaven."

### MCCORMICK & SCHMICK'S  23 | 21 | 22 | $36
*235 SW First Ave. (bet. Oak & Pine Sts.), 503-224-7522;*
*www.mccormickandschmicks.com*
■ "The original McCormick's" that spawned a nationwide school of seafooders, this Downtown "Portland classic" is a "traditional but not stuffy" destination for a "large selection" of "reliable", "fresh" surf 'n' turf and "cheap happy-hour eats"; take in the "dark-paneled elegance" of the "old-style" "cavernous room" and hum along with the weekend "balcony pianist, who looks as if he's sitting in a gilded frame."

### ¡Oba!  24 | 24 | 22 | $34
*555 NW 12th Ave. (Hoyt St.), 503-228-6161; www.obarestaurant.com*
☑ "Spice your night" with the "sumptuous" "Pan-Hispanic flavors" and "exotic drinks" at this "large", "always buzzing" (read: "noisy") Pearl District Nuevo Latino "scene" whose "gorgeous", colorfully "cosmopolitan" decor makes for "sizzling ambiance"; simply "snag a booth to avoid the din" from the "massive meet-market bar", populated by "girls in black" and "hot guys with good jobs."

### PALEY'S PLACE BISTRO & BAR  27 | 22 | 25 | $43
*1204 NW 21st Ave. (Northrup St.), 503-243-2403*
■ At this "quaint Victorian house" in the Nob Hill district, the "fabulous" Northwest-sourced and "French-influenced menu" comes with "stellar wine selections" and a "personal welcome"; the "convivial atmosphere" may "make intimate conversation difficult", given that "you seem to be on top of your neighbors", but it's all part of the pleasure of this piece of "Paris in Portland."

### Pho Van  26 | 24 | 23 | $23
*1012 NW Glisan St. (10th Ave.), 503-248-2172* ☒
*1919 SE 82nd Ave. (bet. Division & Starks Sts.), 503-788-5244*
*11651 SW Beaverton Hillsdale Hwy. (Canyon Rd.), Beaverton,*
*503-627-0822*
☑ These "pho-nominal" hot spots "put Vietnamese food on the haute-cuisine map"; the fare is "reasonably priced", so they're "packed at lunchtime", and be aware that the "friendly, polished service" "can be slow when [things] get hopping"; N.B. the Beaverton branch opened post-*Survey,* and at press time the 82nd Ave. location is planning to close for a two-month revamp of its decor and menu.

### SABURO'S SUSHI HOUSE  27 | 11 | 16 | $21
*1667 SE Bybee Blvd. (bet. 16th & 17th Aves.), 503-236-4237*
☑ "What more could you want", wonder worshipers of this Westmoreland-Sellwood favorite, than the "freshest" "and biggest sushi portions in the city" ("you could take some home and throw it on the grill for a second meal") offered at the "cheapest

prices"?; true, the no-reservations policy and some staffers' "attitude" can be "trying", but the waits are not as "interminable" since a post-*Survey* expansion of the formerly "nondescript, cramped location" nearly doubled seating capacity.

**WILDWOOD**                25 | 23 | 23 | $41

*1221 NW 21st Ave. (Overton St.), 503-248-9663;*
*www.wildwoodrestaurant.com*

☑ Almost "everyone in Portland serves Northwest fare", but fans still go wild for the "fresh, inventive" dishes – including "the best skillet-roasted mussels anywhere" – turned out by celebrity chef-owner, author and "local treasure Cory Schreiber" in his "fast-moving exhibition kitchen"; his "always-crowded", "noisy dining room", complete with works by "the region's best artists", is "a place to be seen" in the Nob Hill area, so be prepared for "fancy food and a side of 'tude" when you come.

# Salt Lake City & Mountain Resorts

## TOP 10 FOOD RANKING

| | Restaurant | Cuisine |
|---|---|---|
| **27** | Tree Room | Regional American |
| | Red Iguana | Mexican |
| | Mariposa | New American |
| **26** | Michelangelo | Italian |
| | Seafood Buffet | Seafood |
| | Glitretind | New American |
| | Fresco Italian Cafe | Northern Italian |
| | Metropolitan | New American |
| | Martine | Mediterranean |
| **25** | Chez Betty | Continental/American |

## ADDITIONAL NOTEWORTHY PLACES

| | |
|---|---|
| Bambara | New American |
| Chimayo | Southwestern |
| Cucina Toscana | Northern Italian |
| L'Avenue | French Bistro |
| Log Haven | Eclectic |
| Lugano | Northern Italian |
| Market St. Grill | Seafood |
| New Yorker Club | American |
| Snake Creek Grill | American |
| Wahso | Asian Fusion |

| F | D | S | C |
|---|---|---|---|

**Bambara**

| 24 | 25 | 24 | $36 |
|---|---|---|---|

*Hotel Monaco, 202 S. Main St. (200 South), 801-363-5454; www.bambara-slc.com*

■ "Bringing energy and style to Downtown", this "hip", "urban" "favorite" in the "trendy Hotel" Monaco boasts a "busy open kitchen" helmed by "talented chef" Robert Barker, whose "dynamite" New American cuisine "excites foodies' imaginations"; with "swanky decor" and a "hip atmosphere", its "great space" (the historic Continental Bank lobby) is a "nice place to impress your date", but it's "not for a quiet romantic dinner" and "not if you're in a hurry" – so just "sit back, have a drink and take it all in."

**Chez Betty**

| 25 | 18 | 24 | $45 |
|---|---|---|---|

*Copperbottom Inn, 1637 Short Line Rd. (Deer Valley Dr.), Park City, 435-649-8181; www.chezbetty.com*

■ "You can *Betty*" that this "jewel" (named after its resident goldfish) "off Main Street" in Park City's Copperbottom Inn is "a delight" thanks to its "consistent", "creative kitchen's" "innovative menu" of "delicious" Continental–Traditional American fare; partisans praise the "superb, personal service" from the "warm, friendly" staff and "romantic, cozy, intimate" environs that "feel like an auberge", even if a few feel that the decor "needs updating"; P.S. there's "always at least one delicious vegetarian plate" on offer.

### CHIMAYO
24 | 25 | 22 | $43

*368 Main St. (4th St.), Park City, 435-649-6222;*
*www.chimayorestaurant.com*

■ "You're immediately engulfed by a ritzy vibe" and "warm ambiance" "reminiscent of Santa Fe in winter" at this Main Street "Park City favorite" where the "charming" "decor and aromas set the perfect mood"; fans are "impressed with" the "wonderful flavors" featured in its "expensive" but "unusual spins on traditional Southwestern-style food", which are "innovative without being weird" and include "great wild-game selections" such as "the best elk in town"; all told, it's "a must-visit."

### Cucina Toscana ⊠
24 | 21 | 24 | $33

*307 W. Pierpont Ave. (300 West), 801-328-3463;*
*www.cucina-toscana.com*

■ The "warm, welcoming staff" will "make you feel at home" when you visit this "gem" "in the Downtown arts district", where *ciao*-hounds dig into "excellent Northern Italian fare" that's "authentic" ("not that sweet, creamy American stuff") and served in a "bustling and fun" "if noisy environment" ("you almost always strike up a conversation about the food with the patrons dining next to you"); the "electric atmosphere" makes it an experience "not to miss", and it's a "great value" to Boot.

### Fresco Italian Cafe
26 | 22 | 24 | $38

*1513 S. 1500 East (bet. Emerson & Kensington Aves.), 801-486-1300*

■ Adoring *amici* swoon over the "fresh", "tasty Northern Italian" dishes on offer at this "romantic little spot" set in a "secluded former home" "tucked away in a quiet Eastside residential neighborhood"; those who find its "intimate" interior a bit "cramped" say it's "best in summer" when one can dine on the "darling patio" surrounded by "beautiful grounds"; P.S. "the place draws a loyal clientele, so be prepared to wait" – and "make your reservations way in advance."

### Glitretind Restaurant
26 | 24 | 26 | $52

*Stein Eriksen Lodge, 7700 Stein Way (Royal St.), Deer Valley,*
*435-645-6455; www.steinlodge.com*

■ Even those who "can't pronounce the name" "love" ascending to the "beautiful alpine setting" of this "Deer Valley treasure" "in the Stein Eriksen Lodge", where a "professional, polished and polite" staff caters to "discerning diners" with "beautifully presented", "manicured meals" of "wonderful, inventive" New American cuisine, accompanied by a "killer wine list" and offered in a "European-feeling" room that's "formal yet comfortable for après-ski"; N.B. if it's "pricey" for your pocketbook, "wait for the summer two-for-one coupons."

### L'Avenue
22 | 25 | 22 | $30

*1355 E. 2100 South (1300 East), 801-485-4494*

Francophiles "love those mussels cooked [one of] five ways" then plated "with the best pommes frites around" by chef Franck Piessel at this "authentic French bistro", a "charming" spot with a "great patio" overlooking Sugarhouse Park on the "urbane" Eastside; a few respondents report "mixed experiences" with the kitchen's creations, but most maintain it's a bastion of "solid sophistication", and the recent "addition of jazz music in the bar on Thursday and Friday nights is a welcome change."

### Log Haven
23 | 27 | 23 | $44

*6451 E. 3800 South (Wasatch Blvd., 4 mi. up Millcreek Canyon), 801-272-8255; www.log-haven.com*

☑ "A magical place" "high in the mountains", this "secluded", "rustic cabin" boasts a "beautiful [Millcreek] Canyon setting" "complete with waterfall"; devotees of "skillful" chef David Jones find his "gourmet" Eclectic fare (with Pacific Rim, New French and Regional American influences) "thoughtfully prepared and delicious", though those who "don't understand the allure" suggest the food is "a bit pricey" and wonder why he "crams so many ingredients into each dish"; still, most insist it all adds up to an "exceptional experience" "to remember."

### Lugano
25 | 19 | 24 | $31

*3364 S. 2300 East (3300 South), 801-412-9994; www.luganorestaurant.com*

■ "It's not uncommon to see" "magnificent chef" and owner Gregory Neville "among the tables" of this "cozy, upscale" Northern Italian in Holladay, "working the crowd" and "ensuring a quality experience"; fans feel that his "reasonably priced", "seasonally changing menu" and "attentive", "knowledgeable staff" "deserve the accolades" regularly "piled upon" them, even if the "lively, upbeat atmosphere" can be more than a little "noisy" ("don't expect to hear everything your date says").

### MARIPOSA, THE
27 | 25 | 25 | $58

*Silver Lake Lodge, Deer Valley Resort, 7600 Royal St. (Rte. 224), Deer Valley, 435-645-6715; www.deervalley.com*

■ Smitten surveyors sum up this "special-occasion" spot in the "world-class Deer Valley" Resort's Silver Lake Lodge as "one of Park City's treasures", touting its "uniformly" "exquisite" New American fare (including a "very good vegetarian tasting menu"), "wonderful wine" list and "consistently superb service"; lauders love the "informal elegance" and "mountain appeal" of its "fabulous" alpine interior, and if you get too "hot sitting next to the fireplace", the signature Chocolate Snowball dessert will cool you off nicely; N.B. open December through mid-April.

### MARKET STREET GRILL
24 | 21 | 22 | $30

*2985 E. 6580 South (3000 East), 801-942-8860*
*48 Market St. (West Temple St., bet. 300 South & 400 South), 801-322-4668*
*www.gastronomyinc.com*

■ Collectively ranked Most Popular among Utah restaurants, this "terrific" twosome "sets the standard" for "excellent seafood" with its "expansive" selection of "reasonably priced" "fresh fish" dishes ("start with" the "superior clam chowder" – a "classic favorite"); whether visiting the "fun Downtown" "institution" or its younger sibling "in the suburbs", which "wows" with "great mountain and creek views", expect "friendly service" and a "packed", "noisy", "high-energy" environment; P.S. the "early-bird special is a wondrous thing."

### Martine ⌧
26 | 23 | 23 | $33

*22 E. 100 South (bet. Main & State Sts.), 801-363-9328*
■ Happy habitués hail the "innovative menu" of "top-notch" "Mediterranean food with serious influences from Morocco and

Spain" (including "inventive tapas") that "leaves diners pleased" at this "well-established Salt Lake classic" set in a "cozy Downtown brownstone"; "romantics" report it's a "great place to bring your main squeeze" thanks to "refined service" from an "attentive staff" and "fine ambiance that feels like a great small restaurant in San Francisco or Boston."

## Metropolitan  ☒    26 | 25 | 24 | $52 |

*173 W. Broadway (300 South, bet. 200 West & West Temple St.), 801-364-3472; www.themetropolitan.com*

☑ "Fine-art platings" of "exquisite food" matched with "incredible wine pairings" are the hallmark of this "excellent-albeit-expensive New American", a "chic" "favorite" whose "cool", "cosmopolitan" interior is manned by "a hip host" and "funky" staffers (some "pierced" and "tattooed") providing "impeccable service"; contrarians contend it "falls short" of its "pretensions" and claim there've been "too many chef changes to ensure consistency", but acolytes aver it's Downtown's "definition of high-end dining"; P.S. its "casual bistro is an escape to NYC, but at SLC prices!"

## MICHELANGELO RISTORANTE  ☒    26 | 14 | 21 | $27 |

*Hyland Plaza Mall, 2156 S. Highland Dr. (2100 South), 801-466-0961; www.michelangeloristorante.com*

☑ "Excellent risottos and housemade pastas" are among the "outstanding" offerings that "consistently impress" at this "authentic" "little trattoria" "in a hard-to-find" Eastside location; fans "love" that it's manned by "actual Italian waiters", though those who find the Sugarhouse "mall basement" setting (with its "kitschy decor" of "travel posters" and "plastic plants") "depressing" hope that "someday these guys may move" to a more "updated locale"; P.S. there's been "a change in ownership", but new proprietor Scott Ashley plans no major modifications at present.

## NEW YORKER CLUB  ☒    25 | 24 | 24 | $45 |

*60 W. Market St. (West Temple St., bet. 300 South & 400 South), 801-363-0166; www.gastronomyinc.com/ny*

☑ The "grand patriarch of Downtown SLC restaurants", this "tasteful, elegant" "classic" is the "always reliable, always appropriate" choice of "well-dressed", "mature" Utahns celebrating "special occasions" and "power brokers" looking to "seal the deal" over "excellent" Traditional American fare (including "great steaks" and "to-die-for soufflés") delivered by a "top-notch" staff; some sigh over the "steep prices" and say it's a "bad thing" that you get a side of "cigarette smoke with your meal", but most say it's "a pleasure" ponying up the nominal membership fee to "join the club."

## RED IGUANA, THE    27 | 12 | 20 | $17 |

*736 W. North Temple St. (800 West), 801-322-1489*

■ Though the "amazing moles" are "the most flavorful north of the border", you "can't go wrong with any dish" from the "impressive menu" of "authentic Mexican" treats at "this crowded joint" in a "sketchy neighborhood" west of Downtown, where the "friendly waiters" keep the "focus on customer service"; sure, it's a bit of a "dive", and you might have to "wait outside" "on the sidewalk" ("the line often snakes down the block"), but spicy-food fanatics "fantasize about" its "fantastic food."

**SEAFOOD BUFFET** ⬛  | 26 | 18 | 22 | $56 |
*Snow Park Lodge, 2250 Deer Valley Dr. (Mellow Mountain Rd.), Deer Valley, 435-645-6632; www.deervalley.com*

■ "Serious overeaters" "skip the slopes" and simply slalom to this "seafood-aficionado's paradise", a "high-end buffet" and bastion of "conspicuous consumption" where the "abundant variety" of "excellent-quality" ocean fare ("incredible fresh fish, oysters, sushi, crab, smoked salmon") and "desserts galore" are an "all-you-can-eat bargain" offered "in a casual atmosphere" that's "great for families and groups"; "pace yourself", though, as "this kind of indulgence requires stamina"; P.S. sadly, it's solely a "ski-season" "event" – "if only it were open year-round!"

**Snake Creek Grill**  | 24 | 18 | 23 | $35 |
*650 W. 100 South (6th St.), Heber City, 435-654-2133; www.snakecreekgrill.com*

■ "Well" "worth the scenic drive to Heber" City, this "hidden" "treasure" in a faux "Old Town", just "off" the main drag, is a "must-visit for anyone serious about food"; the "homestyle meals" remind some of "an old-fashioned dinner at mom's house" thanks to Traditional American fare that's "consistently" "delicious but not pretentious" and served by some of "the nicest, friendliest people" around in a "homey, welcoming atmosphere" – plus the "reasonable prices" make it "a real bargain", to boot.

**TREE ROOM**  | 27 | 27 | 26 | $45 |
*Sundance Resort, Scenic Rte. 92 (off Hwy. 189), Sundance, 801-223-4200; www.sundanceresort.com*

■ "Even the most sophisticated guests are invariably charmed by" this "special place" "surrounded by the splendor of the Sundance" Resort whose "flawless" Rocky Mountain Regional American meals have earned it the No. 1 rating for Food among Utah restaurants; "outstanding service" and the "rustic", "romantic", "relaxed ambiance" of its "beautiful" space with "Native Indian art all around" "only enhance" the "absolutely memorable dining experience", which is made even more "magical" by "frequent Robert Redford sightings" – and yes, there's "a tree growing through the dining room."

**WAHSO**  | 25 | 26 | 23 | $48 |
*577 Main St. (Heber Ave.), Park City, 435-615-0300; www.wahso.com*

■ Slip into "one of the secluded curtained booths for a nice romantic escape" at this "oh-my-God! good" Asian fusion palace where "the decor is stunning and inventive", the "impeccable" fare features "fabulous flavors and textures", the saketinis and other "cocktails are fantastic" and the staff is "informed, friendly and attentive"; gourmets gush that it's chef-owner "Bill White's best", and the one to "try if you have time for only one Park City restaurant" (though his nearby Chimayo is also a "reliable" choice).

# San Diego

## TOP 10 FOOD RANKING

| Restaurant | Cuisine |
|---|---|
| **27** Pamplemousse Grille | New American/New French |
| El Bizcocho | French |
| **26** Tapenade | New French/Provençal |
| Sushi Ota | Japanese |
| WineSellar & Brasserie | New French |
| Laurel | French/Provençal |
| Mille Fleurs | New French |
| Taka | Japanese |
| Sky Room | Continental |
| Donovan's | Steakhouse |

## ADDITIONAL NOTEWORTHY PLACES

| | |
|---|---|
| Arterra | New American |
| A.R. Valentien | Californian |
| Dobson's | Californian |
| George's at the Cove | Californian |
| Rainwater's on Kettner | Steakhouse/Seafood |
| Region | New American |
| Roppongi | Asian Fusion |
| Ruth's Chris | Steakhouse |
| Sammy's Woodfired | Pizza |
| Star of the Sea | Seafood |

| F | D | S | C |
|---|---|---|---|

**Arterra**  25 | 21 | 22 | $46
*San Diego Marriott Del Mar, 11966 El Camino Real (Carmel Valley Rd.), 858-369-6032; www.arterrarestaurant.com*
☑ "Can't believe it's in a Marriott" declare disciples of this Del Mar dining room, whose "imaginative, savory" New American menu is designed by "favorite chef" Bradley Ogden and supervised by local talent Carl Schroeder; some note that "given the prices, they could have done better with the decor" ("too many hard surfaces for a quiet meal") and scold the "inconsistent service"; nevertheless, this newcomer's now "*the* lunch spot for San Diego's high-tech movers and shakers."

**A.R. Valentien**  25 | 26 | 24 | $52
*The Lodge at Torrey Pines, 11480 N. Torrey Pines Rd. (Torrey Pines Golf Course), La Jolla, 858-777-6635; www.lodgetorreypines.com*
■ "Right on the famous Torrey Pines golf course", this "distinctive, Craftsman-style [hotel] restaurant" is an "architectural must-see", with "romantic" "views of the magnificent pines" and ocean; the "formal room" offers "exceptional" Cal cuisine ("the use of local, seasonal produce gives everything a kick"), "elegantly served"; some say it's the "best 19th hole ever", but "if you have to ask the price, wait for a raise" first – or "try lunch on the patio" instead.

### Dobson's ☒ | 25 | 19 | 23 | $43 |

*956 Broadway Circle (2nd Ave.), 619-231-6771;*
*www.dobsonsrestaurant.com*

☑ Owner Paul Dobson "works a room better than Sinatra", which explains why this "local tradition" Downtown remains, "after all these years", a "high-powered, hobnob spot"; the Cal kitchen "serves up delicious, innovative food, along with old standbys" ("have the mussel bisque and think of heaven"); some cavil about the "cramped" digs, but the savvy simply head for the mezzanine tables above the "lively" bar, which provide "a great view, like watching a soap opera" enacted by the suits and "city-hall crowd" at lunch and the "pre-theater diners" at dusk.

### Donovan's Steak & Chop House ☒ | 26 | 24 | 24 | $55 |

*4340 La Jolla Village Dr. (Genesee Ave.), 877-611-6688;*
*www.donovanssteakhouse.com*

■ In La Jolla's trendy Golden Triangle, this "dark" cow palace is "like stepping back in time to a men's club" – one populated by those on "expense-account budgets" since, as steakhouse tradition also dictates, tabs are "on the pricey side"; still, the "beef is unsurpassed", and the "warm, wood-paneled decor" and "courteous staff" combine to create a "classy atmosphere", which explains why some simply "don't eat steaks anywhere else."

### EL BIZCOCHO | 27 | 27 | 26 | $57 |

*Rancho Bernardo Inn, 17550 Bernardo Oaks Dr. (Rancho Bernardo Rd.),*
*Rancho Bernardo, 858-675-8550; www.jcresorts.com*

■ The grande dame "can still tap dance" says the "old-money crowd as well as young in-the-know foodies" who treasure this "luxurious", "romantic" Rancho Bernardo Inn dining room with a mood "as formal as San Diego can muster these days"; what with "live piano music", "rich" French fare "cooked to perfection" (especially at "the beautiful Sunday brunch") and "impeccable" service, it's "deliciously dazzling" on all levels and a "pinnacle experience" perfect "for a splurge" or "to bring guests."

### GEORGE'S AT THE COVE | 25 | 25 | 24 | $50 |

*1250 Prospect St. (bet. Cave St. & Ivanhoe Ave.), La Jolla, 858-454-4244;*
*www.georgesatthecove.com*

■ "A special-occasion place" (with "special-occasion prices"), this "romantic" "pearl" above La Jolla Cove is "recommended" for "exceptional", "imaginative" Cal cuisine by Trey Foshee (a "chef who knows his stuff") backed by a "breathtaking view" without and "beautiful decor" within; "whether dining on the casual rooftop [terrace], in the bar or in the more formal downstairs", the "chic crowd" agrees San Diego's Most Popular stop is not only a "must-go", it's a "place you never want to leave."

### Laurel | 26 | 24 | 24 | $53 |

*505 Laurel St. (5th Ave.), 619-239-2222; www.laurelrestaurant.com*

■ "For big-city dining", San Diegoans designate this destination "near Balboa Park" the city's "signature upscale" eatery; the "swank but not stuffy" setting "forms a perfect backdrop for its sophisticated Provençal" fare and "impressive wine list", proffered by servers who are "helpful and courteous", if "sometimes a bit snobby toward" new faces; still, most laud this "slice of the East Coast" as "worth every nickel"; P.S. "free shuttle" service to the Old Globe Theatre makes it an ideal "stop pre-theater."

## Mille Fleurs
26 | 25 | 25 | $66

*Country Squire Courtyard, 6009 Paseo Delicias (Del Dios Hwy.), Rancho Santa Fe, 858-756-3085; www.millefleurs.com*

🔏 "I only wish my pocketbook could afford this luxury more often" sigh supporters of celebrity owner "Bertrand Hug's original masterpiece" in "posh", "quaint Rancho Santa Fe"; it's "perfect for that romantic occasion", with chef Martin Woesle's New French "works of culinary art" served by an "elegant, refined" staff amid "auberge-style" decor with "miles of pretty Portuguese tiles"; malcontents mutter it can be "snooty", but maybe they just haven't hung around for after-dinner "singing around the piano bar."

## PAMPLEMOUSSE GRILLE
27 | 22 | 24 | $55

*514 Via de la Valle (Jimmy Durante Blvd.), Solana Beach, 858-792-9090; www.pgrille.com*

🔏 "Star of Del Mar Jeffrey Strauss" "stays on top of everything" at his race track–side establishment, which finishes No.1 for Food in San Diego; decorated with "wonderful murals" ("check out the biker painting by the restrooms"), it "attracts all the beautiful people" with a "nice variety" of "extraordinary and creative" New American–New French dishes, served by a "friendly" staff; being "a bit noisy" is its "only fault" – but even so, it's "everyone's secret for a special evening."

## Rainwater's on Kettner
25 | 22 | 23 | $48

*1202 Kettner Blvd. (W. B St.), 619-233-5757; www.rainwaters.com*

■ "They spoil you" at this ultra-"clubby", "East Coast–style" steak-and-seafoodery Downtown, "a great place to drink whiskey and eat hearty"; though it's known for beef, all of the "simple, upscale fare" "possesses a special flair" (including the "unbelievable meatloaf"), further smoothed by a "wine list that goes on and on" and "refined service"; granted, "this place ain't cheap", but it's an "elegant way to spend an evening" whether you're hosting "picky out-of-town guests" or "helping a business deal along."

## Region 🚫
– | – | – | E

*3671 5th Ave. (Pennsylvania Ave.), 619-299-6499*

A trio of partners helms this Hillcrest Contemporary American newcomer – chef Michael Stebner transforms superb local products into picture-perfect palate-pleasers, co-toque Allyson Colwell wheedles the best provender out of top specialty growers and pastry specialist Jack Fisher wows with baked-to-order desserts; its servers dress even more casually than its clientele (no mean feat in come-as-you-are San Diego), but the easygoing mood keeps it jiving until a later hour than most.

## ROPPONGI
25 | 23 | 22 | $42

*875 Prospect St. (Fay Ave.), La Jolla, 858-551-5252; www.roppongiusa.com*

■ "Takes Asian fusion to [the level of] a true art form" fawn followers of this "loud and happening" "place to be seen" (especially by the "outside fire pit" patio) in beautiful Downtown La Jolla; regulars recommend you begin with the "sake sampler", then "stick to" the "selection of starter foods" – "order for the table, share and keep ordering" – being sure to "save room for" "one of the divine desserts"; though "fun" "just about anytime", it's "phenomenal at happy hour" when the "awesome tapas are half-price"; N.B. a sushi bar was recently added.

### RUTH'S CHRIS STEAK HOUSE    25 | 20 | 23 | $52

*1355 N. Harbor Dr. (Ash St.), 619-233-1412*
*11582 El Camino Real (San Dieguito Rd.), Del Mar,*
*858-755-1454*
*www.ruthschris.com*

☑ These two chain steakeries are "always a pleasure" for their "meat masterpieces" – "piping hot, butter-broiled beauties" "so good you forget the cholesterol count", along with "sure-to-please side dishes"; despite its "great views of San Diego Bay", "the Downtown locale has poor acoustics", causing some to find "the Del Mar location superior", "but the well-trained staff is a delight" in either place.

### SAMMY'S WOODFIRED PIZZA    20 | 15 | 17 | $21

*Costa Verde, 8650 Genesee Ave. (bet. La Jolla Vlg. & Nobel Drs.),*
*858-404-9898*
*770 Fourth Ave. (F St.), 619-230-8888*
*Mission Valley Ctr., 1620 Camino de La Reina (Mission Center Rd.),*
*619-298-8222*
*10785 Scripps Poway Pkwy. (east of I-15), 858-695-0900*
*5970 Avenida Encinas (bet. I-5 & Palomar Airport Rd.), Carlsbad,*
*760-438-1212*
*Del Mar Highlands, 12925 El Camino Real (Del Mar Heights Rd.),*
*Del Mar, 858-259-6600*
*565 Pearl St. (Draper Ave.), La Jolla, 858-456-5222*
*www.sammyspizza.com*

☑ Purveyor of the "best original wood-fired pizza in San Diego", this homegrown chain garners "long lines" for its "traditional" and "designer" pies, "unique chopped salads" and trademark "messy sundaes" ("a sinful delight"), consumed on "beautiful patios with ample plants" (at most branches); the "servers tend to be young, so service may vary", and since it's "a casual, family favorite", "the atmosphere is seriously lacking for evening dining"; but "if you're hungry", "it's never a letdown."

### Sky Room    26 | 26 | 27 | $62

*La Valencia Hotel, 1132 Prospect St. (Herschel Ave.), La Jolla,*
*858-454-0771; www.lavalencia.com*

■ A "perfect place for a special occasion", this "intimate" room on the 10th floor of La Jolla's fabled La Valencia Hotel is "just like heaven", with "excellent" Continental fare, famously "romantic" decor and "gracious, professional" service; given the "formal and elegant" ambiance, it's understandably "pricey", but "it's worth any price" if you "book for sundown" and what may be the "best ocean view in Southern California"; N.B. the Food rating may not reflect a post-*Survey* chef change.

### Star of the Sea    25 | 24 | 23 | $50

*1360 Harbor Dr. (Ash St.), 619-232-7408;*
*www.staroftheseaa.com*

■ A "favorite through the years", this Downtowner is "still a star" thanks to the "unbelievable views" from its "beautiful setting" on the Embarcadero, plus "imaginatively prepared" fish fare that "often matches the season" (clearly, "they've got this seafood thing down") and a staff that's "friendly" and "knowledgeable"; in short, it's everything "a San Diego [poisson] palace should be", but be sure to "bring a high-limit credit card"; N.B. the Food rating may not reflect a post-*Survey* chef change.

### SUSHI OTA
26 | 12 | 18 | $36

*4529 Mission Bay Dr. (Bunker Hill), 858-270-5670*

☑ Count on "advance planning" ("businessmen call ahead from Japan") to snare a seat for "the best sushi in San Diego" at "artistic" "genius" Yukito Ota's "hidden gem" near Pacific Beach; "all locals agree" the difficulty of obtaining reservations for a place with often-"abrupt service" and "ho-hum decor" ("ambiance? what ambiance?") may make you feel like you're "living in a *Seinfeld* episode", but think of it as "the price you pay" for a nearly "perfect product" – "and it's not even the most expensive" in town.

### Taka
26 | 19 | 22 | $40

*555 Fifth Ave. (Market St.), 619-338-0555; www.takasushi.com*

■ Taka "a seat at the counter and they'll take very good care of you" at this "urban-chic" sushi source often cited as "the best in Downtown" for fish that tastes "like it jumped out of the ocean and into the hands of the chefs" who, like the servers, are "fast, friendly and no-nonsense"; the "too-small" digs quickly grow "crowded", but if you "get there early, and with reservations", it'll be "the perfect place to start the evening before heading out into the Gaslamp Quarter chaos."

### TAPENADE
26 | 20 | 23 | $52

*7612 Fay Ave. (bet. Kline & Pearl Sts.), La Jolla, 858-551-7500; www.tapenaderestaurant.com*

☑ Chef-owner Jean-Michel Diot "does tradition proud", serving guests "masterly" modern French cuisine "with a Provençal accent" at his "unpretentious" place in Downtown La Jolla; it's "a perennial favorite", drawing an "elegant and intelligent crowd" not only for its "just perfect" cuisine but for its "gorgeous Gallic waiters" (who may be "surfers by day"); however, given the "casual decor", some feel "prices are a bit high" – though not if you go for the "bargain prix fixe lunch" or dinner.

### WINESELLAR & BRASSERIE ⌧
26 | 18 | 25 | $52

*9550 Waples St. (bet. Mira Mesa Blvd. & Steadman St.), 858-450-9557; www.winesellar.com*

■ "Brasserie charm in an industrial-park setting"? – it's possible at this "wine-lover's paradise" ("sister to San Diego's Laurel") whose "quirky location" in Sorrento Mesa doesn't deter disciples from the "fabulous" New French cuisine paired with "sublime" labels "offered at 20 percent above retail" from "the shop on the first floor" ("their whole store is their wine list"); though "hard to find, it's guaranteed to wow your date or spouse", especially given the "impeccable attention" provided by the staff.

# San Francisco Bay Area

## TOP 20 FOOD RANKING

| Restaurant | Cuisine |
|---|---|
| 29 Gary Danko | New American |
| 28 French Laundry | French/New American |
| Masa's | New French |
| Fleur de Lys | New French |
| 27 Le Papillon | French |
| Sushi Ran | Japanese |
| Café La Haye | New American |
| La Toque | French |
| Acquerello | Italian |
| Chez Panisse | Californian/Med. |
| Ritz-Carlton Din. Rm. | New French |
| Marché | New French |
| Fork | Californian/New French |
| Rivoli | Californian/Med. |
| Boulevard | French/New American |
| Marinus | Californian/New French |
| La Folie | New French |
| Hog Island Oyster | Seafood |
| Aqua | French/Seafood |
| Chez Panisse Café | Californian/Med. |

## ADDITIONAL NOTEWORTHY PLACES

| | |
|---|---|
| Bistro Jeanty | French Bistro |
| Campton Place | French/Med. |
| Cortez | Mediterranean |
| Delfina | Northern Italian |
| Farallon | Seafood |
| Fifth Floor | New French |
| Frisson | French/Californian |
| Kabuto Sushi | Japanese |
| Lark Creek Inn | American |
| Michael Mina | New American |
| Oliveto | Northern Italian |
| Piperade | Spanish/Basque |
| Quince | Italian/French |
| Rubicon | Californian/New French |
| Slanted Door | Vietnamese |
| Tartare | New French |
| Terra | New American |
| Town Hall | New American |
| Tra Vigne | Italian |
| Zuni Cafe | Mediterranean |

**Acquerello** ⊠　　27　23　26　$60
*1722 Sacramento St. (bet. Polk St. & Van Ness Ave.), 415-567-5432;*
*www.acquerello.com*
■ It's closed Sunday, but other days are fine times "to worship" at this Italian "in a refurbished chapel" near Polk Street, a "mercifully quiet", "Venetian-themed" "jewel" of "linen tablecloths" and "hand-carved decanters" by an "older" "blue-blooded crowd"; simply "put your faith in Giancarlo Paterlini" who "waits on you hand and foot" and creates some "killer wine pairings" off his "incomparable list", while co-owner/chef Suzette Gresham's "rich" *cucina* "brings you to your knees."

**AQUA**　　27　25　24　$65
*252 California St. (bet. Battery & Front Sts.), 415-956-9662;*
*www.aqua-sf.com*
◪ Take the plunge and "treat yourself" to SF's "best damn seafood" site, which stays "in the swim" under new chef Laurent Manrique; "high ceilings" and "stunning floral displays provide the perfect backdrop" for his "piled-up" French-Cal "feats of fresh fish" and foie gras, offered by "service so polished it shines"; while it's "cacophonous", "crowded and pricey" ("the food's rich, but we weren't after paying the bill"), Downtown power-lunchers and the "breathlessly chic" fall for it hook, line and sinker.

**Bistro Jeanty**　　26　21　23　$45
*6510 Washington St. (Mulberry St.), Yountville, 707-944-0103;*
*www.bistrojeanty.com*
■ Featuring "scrumptious", "soul-satisfying" "classic French bistro cuisine", "quaint" "farmhouse decor" and "*très bien*" service, Philippe Jeanty's "wine-country 'in' spot" "makes you feel" like "you could be in Paris" "right here in Yountville"; *oui*, it's "noisy and cramped", but in the chef-owner's "expanding culinary empire, it remains the stalwart" and "well worth" "*le détour*" – "even if you aren't going to the wineries"; P.S. spontaneous types can "just sit at the bar" or the "communal table for drop-ins."

**BOULEVARD**　　27　25　25　$55
*Audifred, 1 Mission St. (Steuart St.), 415-543-6084;*
*www.boulevardrestaurant.com*
■ There's no better place to "show off our fair city" than at this Embarcadero "icon" that, while "anything but cheap", remains the "sine qua non of SF dining"; in Pat Kuleto's "over-the-top" belle epoque setting, the "brisk" but "professional" "waiters whiz by", serving Nancy Oakes' "extraordinary" French–New American creations ("you feel guilty eating 'cuz they look like works of art"), along with wines that "would turn anyone into a wanna-be sommelier"; P.S. go for "the back with the killer Bay Bridge view."

**Café La Haye**　　27　20　25　$40
*140 E. Napa St. (bet. 1st & 2nd Sts.), Sonoma, 707-935-5994;*
*www.cafelahaye.com*
■ "It's unbelievable what chef John McReynolds creates in his tiny kitchen" at this "always fun" Cal–New American that he co-owns with Saul Gropman, who oversees the "compact", "art"-oriented room and "lovely" service; many feel it's "one of the best in Sonoma", as well as a "value", because the food based on "fresh items from local markets and farms" is "outstanding" and the wine list "worthy" of the locale.

### Campton Place
26　25　26　$67

*Campton Place Hotel, 340 Stockton St. (bet. Post & Sutter Sts.), 415-955-5555; www.camptonplace.com*

■ "Chef Daniel Humm might be young, but he's a genius" gush those who've sampled his "exquisite" Provençal-Med fare (he "should be awarded Best Use of Foam") at this hotel restaurant off Union Square; "ultrasmooth" service, a "classy", "whisper-quiet" room, "wonderful wine list" and "staggering prices" make it "perfect for a special occasion" underwritten by your "rich maiden aunt" or a meal "on the company"; N.B. jackets suggested.

### CHEZ PANISSE ⊠
27　24　25　$69

*1517 Shattuck Ave. (bet. Cedar & Vine Sts.), Berkeley, 510-548-5525; www.chezpanisse.com*

■ "The culinary gene pool of great chefs nationwide", Alice Waters' "legendary" Berkeley establishment "still packs them in" with its "distinctively" "simple" Med-inspired meals that let the "meticulously selected" Cal products "shine through" in an "Arts and Crafts setting that suits" the "subtle" cuisine; you just have to "get past" the "like-it-or-not" set menu and the "expert" staff's "this-is-mecca" 'tude – because while it's "no longer cutting-edge", this "grande dame" has "aged like a fine wine."

### Chez Panisse Café ⊠
27　22　24　$43

*1517 Shattuck Ave. (bet. Cedar & Vine Sts.), Berkeley, 510-548-5049; www.chezpanisse.com*

■ Alice Waters' "more boisterous version of foodie heaven" is "no longer the consolation prize" for not getting into her "flagship" prix fixe downstairs; in fact, it's the preferred choice of "Berkeley intellectuals and tourists in shorts" who come seeking that "Chez Panisse mystique without breaking the bank"; not only do they receive the same "marvelous" Med-influenced "farm-fresh" Cal fare, funky "Arts and Crafts interior" and "impeccable" wine-savvy staff, they get "lots of choice" on the menu.

### Cortez
25　24　21　$46

*Adagio Hotel, 550 Geary St. (Taylor St.), 415-292-6360; www.cortezrestaurant.com*

◪ "Small plates strike again" at this "sceney" Downtown newcomer from "the Bay Bread folks", which many maintain "merits a trip" as much for the "memorable" mix of Mediterranean "masterpieces", "heavenly desserts" and "affable staff" as for the "flatteringly" lit, "numbingly loud" *Sex and the City* atmosphere and "glamorous bar"; however, "prices can sneak up on you", since you "have to order a lot" of the *petit* portions (e.g. "soups that come in shot glasses").

### Delfina
26　19　23　$41

*3621 18th St. (bet. Dolores & Guerrero Sts.), 415-552-4055; www.delfinasf.com*

◪ What's the secret of this small storefront that's "jam-packed" nightly? – it's chef-owner Craig Stoll's "exquisite", "simple" Northern Italian preparations "notched up" with "impeccable, seasonal ingredients", "hot" waitresses who are "always jazzed to serve" and a "Mission-hip-minus-the-attitude" vibe; yes, it's "loud, tight quarters" but that's a "small price to pay" for what's "arguably the best of its kind in San Francisco"; P.S. they now do validated parking, alleviating that "nightmare."

**Farallon**  | 24 | 27 | 23 | $57 |
*450 Post St. (bet. Mason & Powell Sts.), 415-956-6969;*
*www.farallonrestaurant.com*
■ "Dazzle guests" at this "splashy" Downtown fish house; after they "drink in" Pat Kuleto's "nautical fantasyland" decor, they can gobble up Mark Franz's "luscious", "creative" seafood ("with a great wine list to go with it") brought by well-schooled servers who know "when to attend and when to blend into the background"; and while it'll cost you an arm and a gill, the ambiance is refreshingly "less stuffy than at other high-end" piscatorial places.

**Fifth Floor** ⑤  | 26 | 25 | 25 | $78 |
*Hotel Palomar, 12 Fourth St. (Market St.), 415-348-1555*
■ "The elevator stops at the fifth floor, but it's more like heaven" gush those besotted by this "ultramod" yet "clubby" SoMa hotel dining room where chef Laurent Gras' "cerebral" New French menu pairs with an "exceptional" wine list and served with fitting "pomp and circumstance"; although "priced as if the city remained full of dot-com zillionaires", it's still one "tough table to get."

**FLEUR DE LYS** ⑤  | 28 | 27 | 26 | $87 |
*777 Sutter St. (bet. Jones & Taylor Sts.), 415-673-7779;*
*www.fleurdelyssf.com*
■ Be "treated like *un roi*" at Hubert Keller's long-running "flirtation with excess" on Nob Hill that "still amazes after all these years"; the "flawless" staff guides you through an "unparalleled gourmet experience" via the "heart-stopping" New French prix fixes (including a "veritable vegetarian feast") "while you float away" "under the big top" in one of the "prettiest rooms in town" and depart feeling those "big dollars were well spent."

**Fork** ⑤  | 27 | 20 | 23 | $47 |
*198 Sir Francis Drake Blvd. (bet. Bank St. & Tunstead Ave.),*
*San Anselmo, 415-453-9898; www.marinfork.com*
☑ "Big city dining comes to the country" at this Californian–New French in San Anselmo that offers a "spectacular selection of little plates", "perfect for diners who have culinary attention-deficit disorder"; the vibe is "relaxed", the servers seem "knowledgeable" and the "prix fixe is a very good value", but to some, it seems like "the only thing smaller than the plates is the cramped space itself."

**FRENCH LAUNDRY**  | 28 | 26 | 27 | $135 |
*6640 Washington St. (Creek St.), Yountville, 707-944-2380;*
*www.frenchlaundry.com*
■ Enthusiasts are "excited about returning" to Thomas Keller's reopened Yountville institution; the "Herculean effort" "to get a reservation could lead to disappointment" but they "wow you", from the "impeccably served" French–New American menus, "a whirlwind" of tiny tastes and big sensations, to the "gorgeous gardens" or "understated" interior; a few snap it's "stuffy", literally and figuratively, but to most, "no prose can do justice" to this "once-in-a-lifetime experience (twice on someone else's dime)."

**Frisson** ◑  | – | – | – | E |
*244 Jackson St. (bet. Battery & Front Sts.), 415-956-3004;*
*www.frissonsf.com*
This snazzy new French-Cal hopes to create a little frisson Downtown, thanks to a circular, mod, two-tiered sunken dining

room demarcated by honeycomb-shaped Lucite panels and set under a backlit dome; adding to its appeal is a bar (with live DJ), an urban garden patio and chef Daniel Patterson's small-plates menu served until 10 PM, with more casual nibbles available until 1 AM.

### GARY DANKO                                              29 | 26 | 28 | $88
*800 North Point St. (Hyde St.), 415-749-2060;*
*www.garydanko.com*
■ "Danko's is to dining as *The Producers* is to Broadway" – a three-hour "extravaganza" that's "worth every $100 bill" and phone call to get in; "applause goes to Gary" for his "dazzling" New American prix fixes ("if you skip the cheese course, go to foodie jail"), the "beautifully choreographed service" and the "Armani suit"–like ("subdued, elegant") digs; yes, it gets "cramped and loud", but "there's a reason" this Wharf wonder "ends up No. 1 on so many lists" – including this *Survey*'s for SF's Top Food and Most Popular.

### Hog Island Oyster Company & Bar            27 | 18 | 19 | $28
*Ferry Bldg., 1 Ferry Plaza (Market St.), 415-391-7117;*
*www.hogislandoysters.com*
■ Mollusk mavens are in "hog heaven" at this boisterous new oyster bar/shop located in the Ferry Building; "sit, slurp and relax" at the U-shaped bar or "snag a seat outside" and waterside while watching the "spunky staff" shuck the "freshest" Tomales Bay beauties; some "wonder at the wisdom" of the prices, but conclude it's "well worth it" for these "tastes of the sea."

### Kabuto Sushi A & S 🖾                         27 | 14 | 19 | $35
*5121 Geary Blvd. (15th Ave.), 415-752-5652;*
*www.kabutosushi.com*
🗹 Thriving in his "cheerful" new locale, venerable "master chef Sachio Kojima" "reinvents sushi" in the Outer Richmond, with "adventurous" specials, plus "incredibly fresh" fish that's almost "too good to put into a roll"; unfortunately the "smaller location means longer waits", especially given the "slow service" at table.

### La Folie 🖾                                  27 | 22 | 25 | $80
*2316 Polk St. (bet. Green & Union Sts.), 415-776-5577;*
*www.lafolie.com*
■ On Polk Street, "passionate" Roland Passot, "with precision and panache", "prepares to perfection" New French fare at this "foodies' underground favorite"; within the "whimsical", small but "charming" room, the chef-owner and his wife, Jamie, "go out of their way to make everyone feel welcome", so although the "prices are astronomical", the experience "is also out of this world."

### Lark Creek Inn, The                          26 | 25 | 24 | $52
*234 Magnolia Ave. (Madrone Ave.), Larkspur, 415-924-7766;*
*www.larkcreek.com*
■ Bradley Ogden's Larkspur "flagship" "temple to farm-fresh fare" is "something of an icon", proffering "polished", "plentiful" and "perfected" portions of "grandma's cooking", a "strictly American wine list" and a staff that "knows how to make guests feel at home"; the "picturesque" "100-year-old Victorian" house's "out-of-the-way location" discourages eating here on a lark, but a meal "on the sublime patio" "surrounded by redwood groves" is "worthy of a long drive" from anywhere.

### La Toque
27 | 24 | 27 | $93 |

*1140 Rutherford Rd. (Hwy. 29), Rutherford, 707-963-9770;*
*www.latoque.com*

■ From the "exquisite" menus du jour to the suggested "dress code" to the "serene" room, this Rutherford refuge is "French in every classic sense of the word, and yet it's definitely Napa Valley" thanks to "minimal pretension"; "great" as the Gallic gastronomy is, "what really shines is the service", from the sommelier who "recommends wineries to visit" to chef-owner Ken Frank himself who "comes out to shave the truffles" on your dinner, if you're there "in January, when they're featured."

### LE PAPILLON
27 | 23 | 27 | $62 |

*410 Saratoga Ave. (Kiely Blvd.), San Jose, 408-296-3730;*
*www.lepapillon.com*

■ Although "nondescript on the outside", this "classy French" is "excellent in all respects inside", offering "the real-deal" fine-dining experience – the kind with "old-fashioned fussing over the customers" and "beautifully presented" tasting menus that culminate with soufflés slashed open tableside; no wonder that for nearly 30 years it's been seen as "San Jose's finest" for "a special-occasion meal for that special someone" (with "top-tier" tabs to match).

### Marché ⊠
27 | 24 | 25 | $61 |

*898 Santa Cruz Ave. (University Dr.), Menlo Park, 650-324-9092*

■ "It's just Menlo Park", but it "feels like you're in the big city" (with metropolitan prices to boot) at chef-owner Howard Bulka's "posh" "destination"; his daily changing New French à la carte and tasting menus – "based on the seasons and the market" ("as the name implies") – and the "brilliant wine selections" are "serious business", but what seals the deal is the service, from the "chef's visits to each table" to the crew of "friendly, professional" servers who "remember diners."

### Marinus
27 | 26 | 25 | $72 |

*Bernardus Lodge, 415 Carmel Valley Rd. (Laureles Grade Rd.),*
*Carmel, 831-658-3500; www.bernardus.com*

■ "The absolute star of the Carmel dining scene" resides at this "pastoral" "getaway"; be sure to "wear a belt you can loosen a notch" and then "sit back and be pampered" by "perfectly professional servers" dishing up "insanely delicious" Cal–New French cooking and a "bank-breaking wine list" (weighted with Bernardus Winery bottlings) in "one of the all-time great dining rooms" – "elegant, yet rustic" when "next to the cozy fireplace"; P.S. true sports can "spend the weekend" at the lodge.

### MASA'S ⊠
28 | 25 | 27 | $93 |

*Hotel Vintage Ct., 648 Bush St. (bet. Powell & Stockton Sts.),*
*415-989-7154*

■ Celebrated chef Ron Siegel, who restored this legendary Downtowner to "days of glory", has departed post-*Survey*, but the arrival of co-chefs Richard Reddington and Gregory Short (ex French Laundry) should ensure this "crème de la crème" will continue the New French cuisine that inspires "transports of delight"; fans feel the front-of-the-house staff will "uphold its reputation" for treating guests "like royalty" in the "hushed", stylishly "updated, urbane" digs.

### Michael Mina
| – | – | – | E |

*Westin St. Francis, 335 Powell St. (bet. Geary & Post Sts.), 415-397-9222*
Michael Mina's new, eponymous Downtown dining room features 35-ft. ceilings, Ionic columns and a sea of crème-colored drapery and celadon armchairs, a fitting backdrop for his super-luxe, high-concept New American prix fixe menu built around a single ingredient prepared three ways on the same plate; guests can also choose among the classics from his 11 years at Aqua, along with a 1,000-label wine list overseen by Rajat Parr (ex Fifth Floor).

### Oliveto Cafe & Restaurant
| 25 | 22 | 21 | $47 |

*5655 College Ave. (Shafter Ave.), Oakland, 510-547-5356;*
*www.oliveto.com*
☑ It's "great on a normal night and amazing" on a "special themed one" attest acolytes of Oakland's "casually elegant" "temple" to chef/co-owner Paul Bertolli's "handcrafted" "take on Northern Italian" fare; while heretics huff that portions are "absurdly small" and the "staff takes itself oh-so-seriously", all agree the downstairs cafe is "wonderful" "at a fraction of the price."

### Piperade ⌧
| 25 | 21 | 21 | $43 |

*1015 Battery St. (Green St.), 415-391-2555; www.piperade.com*
■ Everyone seems to be "basking in the pleasure" of chef-owner Gerald Hirigoyen's Downtown paean to the Pyrénées, including the "omnipresent" maestro himself, "working the room" and making fast friends at the communal table; perhaps they could "use a few more waiters on the floor", but the "haute and folksy Basque cuisine", regional wines that "you won't see anywhere else", "cozy" bistro feel and "easy parking" ensure a "smash hit" here.

### Quince
| 25 | 23 | 25 | $55 |

*1701 Octavia St. (bet. Bush & Pine Sts.), 415-775-8500;*
*www.quincerestaurant.com*
■ Lindsay and Michael Tusk's "pricey" "hot" "newcomer" in a converted Pacific Heights apothecary is "earning some stripes"; "she makes customers feel special" in the "refined", albeit "noisy", 15-table dining room, while his startlingly "simple" yet "superlative" Italian-French multicourse menu of seasonal, "edible shrines to a few good ingredients" "leaves you wanting more" – and not just because "the portions are small."

### Ritz-Carlton Dining Room ⌧
| 27 | 27 | 28 | $86 |

*Ritz-Carlton Hotel, 600 Stockton St. (bet. California & Pine Sts.),*
*415-773-6198; www.ritzcarlton.com*
■ "For truth in advertising, they could have named it" the "technically perfect" dining room, fawn fanciers of this "formal" Nob Hill address offering a "privileged" experience in the "grand European tradition"; the setting's "splendor" is outranked only by a "first-class" staff that serves from "so many carts, you lose count"; note that the Food score doesn't reflect the arrival of chef Ron Siegel (ex Masa's) who's expected to add slight Asian influences to the "heavenly" New French menu.

### Rivoli
| 27 | 23 | 24 | $42 |

*1539 Solano Ave. (bet. Neilson St. & Peralta Ave.), Berkeley,*
*510-526-2542; www.rivolirestaurant.com*
■ "It would be a perfect world if all neighborhoods had restaurants this good" fantasize fanciers of Wendy Brucker's Cal-Med whose

ambiance, "expressive, straight-shootin'" fare and "gracious" service are "comparable to the best SF haunts but at Berkeley prices"; the "snug" dining room, with its "windows overlooking a peaceable garden" lets you watch what the "local wildlife" eats for dinner, even as you enjoy yours; P.S. "the bar is a great place for a quick bite."

### Rubicon ⌧
23 | 20 | 23 | $57

*558 Sacramento St. (bet. Montgomery & Sansome Sts.), 415-434-4100; www.sfrubicon.com*

■ Oenophiles happily "cross this Rubicon" just to get a little "tableside education" from Larry Stone, aka "the king of wine"; while his "famous list" of 1,600 labels "rules the roost", there is an "excellent" Cal–New French eatery "attached to it", sporting an "old-school-men's-club-meets-California-chic" air and attracting an "A-list" and "business-suit crowd" with its "smart service"; N.B. scores may not reflect chef Stuart Brioza's arrival.

### Slanted Door, The
26 | 20 | 21 | $40

*Ferry Bldg., 1 Ferry Plaza (Market St.), 415-861-8032; www.slanteddoor.com*

◪ There's almost "nothing askew" now that Charles Phan's "mom-and-pop organization" has relocated to "ultrachic" Ferry Building digs (a move the scores may not fully reflect); it's "the paragon of Southeast Asian dining" where an "eager-to-please wait staff" proffers "intriguing" "modernized Vietnamese" chow and "a hugely innovative" wine list; a few opponents opine it's "overrated and overpriced", but most folks "have never been disappointed, except when they can't get a reservation."

### Sushi Ran
27 | 20 | 21 | $44

*107 Caledonia St. (bet. Pine & Turney Sts.), Sausalito, 415-332-3620; www.sushiran.com*

■ "In a town that knows good, fresh fish", this "Tokyo-class" Japanese stalwart in Sausalito has achieved "near-cult status" for its "artistically presented" "Ameri-makis" and sashimi, as well as "innovative Cal-Japanese" cooked offerings "for those who stay away from the raw stuff"; it also "scores high on the trend-o-meter" with "chichi crowds" peopling the "lovely Zen-like room" or cooling their jets on the patio of the stellar sake bar as they wait for a table (which "can take forever", some grouse).

### Tartare ⌧
– | – | – | E

*550 Washington St. (bet. Montgomery & Sansome Sts.), 415-434-3100; www.tartarerestaurant.com*

Chef George Morrone (ex Fifth Floor) is back wowing Downtowners at this smart New French newcomer whose menu may be half-baked – it's built around five tartares (including ostrich, fruit and ahi versions), two carpaccios and raw oysters, along with heated entrees – but is hardly un-thought-out; the small, cozy rectangular dining room features warm, wood-toned walls and a black-leather-lattice arched ceiling.

### Terra
26 | 24 | 25 | $60

*1345 Railroad Ave. (bet. Adams & Hunt Sts.), St. Helena, 707-963-8931; www.terrarestaurant.com*

■ "Trust your culinary fortunes to Hiro Sone and his wife, Lissa Doumani", who deliver "all the bang-for-big-bucks" with an "exquisite", "flawlessly executed" New American roster (with

Southern French and Northern Italian influences) at their Napa Valley "destination" housed in a "beautiful" fieldstone building; the "wine list is like a dictionary", and the staff so "knowledgeable it was as if they were in the kitchen preparing the food."

**Town Hall**    23 | 21 | 20 | $45
*342 Howard St. (Fremont St.), 415-908-3900; www.townhallsf.com*
☑ Rub elbows with "politicos and socialites" and tuck into "creative" "New Orleans–influenced" New American cuisine and "upstaging desserts" at this "new new thing" in SoMa from chef-brothers Mitchell and Steven Rosenthal and "quintessential host Doug Washington"; though critics cavil about the "acoustically challenged" interior and service "jitters" that "need to be worked out", most agree the "food is worthy of a repeat visit."

**Tra Vigne**    24 | 25 | 22 | $48
*1050 Charter Oak Ave. (Hwy. 29), St. Helena, 707-963-4444;*
*www.travignerestaurant.com*
■ A stop at St. Helena's "quintessential Napa Valley restaurant" is like being "wined and dined at a private Tuscan villa" by "attentive" hosts who "know every wine and every vineyard"; dazzled devotees can't decide whether the "excellent" Italian fare "enhances the sun-dappled courtyard setting, or the other way around", but it's moot for most who think this is the best way "to spend a romantic afternoon before hitting the wineries"; P.S. the "bar is a great place" to "drop in without a reservation" and "meet local vintners."

**Zuni Cafe** ◐    24 | 20 | 20 | $43
*1658 Market St. (bet. Franklin & Gough Sts.), 415-552-2522*
☑ "One of the great SF dining parties" takes place nightly at Judy Rodgers' perennially hot boîte, where the "who's who" "meet and eat" "till the wee hours" in a "fab glass-walled" space "with a Market Street view"; after 25 years, "she may be tired of making the roasted chicken and bread dish, but that's too darn bad", because it's so darn good – as are the "perfect burger" and Med dishes "cooked over an open fire"; "service is sometimes snooty, but if you can overlook that", you'll have a "phenomenal" time.

# Seattle

## TOP 20 FOOD RANKING

| Restaurant | Cuisine |
|---|---|
| **29** Mistral | New American/New French |
| **28** Cafe Juanita | Northern Italian |
| Nishino | Japanese |
| Herbfarm, The | New American |
| Tosoni's | Continental |
| Rover's | New French |
| **27** Harvest Vine | Spanish |
| Campagne | French |
| Inn at Langley | Pacific Northwest |
| Izumi* | Japanese |
| JaK's Grill | Steakhouse |
| Lampreia | Pacific NW/New American |
| **26** Shiro's Sushi | Japanese |
| Canlis | American/Pacific NW |
| Shoalwater | Pacific NW/Seafood |
| Dahlia Lounge | Pacific Northwest |
| Monsoon | Vietnamese |
| Il Terrazzo Carmine | Italian |
| Kingfish | Southern |
| Cafe Campagne | French Bistro |

## ADDITIONAL NOTEWORTHY PLACES

| | |
|---|---|
| Brasa | Mediterranean |
| Cascadia | Pacific Northwest |
| El Gaucho | Steakhouse |
| Flying Fish | Seafood |
| Georgian, The | Pacific Northwest |
| Kaspar's | Pacific Northwest |
| Lark | New American |
| Le Gourmand | French |
| Le Pichet | French Bistro |
| Matt's in the Market | Seafood |
| Metropolitan Grill | Steakhouse |
| Nell's | New Amer./Pacific NW |
| Oceanaire Seafood Rm. | Seafood |
| Palace Kitchen | New American |
| Ray's Boathouse | Seafood/Pacific NW |
| Restaurant Zoë | New American |
| Szmania's | German |
| Union | New American |
| Union Bay Cafe | Pacific NW/New American |
| Wild Ginger | Pacific Rim |

---

\* Indicates a tie with restaurant above

### Brasa ◗　　　　　　　　　　25 | 24 | 22 | $45
*2107 Third Ave. (bet. Blanchard & Lenora Sts.), 206-728-4220;*
*www.brasa.com*
■ "Everything's a winner" – from the "unforgettable, creative"
Mediterranean cuisine to the "sleek", "beautiful interior" "glowing
with golden light" to the "attentive, discreet" service – at this
"very upscale" Belltown "class act"; chef/co-owner Tamara
Murphy's "imaginative" dishes are all the more "memorable"
when paired with choices from the "thoughtful wine list" "filled
with obscurities"; P.S. bargain-hunters ballyhoo the "amazing bar
menu", which goes half-price during the "best happy hour in town."

### Cafe Campagne　　　　　　　26 | 23 | 22 | $33
*Pike Place Mkt., 1600 Post Alley (bet. First & Pine Sts.), 206-728-2233*
■ "In some ways more fun" than Campagne, its "grown-up brother"
upstairs, this casual Pike Place Market "favorite" provides the
"perfect combination" of "*romantique*" ambiance and "excellent
French bistro fare" ("*vive le steak frites!*") and the "pâté of
champions"); its "great list of [Gallic] wines", "gracious service",
sidewalk seating and "reasonable prices" add to the appeal.

### CAFE JUANITA　　　　　　　28 | 22 | 26 | $44
*9702 NE 120th Pl. (97th St.), Kirkland, 425-823-1505; www.cafejuanita.com*
■ "It just keeps getting better" gush groupies of chef-owner Holly
Smith's "magical" Northern Italian that's considered "a must" for
special "celebrations" ("secluded" location notwithstanding); its
"transporting" "meals to remember" are composed of "sublime",
"perfectly" prepared cuisine making "great use of seasonal
ingredients", "outstanding wine" selections and "terrific service";
P.S. "are we sure this is Kirkland and not Liguria?"

### Campagne　　　　　　　　　27 | 24 | 25 | $51
*Pike Place Mkt., 86 Pine St. (1st Ave.), 206-728-2800*
■ "Still one of the best in Seattle", this Pike Place Market Country
French "classic" is "strong all around", from the "take-your-breath-
away quality" of its "sophisticated" cuisine and "superior" wine
list to its "elegant" interior to its "formal but relaxed" service;
sure, it's "expensive", but devotees resoundingly vote it "worth
every penny", especially for celebrating "special occasions", so
"save up, skip lunch" and indulge.

### CANLIS ⊠　　　　　　　　　26 | 27 | 27 | $60
*2576 Aurora Ave. N. (Halladay St., south of Aurora Bridge),*
*206-283-3313; www.canlis.com*
■ "Family-owned" for more than half a century, this "Seattle
institution" "perched above Lake Union" is the "ultimate" "special-
occasion" destination thanks to its "can't-be-beat ambiance"
and "phenomenal view", "divine" NW-accented surf 'n' turf
menu, which "pleases every palate" by managing to be "old-
fashioned and modern at the same time", 1,000-plus-label wine
list brimming with "endless charms" and "gracious", "intuitive"
service; this *très* spendy "classic" just "grows better with age."

### Cascadia ⊠　　　　　　　　24 | 26 | 24 | $63
*2328 First Ave. (bet. Battery & Bell Sts.), 206-448-8884;*
*www.cascadiarestaurant.com*
■ "Absolutely wonderful" rave reviewers of this Belltown NWer
where chef-owner Kerry Sear's "spectacular" cuisine composed

of "seasonal" ingredients from the Cascade Mountain region is nothing less than a "lesson in culinary craft" (especially the "not-to-be-missed" tasting menu options), backed by an "excellent" wine list overseen by "helpful" staffers who brim with "great pairing" suggestions; "beautiful" decor (including a "waterfall") completes the "truly amazing" experience.

### DAHLIA LOUNGE
26 | 25 | 23 | $42

*2001 Fourth Ave. (Virginia St.), 206-682-4142; wwww.tomdouglas.com*
■ "Still strong after all these years", Tom Douglas's "first" (and "best") eatery continues to set hearts swooning with its "bold" "showcase of NW flavors" reflecting a "Pacific Rim" "twist", "warm yet sophisticated" decor (including "sumptuous red walls") and a "sterling" staff; yes, everyone "loves the coconut cream pie", which is available to-go from "the Dahlia Bakery next door."

### El Gaucho ◗
25 | 24 | 24 | $63

*2505 First Ave. (bet. Vine & Wall Sts.), 206-728-1337*
*2119 Pacific Ave. (S. 21st St.), Tacoma, 253-272-1510*
*www.elgaucho.com*
■ Imagine a "NY supper club straight out of a Frank Sinatra flick" and you've got this "dark, sexy", "retro"-styled Belltown steakhouse "known for its prime beef" and "near-perfect" Caesar salads "expertly prepared tableside"; for such "swanky" experiences, including "superb", "prepare-to-be-pampered" service, it's no surprise tabs are "very spendy" ("go on an expense account" or brace for "el oucho in the pocketbook").

### Flying Fish ◗
25 | 21 | 22 | $39

*2234 First Ave. (Bell St.), 206-728-8595; www.flyingfishseattle.com*
■ Christine Keff and her team "make anything that swims taste divine" at this "vibrant" Belltown stand-out seafooder offering "interesting" twists, often with "an Asian flair", on "exotic and local fish" ("love the whole fried snapper"), all of which "match well" with selections from the "excellent" wine list; it's also a "great late-night" choice (though the "festive" quarters can get "cramped" and "noisy as the evening" wears on) and "fun" just for "apps at the bar"; N.B. it now serves lunch and takeout.

### Georgian, The
26 | 26 | 27 | $52

*Fairmont Olympic Hotel, 411 University St. (bet. 4th & 5th Aves.), 206-621-7889*
■ The yellow-toned interior of this "grand old" Downtown "hotel dining room" remains "one of the classiest" "fancy" places in Seattle, but "without being too stuffy"; the "top-rate" NW cuisine with its "beautiful presentations", extensive, regionally focused wine list and "exquisite service" conspire to make "special occasions extra-special" at this ultimate "place to impress."

### Harvest Vine, The ⊠
27 | 17 | 22 | $36

*2701 E. Madison St. (27th Ave.), 206-320-9771*
■ At Joseph Jimenez de Jimenez's "tiny Madison Park Basque", the "best seats are at the copper-topped bar", where "the chefs in front of you" craft "exquisite tapas" "like nothing else", so "taste everything they offer", choose from the "extensive wine list" and don't forget to "save room for pastry chef Carolin Jimenez's creations"; the "waits can be long" in the restaurant, where there are "no reservations", but you can book ahead for the cellar room.

### HERBFARM, THE
28 | 26 | 26 | $152

*Willows Lodge, 14590 NE 145th St. (Woodinville-Redmond Rd.),*
*Woodinville, 206-784-2222; www.theherbfarm.com*
■ Prepare for the "meal of a lifetime" at this "legendary"
Woodinville New American where "four-hour-plus" prix fixe
evenings are centered around "master" chef Jerry Traunfeld's
"rigorously seasonal" "nine-course [menu of] gourmet wonders"
that celebrates "the bounty of the NW", with "herbs in everything"
down to "the sparkling wine"; "nothing is lacking", from the
"superb" service to the "wonderful atmosphere" to the substantial
tab; P.S. for the ultimate, "plan to stay the night" at the Lodge.

### Il Terrazzo Carmine ⧄
26 | 24 | 25 | $44

*411 First Ave. S. (bet. Jackson & King Sts.), 206-467-7797*
■ "Astounding" "traditional Italian" cuisine featuring "simple
preparations and the best ingredients" is what comes out of the
kitchen at this "friendly" "jewel in the middle of Pioneer Square";
"upscale" but "not stuffy" decor, "honest-to-goodness pro waiters"
and a "wonderful wine list" make for a truly "delightful evening",
whether "entertaining clients" or celebrating "special occasions."

### Inn at Langley
27 | 22 | 24 | $63

*Inn at Langley, 400 First St. (bet. Anthes & Park Aves.), Langley,*
*360-221-3033; www.innatlangley.com*
■ Simply "outstanding" "fresh and creative" seasonal NW cuisine
is showcased in "six-course extravaganzas" at this Whidbey
Island inn, where evenings are centered around the "spectacle" of
"watching" chef/innkeeper Matt Costello prepare the meal before
diners' eyes as he "comments on ingredients and techniques";
it's an all-around "wonderful dining experience."

### Izumi
27 | 17 | 24 | $22

*Totem Lake West Ctr., 12539 116th Ave. NE (124th St.), Kirkland,*
*425-821-1959*
■ It's "hard to beat" the "excellent sushi" sliced up at this
popular, "traditionally" appointed Japanese unexpectedly
located in a Kirkland "strip mall", where the "witty chef" might
just give you "things to try that aren't on the menu" while you're
"sitting at the bar" trying to choose among the myriad "catch-of-
the-day" options; in addition to the "very fresh" fish, regulars
appreciate being "treated extremely well" by the "friendly"staff.

### JaK's Grill
27 | 17 | 22 | $32

*4548 California Ave. SW (bet. Alaska & Oregon Sts.), 206-937-7809*
*3701 NE 45th St. (37th Ave.), 206-985-8545*
*14 Front St. N (Sunset Way), Issaquah, 425-837-8834*
■ The "superb" beef in "tremendous" portions served up at this
West Seattle–Issaquah "terrific neighborhood steakhouse" trio
"competes with the big names"; given such "marvelous" quality,
no-"attitude" service and atmosphere, not to mention "excellent-
value" prices, it's no wonder it's made "regulars" even of surveyors
who "relish the food" but not the "no-reservations" policy that
ensures a "long wait" unless you "get there early."

### Kaspar's ⧄
25 | 22 | 24 | $40

*19 W. Harrison St. (1st Ave.), 206-298-0123; www.kaspars.com*
■ Swiss-born chef-owner Kaspar Donier "loves what he does,
and it shows" in the "masterful cuisine" at this Queen Anne

Northwestern where the "interesting seasonal" lineup is especially strong on locally sourced seafood and backed by a "great wine cellar"; this "first-class" "favorite" features "impeccable" service and a room that's "quiet and pleasant", and oenophiles tout the wine bar's "nice by-the-glass selection and reasonable menu"; N.B. the Decor rating may not reflect a post-*Survey* renovation.

**Kingfish** 26 22 20 $27
*602 19th Ave. E. (Mercer St.), 206-320-8757*
■ "Heaven-sent" soul food to "remind a Southern boy of home" draws diners in droves to this Capitol Hill "favorite" boasting a "simple yet sophisticated" setting and "gracious" service; the only thing to "hate" is "the long wait" ("be there when they open to get a table"), but for most it's more than "worth it"; P.S. "save room for" the "red velvet cake."

**Lampreia** 🖾 27 20 22 $58
*2400 First Ave. (Battery St.), 206-443-3301;*
*www.lampreiarestaurant.com*
◨ "Genius" chef-owner Scott Carsberg has "perfected his art" and "continues to innovate" at this "sophisticated", albeit pricey, Belltown NW–New American where the "exquisite" cuisine employing "beautiful", "interesting ingredients" is considered the ultimate for "celebrating a special occasion"; still, despite its undisputed gustatory "excellence" and generally solid service rating, there are gripes that this "food church" serves up a "heaping helping of attitude" along with its other "sublime" offerings.

**Lark** – – – E
*926 12th Ave. (bet. Marion & Spring Sts.), 206-323-5275*
At this Capitol Hill spot owned by celebrated chef Jonathan Sundstrom, his wife, J.M. Enos, and their partner, Kelly Ronan, you can expect a similar regional, seasonal emphasis on its New American menu, as perfected at his previous post, including bread from neighbor La Panzanella and coffee roasted just blocks away at Caffe Vita; warm colors and textures set the mood for a comforting dining experience.

**Le Gourmand** 🖾 26 20 26 $54
*425 NW Market St. (6th Ave.), 206-784-3463*
■ "You'd never suspect" that "one of the finest dining experiences in Seattle" is on a busy Ballard thoroughfare "hidden behind an extremely unassuming facade", but once inside this "secret hideaway" you'll find a pleasantly "non-pompous" setting for "wonderful seasonal" French fare "with a bit of NW" flair à la chefs-owners Bruce and Sara Naftaly; the menu's "reasonably priced", the "wine list excellent" and the staff near-"perfect", meaning that while it may "not be the trendiest" place in town, it certainly is one of the most "amazing"; N.B. the next-door bar/casual eatery, Sambar, is one of the trendiest spots in town.

**Le Pichet** ◑ 23 20 21 $30
*Pike Place Mkt., 1933 First Ave. (Virginia St.), 206-256-1499*
■ "The fastest and cheapest way to visit France" without leaving Pike Place Market, this "slice-of-Paris" "charmer" is home to "French bistro cuisine at its best", providing "pâté fixes" amid an "authentically" "noisy", "jam-packed", zinc-bar-and-banquette-appointed interior; the "terrific fun" here is enhanced by an "unpretentious" wine list that allows you to "experiment" with

different sizes of *pichets* (pitchers); N.B. snackers take note: the *casse-croûte* menu's served all day long.

### Matt's in the Market ⊠   25 | 16 | 22 | $29
*Pike Place Mkt., 94 Pike St. (1st Ave.), 206-467-7909*

■ "Hard to find" but a "true Pike Place Market gem" worth seeking out, this "tiny" seafooder has but a "two-burner kitchen" in which owner Matt Janke and his "fast, friendly" staff produce "some of Seattle's best fish dishes" in full view of the "counter seats"; at lunchtime "exceptional" catfish sandwiches and other easygoing eats ensure it "fills up in about five minutes", while at dinner it features a "wonderful" "short menu" of more sophisticated dishes that really show off "fresh, local, seasonal" Market products.

### METROPOLITAN GRILL   26 | 21 | 23 | $50
*820 Second Ave. (Marion St.), 206-624-3287;*
*www.themetropolitangrill.com*

■ "Where the power elite come to eat meat", this "pricey" Downtown "quintessential traditional steakhouse" "never disappoints" with its "whole-cow" portions of "thick, well-marbled", "cooked-to-perfection" beef and "delicious" sides supported by a "fabulous" 600-label wine list; add the pleasingly "old-school" "chophouse atmosphere" ("busy", "noisy") and "knowledgeable, courteous" service, and it's no wonder the "fat cats" who frequent this "Seattle classic" don't mind opening their wallets for the privilege.

### MISTRAL ⊠   29 | 23 | 25 | $85
*113 Blanchard St. (bet. 1st & 2nd Aves.), 206-770-7799;*
*www.mistralseattle.com*

■ "Out of this world" (and No. 1 for Food among Seattle-area restaurants), this Belltown New American–New French features cuisine that's simply "outstanding in every way" thanks to "exacting" chef-owner William Belickis' "uncompromising" use of "seasonal ingredients" and "creative" techniques imparting an "astonishing" "clarity of flavors" and resulting in "one-of-a-kind" "gastronomic experiences"; the multicourse format makes for "relaxing" dinners that amount to an "evening's entertainment" – and are priced accordingly.

### Monsoon   26 | 20 | 20 | $30
*615 19th Ave. E. (bet. Mercer & Roy Sts.), 206-325-2111;*
*www.monsoonseattle.com*

☑ At this "destination" eatery in an out-of-the-way Capitol Hill "enclave", chef-owner Eric Banh produces "excellent Vietnamese food with flair", "delighting the senses" with an "ever-changing" menu of "innovative, well-prepared" dishes plus "specials that are worth exploring"; the "stark", "contemporary" room can get "noisy", but that doesn't deter the "crowds" from coming, meaning there's often an "unbearable wait" for a table; P.S. check out the "first-rate wine list."

### Nell's   25 | 21 | 25 | $47
*6804 E. Green Lake Way N. (bet. 2nd & 4th Aves.), 206-524-4044*

■ "Even if you're totally jaded", this Green Lake New American's "exceptional" cuisine will "break through" your gustatory cynicism with an "innovative" bill of fare "that sings" with distinctive NW touches from "superb" chef-owner Philip Mihalski (the "excellent-value tasting menu" is a "gourmand's delight"); its "oasis-of-serenity" interior and "friendly" pro service are the crowning touches on an evening that's "first-class" all the way.

### NISHINO                    28 | 22 | 24 | $38
*3130 E. Madison St. (Lake Washington Blvd.), 206-322-5800*
■ "No need to fish for compliments" here – they abound from finatics who say this "elegant, relaxed" Madison Park Japanese offers "a virtually perfect sushi experience", not to mention "divine" cooked dishes; for many the multicourse "omakase meal remains a reason to wake up in the morning" ("remember to order it 24 hours ahead") – just "turn your taste buds over" to "creative" chef-owner Tatsu Nishino and "you won't go wrong."

### Oceanaire Seafood Room       24 | 23 | 24 | $44
*1700 Seventh Ave. (Olive Way), 206-267-2277; www.theoceanaire.com*
■ An "outstanding" "contender" on the "fish-house" scene, this "bustling" Downtown link of a national chain "has it all down" – "fantastic", "very fresh" seafood notable for its "inventive but not way-out" preparations and "mammoth portions" (regulars suggest "splitting"), truly "impeccable service" that's already among the best in town and "classy", "retro"-style decor replete with "red leather and wood."

### Palace Kitchen ◗            25 | 22 | 22 | $36
*2030 Fifth Ave. (Lenora St.), 206-448-2001; www.tomdouglas.com*
■ "Food fit for royalty in a laid-back setting" is the allure of this Downtown New American (to some, the "best" of the Tom Douglas–owned eateries); considering the "great cocktails" and "highly creative", "sensational food", it's no wonder this "energetic, vibrant" place is "always bustling", especially "late night" (the kitchen's open till 1 AM); all in all, it's considered the "quintessential Seattle experience."

### Ray's Boathouse             24 | 24 | 22 | $38
*6049 Seaview Ave. NW (Market St.), 206-789-3770; www.rays.com*
■ "Always tops", this "old-school" Shilshole "institution" is among the "best places for visitors to get their fill of really good salmon" and other "fantastic" seafood prepared with "classic NW" touches while taking in a "million-dollar view over Puget Sound to the Olympic Mountains"; also contributing to the "pleasurable experiences" here is a "voluminous wine list" offering myriad "domestic and import choices" for oenophiles.

### Restaurant Zoë              26 | 23 | 24 | $40
*2137 Second Ave. (Blanchard St.), 206-256-2060;*
*www.restaurantzoe.com*
■ "One of Belltown's best", this "happening" New American succeeds on the strength of its "stellar", "creative" cuisine based on local, seasonal ingredients, "fantastic" pro service and "warm, glowing, inviting" ambiance, all overseen by chef-owner Scott Staples, "a great guy" who "always seems to know what's going on in his dining room"; though all appreciate the "hip", "see-and-be-seen" setting and "people-watching" opportunities, tender ears wish they could "cut the decibels" a bit.

### ROVER'S ⊠                   28 | 23 | 27 | $88
*2808 E. Madison St. (28th Ave.), 206-325-7442; www.rovers-seattle.com*
■ Expect "an unforgettable dining experience" at chef-owner Thierry Rautureau's "world-class" Madison Valley New French

showing "first-rate" "attention to detail", from the "perfectly executed" cuisine with "wonderful matched wines" to the "impeccable" staff to the "elegant" decor that's "unexpectedly relaxed"; just find "somebody else to pay the bill" because it's "breathtakingly expensive", though "worth every penny."

### Shiro's Sushi
26 | 15 | 20 | $35

*2401 Second Ave. (Battery St.), 206-443-9844*
■ Some of "the best sushi in Seattle" is sliced up at this Belltown Japanese where chef-owner Shiro Kashiba ("a true master") works "inventive" spins on "succulent", pristinely "fresh" fish, "setting the bar that others aspire to"; such "top-quality" tastes "almost make you forget" the "spartan" surroundings and service that, while "friendly", can lack polish.

### Shoalwater
26 | 24 | 26 | $43

*Shelburne Inn, 4415 Pacific Hwy. (45th St.), Seaview, 360-642-4142;*
*www.shoalwater.com*
■ "Owner Tony Kischner treats you and your appetite right" at this Long Beach Peninsula destination for "fabulous NW cuisine" with an emphasis on seafood; the "beautiful setting" (the landmark Shelburne Inn), near-"miraculous wine list" and top-notch service are the crowning touches on this overall "outstanding" experience.

### Szmania's
25 | 24 | 23 | $37

*3321 W. McGraw St. (34th Ave.), 206-284-7305*
*Kirkland Waterfront Market Bldg., 148 Lake St. S. (Kirkland Ave.),*
*Kirkland, 425-803-3310*
*www.szmanias.com*
■ At this "innovative" Magnolia Deutschlander, "charming", "deft" chef-owner Ludger Szmania's "fabulous schnitzel" and other "top-notch" dishes "elevate German food to a high gourmet level" while "making good use" of NW ingredients, and aspiring toques seek out the "seasonal cooking demonstration dinners"; a "well-trained staff" and "fun" vibe round out the "enjoyable dining experience"; N.B. the Kirkland branch recently changed its name to Jäger.

### TOSONI'S
28 | 16 | 26 | $41

*14320 NE 20th St. (bet. 140th & 148th Aves.), Bellevue, 425-644-1668*
■ "One of Bellevue's best-kept secrets", this Continental "diamond in the strip-mall rough" is where "welcoming" chef-owner Walter Walcher creates "outstanding" retro classics like steak tartare and duck à l'orange (he really "knows his craft"), but "just don't ask for a menu" because the lineup changes daily; add "personal service" and a "great wine list", and it's all "worthy of a splurge", even if the "interior is a little tired."

### Union
– | – | – | E

*1400 First Ave. (Union St.), 206-838-8000*
This inviting New American is a stylish venue for dining Downtown, with a menu that's in constant flux, much of it varying daily to follow the ebb and flow of seasonal ingredients, giving chef-owner Ethan Stowell full creative freedom to follow his delicious whims (his multicourse prix fixe is easily one of the best dining deals in town).

### Union Bay Cafe
25 | 22 | 24 | $36

*3515 NE 45th St. (bet. Mary Gates Dr. & 36th Ave.), 206-527-8364*
■ Everyone from "academics to old money" can be found at this "delightful, intimate, sophisticated" Laurelhurst NW–New

American that has the "relaxed" feel of a "well-done upscale bistro"; chef-owner Mark Manley "consistently turns out imaginative seasonal dishes" on a "unique", daily changing menu "that calls you back for more", while the "knowledgeable staff" and "excellent wine list" conspire to make experiences here near-"perfect."

**WILD GINGER** 26 | 23 | 21 | $36
*1401 Third Ave. (Union St.), 206-623-4450*
■ Once again voted the Most Popular restaurant in Seattle, this simply "superb" Downtown "Pacific Rim delight" "continues to charm" with "the best fragrant duck" and other "innovative, delicious dishes" savored amid "big, noisy", "high-energy" yet "elegant" environs; given such "stunning" "excellence", it's no wonder that the throng of "too-chic-for-words" patrons "never dwindles", meaning it "can be hard to get a table" (even booking ahead, regulars report an "indifference to reservation times"), though "once you get past the hostess it's smooth sailing."

# St. Louis

## TOP 10 FOOD RANKING

| Restaurant | Cuisine |
|---|---|
| *27* Tony's | Italian |
| Sidney Street Cafe | New American |
| Trattoria Marcella | Italian |
| *26* Crossing, The | New American |
| Dominic's | Italian |
| Al's | Steakhouse |
| Nippon Tei | Asian Fusion |
| Kemoll's | Italian/Continental |
| Zinnia | New American |
| Giovanni's | Italian |

## ADDITIONAL NOTEWORTHY PLACES

| | |
|---|---|
| Annie Gunn's | American |
| Arthur Clay's | New American |
| Frazer's | New American |
| Harvest | New American |
| Monarch | Eclectic |
| 1111 Mississippi | Italian/Californian |
| Pho Grand | Vietnamese |
| Pueblo Solis | Mexican |
| Remy's Kitchen | Mediterranean |
| Restaurant Figaro | Mediterranean |

| F | D | S | C |
|---|---|---|---|

**Al's Restaurant** ☒

| 26 | 19 | 24 | $51 |
|---|---|---|---|

*1200 N. First St. (Biddle St.), 314-421-6399;*
*www.alsrestaurant.net*

■ Entering Al Barroni's "classic" steakhouse is "like stepping back in time", and no wonder – this Downtown "benchmark" with a "men's club feel", one of the city's oldest restaurants, has been serving "superb meat and seafood" since 1925; instead of a menu, the "accommodating staff" presents "a fabulous platter" of raw materials that can be prepared with all the "fixings"; if a few yawn it's a "bit tired", fans find it "reassuring" that it "never changes."

**ANNIE GUNN'S**

| 25 | 21 | 22 | $36 |
|---|---|---|---|

*16806 Chesterfield Airport Rd. (Baxter Rd.), Chesterfield,*
*636-532-7684*

☑ Chef Lou Rook III "keeps the Chesterfield–West County set happy" with his "sublime" American fare, including "hearty portions" of "heavenly" steaks and the "freshest fish" "served with hospitality" and accompanied by an "extensive wine list"; "guys and gals appreciate" the "snuggle booths", "clubby atmosphere" and "attached Smokehouse Market" for "high-end grocery items"; call weeks ahead for weekend reservations or "be prepared" for an "unbearable wait."

### Arthur Clay's ⊠

– | – | – | E

*7266 Manchester Rd. (Southwest Ave.), Maplewood, 314-645-0300;*
*www.arthurclays.com*

Yet another reason Maplewood's Manchester Road is becoming a diners' destination district is this New American from Stephen and Kerri Scherrer and their veteran staff; though the slate changes daily, expect to find global flourishes (spaetzle, sticky rice, edamame), vegetarian options and an interesting 80-label wine list; the dining room has classic exposed brick and hardwood floors, with a few 21st-century accents (hanging metal art, a concrete bar), and sidewalk seating provides an alfresco alternative.

### CROSSING, THE ⊠

26 | 20 | 25 | $43

*7823 Forsyth Blvd. (Central Ave.), Clayton, 314-721-7375;*
*www.thecrossingstl.com*

■ "Breathtaking from every angle", this "chic", candlelit New American "star of Clayton" brings together regional ingredients from around the country, dishing up a "sublime experience" with "phenomenal" fare and a "tasting menu to die for"; chef-owner Jim Fiala was "trained in New York and you can tell" beam boosters who make a beeline to "savor every mouthful."

### DOMINIC'S ⊠

26 | 24 | 26 | $44

*5101 Wilson Ave. (Hereford St.), 314-771-1632;*
*www.dominicsrestaurant.com*

■ "Still a must if you enjoy classic Italian cuisine", this "fab" family-owned "favorite" "place to celebrate" "that special occasion" in the Hill district is also a "top choice for a romantic night out"; it's "elegant in every respect", from the "impeccable service" and "large portions" of "flavorful food" to the "lovely", "outstanding decor" and "wonderful atmosphere" – indeed, gastronomes gush it's "worth the splurge."

### 1111 Mississippi ⊠

– | – | – | E

*1111 Mississippi (Chouteau Ave.), 314-241-9999; www.1111-m.com*

Once a shoe factory, this 1922 brick building in Lafayette Square has been rehabbed into an upscale eatery with an open kitchen, two fireplaces, a loft lounge and a glass-enclosed, eat-in wine cellar; chef Ivy Magruder's Tuscan-Californian cuisine (signature dishes include braised rabbit and potato wrapped grouper) and a solid list of American and Italian vintages all come to your table courtesy of a carefully schooled staff.

### Frazer's Traveling Brown Bag ⊠

23 | 18 | 21 | $28

*1811 Pestalozzi St. (Lemp Ave.), 314-773-8646; www.frazergoodeats.com*

■ Frazer Cameron's "offbeat" "little place on Pestalozzi" in Benton Park, across the highway from Anheuser-Busch, has "vaulted" "up a notch" spacewise, growing from "hip" to even "hipper"; nevertheless, the "really original" New Orleans–accented New American "food stays consistently" "delicious" – "and the crowds waiting for tables know it"; admirers also adore the "relaxed vibes and arty decor" as well as the "passionate staff."

### Giovanni's ⊠

26 | 23 | 25 | $44

*5201 Shaw Ave. (Marconi Ave.), 314-772-5958;*
*www.giovannisonthehill.com*

■ "The crown of the Hill, worthy of a president's palate" (Reagan, Bush, Clinton, to date), this "excellent, expensive", "elegant" Italian offers a "wonderful romantic experience" replete with "tableside finishing of dishes" and "primo", "polished but not fussy service"; longtime owner Giovanni Gabriele has turned the kitchen reins over to son Francisco Paolo, who whips up "sublime food" that's "perfect for a special occasion" (hint: it's one of "the best places to impress a woman").

## HARVEST
24 | 23 | 23 | $39 |

*1059 S. Big Bend Blvd. (Clayton Rd.), Richmond Heights, 314-645-3522; www.harveststlouis.com*

■ "Talented chef"-owner Steve Gontram operates "a well-run restaurant" in the Clayton–Richmond Heights corridor with an "always changing" seasonal New American menu "that has something to offer all eaters", "excellent wine choices" and a "homey atmosphere", "especially in the winter when the fire is going"; it's a "favorite" for "soulfully satisfying inventive dishes" (including "bread pudding like manna") that "really make you feel like you're somewhere special"; still, a smattering snipe "everything is nice but the noise level."

## Kemoll's ☒
26 | 24 | 25 | $41 |

*Metropolitan Square Bldg., 1 Metropolitan Sq. (Pine St.), 314-421-0555; www.kemolls.com*

■ An "oldie but goodie", this fourth-generation family-owned Italian-Continental "treasure", in the marble lobby of Downtown's Metropolitan Square, "deserves its status" as a "local legend"; the smitten swoon over the "superb service" and "sumptuous surroundings" as well as the "delicious food" (the "divine" "cheese garlic bread is worth the trip" alone); granted, it "ain't cheap", but it's a "great place for a fancy night out."

## Monarch ☒
– | – | – | E |

*7401 Manchester Rd. (Sutton Ave.), Maplewood, 314-644-3995; www.monarchrestaurant.com*

Owners Jeff Orbin and Aaron Teitelbaum hope to make downtown Maplewood the next must-visit neighborhood with this imaginative Eclectic that boasts an elegant dining room and a trendy bistro coexisting around a comfortable bar; in the kitchen, well-regarded chef Brian Hale brings complementary Asian and American flavors to dishes such as grilled halibut, spicy pork tenderloin and a short rib sandwich – all stylishly presented and accompanied by a fine, well-priced wine list.

## Nippon Tei
26 | 24 | 22 | $28 |

*14025 Manchester Rd. (Weidmann Rd.), Ballwin, 636-386-8999*

■ A "wonderful respite from the everyday grind", this Ballwin "favorite" provides everything "you hope for in Asian fusion cuisine", from "creative tableside sukiyaki" and shabu shabu to "some of the best sushi around"; "the greetings you receive are warm", "the service outstanding" and the "presentation superb", plus the "elegant setting" boasts "hip" colorful, "transporting decor" – so "don't be fooled by the strip-mall location."

## Pho Grand
24 | 17 | 21 | $15 |

*3195 S. Grand Blvd. (bet. Connecticut & Wyoming Sts.), 314-664-7435; www.phogrand.com*

■ This Grand Boulevard "hideaway" in "charming" "new digs" on a "street of funky storefronts", offers a "screaming value" on the "best, most authentic Vietnamese" "in town" and service so "fast" and "friendly" your order may arrive "before you work up an appetite"; the "delicious dishes" have "heat in all the right places", plus there are "enough selections so you never get bored"; the "only drawback: everyone else loves it too, so the wait seems like an eternity."

### Pueblo Solis 23 | 16 | 19 | $23
*5127 Hampton Ave. (bet. Delor & Itaska Sts.), 314-351-9000*
■ "Masterly Mama Solis" is no longer cooking at this South City "treasure", but it's still "one of the best Mexicans" in town, starting with the "fab margaritas and sangria" and moving on to "killer guacamole" and "amazing fish entrees"; "friendly" service and a colorful, "festive" atmosphere help compensate for "long waits" in the "tiny interior."

### Remy's Kitchen & Wine Bar ⊠ 24 | 20 | 22 | $30
*222 S. Bemiston Ave. (bet. Bonhomme Ave. & Forest Park Pkwy.), Clayton, 314-726-5757; www.remyskitchen.net*
■ Offering a "refreshing interpretation of Med cuisine" paired with "fun flights of wine", Tim Mallett's "casual, comfortable" Clayton boîte with a "beautiful bar" is "appropriate for business occasions, a date" or "late-night snacking"; "unique entrees" play "second fiddle" to the "tapaslike", "inventive" small plates boasting "wonderful" "flavors, textures and spices."

### Restaurant Figaro − | − | − | E
*15 N. Meramec Ave. (Forsyth Blvd. & Maryland Ave.), Clayton, 314-726-5007*
Highly skilled veteran chef Mike Johnson brings his expertise to this Mediterranean in Clayton, one of the area's hottest dining neighborhoods; Moroccan-style lamb tagine is a highlight, and there's a good selection of pizzas and pastas to boot; other attractions include the comfortable room, slick service and fine, expensive wine list.

### SIDNEY STREET CAFE ⊠ 27 | 24 | 26 | $38
*2000 Sidney St. (Salena St.), 314-771-5777; www.sidneystreetcafe.com*
■ "Tucked away in a building" dating back to 1885, this "oh-so-romantic" storefront Benton Park beacon decorated with "exposed-brick walls" and lit by "flickering candles" "continues to live up to its reputation" for "innovative" New American cuisine; the "very friendly staff" presents the "menu on a chalkboard" and generously bestows "baskets of steaming hot, impossibly soft beignets" (don't "overdose"); "reserve well in advance, as they book up quickly", and remember: it's also "fun to sit" in the "cool" "old bar."

### TONY'S ⊠ 27 | 25 | 27 | $57
*410 Market St. (4th St.), 314-231-7007; www.tonysstlouis.com*
■ Elected the city's No. 1 venue for Food, this Downtown "icon" sets the standard by which "all other St. Louis restaurants are judged", with "superlative", "classic" Italian fare that's "never less than absolutely divine" bolstered by "very visible" owners and an "unobtrusive" staff that "treats you like royalty"; enthusiasts exclaim it's "definitely a destination for special celebrations" – as well as *the* "place to go to drop serious money on dinner" – but thankful trenchermen report that "portions are hearty for such a fancy place."

## TRATTORIA MARCELLA 🖾

27 | 19 | 24 | $33

*3600 Watson Rd. (Pernod Ave.), 314-352-7706*

■ Brothers Steve and Jamie Komorek "have a great thing going" at their "cozy", "bistro-style" Italian "gem" on the South Side where fans flock for "tremendously good", "rustic" yet "innovative meals" capped with a "fine choice of wine" and "hip service"; while grumblers gripe it can be as "loud as a hockey game", especially on the "newer side", and "dang hard to get into", mavens maintain it's "worth it."

### Zinnia

26 | 20 | 25 | $35

*7491 Big Bend Blvd. (Shrewsbury Ave.), Webster Groves, 314-962-0572; www.zinniarestaurant.com*

■ A perennial "purple" "favorite" "year in and year out", this "charmingly decorated" "gourmet delight" set in a "converted gas station" in Webster Groves "lives up to its reputation" with "daring" New American "preparations that make for a superb evening"; the "quaint" porch-style "patio is one of the best places to dine", plus the "great" staff is "very helpful"; P.S. "make reservations – it's not that big" a space.

# Tampa/Sarasota

## TOP 10 FOOD RANKING

| Restaurant | Cuisine |
|---|---|
| **28** Beach Bistro | Floribbean |
| Café B.T. | French/Vietnamese |
| **27** SideBern's | New American |
| **26** Six Tables | New French/Continental |
| Selva Grill | Peruvian |
| Pane Rustica | Bakery/Sandwich Shop |
| Bijou Café | Continental |
| Black Pearl | New American |
| Euphemia Haye | Eclectic |
| Armani's | Northern Italian |

## ADDITIONAL NOTEWORTHY PLACES

| | |
|---|---|
| Bern's | Steakhouse |
| Columbia | Spanish/Cuban |
| Michael's on East | Continental |
| Mise en Place | New American |
| Ophelia's | Continental |
| Pelagia Trattoria | Mediterranean |
| Roy's | Hawaii Regional |
| Salt Rock Grill | Seafood |
| Water, Unique Sushi | Japanese/Pan-Asian |
| Zoria | Continental/Eclectic |

| F | D | S | C |
|---|---|---|---|

**ARMANI'S** ☒     | 26 | 26 | 25 | $60 |

*Grand Hyatt Tampa Bay, 2900 Bayport Dr. (Hwy. 60), Tampa,
813-207-6800; www.armanisrestaurant.com*

■ "Wear Armani" and arrive "one hour before sunset" for "a
spectacular view of Tampa Bay" from this "swanky" Northern
Italian atop the Grand Hyatt Tampa Bay; the "veal is the specialty"
but the "antipasto from heaven" is also a "must"; a staff that
"treats you like a big shot" and a setting that's "elegant" "without
feeling musty" make this the place to "celebrate and impress",
though some gripe about sticker-shock prices and a "snooty"
attitude; N.B. "seafood lovers" who "wish for fish" might swim
on over to the Hyatt's Oystercatchers, which is said to offer a
"fantastic" buffet brunch.

**BEACH BISTRO**     | 28 | 23 | 27 | $58 |

*6600 Gulf Dr. (66th St.), Holmes Beach, 941-778-6444;
www.beachbistro.com*

■ At this Anna Maria Island cubbyhole, voted No. 1 for Food on
the Gulf Coast, "a chef with sand between his toes" conjures up
"exceptional" Floribbean fare (plus bouillabaisse "even the French
can't duplicate") accompanied by 300-plus wines and served by
a "personable" staff; though it can be "crowded and noisy", not

to mention "expensive", bistrophiles say "it's worth it": "even death would be a treat if these folks had cooked it!"

**BERN'S STEAK HOUSE**　　25 | 19 | 26 | $55

*1208 S. Howard Ave. (bet. Marjorie & Watrous Sts.), Tampa, 813-251-2421; www.bernssteakhouse.com*

■ "Red meat, red wine and red walls": such are the robust joys of this "iconic" "carnivores' delight" (voted the Gulf Coast's Most Popular), with its "plate-sized" steaks, hundreds of thousands of bottles and "Barbary Coast/brothel" interiors; "well-versed" servers lead "unbelievable" kitchen and cellar tours, and for sugar junkies the dessert room upstairs is "as much fun as you can have" – even if prices leave you in the red; P.S. walk-ins can eat in the bar and "enjoy the experience on a budget."

**BIJOU CAFÉ**　　26 | 24 | 25 | $47

*1287 First St. (Pineapple Ave.), Sarasota, 941-366-8111; www.bijoucafe.net*

■ No longer a diamond in the rough, this Downtown Continental (once a gas station) is now a "beautifully remodeled" "little jewel", gratifying regulars with "rack of lamb to die for" and shrimp piri piri courtesy of chef-owner Jean-Pierre Knaggs and a "precise, friendly" staff that "treats you like family"; even post-expansion, book way ahead in winter to beat opera-bound crowds worried about curtain time.

**Black Pearl**　　26 | 21 | 26 | $44

*315 Main St. (Broadway St.), Dunedin, 727-734-3463; www.theblackpearlofdunedin.com*

■ The few who have discovered this "rare pearl" in the "delightful small town" of Dunedin say the tiny New American is an "excellent value" for its "delicious" twice-cooked Long Island duck and Maryland crab cakes, served up by a "superbly knowledgeable" staff"; eating here is "like eating at a close friend's house", but if you want to woo your honey at this "cozy, quiet and romantic" hideaway, you'd better "make your reservations well in advance of Valentine's Day."

**CAFÉ B.T.** 🖼　　28 | 18 | 24 | $34

*3324 W. Gandy Blvd. (bet. Sheridan Rd. & Sherwood Ave.), Tampa, 813-831-9254; www.btrestaurants.com*

■ "Who could believe" such "simply superb" French-Vietnamese concoctions could be found in a Tampa "strip mall"? – but there's "an artist in the kitchen" of this "small restaurant serving big-time food", making it "an excellent choice for a light dinner": the "chef's seafood specials" paired with (only) beer and wine create an "outstanding", "creative", "refreshing experience for the taste buds", say dazzled devotees, who conclude it's "easy to drive past" this unassuming spot – "but don't."

**COLUMBIA**　　20 | 21 | 19 | $33

*1241 Gulf Blvd. (½ mi. south of Sand Key Bridge), Clearwater, 727-596-8400*
*411 St. Armands Circle (Blvd. of the Presidents), Sarasota, 941-388-3987*
*St. Petersburg Pier, 800 Second Ave. (Beach Dr.), St. Petersburg, 727-822-8000*
*2117 E. Seventh Ave. (bet. 21st & 22nd Sts.), Ybor City, 813-248-4961*
*www.columbiarestaurant.com*

☑ "If it didn't exist, Hemingway would have invented it": this venerable indoor/outdoor Ybor City Spanish/Cuban, the first of the

Gonzmart family's statewide chain, delivers a "festive", "authentic" Iberian interlude (with flamenco dancers, even!) in a historic tiled building; perennials like the 1905 salad (so called to commemorate the restaurant's founding), black bean soup, paella and sangria are strongest here, but St. Petersburg's pier view and the people-watching at Sarasota's St. Armands Circle are compensations.

**Euphemia Haye ☽** 26 | 22 | 24 | $53
*5540 Gulf of Mexico Dr. (Gulf Bay Rd.), Longboat Key, 941-383-3633; www.euphemiahaye.com*
☑ "Don't blink or you'll miss the turn" for chef-owner Raymond Arpke's "expensive" Eclectic, "hidden in the trees" on Longboat Key; admirers adore its "prime pepper steak" and duck "still on the wing", served by a "loyal" staff in a formal dining room that's "like a private club in the tropics", but skeptics ask "what the Haye happened?" – this "old standby" "ain't what she used to be"; P.S. for lighter dishes and "fabulous" desserts, there's the casual HayeLoft upstairs.

**Michael's On East ⍉** 25 | 24 | 24 | $48
*1212 East Ave. S. (Bahia Vista St.), Sarasota, 941-366-0007; www.bestfood.com*
☑ Sarasota's "sleek, stylish and consistent" Continental certainly has "high snob appeal" ("take your mother-in-law, boss or fiancée" to "watch the crowd strut about"); aficionados applaud "one of the best kitchens in the region", "exceptional wines" from the sibling shop next door and "attentive" staffers, but detractors demur, calling it "trendy but not always wonderful" and charging that this "flashy" "joint" "suffers" because owners Phil Mancini and Michael Klauber are "more focused on catering."

**Mise en Place ⍉** 25 | 22 | 23 | $44
*442 W. Kennedy Blvd. (Grand Central Pl.), Tampa, 813-254-5373; www.miseonline.com*
■ "This is where Niles and Frasier would dine in Tampa", declare gourmands who glorify chef-owner Marty Blitz's New American Downtowner, a "solid price-performer" where "any foodie worth his sea salt" can find cuisine that "rewards an adventurous palate"; meanwhile, a "doting" staff maintains the "high energy" at this "chichi" "watering hole"; a few cavil, though, that "ingredients can be overly complicated" (jokers jest "does everything have to be served with a purée of glazed walnuts and blueberry chutney?").

**Ophelia's on the Bay** 24 | 24 | 23 | $48
*9105 Midnight Pass Rd. (south of Turtle Beach), Siesta Key, 941-349-2212; www.opheliasonthebay.net*
■ Sit near a window or on the bayside patio for "breathtaking water views", courtesy of this "pearl" at the south end of Siesta Key; it may be "expensive", but for a "special occasion" diners can expect a "charming", "quiet setting without tourist kitsch"; the Continental menu's "sophisticated" and "creative" and the staff is "friendly", but in the end "atmosphere is what it's all about."

**Pane Rustica** 26 | – | 19 | $13
*3225 S. MacDill Ave. (Bay to Bay Blvd.), Tampa, 813-902-8828*
■ "The angels bake bread here" say loaf-ers who love the "world-class artisanal" goodies at this Tampa lunch favorite: "thin and crispy" pizzas, "spectacular" sandwiches and homemade soups

"make eating carbs fashionable again", even if the "creative and friendly staff" does sometimes "run out of the best daily choices"; "finding a table" during peak hours can be "difficult", but hey, there's always takeout; N.B. a post-*Survey* move to larger digs has outdated the Decor score.

### Pelagia Trattoria　　　　　– | – | – | E
*Renaissance Tampa Hotel Intl. Plaza, 4200 Jim Walter Blvd. (Bay St.), Tampa, 813-313-3235; www.renaissancetampa.com*
Big buzz surrounded this upscale trattoria's August 2004 opening as part of the Renaissance Tampa Hotel International Plaza, and nowadays a stylish crowd comes here clamoring for chef Fabrizio Schenardi's lush Mediterranean cuisine (cinnamon–juniper berry marinated quail, pistachio-crusted rack of lamb with fig-merlot sauce); a bold, colorful dining room, with hand-glazed tiles and custom ironwork, recalls the region as well.

### Roy's　　　　　25 | 23 | 24 | $48
*4342 W. Boy Scout Blvd. (bet. Lois Ave. & Westshore Blvd.), Tampa, 813-873-7697; www.roysrestaurant.com*
■ "So much for a jaded palate", lei people say of their meals at this outpost of Roy Yamaguchi's "pricey" Hawaii Regional chain: "inspired, almost over-the-top" seafood entrees and the signature "oozy chocolate soufflé" "with a molten lava center" wake up "weary taste buds"; meanwhile, an "attentive but not obtrusive" staff steers island-hoppers through this Pacific passage amid an atmosphere that some call "lively" and others "loud."

### Salt Rock Grill　　　　　24 | 23 | 19 | $42
*19325 Gulf Blvd. (1 mi. north of Park Blvd.), Indian Shores, 727-593-7625; www.saltrockgrill.com*
■ Expect fish "so fresh it may still be swimming" plus a 790-label wine list at this Intracoastal Waterway seafoodery: they cook their own catch "over a wood-burning grill" to produce "the best-tasting" steaks, seared ahi tuna and crab legs that "sizzle" – even if service sometimes "fizzles"; the "bustle" can be "fun" (or "loud"), and a "come-as-you-are" policy means "both tuxedos and flip-flops" make the scene – hence it's "always packed"; P.S. the under-$10 early-bird menu is downright "reasonable."

### SELVA GRILL　　　　　26 | 14 | 20 | $34
*2881 Clark Rd. (Swift Rd.), Sarasota, 941-927-3500; www.selvagrill.com*
■ "Viva Peru!" cheer the happy few who have explored this unassuming Peruvian dinner-only "gem" in a Sarasota "strip center"; chef-owner Darwin Santa Maria "cooks with great gusto", "speaking fluent cilantro" with a Nuevo Latino accent and creating special seviche that manages to be "very flavorful" yet "not too spicy for aging taste buds"; though the decor is "minimal", a "charming staff" makes it "a pleasure to go there."

### SIDEBERN'S ⊠　　　　　27 | 24 | 23 | $45
*2208 W. Morrison Ave. (S. Howard Ave.), Tampa, 813-258-2233; www.bernssteakhouse.com*
■ This "offspring" of Bern's Steak House "should make the parent proud"; surveyors call it a "gastronomic tour de force" thanks to chef-partner Jeannie Pierola's "masterful" New American "creations" (e.g. "to-die-for" dim sum and desserts "that draw stares"); sure, prices are a bit steep, but this "contemporary

stunner" brings in an "upbeat, fast-paced" crowd and staffers meet "your every need"; N.B. thrifty oenophiles buy a bottle of wine at the attached store, pay the corkage fee and save big.

### SIX TABLES
26 | 21 | 28 | $70

*1153 Main St. (Pinehurst Rd.), Dunedin, 727-736-8821*
*The Peninsula Inn & Spa, 2937 Beach Blvd. (54th St.), Gulfport, 727-346-9800* ☒
*118 W. Bay Dr. (west of RR tracks), Largo, 727-518-1123*
*4267 Henderson Blvd. (south of JFK Blvd.), Tampa, 813-207-0527*
*www.sixtables.com*
■ At these four prix fixe New French–Continentals (each serving half a dozen parties at one nightly seating) chef-founder Roland Levi (once Brooke Astor's private toque) puts forth a sextet of "impeccably prepared" courses, including baked Chilean sea bass, sole meunière and duckling à l'orange; thanks to his "detailed" presentations in the "intimate", "quiet" and "very romantic" dining rooms, "gastronomically blessed" respondents feel like "invited guests" who are "eating at a good friend's house."

### Water, Unique Sushi ☒
– | – | – | I

*1015½ S. Howard Ave. (W. Morrison Ave.), Tampa, 813-251-8406;*
*www.ciccioandtonys.com*
With Culinary Institute of America graduate Erin Van Zandt at the helm, this new Japanese–Pan-Asian has become a neighborhood foodie fave; the fin fare focuses on what the chef calls 'clear rolls' (sushi wrapped in rice paper instead of nori), paired with zingy sauces and sizzling side dishes; simple aquatic-themed decor, with turquoise walls and azure stained glass, makes the small room feel like Tampa's own blue grotto; N.B. beer and wine only.

### Zoria ●
25 | 24 | 23 | $44

*1991 Main St. (bet. Links Ave. & US 301), Sarasota, 941-955-4457;*
*www.zoria.net*
■ Formerly of Hillview Street, this Continental-Eclectic has redeemed a once-jinxed Downtown Sarasota location; the "chic clientele" calls the move a "huge improvement", "watching the movie crowd" while seated at the outdoor tables and praising the "much quieter digs inside"; meanwhile, the three chef-owners' "fusion of exotic and familiar flavors" in "exquisite" dishes served by a "cheerful", "knowledgeable" staff still impresses, and the expanded bar offers a menu that's "great for a light bite."

# Tucson

## TOP 10 FOOD RANKING

| | Restaurant | Cuisine |
|---|---|---|
| **28** | Dish, The | New American |
| **27** | Grill at Hacienda del Sol | New American |
| **26** | Vivace | Northern Italian |
| | Ventana Room | New American |
| | Janos | Southwestern |
| | Le Rendez-Vous | French |
| **25** | Cafe Poca Cosa | Mexican |
| | Wildflower | New American |
| | Gold Room | SW/Continental |
| **24** | Jonathon's Tucson Cork | SW/Steakhouse |

## ADDITIONAL NOTEWORTHY PLACES

| | |
|---|---|
| Anthony's/Catalinas | Continental |
| Arizona Inn | Continental |
| Bistro Zin | New American |
| Cuvée World Bistro | Eclectic |
| Feast | Eclectic |
| Fuego! | Southwestern |
| J Bar | Nuevo Latino |
| Kingfisher | New American/Seafood |
| McMahon's Prime | Steakhouse |
| Mi Nidito | Mexican |

| F | D | S | C |
|---|---|---|---|

**Anthony's in the Catalinas** 🗷    | 22 | 24 | 22 | $50 |
*6440 N. Campbell Ave. (E. Skyline Dr.), 520-299-1771*
▣ Though you may "need two credit cards to pay for dinner", this "beautiful" Continental showplace's "legendary wine list" and "dynamite city views" are "first class"; disappointed diners, however, cite the "old-fashioned menu" and "pretentious" service as proof that it's "overrated" and lament that it's now a mere "shadow of what used to be a great Tucson experience."

**Arizona Inn**    | 21 | 25 | 23 | $42 |
*Arizona Inn, 2200 E. Elm St. (bet. N. Campbell Ave. & N. Tucson Blvd.), 520-325-1541; www.arizonainn.com*
■ Graced with a timeless "serenity", this "lovely" Continental "throwback" in a "secluded" old hotel is revered for its "exquisite" gardens and "solicitous", "old-style" service, capturing the "understated elegance" of the "'30s West"; it may "not be a place for the young crowd", but it does provide a "charming" glimpse of "old Arizona at its best", especially at "afternoon tea" during winter.

**Bistro Zin**    | 23 | 22 | 23 | $38 |
*1865 E. River Rd. (Campbell Rd.), 520-299-7799; www.tasteofbistrozin.com*
■ "Wear black and bring a megaphone" if you visit this "big-city" bistro (owned by Sam Fox of Wildflower) because it's as "chic" as

it is "noisy"; the main draw is the "impressive" selection of wines by the glass (also offered in nearly two dozen "interesting flights"), and "knowledgeable" servers can suggest pairings to match the "excellent" French-accented New American dishes; P.S. "don't miss the chocolate desserts."

### CAFE POCA COSA ⚠ | 25 | 21 | 21 | $26 |
*Clarion Santa Rita Hotel, 88 E. Broadway Blvd. (Scott Ave.), 520-622-6400*
■ "Rollicking yet somehow intimate", this Downtown "treasure" with a "unique" vibe is a popular "spot to take out-of-town guests" thanks to Suzana Dávila's "amazing" Mexican fare (her chalkboard menu changes twice daily, but you "can't go wrong with the chef's tasting plate"); adding to the "festive" atmosphere are the colorful Oaxacan masks mounted on bright walls and the south-of-the-border music, making this an "absolutely essential dining experience in Tucson."

### Cuvée World Bistro ⚠ | – | – | – | M |
*Rancho Ctr., 3352 E. Speedway Blvd. (bet. Alvernon Way & Country Club Blvd.), 520-881-7577; www.cuveebistro.com*
Like the method of champagne-making that inspired its name, this casual but elegant newcomer reflects a blending of elements, both in its exotic design (Moroccan archways, Italian pillars, palace doors from India) and wide-ranging Eclectic cuisine; though it's too soon to tell, chef-owner Mitch Levy's potato-basil-crusted salmon and single-malt butterscotch pudding may become mainstays of his seasonal menu, which includes wine-pairing suggestions for every course.

### DISH, THE ⚠ | 28 | 19 | 25 | $38 |
*3200 E. Speedway Blvd. (Country Club Blvd.), 520-326-1714; www.dishbistro.com*
■ "Wow!" exclaim enthusiasts about this "tiny" New American "diamond" ranked No. 1 for Food in Tucson; they call it a "perfect place for a quiet dinner" over "original" "dishes of delectable delights", accompanied by a "fantastic wine selection" and presented by a "knowledgeable" staff; it may be "cramped" (there are "very few tables", so "reservations are a must"), "but who cares given the quality and service?"

### Feast | ▽ 25 | 15 | 19 | $21 |
*4122 E. Speedway Blvd. (bet. Alvernon Way & Columbus Blvd.), 520-326-9363; www.eatatfeast.com*
■ "What a find!" exclaim enthusiasts of this "casual" Eclectic gem where "wonderful cook" Doug Levy (ex The Dish) "challenges the senses" with his "monthly changing menu" of "imaginative", "amazing" "gourmet" treats; though it's mostly known as a "take-out heaven" that "makes a mockery of fast-food joints", a recent expansion of its "small" but "comfy" dining space now allows 50-plus people to eat on the premises; N.B. closed Mondays.

### Fuego! | 23 | 17 | 21 | $38 |
*6958 E. Tanque Verde Rd. (Sabino Canyon Rd.), 520-886-1745; www.fuegorestaurant.com*
☑ "Local personality" Alan Zeman "keeps his eye on the details" at his "festive" Southwestern bistro (the name means 'fire' in Spanish) where the "innovative" menu highlights "flaming platters" of "devilishly good" appetizers and wild game; though he exhibits a particularly "deft hand" with exotica like ostrich, all his creations

offer a "successful combination of flavors and textures", so despite "inconsistent" service, fired-up fans swear it's "well worth it"; N.B. closed Mondays.

### Gold Room     25 | 26 | 23 | $48

*Westward Look Resort, 245 E. Ina Rd. (bet. N. 1st Ave. & Oracle Rd.), 520-297-1151; www.westwardlook.com*

☑ "Sublime views" of Downtown enhance the experience at this "magical" dining room, "a major treat for the eyes and palate"; the newly refreshed, "lovely surroundings", "superb" Southwestern-Continental cuisine and "exhaustive wine list" bolster its reputation as an "elegant" "celebration place", but be forewarned that some say the "snotty" staff ("pretentious to the nth degree") "can leave you wondering if you're invisible"; N.B. a post-*Survey* chef change may outdate the above Food score.

### GRILL AT HACIENDA DEL SOL     27 | 27 | 24 | $51

*Hacienda del Sol, 5601 N. Hacienda del Sol (bet. E. River Rd. & E. Sunrise Dr.), 520-529-3500; www.haciendadelsol.com*

☑ Once a "favorite rendezvous spot for Tracy and Hepburn", this "romantic jewel on a hill" – the city's Most Popular restaurant – epitomizes "Tucson's casual elegance"; surveyors suggest you "get a window table" in the "gorgeous" dining room to best enjoy the "city lights" (a "memorable view") while splurging on "fabulous" New American fare; the smitten insist that it's a "must for a special occasion", but cynics feel it "doesn't live up to expectations"; N.B. the Food rating may not reflect a post-*Survey* chef change.

### JANOS  ☒     26 | 25 | 24 | $57

*Westin La Paloma, 3770 E. Sunrise Dr. (bet. N. Campbell Ave. & N. Swan Rd.), 520-615-6100; www.janos.com*

☑ "Still one of Arizona's best" for "special-occasion" dining, this "formal" "oasis" in the foothills of the Catalinas is the brainchild of Janos Wilder, whose "sublime" French-inspired Southwestern cooking is "inventively presented" and beautifully paired with a winning wine list; turned out in an "exquisite" setting with a "spectacular view of Tucson", dinner here is "always an exciting surprise", even if dissenters declare that it's "too pricey for the portions" and "too pretentious for this town."

### J Bar  ☒     23 | 22 | 22 | $31

*Westin La Paloma, 3770 E. Sunrise Dr. (bet. N. Campbell Ave. & N. Swan Rd.), 520-615-6100; www.janos.com*

■ Cost-conscious connoisseurs crow about getting "Janos Wilder's food at half the price" at his "spirited" and far more "casual" offshoot (adjacent to Janos); from the open kitchen emerge grilled Nuevo Latino specialties infused with "wonderfully original flavors" (the "jerked pork is fantastic"), while the handsome bar, custom-made of tin and mirrors, hosts a convivial social scene; "big food without big attitude" plus "a mean margarita" – "you can't ask for much more."

### Jonathan's Tucson Cork     24 | 19 | 21 | $34

*6320 E. Tanque Verde Rd. (bet. E. Pima St. & N. Wilmot Rd.), 520-296-1631; www.jonathanscork.com*

■ Loyalists continue to beat a path to this "dependable" '60s-era steakhouse for its "great" Southwestern spin on certified Angus beef, as well as its "well-prepared" game dishes ("outstanding ostrich"); regulars report it's "always a pleasure" to dine here because they get a "friendly greeting" and an "excellent meal for the price" (it's "been on the Tucson scene for a long time, and it knows its business").

**Kingfisher Bar & Grill** ❶                    22   17   21   $32
*2564 E. Grant Rd. (N. Tucson Blvd.), 520-323-7739;*
*www.kingfisherbarandgrill.com*
■ Though the decor at this New American seafood house draws divided opinions – "weird" vs. "cool" – the menu (starring some of the "freshest fish without a sea nearby") is praised as one of the most "original" in Tucson; backed by a "great" wine list and "exceptionally accommodating" service, it's "excellent across the board", and "thank goodness there's a fine restaurant that's still open after a play or concert."

**Le Rendez-Vous**                    26   17   22   $44
*3844 E. Ft. Lowell Rd. (N. Alvernon Way), 520-323-7373;*
*www.lerendez-vous.com*
■ Tucson Francophiles finagle a "trip to France without leaving town" by visiting this time-honored "quality act" where the "honest, authentic" cooking is "rich" and "wonderfully decadent"; the "traditional" slate may hold "no surprises", but when "classics" such as duck à l'orange, sweetbreads and crêpes suzette are "prepared so artfully with top-notch ingredients", who cares? N.B. closed Mondays.

**McMahon's Prime Steakhouse**                    21   24   20   $50
*2959 N. Swan Rd. (bet. E. Ft. Lowell Rd. & E. Glenn St.), 520-327-2333;*
*www.metrorestaurants.com*
◪ "Contemporary Western art" provides a "stylish" backdrop for the "local power brokers" who patronize this "elegant" "expense-account enclave", long a "favorite" for "fine cuts of meat", an "outstanding wine cellar", an "excellent" piano lounge with live music several nights a week and a "great cigar bar"; the less impressed stress "everything is good but overpriced."

**Mi Nidito**                    23   15   18   $17
*1813 S. Fourth Ave. (bet. 28th & 29th Sts.), 520-622-5081;*
*www.minidito.net*
■ "All the locals" (not to mention former President Bill Clinton) go to this "bargain" Mexican "hideaway" when they want a "quintessential South Tucson experience": "generous portions" of "super Sonoran" *comida* to "eat *con mucho gusto*" in a "comfortable atmosphere" of serape-stripe upholstery, tiled hallways, painted stucco walls and beamed ceilings, where "congenial servers" ferry food to and fro till 2 AM on Fridays and Saturdays; be warned, though, that the no-reservations policy means "long lines"; N.B. closed Monday–Tuesday.

**VENTANA ROOM** ⊠                    26   27   26   $63
*Loews Ventana Canyon Resort, 7000 N. Resort Dr. (N. Kolb Rd.),*
*520-299-2020; www.ventanaroom.com*
■ Change is the order of the day at this "fancy" "gem" ("a hotel restaurant of the best kind") nestled in the foothills that's known for its "beautiful city view" as well as "outstanding" cuisine, an "excellent wine list" and "crisp" service; French chef Philippe Trosch, a post-*Survey* arrival, oversees a formal New American menu, and a recently completed renovation has added European overtones to the "elegant", "romantic" setting, thereby enhancing

an already "superlative dining experience"; N.B. these alterations may not be reflected in the above scores.

### VIVACE ⊠

26 | 22 | 25 | $37

*St. Philip's Plaza, 4310 N. Campbell Ave. (River Rd.), 520-795-7221*
■ Loquacious locals can't say enough about chef-owner Daniel Scordato's Northern Italian "class act" (he "deserves more credit than he gets"); better "forget about your diet" here because his "inspired" cooking makes it hard to stop eating the "amazing pesto olive oil dip", "divine fish" and "desserts that give new meaning to fruit"; consider too the "wonderful" atmosphere ("never stuffy") and "attentive yet unobtrusive" service and it's easy to see why regulars come "back for more again and again."

### Wildflower

25 | 21 | 21 | $32

*Casas Adobes, 7037 N. Oracle Rd. (Ina Rd.), 520-219-4230;*
*www.foxrestaurantconcepts.com*
✓ A trompe l'oeil ceiling depicting clouds and giant paintings of wildflowers give this "hot spot" a "stylish" look despite its "strip-mall" setting; it's an "excellent choice" for "exceptional" New American fare (including "can't-miss" desserts) and a "solid wine list" presented by a staff that treats each guest "with care"; for a "quieter but still lively" experience, regulars "recommend" the "pretty" covered patio with a view of the mountains; N.B. the Decor rating may not reflect a post-*Survey* spruce-up of the interior.

# Washington, DC

## TOP 20 FOOD RANKING

| Restaurant | Cuisine |
|---|---|
| *28* Makoto | Japanese |
| Inn at Little Washington | New American |
| Maestro | Italian |
| Citronelle | New French |
| L'Auberge Chez François | French |
| *27* Marcel's | Belgian/French |
| Gerard's Place | New French |
| Restaurant 2941 | New American |
| L'Auberge Provençale | French |
| Obelisk | Italian |
| Ray's The Steaks | Steakhouse |
| *26* Kinkead's | New American/Seafood |
| Prime Rib | Steakhouse |
| Melrose | New American |
| La Bergerie | French |
| Rabieng | Thai |
| Asia Nora | Pan-Asian |
| El Pollo Rico | Peruvian |
| Nora | New American |
| Galileo/Il Laboratorio | Italian |

## ADDITIONAL NOTEWORTHY PLACES

| | |
|---|---|
| Bis | French Bistro |
| Bombay Club | Indian |
| Bread Line | Bakery/Cafe |
| Café Atlántico | Nuevo Latino |
| Cashion's Eat Place | New American |
| Ceiba | Nuevo Latino |
| DC Coast | New American |
| Equinox | New American |
| Eve | New American |
| Jaleo | Spanish/Tapas |
| Johnny's Half Shell | Seafood |
| Majestic Cafe | New American |
| Palena | New American |
| Pizzeria Paradiso | Pizza |
| 1789 | New American |
| Taberna del Alabardero | Spanish/Tapas |
| TenPenh | Pan-Asian |
| Tosca | Northern Italian |
| Vidalia | New American |
| Zaytinya | Mediterranean |

### Asia Nora ☒          26 | 24 | 23 | $51
*2213 M St., NW (bet. 22nd & 23rd Sts.), 202-797-4860; www.noras.com*
☑ An "air of luxury and mystery" pervades Nora Pouillon's West End "subterranean gem" where, arguably, DC's "most inventive" Pan-Asian fare comes from a kitchen that "takes sourcing seriously", with ingredients as "organic" and "local as possible"; the "tiny portions" of "succulent appetizers" and "gorgeous entrees" are as "elegant" as the "intimate" surroundings, which are staffed by "attentive" if "pretentious" servers, causing devotees to sigh that they "love everything but the price – though it's worth it."

### Bis          24 | 23 | 21 | $48
(aka Bistro Bis)
*Hotel George, 15 E St., NW (bet. N. Capitol St. & New Jersey Ave.), 202-661-2700; www.bistrobis.com*
■ Stop by this "stunning", "modern" bistro near the Capitol "at lunch when the Senate checks in" and experience a "power-dining spot if ever there was one": a "stylish" yet "relaxed" operation with "comfy" nooks and a "hoppin' bar"; the "fine" "French favorites" "shine", and the "knowledgeable" sommelier will guide you through "wonderful" regional wines and "tremendous" cheese selections, all "preferably expensed."

### Bombay Club          23 | 25 | 24 | $43
*815 Connecticut Ave., NW (H St.), 202-659-3727; www.bombayclubdc.com*
■ "Dine where former presidents have, a stone's throw from the White House", at this "elegant" South Asian that cossets the "politico" caste at "well-spaced tables" in an "exquisite" "setting with palm trees" straight out of "*A Passage to India*"; lulled by "live piano", you'll "luxuriate" as a staff that "takes care of every need" ferries "refined" dishes at prices that "won't break the bank", making it "great for business" or a "delicious, reasonably priced romantic night"; in short, it's "the best non–dues paying club you'll ever join."

### Bread Line ☒          23 | 9 | 13 | $14
*1751 Pennsylvania Ave., NW (bet. 17th & 18th Sts.), 202-822-8900*
☑ "Crusty" loaves "star" at this White House–area bakery/cafe where "everything is inventive" and "homemade", from "terrific" knishes to "fantastic fries", "savory" soups, "incredible" salads, "to-die-for" cookies and "monstrous" "bread-oriented" belly busters, served amid "organized chaos" in an "eat-and-run" setting; while the "line moves fast", it's best to "know what you want", "sit outside", expect "pricey" tabs and concede that it's "hard to go back to a regular tuna sandwich after trying theirs."

### Café Atlántico          23 | 22 | 21 | $42
*405 Eighth St., NW (bet. D & E Sts.), 202-393-0812*
☑ "Walk on the culinary wild side" in this "stylish" Penn Quarter Nuevo Latino's "airy, multilevel" digs; its menus are filled with the "unexpected", from "divine guacamole made tableside" to "outstanding" 'dim sum' brunch and a "most impressive" pre-theater deal; at its copper-clad, six-seat "experimental" Minibar influenced by Spain's fabled El Bulli, "30 or more unique bites" jump-start "jaded foodies" who testify that if some dishes are "too creative" and "service is sometimes a little lax", at least you'll "never be bored."

### Cashion's Eat Place
25 | 20 | 21 | $42

*1819 Columbia Rd., NW (bet. Biltmore St. & Mintwood Pl.), 202-797-1819;*
*www.cashionseatplace.com*

■ "Inventive use" of "the freshest ingredients" "stretches the boundaries" "without getting scary" at this "chic" New American "treasure" from Adams Morgan, whose "delightful" staff is "there when needed"; the decor strikes a "balance with masculine dark wood and soothing soft lights and fabrics", and though the "tables can be close", the "high ceiling makes things feel spacious"; P.S. its "fantastic" brunch is "the best way to start a tired Sunday."

### Ceiba ⊠
24 | 24 | 23 | $45

*701 14th St., NW (G St.), 202-393-3983; www.ceibarestaurant.com*

■ "Daringly" different, this "vibrant" Downtown "hot spot" from the TenPenh team wows with "clever" takes on Latin "flavors from mild to wild" in "sophisticated" surroundings accented with dark woods, arty photos and "tropical" touches; servers act as your "adventure" guides, "taking the time" to explain "what's what" on the "surprising" menu; sure, the "hyped" yearling has some "kinks", but reviewers rave that "all the excitement is justified."

### CITRONELLE
28 | 25 | 26 | $80

(aka Michel Richard's Citronelle)
*Latham Hotel, 3000 M St., NW (30th St.), 202-625-2150;*
*www.citronelledc.com*

■ "Playful" Michel Richard plates "dazzling" dishes that look "almost too creative to eat, but [taste] too good not to" at this top French; add a "classy", jacket-required Georgetown setting with a color-changing mood wall, "impeccable" staff and a "wonderful wine cellar", and the result is an "expensive" yet "truly fabulous dining experience" that you'll "never want to [have] end" and "will never forget"; P.S. the chef's table is a "gastronomic epiphany."

### DC Coast ⊠
25 | 23 | 22 | $48

*Tower Bldg., 1401 K St., NW (14th St.), 202-216-5988; www.dccoast.com*

■ A bar swimming with "young sophisticates" is awash in "the energy of the city" at this "swanky" Downtown New American that offers "the best of everything": "fantastic seafood", "style, service and presentation" in a "sweeping, bustling" deco-detailed room; it's a "great scene if you're looking down from the balcony" where it's a bit "quieter"; downstairs the "buzz" makes it "hard to converse", but the "delicious food more than makes up for it."

### El Pollo Rico ⊅
26 | 5 | 17 | $9

*932 N. Kenmore St. (Fairfax Dr.), Arlington, VA, 703-522-3220*
*2541 Ennalls Ave. (Veirs Mill Rd.), Wheaton, MD, 301-942-4419*

■ The "fragrant, perfectly seasoned", "cravable" spit-roasted chicken and "great" fries are an "unbeatable value" at these Peruvian "cult favorites" with "zilch" ambiance and "lines out the door"; amid Wheaton's "strip-mall funk" or newer, "bigger digs" in Arlington, the "lip-smacking", "super-juicy" birds are "served fast and hot" and mostly for takeout to a "diverse clientele."

### Equinox
25 | 19 | 23 | $55

*818 Connecticut Ave., NW (bet. H & I Sts.), 202-331-8118;*
*www.equinoxrestaurant.com*

■ It's "no frills, just thrills" courtesy of Todd Gray's "skill" at this "welcoming" White House–area destination he co-owns with wife

Ellen; the New American tasting menu shows what a "confident chef at the top of his game can do" with "top-notch ingredients at their seasonal peak", delivered by a "delightful staff" that makes diners "comfortable" in an enclosed terrace and rooms where "you can actually talk"; "those who poo-poo the aesthetics" as in need of "pizzazz" should try a "group dinner in the wine cellar – it rocks!"

### Eve ⊠ ─｜─｜─｜ E

*110 S. Pitt St. (bet. King & Prince Sts.), Alexandria, VA, 703-706-0450; www.restauranteve.com*

Chef-owner Cathal Armstrong (ex Bis) and his wife, Meshelle, have fashioned a multifaceted Old Town showplace for his seasonal New American cuisine employing locally sourced ingredients, some of which have been specially grown for the restaurant; there's a lounge, an intimate tasting room with daily changing prix fixe menus and a dining room with a brick fireplace and garden (natch) where comforting bistro fare is served.

### Galileo/Il Laboratorio del Galileo 26｜22｜22｜$69

*1110 21st St., NW (bet. L & M Sts.), 202-331-0880; www.galileodc.com*

☑ The namesake astronomer "would be proud": "Roberto Donna isn't a star – he's a whole galaxy" at this "superlative" Italian in the Golden Triangle; inside Il Laboratorio, the glass-walled dine-in kitchen, he performs tasting-menu "magic" matched by "stunning" wines for an "experience like no other", "and priced accordingly", while in the bar and adjacent dining areas his under-$10 trattoria is served; even critics who decry the main room's "dull" decor, "stuffy" service and "inconsistent" fare agree the cooking crew is "unmatched when it's on."

### Gerard's Place ⊠ 27｜21｜24｜$69

*915 15th St., NW (bet. I & K Sts.), 202-737-4445*

■ At his Downtown "culinary destination", "genius" Gerard Pangaud creates Modern French "interpretations of the classics" in a "serene", "understated" setting reminiscent of "charming" small restaurants in NYC, Paris or Lyons; it's the "perfect place for that special dinner" when "privacy", "pristine quality" and "flawless", "unobtrusive" service matter most; each "memorable" meal with "wonderful" wines is "expensive and worth it", and the $29.50 prix fixe lunch "cannot be beat for taste or price."

### INN AT LITTLE WASHINGTON 28｜28｜28｜$129

*The Inn at Little Washington, Main & Middle Sts., Washington, VA, 540-675-3800; www.theinnatlittlewashington.com*

■ For over a quarter century, this "luxurious" Virginia inn has been a "gastronomic heaven" where Patrick O'Connell transforms the "freshest" ingredients into an "exceptional" New American prix fixe menu; "total pampering" and "rich", "romantic", "theatrical" decor add to the "truly fantastical experience" that's "worth the journey" and "every one of its many pennies"; P.S. to fully realize the "dream of paradise", "stay overnight."

### JALEO 23｜20｜19｜$31

*480 Seventh St., NW (E St.), 202-628-7949 ●*
*7271 Woodmont Ave. (Elm St.), Bethesda, MD, 301-913-0003*

■ With a name meaning both 'revelry' and 'racket', it's no surprise these "high-energy" tapas siblings are "buzzing" with "big groups" indulging in little plates that present "many different", "zesty" Spanish flavors ("don't worry about choosing something you don't like – there'll be something good coming right behind it"); patrons enjoy "sangria-filled dinners outside" in Bethesda and in Penn Quarter "after a show at the Shakespeare", and on some nights, entertainers "do a mean flamenco", making these "vibrant" spots even more "fun."

### Johnny's Half Shell ☒　　　23 | 16 | 20 | $37
*2002 P St., NW (bet. 20th & 21st Sts.), 202-296-2021*
■ This "unpretentious" Dupont Circle "favorite" serves "splendid" seafood, "crisp white wines aplenty" and much more, "without a huge price tag"; it's "wonderfully alive", with "first-rate" cooking, a "classic" oyster-house feel and a "neighborly" bar that's a favored "perch" for "wonk sightings and soft-shell crab"; "deterrents" such as "long waits and no reservations" can be side-stepped by visiting at lunch for "great po' boys and hot dogs."

### KINKEAD'S　　　26 | 21 | 24 | $55
*2000 Pennsylvania Ctr., 2000 Pennsylvania Ave., NW (I St.), 202-296-7700; www.kinkead.com*
☑ "You may run into your congressman" dining on "fabulous seafood" at this Most Popular of DC restaurants, a "venerable" New American haunt for "high rollers and power brokers" in Foggy Bottom; using the "best ingredients, creativity and presentation", Bob Kinkead plates meals made to "impress clients", which are "matched by solicitous service" and a "wine list from heaven"; since a mid-*Survey* "face-lift", the atmosphere is more "inviting and airy", but the place still has "attitude" according to those who claim the "less fabulous are often relegated to Siberia."

### La Bergerie　　　26 | 21 | 25 | $54
*218 N. Lee St. (bet. Cameron & Queen Sts.), Alexandria, VA, 703-683-1007; www.labergerie.com*
■ Fans of "traditional" methods say "a lesson in how French cooking should be done" can be had at this "elegant" restaurant; "if you are fond of goose livers", "real quenelles" and "scrumptious soufflé", you'll savor its "exquisitely prepared" dishes, and the "sophisticated" ambiance contributes to "a truly adult experience" that "makes you want to get dressed up"; perhaps they're "a little stuck up", but what do you expect when they keep hearing they're "the tops in Old Town"?

### L'AUBERGE CHEZ FRANÇOIS　　　28 | 27 | 28 | $68
*332 Springvale Rd. (Beach Mill Rd.), Great Falls, VA, 703-759-3800; www.laubergechezfrancois.com*
■ The "magical esprit" of the Haeringer family pervades their "enchanting" Alsatian farmhouse "tucked in the windy roads of Great Falls", where "memorable" evenings include "delicious" regional dishes, "gracious" treatment and "just the right amount of homey-ness"; with its "charming", rustic rooms and "gorgeous garden", it's a "special place from an earlier time that hugs you like grandma did when you were little" – that is, after you get through the "hassle" of making reservations.

### L'Auberge Provençale　　　27 | 26 | 26 | VE
*L'Auberge Provençale, 13630 Lord Fairfax Hwy. (Rte. 50), Boyce, VA, 540-837-1375; www.laubergeprovencale.com*
■ Your "short ride" through the Virginia countryside is "just enough time to anticipate the surroundings and fabulous fare" at this "wonderful" Provençal-style "country inn" where the French

cuisine and rare wines are "heaven on the tongue"; the prix fixe meals are so "breathtaking", you "won't want the evening to end" – but "if you are staying the night", you have "an over-the-top fantastic breakfast" to look forward to in the morning.

### MAESTRO ⊠       28 | 27 | 28 | $98

*Ritz-Carlton Tysons Corner, 1700 Tysons Blvd. (International Dr.), McLean, VA, 703-917-5498; www.ritzcarlton.com*

■ Take a "front-row seat" near "star" Fabio Trabocchi's open kitchen to watch his "elegant precision" and "amazing" creativity in action; "interpretive" cuisine with a "depth of flavor" on a par with "Italy's best", matched by "fantastic sommelier" Vincent Feraud's "beyond-extensive" wine list, gives front-runners like "Inn at Little Washington a run for their money" in the ratings, while the "impeccable" staff at this "luxurious" Ritz-Carlton "splurge" provides top service.

### Majestic Cafe       22 | 19 | 21 | $36

*911 King St. (bet. Alfred & Patrick Sts.), Alexandria, VA, 703-837-9117*

☑ "Creative" chef Susan Lindeborg's "sizzling", "Southern-inspired" New American "home cooking" and "gracious" spirit fill one of Old Town's "happiest-looking rooms" at this "cool", "retro" redo of a '40s classic cafe; her crew mixes a "great New York–style martini", bakes the "best" "old-fashioned layer cake" and keeps it all "fresh", "unpretentious" and "within reason", say fans, while the "unimpressed" dis the "crowds" and "noise", and claim the "food doesn't live up to its p.r."

### MAKOTO       28 | 22 | 27 | $61

*4822 MacArthur Blvd., NW (U St.), 202-298-6866*

☑ "Nothing is lost in translation" at this "authentic Japanese" "favorite" in the Palisades whose "dedication to excellence" has earned it the ranking of "No. 1" for Food among DC restaurants; each "heavenly" course of its "exquisite" omakase tasting menu "is a work of art with subtle flavors, lots of textures and beautiful composition" that's "impeccably served" in a "tiny", "traditional" "studio" akin to "an old Kyoto *kappo*"; P.S. "be prepared to take off your shoes" before settling into one of the "uncomfortable seats."

### Marcel's       27 | 23 | 25 | $67

*2401 Pennsylvania Ave., NW (24th St.), 202-296-1166; www.marcelsdc.com*

■ "Every dish" by chef-owner Robert Wiedmaier "explodes with flavor" at this "luscious" Belgian-French "stunner" whose "comfortably urbane" digs are "lovely for anything from a date" to a "family occasion" to a "business meeting"; its "prix fixe, pre-theater menu" is "excellent" and "reasonably priced", making it "de rigueur" for "divine" "dining before Kennedy Center events" – and "as a bonus they provide" a "complimentary limo" to "take you to" the venue or bring you "back after the performance for dessert", live "jazz and drinks."

### Melrose       26 | 23 | 25 | $55

*Park Hyatt Washington, 1201 24th St., NW (M St.), 202-955-3899; www.parkwashington.hyatt.com*

■ "When money is no object and quality counts", "you can't beat" the "dazzling" New American creations of Park Hyatt chef Brian McBride; an "attentive and unobtrusive" staff delivers his "sublime" goods in this "ultra-sophisticated" West Ender with "sunlight" streaming through the "airy" space and "plenty of room between tables for business meetings or romantic interludes"; "well-dressed" dancers spin to live salsa on Fridays and swing on Saturdays, and it's "especially nice for Sunday brunch."

### Nora 🗷                                        26  22  24  $56
2132 Florida Ave., NW (bet. Connecticut & Massachusetts Aves.), 202-462-5143; www.noras.com

☑ "Organic before it was in", Nora Pouillon's "exceptional" Dupont Circle New American uses the "freshest" seasonal ingredients in "innovative" dishes that are "indulgent" and "delicious", yet leave her fans feeling that they've "done something healthy" for themselves; there are "DC hotshots everywhere you look", soaking up the "caring" ambiance of a "picture-perfect" carriage-house setting complete with "handmade quilts"; nevertheless, critics say this "special-occasion" spot is "skating by on reputation."

### Obelisk 🗷                                       27  20  26  $65
2029 P St., NW (bet. 20th & 21st Sts.), 202-872-1180

■ At this "popular" Dupont Circle townhouse, Peter Pastan's "Italian sensibilities" allow "superb ingredients to shine with a minimum of fuss" in daily changing, five-course prix fixe menus; "no-attitude" "foodie waiters" help diners "explore" the "flawless, multilayered flavors" and "excellent" wines from small vintners in a "spare" but "lovely" and "intimate" room that's "perfect" for "romance"; the only complaint is that it's "hard to get into."

### Palena 🗷                                        25  21  22  $58
3529 Connecticut Ave., NW (bet. Ordway & Porter Sts.), 202-537-9250; www.palenarestaurant.com

☑ "Prepare to be amazed" at this "civilized" Cleveland Park New American where "perfectionist" Frank Ruta offers "good value for the money", with the option of "marvelous" "bar food in the front" at an under-$10 "steal"; in the "luxuriously cozy" back room, "a conversation can be had" over a "superb" prix fixe that reminds *bec fins* of "intimate European" destinations; co-owner Ann Amernick's desserts are equally "fantastic", but impatient eaters cite "slow service" as a drawback.

### Pizzeria Paradiso                                 24  15  17  $21
3282 M St., NW (bet. 32nd & 33rd Sts.), 202-337-1245
2029 P St., NW (bet. 20th & 21st Sts.), 202-223-1245

■ "Pizza delivery is a thing of the past" after the "first slice" of a wood-baked pie from these Dupont Circle and Georgetown "boutiques"; the "freshest" ingredients top their "crispy", "smoky crusts", which are accompanied by "wonderful antipasto" and "rustic wines by the glass" and served at "cozy" tables that "invite conversation"; the "only problem is the crowds", so "go at off hours to avoid the lines."

### Prime Rib 🗷                                      26  24  25  $62
2020 K St., NW (bet. 20th & 21st Sts.), 202-466-8811; www.theprimerib.com

☑ "Deals get done over a nice, juicy" namesake the "size of a sofa" at this Golden Triangle "grand supper club" (part of a "swanky" chain) where the wine list, as well, "can't be beat"; you must "get dressed in jacket and tie" for a seat in its "uptown leopard-print, chrome and black-leather" space, where you'll be serenaded by the "tinkling" of the baby grand and the thrum of the upright bass;

hipsters might call it a "stuffy" "time warp", but traditionalists say it's "the last vestige of civilization in an age of casual-gone-amok."

### Rabieng                    26  17  20  $23
*Glen Forest Shopping Ctr., 5892 Leesburg Pike (Glen Forest Dr.), Falls Church, VA, 703-671-4222; www.duangrats.com*

■ A Falls Church "gem that sparkles", this "fantastic" Thai serves up a "wide and varied" menu with "perfectly balanced flavors"; the "skillful kitchen's" "spicy" stuff is "not for the faint of tongue", but the "cheap" prices are perfect for the faint of wallet, and an "attentive" staff and "super" Sunday dim sum "just seal the deal."

### Ray's The Steaks           27  11  21  $36
*Colonial Village, 1725 Wilson Blvd. (Rhodes St.), Arlington, VA, 703-841-7297*

■ The "lights are bright", the "walls are white", but the steak is "as good as you can get in DC", for "much less money" than at the "expense-account" joints, at this "no-frills" Arlington strip-mall beefery; "charming owner, knowledgeable sommelier" and crack chef Mike (Ray) Landrum "walks around in a working apron, talks to everyone and adds to the fun", while "the decor, or lack thereof, gives you nothing to focus on besides the taste" of the "delicious" prime cuts; P.S. word is out, so "reservations are a must."

### Restaurant 2941            27  27  24  $58
*2941 Fairview Park Dr. (Arlington Blvd.), Falls Church, VA, 703-270-1500; www.2941.com*

■ An "entrancing restaurant in a Falls Church office park" "mere seconds from the Beltway", this "superb" New American "retreat" serves "marvelous" meals distinguished by "wonderful, rich reductions" and "quality ingredients"; set among trees and overlooking a lake, the "dramatic" place is a "romantic" modern "winner", from the "ponds of koi as you arrive" to the "best meeting rooms" to the take-home baguette baked by the chef's "papa."

### 1789                       25  25  25  $58
*1226 36th St., NW (Prospect St.), 202-965-1789; www.1789restaurant.com*

■ "The ambiance is colonial and the clientele is Kennedy"-esque at this "old-money" "crowd-pleaser" of "the Georgetown scene" where the "food, service and cozy, romantic ambiance [especially downstairs] are all top-notch"; chef Ris Lacoste "pleases the demanding palate", crafting "terrific, seasonal" New American menus with "multigenerational" appeal, which are served to a "formal", "dressy" group (jacket required) within a "wood-paneled" space that's perfect for "special occasions" – just "don't look for a loud, wild time or a small tab."

### Taberna del Alabardero ⌦   25  25  25  $56
*1776 I St., NW (18th St.), 202-429-2200; www.alabardero.com*

■ "Get dressed up, put on your best manners", enter this taberna through its door on 18th Street and you're "suddenly whisked to Madrid" to "savor" "extraordinary" tapas at the bar (a "nice secret for lunch") or "wonderful", "hearty" Iberian classics "prepared with modern flair" and matched by "a great selection of top Spanish wines"; the "sumptuously decorated" dining room "sparkles" at night, and so will you when you're "coddled" in its "grand atmosphere", which has expats crying "bravo."

## TENPENH ⊠     | 25 | 24 | 23 | $46 |

*1001 Pennsylvania Ave., NW (10th St.), 202-393-4500; www.tenpenh.com*

■ "A treat for the senses", this "Penh-ominal" Downtown venue is blessed with chef Jeff Tunks' "unique and successful take" on Pan-Asian fare, which renders an "intriguing menu" filled with dishes so "delicious" you'll be tempted to "lick your plate clean"; "striking decor", a "friendly, knowledgeable staff" and a "lively bar" that "buzzes with energy" further cement its status as the "perfect place" to "prove to your New York friends that Washington is not a dining wasteland" – but be prepared for "prices that match the high ceilings."

## Tosca     | 25 | 23 | 24 | $55 |

*1112 F St., NW (bet. 11th & 12th Sts.), 202-367-1990; www.toscadc.com*

■ The "flavors are as dynamic and colorful as a Clinton denial" at this "wonderful" Penn Quarter place, the "Armani" of Northern Italians, where the "daring" yet "luscious" cooking "rivals the city's best", the "sharp, contemporary" room "oozes" "minimalist" "subtlety" and the "warm, welcoming" staff "knows what it's recommending"; it's a "top pick" when you're looking to "impress a new customer", and it can be "surprisingly affordable" if you take advantage of the "great-value" early-bird menu.

## Vidalia     | 25 | 23 | 24 | $54 |

*1990 M St., NW (bet. 19th & 20th Sts.), 202-659-1990; www.vidaliadc.com*

■ "The South rises victorious from every plate" at this Golden Triangle New American where "dynamite" dishes with Dixie "flair" are served up with "passion and care"; "down-home was never this good", and a meal here now is "better than ever" since the joint has been "reinvigorated" with a "stylish makeover" resulting in "fabulous new digs" that feature "lavish" leather banquettes, rippled glass and more "open" space; P.S. there's also a "fantastic wine list."

## Zaytinya ◑     | 25 | 26 | 21 | $37 |

*701 Ninth St., NW (G St.), 202-638-0800; www.zaytinya.com*

■ Set in a "spectacular", "soaring" "glass, chrome and marble" space, this "stunning" sophisticate "has lit up the Penn Quarter", drawing "beautiful people" with its "culinary tour of the Eastern Mediterranean"; "you can't stop eating" its "incredible selection" of Greek, Lebanese and Turkish meze and sipping its "excellent", "unusual" wines, and at these "surprisingly" "affordable" prices, why should you?; still, "noise" and "long waits" (no reservations are taken) cause admirers to sigh "if it weren't so trendy and popular it would be even better."

# Westchester/ Hudson River Valley

## TOP 20 FOOD RANKING

| Restaurant | Cuisine |
|---|---|
| **29** Xaviar's at Piermont | New American |
| Freelance Café | New American |
| **28** Arch | French/Continental |
| La Panetière | New French |
| **27** Il Cenàcolo | Northern Italian |
| Zephs' | Eclectic/New American |
| L'Europe | French/Continental |
| Escoffier, The | French |
| La Crémaillère | French |
| Buffet de la Gare | French |
| **26** Busy Bee Cafe | New American |
| Equus | French/American |
| Rest. X & Bully Boy Bar | New American |
| DePuy Canal House | American/Eclectic |
| Le Pavillon* | French |
| Iron Horse Grill | New American |
| Mina | New American |
| Terrapin | New American |
| **25** American Bounty | New American |
| Azuma Sushi | Japanese |

## ADDITIONAL NOTEWORTHY PLACES

| | |
|---|---|
| Aroma Osteria | Italian |
| Aubergine | French/New American |
| Bear Cafe | New American |
| Blue Hill at Stone Barns | New American |
| Cafe Mezé | Mediterranean |
| Cafe Tamayo | New American |
| Caterina de Medici | Italian |
| Crabtree's Kittle House | New American |
| F.I.S.H. | Med./Seafood |
| French Corner | French |
| Gigi Trattoria | Italian/Med. |
| Harvest on Hudson | Mediterranean |
| Koo | Japanese |
| Le Canard Enchainé | French Bistro |
| Lu Shane's | American |
| McKinney & Doyle | New American |
| Mulino's | Northern Italian |
| Sonora | Nuevo Latino |
| Trotters | Mediterranean |
| Would, The | New American |

---

\* Indicates a tie with restaurant above

### American Bounty Restaurant ⊠     25 | 24 | 24 | $48
*Culinary Institute of America, 1946 Campus Dr. (Rte. 9), Hyde Park, 845-471-6608; www.ciachef.edu*
■ "This cooking school restaurant gets an A+" enthuse gourmets grading this Hyde Park New American training ground for CIA students; expect "perfectly presented" "excellent food" using local products, a "well-constructed wine list", an "elegant", newly decorated dining room and an "unrushed" atmosphere; the staff may "need more practice" but is "earnest" and "enthusiastic."

### ARCH     28 | 25 | 27 | $62
*Rte. 22N (end of I-684), Brewster, 845-279-5011; www.archrestaurant.com*
■ "Fabulous food", "impeccable service" and a "romantic", "unstuffy" "country-inn" setting ("dine in the atrium" or on the patio in summer) combine to make this "pricey" Brewster "French-Continental haven" "a true gem"; the "chocolate soufflé is the best anywhere" and "Sunday brunch is a winner" too, so is it any wonder "this is a blueprint for other places that want to do it right"?

### Aroma Osteria     25 | 17 | 22 | $38
*114 Old Post Rd. (Rte. 9), Wappingers Falls, 845-298-6790*
■ "A wonderful touch of Tuscany" in Wappingers Falls, this "popular", "unpretentious" Italian showcases "generous portions" of chef Eduardo Lauria's "terrific" food ("try the bread salad"), served by a crack staff overseen by wife Lucia; aesthetes add that the "charming", "comfortable" setting was expanded to include both public and private dining rooms.

### Aubergine     25 | 24 | 23 | $57
*Aubergine Fine Food & Lodging, Rtes. 22 & 23, Hillsdale, 518-325-3412*
■ Those in search of "excellent French country cuisine" jazzed up with a touch of American flair can find it at this "lovely shabby-chic country inn" in Columbia County where chef-owner David Lawson's "delightful" fare is "presented with panache"; located "way out in the sticks", this 18th-century auberge is a "warm and enticing retreat" worth "building a trip around", though some might find it a tad "too formal for the area."

### Azuma Sushi     25 | 13 | 17 | $39
*219 E. Hartsdale Ave. (Bronx River Pkwy.), Hartsdale, 914-725-0660*
■ "Perfect", incredibly "fresh" raw fish is the draw at this "small", "unassuming" Hartsdale Japanese where regulars say "don't even think of eating at the sushi bar unless you mean business"; despite quibbles about "somewhat indifferent service" and digs that are "not much to look at", foodwise, there's now "no need to venture to Manhattan"; P.S. "make a reservation or plan on waiting a long time."

### Bear Cafe     24 | 22 | 20 | $39
*295 Tinker St. (Rte. 212), Bearsville, 845-679-5555; www.bearcafe.com*
☑ "A classic Woodstock dining experience" awaits visitors to this "comfy, rustic" New American where locals and "well-to-do weekenders" mingle at the "happening bar" then take in the "beautiful view of the woods and stream" over "delicious", "inventive" cuisine, conveyed by a "down-to-earth" staff; in sum, it "continues to set the pace in Ulster County", so "book ahead."

### Blue Hill at Stone Barns　– – – E
*Stone Barns Center for Food & Agriculture, 630 Bedford Rd. (Lake Rd.), Pocantico Hills, 914-366-9600; www.bluehillstonebarns.com*
Chef-owner Dan Barber and family (of NYC's highly rated Blue Hill) have opened this much-anticipated New American in a Norman-style barn on the 4,000-acre Rockefeller State Park Preserve in Pocantico Hills; the restaurant showcases executive chef Michael Anthony's seasonal dishes, which use sustainable agricultural products from the premises' working farm (be sure to take a tour) and from local growers, while complementary education programs include wine tastings, cooking classes and garden tours.

### Buffet de la Gare ⊠　27 21 25 $56
*155 Southside Ave. (Spring St.), Hastings-on-Hudson, 914-478-1671*
■ "An amazing culinary experience" "brings back memories of Paris" to guests of this "romantic" Hastings French high-achiever set in various "artifact-filled" "rooms in an old house"; chef Gwenael Goulet's French preparations are called "*fantastique*" – "wonderful cassoulet", "to-die-for coq au vin", "superb housemade terrine of foie gras" – while wife Annie and the staff are "ever-present and helpful."

### Busy Bee Cafe ⊠　26 13 20 $28
*138 South Ave. (Reade Pl.), Poughkeepsie, 845-452-6800*
■ Aficionados are abuzz over this "tiny" Poughkeepsie "gem" that looks like a smart luncheonette but is actually a "gourmet bistro", serving "innovative", "lovingly prepared" New American entrees and "to-die-for" desserts; what's more, though the "tables are tight, the hive is friendly" and the staff "helpful and efficient"; N.B. call ahead for hours.

### Cafe Mezé　23 18 20 $46
*20 N. Central Ave. (Hartsdale Ave.), Hartsdale, 914-428-2400; www.cafemeze.com*
■ Diners seeking "something special in Westchester" steer over to this rustic, "charming", "cozy" and "crowded" Hartsdale Mediterranean "find", "one of the Livanos family's" properties; the "intriguing entrees", including "unusual pasta dishes" and "excellent fish", are "delicious" – "superb" "chef Mark Filippo keeps this kitchen up to date" – plus the wine list showcases "some choice spirits to wet your whistle"; service is "polite and attentive", inspiring the enchanted to exclaim "can't wait to go again!"

### Cafe Tamayo　23 20 19 $41
*89 Partition St. (Main St.), Saugerties, 845-246-9371; www.cafetamayo.com*
■ It's "easy to feel life is good" at this Saugerties New American where chef-owner James Tamayo's "menu features game" and other "terrific comfort food" ("amazing duck confit"), augmented by an "exceptional" cellar; a "tin ceiling" and "Rube Goldberg–like fans" in the "inviting bar" add to the "lovely old-fashioned" feel of this 1864 structure, which also has a pleasant garden patio.

### Caterina de Medici ⊠　25 25 24 $47
*Colavita Center for Italian Food and Wine, Culinary Institute of America, 1946 Campus Dr. (Rte. 9), Hyde Park, 845-471-6608; www.ciachef.edu*
■ Would-be chefs and restaurateurs (aka CIA students) run this Italian at Hyde Park's prestigious culinary school, where the

"wonderful" seasonal cuisine is served in a "beautiful" "Tuscan-like setting" that includes an open kitchen; the staff is "friendly" and "conscientious" too (and no wonder, as "they're all being graded"), so all in all, this is a "place for a memorable meal."

### CRABTREE'S KITTLE HOUSE — 25 | 25 | 24 | $54

*Crabtree's Kittle House Inn, 11 Kittle Rd. (Rte. 117), Chappaqua, 914-666-8044; www.kittlehouse.com*

■ "Exactly what a top-notch restaurant should be" and the area's Most Popular eatery, this "charming", "picturesque" historic inn "tucked away" in Chappaqua captivates diners with "beautifully presented", "gloriously delicious" New American fare "served with aplomb" and coupled with a 5,500-label wine list; while some reserve it for a "special occasion", regulars reveal that the "delightful atmosphere" makes it a "favorite" spot to "dine with friends anytime"; P.S. "Sunday buffet brunch is a treat."

### DePuy Canal House — 26 | 26 | 25 | $60

*Rte. 213 (Lucas Tpke.), High Falls, 845-687-7700; www.depuycanalhouse.net*

■ Chef-owner John Novi is "still at his old tricks" at this High Falls American-Eclectic where "gastronomy doesn't get any better" and "some of the wackiest combinations" result in "sublime" dishes; the "elegant, rustic-chic" decor at the "romantic 18th-century inn" creates a "delightful" mood where you can "relax and feel attended to", perhaps more so "if you're on an expense account."

### Equus — 26 | 29 | 26 | $65

*Castle at Tarrytown, 400 Benedict Ave. (bet. Maple St. & Martling Ave.), Tarrytown, 914-631-3646; www.castleattarrytown.com*

■ This "enchanted" restaurant in the "deliciously luxurious" hilltop Castle at Tarrytown hotel allows you to "play king and queen for an evening" – if you can afford the princely "ransom to pay for it"; expect "wonderfully indulgent" French-American fare and an "impeccable" staff that treats you "like royalty" whether you drink in the "spectacular" Hudson views from the Garden Room, delight in the "voluptuous interior" of the Oak or Terrace Room or share a "special celebratory dinner" on the terrace.

### Escoffier, The ⊠ — 27 | 25 | 24 | $55

*Culinary Institute of America, 1946 Campus Dr. (Rte. 9), Hyde Park, 845-471-6608; www.ciachef.edu*

■ "Be prepared for a culinary treat" at this Hyde Park Classic French bastion that may be "the best of the CIA restaurants" thanks to "delectable food" with "fancy sauces", "beautiful" decor and an "eager-to-please" staff (though "flaming desserts made tableside" by students might not be for the "faint of heart"); tip: try to "get a table with a kitchen view to watch the future masters at work."

### F.I.S.H. — ▽ 24 | 18 | 21 | $53

*102 Fox Island Rd. (Grace Church St.), Port Chester, 914-939-4227; www.fishfoxisland.com*

■ "It's so nice to have a chic, citified eatery" in Port Chester, state supporters of this Mediterranean seafooder where the "delicious" dishes from a wood-burning stove are prepared with "creative verve" and served amid "fab" industrial environs; early-birders who place their orders by 6:30 PM receive a complimentary bottle of wine, while owls can take advantage of the late-night menu, available Thursday–Saturday until the bar closes.

### FREELANCE CAFÉ & WINE BAR, THE ⌿    29 | 19 | 25 | $45

*506 Piermont Ave. (Ash St.), Piermont, 845-365-3250; www.xaviars.com*

■ Another of chef-owner Peter Kelly's "masterpieces", this Piermont New American is a "casual yet sophisticated gourmet paradise" where the "food is as sensational" as it is at the Xavier's "mother ship" next door (but "more affordable"), the wine list is "fantastic", the "tiny room" "intimate" and "welcoming" and the staff "well trained" and "warm"; "the only problem is the no-reservations policy", but converts coo that "even waiting for a table is a pleasure" because "Ned Kelly is a most gracious host."

### French Corner    – | – | – | E

*3407 Cooper St. (Rte. 209), Stone Ridge, 845-687-0810; www.frcorner.com*

Top NYC toque Jacques Qualin bid au revoir to Manhattan and sashayed up to Stone Ridge to open this classic French boîte, where he's feeding lucky locals the likes of his signature turbot in champagne sauce; Gallic antiques, including a painted grandfather clock, warm up the smart makeover of this village eatery, as does wife Leslie Flam, who meets and greets.

### Gigi Trattoria    23 | 20 | 18 | $36

*6422 Montgomery St./Rte. 9 (Livingston St.), Rhinebeck, 845-876-1007; www.gigitrattoria.com*

■ "Arrive early" or "be prepared to wait" at this "lively", "upscale" "hot spot" in Rhinebeck where the Italian-Med offerings are "delicious" ("crisp, creative" pizzas, risottos and homemade pastas) and the "charming building" is so "cool"-looking it's hard to believe it was "originally a garage"; while "good for people-watching", it's also "noisy" and a "bit too city-chic for upstate."

### HARVEST ON HUDSON    21 | 25 | 19 | $47

*1 River St. (¼ mi. north of Hastings-on-Hudson RR), Hastings-on-Hudson, 914-478-2800; www.harvest2000.com*

☑ "Romantic as heck", this "divine treat" in Hastings-on-Hudson "feels like a vacation to Napa" thanks to "well-executed" Med food, "cozy fires" in the winter and "spectacular" summer outdoor seating that overlooks the Palisades; better yet, make a sunset toast out "among the vegetable" gardens; N.B. new chef Vincent Barcelona (formerly of NYC's Le Bernardin) sailed upstream to add his signature dishes just at press time.

### IL CENÀCOLO    27 | 19 | 25 | $53

*228 S. Plank Rd. (bet. New Rd. & Paffendorf Dr.), Newburgh, 845-564-4494*

■ A long list of "incredible specials" and a "to-die-for antipasti table as you walk in" fuel the raves for this "unlikely jewel" in Newburgh where the "imaginative", "exceptional" and "pricey" Northern Italian cuisine "never wavers in quality"; a "deep" wine selection and "knowledgeable" staffers are other reasons it's "really a marvel for an exurban location" and "worth every penny."

### Iron Horse Grill ⧈    26 | 22 | 24 | $52

*20 Wheeler Ave. (Manville Rd.), Pleasantville, 914-741-0717; www.ironhorsegrill.com*

■ We've found "heaven in Pleasantville" gloat gourmets gaga over chef-owner Philip McGrath's grill, where he creates "fantastic", "imaginative" seasonal New American entrees; a "renovated train station" setting makes for "irreplaceable ambiance" and the "friendly" staff provides "wonderful tableside care."

## Koo — | — | — | VE |

*17 Purdy Ave. (2nd St.), Rye, 914-921-9888; www.koorestaurant.com*

Yellowtail sashimi topped with paper-thin slices of jalapeño illustrates the sophisticated global-influenced contemporary Japanese menu at this 90-seat Rye entry just off the city's main thoroughfare; highlights include spare, muted decor emphasizing the serenity of nature, flashy cocktails, a raw-fish bar in back and a cool crowd; just be forewarned, the check isn't nearly as easy on the wallet as the gorgeously presented dishes are on the eyes.

## La Crémaillère | 27 | 26 | 25 | $68 |

*46 Bedford-Banksville Rd. (Roundhouse Rd.), Banksville, 914-234-9647; www.cremaillere.com*

■ The Meyzen family has "sustained a remarkably high standard for decades" at this "superior" Banksville French where a staff that's "beyond reproach" serves a "dressy" crowd "upper-crust" "delicacies like escargots and foie gras" (not to mention "fabulous ice cream"); the "picture-perfect" Provençal "country-inn" setting includes slate floors, sconces and murals depicting regional dress.

## LA PANETIÈRE | 28 | 27 | 27 | $70 |

*530 Milton Rd. (Oakland Beach Ave.), Rye, 914-967-8140; www.lapanetiere.com*

■ Rye's "quiet", "elegant" Provençal-style New French "grande dame" has patrons praising its "rich", "decadent meals" (including a six-course tasting menu), "fabulous" (if "pricey") wine list "that should be framed" and "flawless" staff overseen by impeccably groomed owner Jacques Loupiac; ladies, take note, if your boyfriend "brings you here, you know he's got an engagement ring" in his "deep pocket."

## Le Canard Enchainé | 25 | 22 | 22 | $40 |

*276 Fair St. (bet. John & Main Sts.), Kingston, 845-339-2003; www.lecanard-enchaine.com*

■ "Chef-owner Jean-Jacques Carquillat brings a bit of Paris to Kingston" via this "authentic" bistro where the "cassoulet is divine", the duck delivers ("why go anywhere else for it?") and the other fine fare is "served with style" by a "usually lovely Gallic-accented staff"; add a "fairly priced" all-French *carte du vin* and a "great buzz on weekends" from "jazz in the comfortable lounge" and this place can "feel like a mini-vacation."

## Le Pavillon 🈂 | 26 | 20 | 23 | $44 |

*230 Salt Point Tpke./Rte. 115 (N. Grand Ave.), Poughkeepsie, 845-473-2525; www.lepavillon.home-page.org*

■ It's "worth using your car's GPS to find" this "out-of-the-way" Poughkeepsie French "veteran" where chef-owner Claude Guermont "is still in top form" turning out "wonderful food" ("great soufflés") complemented by a "reasonably priced wine list"; the "warm, cozy old farmhouse" makes for a "romantic", "quiet dinner", and the five-course prix fixe means "you don't have to save it just for special occasions."

## L'Europe Restaurant | 27 | 24 | 27 | $56 |

*407 Smith Ridge Rd./Rte. 123 (Tommys Ln.), South Salem, 914-533-2570; www.leuroperestaurant.com*

■ "The only casualty is your diet" at this "quiet", "relatively undiscovered gem" in South Salem where "diners still dress appropriately" for "special-occasion" meals of "impeccable" French-Continental specialties like "outstanding rack of lamb", "wonderful soufflés" and flaming desserts; "old-world service" and an impressive Sunday brunch are further inducements.

### Lu Shane's                                    24 | 19 | 20 | $46
*8 N. Broadway (bet. Main & New Sts.), Nyack, 845-358-5556; www.lushanes.com*
■ This "trendy" American in Nyack has a "great raw bar" (note: "prices add up quickly") and serves "delicious", "innovative cuisine" from an "eclectic menu" with "unusual touches, like game"; the "SoHo-style atmosphere" includes weekend jazz and a copper-clad "bar that's always hopping" ("bring earplugs").

### McKinney & Doyle Fine Foods Cafe    24 | 18 | 21 | $37
*10 Charles Coleman Blvd. (Main St.), Pawling, 845-855-3875*
■ Brian Doyle has ducked out, but Shannon McKinney is still serving "country favorites" at this New American in the "middle of nowhere" (aka Pawling); from the "excellent soups" to the "heavenly desserts", "there are no bad choices", and the "comfy" vibe has some "folks driving two hours" to come here.

### Mina                                         26 | 18 | 24 | $41
*29 W. Market St. (Rte. 9), Red Hook, 845-758-5992; www.minarestaurant.com*
■ "Not a detail is overlooked" at this Red Hook New American; a market-based, weekly changing menu of "sophisticated food for grown-ups" is prepared by "inspired chef" Natalie Steward and served in a "casual but elegant" setting by the "best-looking staffers" (they're "well informed" and "attentive" too); N.B. in winter, open Friday–Sunday only.

### Mulino's of Westchester ●Ⓩ        24 | 23 | 24 | $53
*99 Court St. (bet. Martine Ave. & Quarropas St.), White Plains, 914-761-1818*
■ The "who's who of Westchester" has warmed to this "high-powered" White Plains Northern Italian because of "excellent" fare that "pleases even skeptics" and service so "attentive" you "feel like you're the only one there"; though it can get "hectic" on Saturdays, the "enchanting" room and "romantic" setting are "hard to beat", especially "at Christmas."

### RESTAURANT X & BULLY BOY BAR    26 | 25 | 24 | $51
*117 Rte. 303 (bet. Lake Rd. & Rte. 9W), Congers, 845-268-6555; www.xaviars.com*
■ "X marks the spot" for "fabulous" New American cuisine at this Congers branch of owner Peter Kelly's culinary "empire"; while it's "less formal" than his other places, Xaviar's and Freelance Café, diners can still "expect the best of everything", including a "professional", "well-trained staff", an "excellent and reasonable wine list" and "terrific ambiance" thanks to a "bright, cheerful" room overlooking "charming ducks on a pond"; N.B. the $20.04 prix fixe lunch is the best bet for bargain-hunters.

### Sonora                                       23 | 23 | 20 | $46
*179 Rectory St. (Willett Ave.), Port Chester, 914-933-0200; www.sonorarestaurant.com*
■ "Hidden on a nondescript street" in Port Chester, this "inviting" Nuevo Latino entry is a "lively, happening" place "to seek out"

Rafael Palomino's "inventive" cuisine that's an "extraordinary confluence of flavors"; the staff, moreover, "exudes as much energy and personality as the kitchen", and the "delicious" cocktails and sangria leave tipplers tickled.

### Terrapin ●                                      26 | – | 21 | $42
6426 Montgomery St. (Livingston), Rhinebeck, 845-876-3330;
www.terrapinrestaurant.com
■ Chef Josh Kroner is ensconced at last in his new Rhinebeck digs and he's making the most of the former church's architecture; the more formal room's soaring ceilings and mezzanine add drama to the experience of sampling his creative New American cuisine; some dishes (including the signature barbecued duck quesadillas) also turn up on the more casual menu in the bistro section, where on Friday nights, diners dance the night away to a DJ.

### Trotters ● 🖻                                   22 | 20 | 20 | $37
175 Main St. (Court St.), White Plains, 914-421-5012; www.trottersny.com
■ "One of the best choices for dining in Downtown" White Plains, particularly for suits scheduling "business power meals", is this "beautifully remodeled" Med that oozes "NYC sophistication" with its "art deco–themed" setting, urbane dishes like potato-crusted sea bass ("the kitchen knows how to cook fish") and daily tasting menu; a post-Survey revamp increased dining space, while a new tapas menu served from 10 PM to 2 AM attracts off-duty chefs and other night-owls.

### Would, The                                     25 | 17 | 21 | $41
Inn at Applewood, 120 North Rd. (Rte. 9W), Highland, 845-691-9883;
www.thewould.com
■ This "out-of-the-way treasure" offers "artfully presented" "inspired New American cuisine" ("wonderful breads, excellent soups", "divine desserts") declare devotees of this Ulster County secret; pet "chickens walking around" "add character" to the "dumpy outside", while inside, a new paint job and ongoing renovations are giving a "much-needed boost" to the decor.

### XAVIAR'S AT PIERMONT ⌀                          29 | 25 | 28 | $73
506 Piermont Ave. (Ash St.), Piermont, 845-359-7007; www.xaviars.com
■ "Divine" New American fare from chef-owner Peter Kelly and a staff that dances a "ballet of perfection" have dazzled diners declaiming that this "little jewel box", the region's No. 1 for Food, is "heaven on earth in Piermont"; regarding everything "from table settings to sumptuous desserts", reviewers report it's a "magical dining experience"; the $60 prix fixe menu ($35 for brunch) means the "tab will be high", but go and "treat yourself royally" – just remember jackets are required and "no credit cards" are accepted, so "bring lots of cash" or "your checkbook."

### Zephs'                                         27 | 16 | 24 | $47
638 Central Ave. (bet. Nelson Ave. & Water St.), Peekskill, 914-736-2159
■ "Don't let its location fool you": "you'll dine, not just eat" when you visit this Eclectic–New American "culinary gem" in a "small", recently revamped "converted Peekskill grist mill"; "talented", "accomplished chef" Victoria Zeph turns out a "short" seasonal menu of "wonderful", "interesting" dishes that "challenge your expectations", and brother Michael ("a superb host") supervises a "staff as professional as at any upscale Manhattan restaurant"; in sum, it's a "real find."

# Indexes

# CUISINES BY AREA

## Atlanta

*American (New)*
Aria
Bacchanalia
BluePointe
Buckhead Diner
Canoe
dick and harry's
Food Studio
ONE.midtown kitchen
Park 75
Rathbun's
Wisteria

*American (Traditional)*
Thumbs Up

*Asian*
BluePointe
Sia's

*Chinese*
Hsu's Gourmet

*Coffee Shops/Diners*
Thumbs Up

*Continental*
Iris
Nikolai's Roof
Pano's & Paul's
Seeger's

*European*
Babette's Cafe

*French*
Floataway Cafe
Nikolai's Roof

*French (Bistro)*
Brasserie Le Coze

*French (New)*
Brasserie Le Coze
Joël
Ritz-Carlton Din. Rm.

*Indian*
Madras Saravana

*Italian*
*(N=Northern)*
di Paolo (N)
Floataway Cafe
La Grotta (N)
La Tavola
Sotto Sotto (N)

*Japanese*
*(\* sushi specialist)*
MF Sushibar\*
Sushi Avenue\*

*Pan-Latin*
Tierra

*Seafood*
Atlanta Fish Market
Chops/Lobster Bar
dick and harry's

*Small Plates*
Buckhead Diner

*Southern*
Blue Ridge Grill
South City Kitchen
Wisteria

*Southwestern*
Nava
Sia's

*Steakhouses*
Bone's
Chops/Lobster Bar
McKendrick's

*Thai*
Nan
Tamarind

*Vegetarian*
Madras Saravana

## Atlantic City

*American (Traditional)*
Alfonso's City Grill
Dock's Oyster

*Asian Fusion*
Mixx

*Chinese*
Suilan

*Cuban*
Babalu Grill

*French*
Suilan

*Italian*
*(S=Southern)*
Capriccio
Chef Vola's
Girasole (S)

*Pan-Latin*
Mixx

*Sandwiches*
White House

*Seafood*
Dock's Oyster

*Steakhouses*
Brighton

## Baltimore/Annapolis

*Afghan*
Helmand

*American (New)*
Charleston
Corks

Hampton's
Linwoods
Paul's Homewood
*American (Traditional)*
Cheesecake Factory
Clyde's
*Asian Fusion*
Soigné
*Crab House*
Mr. Bill's Terrace Inn
*Dessert*
Cheesecake Factory
*Eclectic*
Bicycle
*French (Bistro)*
Les Folies Brasserie
*Greek*
Samos
*Hamburgers*
Clyde's
*Italian*
*(N=Northern)*
Boccaccio (N)
*Japanese*
*(\* sushi specialist)*
Joss Cafe/Sushi Bar*
*Mediterranean*
Soigné
*Pub Food*
Clyde's
*Seafood*
Les Folies Brasserie
McCormick & Schmick's
Mr. Bill's Terrace Inn
O'Learys Seafood
*Steakhouses*
Lewnes'
Prime Rib
Ruth's Chris

## Boston
*Afghan*
Helmand
*American (New)*
Clio
Excelsior
Franklin Café
Hamersley's Bistro
Icarus
Meritage
Olio
Sage
Salts
UpStairs on the Square
*Asian Fusion*
Blue Ginger
Restaurant L

*Barbecue*
East Coast Grill
*Chinese*
Jumbo Seafood
*Continental*
Locke-Ober
*French*
Dining Room/Ritz-Carlton
Le Soir
Mistral
No. 9 Park
*French (Bistro)*
Coriander Bistro
Craigie St. Bistrot
Hamersley's Bistro
Pigalle
Troquet
*French (New)*
Aujourd'hui
Clio
L'Espalier
Lumière
Radius
*Italian*
*(N=Northern; S=Southern)*
Bricco
Il Capriccio (N)
No. 9 Park
Sage (N)
Taranta (S)
Terramia
Trattoria a Scalinatella
*Japanese*
*(\* sushi specialist)*
Oishii*
*Mediterranean*
Caffe Bella
Mistral
Oleana
Rialto
*Persian/Iranian*
Lala Rokh
*Seafood*
East Coast Grill
Jumbo Seafood
Legal Sea Foods
*Small Plates*
Restaurant L
*Spanish*
*(\* tapas specialist)*
Dalí*

## Charlotte
*American (New)*
Barrington's
Bonterra Dining/Wine
Carpe Diem
Guytano's

*Malaysian*
  Bentara
*Nuevo Latino*
  Roomba
*Pan-Asian*
  Ching's Table
*Pizza*
  Frank Pepe
  Harry's Pizza
  Sally's Apizza
*Seafood*
  Alta Rest.
  Max's Oyster
*Spanish*
  Ibiza
  Meigas
*Steakhouses*
  Carmen Anthony
  Max Downtown

## Dallas

*American (New)*
  Aurora
  Café on the Green
  Grape, The
  Green Room
  Iris
  Lola
  Mercury Grill
  Nana
  Tramontana
  2900
  York Street
*American (Traditional)*
  French Room
*Brazilian*
  Fogo de Chão
*Chinese*
  P.F. Chang's
*Continental*
  Hôtel St. Germain
  Old Warsaw
*Eclectic*
  Abacus
*French*
  French Room
  Hôtel St. Germain
  Old Warsaw
*French (Bistro)*
  L'Ancestral
  Lavendou
*Hawaii Regional*
  Roy's
*Italian*
*(N=Northern)*
  Il Mulino
  Il Sole

  Mi Piaci (N)
  Modo Mio Cucina (N)
*Japanese*
*(\* sushi specialist)*
  Steel
  Tei Tei Robata Bar
  Teppo*
*Mediterranean*
  Suze
*Pan-Latin*
  La Duni Latin Café
*Seafood*
  Cafe Pacific
  Oceanaire
*Southeast Asian*
  Steel
*Southwestern*
  Mansion on Turtle Creek
*Steakhouses*
  Al Biernat's
  Bob's
  Capital Grille
  Chamberlain's
  Del Frisco's
  Fogo de Chão
  Nick & Sam's
  Pappas Bros.
*Thai*
  Chow Thai

## Denver Area & Mountain Resorts

*American (New)*
  Adega Rest./Wine
  Emma's
  Flagstaff House
  Highlands Garden
  John's
  Kevin Taylor
  Keystone Ranch
  Mel's Rest./Bar
  Mizuna
  Montagna
  Opus
  Potager
  Q's
  Six89 Kitchen/Wine
  Solera Rest./Wine
  Splendido
  Sweet Basil
  Syzygy
  240 Union
  Wildflower
*American (Regional)*
  Grouse Mountain Grill
  Piñons

*American (Traditional)*
Alpenglow Stube

*Asian Fusion*
Zengo

*Brazilian*
Cafe Brazil

*Colombian*
Cafe Brazil

*Continental*
John's

*Delis*
Parisi

*Eclectic*
Flagstaff House

*French*
L'Atelier
Left Bank
Tante Louise

*German*
Alpenglow Stube

*Italian*
*(N=Northern)*
Barolo Grill (N)
Full Moon Grill (N)
Luca d'Italia
Panzano (N)
Parisi

*Japanese*
*(\* sushi specialist)*
Matsuhisa\*
Sushi Den\*

*Nuevo Latino*
Zengo

*Seafood*
Jax Fish House
240 Union

*Small Plates*
Zengo

*Steakhouses*
Capital Grille
Del Frisco's
Morton's

*Vietnamese*
New Saigon

## Detroit

*American (New)*
Beverly Hills Grill
Five Lakes Grill
Grill/Ritz-Carlton
West End Grill

*American (Traditional)*
Opus One
Rugby Grille

*Asian Fusion*
Tribute

*Continental*
Lark, The
Opus One
Rugby Grille

*Delis*
Steve's Deli
Zingerman's

*French (New)*
Cafe Bon Homme
Emily's
Tribute

*Italian*
Bacco
Il Posto
Rist. Café Cortina

*Mediterranean*
Emily's

*Seafood*
Common Grill
No. VI Chop Hse.

*Steakhouses*
Capital Grille
No. VI Chop Hse.
Rochester Chop Hse.
Ruth's Chris

## Ft. Lauderdale

*American (New)*
By Word of Mouth
Darrel & Oliver's
Sunfish Grill

*American (Traditional)*
Cheesecake Factory
Houston's

*Brazilian*
Chima

*Chinese*
Silver Pond

*Continental*
Black Orchid Cafe

*Dessert*
By Word of Mouth
Cheesecake Factory

*Eclectic*
Darrel & Oliver's
Le Bistro

*Floribbean*
Johnny V's
Mark's Las Olas

*Italian*
Cafe Martorano
Cafe Vico/Vico's Downtown
Casa D'Angelo

*Mediterranean*
La Brochette Bistro
Trina

*Mexican*
  Eduardo de San Angel
*Seafood*
  Sunfish Grill
*Southwestern*
  Canyon
*Steakhouses*
  Chima
  Outback
  Ruth's Chris

**Ft. Worth**

*American (New)*
  Bistro Louise
  Cafe Aspen
  Rough Creek Lodge
*American (Regional)*
  Lonesome Dove
*American (Traditional)*
  Babe's Chicken
  Classic Cafe
*Barbecue*
  Angelo's Barbecue
*Brazilian*
  Boi NA Braza
  Texas de Brazil
*French*
  Cacharel
  Saint-Emilion
*Hamburgers*
  Kincaid's
*Italian*
  La Piazza
  Piccolo Mondo
*Mediterranean*
  Bistro Louise
  Pegasus, The
*Mexican*
  Joe T. Garcia's
*Southwestern*
  Reata
*Steakhouses*
  Chop House
  Del Frisco's
  Silver Fox
  Texas de Brazil

**Honolulu**

*American (New)*
  Orchids
*Asian*
  Indigo
*Chinese*
  Golden Dragon
*Dessert*
  Hy's Steak House
  3660 on the Rise

*Eclectic*
  Indigo
*French*
  Padovani's Rest./Wine
*French (New)*
  Chef Mavro
  La Mer
*Hawaii Regional*
  Alan Wong's
  Chef Mavro
  Diamond Head Grill
  Pineapple Room
  Roy's
*Hawaiian*
  Side Street Inn
*Italian*
  Longhi's
*Japanese*
  L'Uraku
*Mediterranean*
  Longhi's
  Padovani's Rest./Wine
*Pacific Rim*
  Bali By The Sea
  Hoku's
  Sansei
  3660 on the Rise
*Seafood*
  Orchids
  Sansei
*Steakhouses*
  Hy's Steak House
  Ruth's Chris
*Thai*
  Mekong Thai

**Houston**

*American (New)*
  Aries
  Artista
  benjy's
  Daily Review Café
  Mark's American Cuisine
  Mockingbird Bistro
  Quattro
  Ruggles
  17
  Shade
  Zula
*American (Regional)*
  Rainbow Lodge
*Barbecue*
  Goode Co. Texas BBQ
*Brazilian*
  Fogo de Chão
*Cajun*
  Tony Mandola's

# Cuisines by Area Index

*Continental*
Tony's
*Creole*
Brennan's of Houston
*Eclectic*
Shade
*French*
Brennan's of Houston
Chez Nous
*German*
Charivari
*Hamburgers*
Lankford Grocery
*Indian*
Ashiana
Indika
*Italian*
*(N=Northern)*
Da Marco
Damian's Cucina Italiana
La Griglia
La Mora Cucina (N)
Quattro
Simposio (N)
Tony Mandola's
*Japanese*
*(\* sushi specialist)*
Azuma
Kubo's*
*Mediterranean*
t'afia
*Mexican*
Hugo's
*Seafood*
Goode Co. Texas Seafood
Pesce
Tony Mandola's
*South American*
Américas
Churrascos
*Southwestern*
Cafe Annie
*Steakhouses*
Capital Grille
Churrascos
Fleming's Prime
Fogo de Chão
Pappas Bros.
Ruth's Chris

## Kansas City
*American (New)*
American Rest.
Bluestem
Café Sebastienne
40 Sardines
Grille on Broadway

Starker's Reserve
zin
*American (Traditional)*
Stroud's
*Barbecue*
Danny Edwards'
Fiorella's Jack Stack
Oklahoma Joe's
*Delis*
d'Bronx
*Dessert*
André's Confiserie Suisse
*Eclectic*
Grand St. Cafe
Pachamama's
*French*
Tatsu's
*French (Bistro)*
Le Fou Frog
*Italian*
*(N=Northern)*
Lidia's (N)
*Pizza*
d'Bronx
*Seafood*
McCormick & Schmick's
*Steakhouses*
Plaza III
*Swiss*
André's Confiserie Suisse

## Las Vegas
*American (New)*
Aureole
Bradley Ogden
Rosemary's
Sterling Brunch
*Asian Fusion*
Malibu Chan's
*Cajun*
Commander's Palace
Emeril's
*Californian*
NOBHILL
*Chinese*
Mayflower Cuis.
*Continental*
Hugo's Cellar
Michael's
3950
*Creole*
Commander's Palace
Emeril's
*Eclectic*
Bellagio Buffet
*French*
Andre's
Eiffel Tower

Mayflower Cuis.
Pamplemousse
*French (Bistro)*
Bouchon
*French (New)*
Alizé
Le Cirque
Picasso
Renoir
*Hawaii Regional*
Roy's
*Italian*
*(N=Northern)*
Gaetano's (N)
Osteria del Circo (N)
Piero's Tratt. (N)
Valentino (N)
*Japanese*
*(\* sushi specialist)*
Nobu\*
Shintaro\*
*Mediterranean*
Medici Café
*Pacific Rim*
Malibu Chan's
*Pizza*
Piero's Tratt.
*Seafood*
Craftsteak
Emeril's
Michael Mina
Seablue
*Spanish*
*(\* tapas specialist)*
Firefly\*
*Steakhouses*
Craftsteak
Del Frisco's
Delmonico
N9ne Steakhse.
Prime
Pullman Grille
Steak House
*Thai*
Lotus of Siam

## Long Island
*American (New)*
Barney's
Collins & Main
Coolfish
Mill River Inn
Palm Court
Panama Hatties
Piccolo
Plaza Cafe
Polo

*American (Traditional)*
American Hotel
Cheesecake Factory
*Continental*
Barolo
Dave's Grill
Palm Court
1770 House
*Dessert*
Cheesecake Factory
*Eclectic*
Collins & Main
La Plage
Mill River Inn
Mirko's
*French*
American Hotel
Barney's
L'Endroit
Le Soir
Mirabelle
Stone Creek
*French (Bistro)*
Kitchen a Bistro
*French (New)*
Chez Noëlle
Louis XVI
*Italian*
*(N=Northern)*
Barolo
Dario (N)
Da Ugo
Giulio Cesare
Harvest on Ft. Pond (N)
La Pace (N)
La Piccola Liguria (N)
Pasta Pasta
Piccolo
Rialto (N)
Robert's
Solé
*Japanese*
*(\* sushi specialist)*
Kotobuki\*
*Mediterranean*
Harvest on Ft. Pond
Nick & Toni's
Stone Creek
*Pizza*
Nick & Toni's
*Seafood*
Bryant & Cooper
Coolfish
Dave's Grill
Kitchen a Bistro
Plaza Cafe
Tellers

# Cuisines by Area Index

**Steakhouses**
Bryant & Cooper
Jimmy Hay's
Peter Luger
Tellers

*Thai*
Siam Lotus

## Los Angeles

*American (New)*
Belvedere
Derek's
Grace
Josie
Mélisse
Saddle Peak

*American (Traditional)*
Grill on the Alley

*Asian*
Chaya Brasserie
Shiro

*Californian*
A.O.C.
Bel-Air Hotel
Bistro 45
Café Bizou
Campanile
Christine
Derek's
JiRaffe
Joe's
Patina
Shiro
Spago

*Delis*
Brent's Deli

*Dessert*
Sona
Spago

*Eclectic*
Chaya Brasserie
Depot

*Eurasian*
Chinois on Main

*French*
A.O.C.
Bastide
Bel-Air Hotel
Bistro 45
Café Bizou
La Cachette
L'Orangerie
Mélisse
Patina

*French (Bistro)*
Mimosa

*French (New)*
Joe's
Sona

*Italian*
Angelini Osteria
Capo
Valentino

*Japanese*
*(\* sushi specialist)*
Katsu-ya\*
Matsuhisa\*
Mori Sushi\*
Nobu Malibu\*
Sushi Nozawa\*
Sushi Sasabune\*
Takao\*

*Mediterranean*
A.O.C.
Campanile
Christine

*Pizza*
Spago

*Sandwiches*
Brent's Deli

*Seafood*
Shiro
Water Grill

*Small Plates*
A.O.C.

*Steakhouses*
Mastro's
Palm

## Miami

*American (New)*
Nemo
Wish

*American (Traditional)*
Cheesecake Factory
Roger's

*Argentinean*
Graziano's Parrilla

*Barbecue*
Pit Bar-B-Q

*Caribbean*
Azul
Ortanique on Mile

*Chinese*
*(\* dim sum specialist)*
Tropical Chinese\*

*Continental*
Forge, The

*Cuban*
Versailles

*Dessert*
Cheesecake Factory

*Floribbean*
  Mark's South Beach
*French (New)*
  Azul
  Blue Door
  Pascal's on Ponce
*Italian*
*(N=Northern)*
  Acqua (N)
  Café Ragazzi
  Casa Tua (N)
  Escopazzo
  Osteria del Teatro (N)
  Romeo's Cafe (N)
*Japanese*
*(\* sushi specialist)*
  Matsuri\*
  Nobu Miami Beach\*
  Shibui\*
  Toni's Sushi Bar\*
*Mediterranean*
  AltaMar
  La Dorada
*New World*
  Chef Allen's
  Mundo
  Norman's
*Nuevo Latino*
  Cacao
  Carmen The Restaurant
  Chispa
*Pan-Asian*
  Pacific Time
*Peruvian*
  Francesco
*Seafood*
  AltaMar
  Francesco
  Garcia's
  Joe's Stone Crab
  La Dorada
  Prime 112
*Spanish*
*(\* tapas specialist)*
  Casa Juancho\*
  La Dorada
*Steakhouses*
  Capital Grille
  Forge, The
  Graziano's Parrilla
  Prime 112
*Vietnamese*
  Miss Saigon Bistro

## Milwaukee
*American (New)*
  Bacchus
  Dream Dance

  Heaven City
  Sanford
*American (Traditional)*
  Eddie Martini's
  Jackson Grill
  Riversite, The
*Chinese*
  P.F. Chang's
*Eclectic*
  Immigrant Rm./Winery
*French (Bistro)*
  Coquette Cafe
  Lake Park Bistro
*Indian*
  Dancing Ganesha
*Italian*
*(N=Northern; S=Southern)*
  Maggiano's (S)
  Osteria del Mondo (N)
  Ristorante Bartolotta (N)
*Seafood*
  Eddie Martini's
  Moceans
  River Lane Inn
  Watermark Seafood
*Serbian*
  Three Brothers
*Steakhouses*
  Eddie Martini's
  Jackson Grill
*Thai*
  Singha Thai

## Minneapolis/St. Paul
*American (New)*
  Alma
  Bayport Cookery
  Goodfellow's
  Levain
  Lucia's
  Vincent
  Zander Cafe
*American (Regional)*
  Heartland
*American (Traditional)*
  St. Paul Grill
*Bakeries*
  Bakery on Grand
*French (Bistro)*
  Bakery on Grand
  Vincent
*French (New)*
  La Belle Vie
*Italian*
*(N=Northern)*
  D'Amico Cucina (N)
  Ristorante Luci

# Cuisines by Area Index

*Japanese*
*(\* sushi specialist)*
   Origami\*
*Mediterranean*
   La Belle Vie
*Pizza*
   Punch Neapolitan
*Seafood*
   Kincaid's
   Oceanaire
*Spanish*
*(\* tapas specialist)*
   Solera\*
*Steakhouses*
   Kincaid's
   Manny's
*Thai*
   True Thai

## New Jersey
*American (New)*
   Amanda's
   Bernards Inn
   Daniel's on B'way
   Dining Room
   Doris & Ed's
   Ebbitt Room
   Frog & Peach
   Highlawn Pavilion
   Joe & Maggie's
   Nicholas
   Saddle River
   Union Park
   Waters Edge
   Whispers
*American (Traditional)*
   Doris & Ed's
   Latour
   Washington Inn
*Caribbean*
   410 Bank St.
*Creole*
   410 Bank St.
*Eclectic*
   Cafe Matisse
   Cafe Panache
   Savaradio
*French*
   Jocelyne's
   La Campagne
   Latour
   Saddle River
   Siri's Thai French
*French (New)*
   Origin
   Rat's
   Ryland Inn

   Serenäde
   Stage House
*Italian*
*(N=Northern)*
   Fascino
   Giumarello's (N)
   Scalini Fedeli (N)
*Japanese*
*(\* sushi specialist)*
   K.O.B.E.\*
   Robongi\*
*Nuevo Latino*
   Zafra
*Pan-Asian*
   Ritz Seafood
*Pizza*
   DeLorenzo's
*Seafood*
   Blue Point Grill
   Daniel's on B'way
   Doris & Ed's
   Ritz Seafood
*South American*
   Cucharamama
*Steakhouses*
   Bay Point Prime
   River Palm
*Thai*
   Origin
   Siri's Thai French

## New Orleans
*American (New)*
   Bayona
   Dakota, The
   Gautreau's
   Herbsaint
   Pelican Club
   Stella!
*Asian*
   Kim Son
*Cajun*
   K-Paul's
   Uglesich's
*Caribbean*
   Martinique Bistro
*Chinese*
   Nine Roses
*Contemporary Louisiana*
   Brigtsen's
   Emeril's
   Gabrielle
   La Petite Grocery
   Mr. B's Bistro
   New Orleans Grill
   NOLA
   Peristyle

*Continental*
  New Orleans Grill
  Rib Room
*Creole*
  Antoine's
  Arnaud's
  Brennan's
  Clancy's
  Commander's Palace
  Dick and Jenny's
  Eleven 79
  Gabrielle
  Galatoire's
  Jacques-Imo's Cafe
  Muriel's
  NOLA
  Sal & Judy's
  Uglesich's
  Upperline
*Dessert*
  Commander's Palace
*French*
  Antoine's
  Brennan's
  Dick and Jenny's
  La Provence
  Peristyle
*French (Bistro)*
  La Petite Grocery
  Martinique Bistro
  René Bistrot
*French (New)*
  August
  Gautreau's
  Herbsaint
*Italian*
*(S=Southern)*
  Eleven 79
  Irene's Cuisine
  Mosca's
  Sal & Judy's (S)
*Po' Boys*
  Crabby Jack's
*Seafood*
  Arnaud's
  Crabby Jack's
  Martinique Bistro
  RioMar
  Uglesich's
*Soul Food*
  Jacques-Imo's Cafe
*Spanish*
  RioMar
*Steakhouses*
  Rib Room
  Ruth's Chris

*Vietnamese*
  Nine Roses

# New York City
*American (New)*
  Aureole
  Blue Water
  Craft
  davidburke/donatella
  Eleven Madison
  Gotham B&G
  Gramercy Tavern
  Ouest
  per se
  River Cafe
  Tasting Room
  21 Club
  Union Sq. Cafe
  Veritas
*American (Traditional)*
  Bayard's
  Tavern on Green
  21 Club
*Austrian*
  Danube
*Chinese*
  Shun Lee Palace
*Delis*
  Carnegie Deli
*French*
  Bayard's
  Café Boulud
  Café des Artistes
  Le Bernardin
  Montrachet
  per se
*French (Brasserie)*
  Balthazar
*French (New)*
  Alain Ducasse
  Asiate
  Bouley
  Chanterelle
  Daniel
  Jean Georges
  Picholine
*Greek*
  Milos
*Italian*
*(N=Northern)*
  Babbo
  Fiamma Osteria
  Il Mulino (N)
  L'Impero
  Scalini Fedeli (N)
  Trattoria L'incontro

Higgins
Joel Palmer
Paley's Place
Wildwood
*Seafood*
Jake's Famous Crawfish
McCormick & Schmick's
*Steakhouses*
El Gaucho
*Thai*
Lemongrass
*Vietnamese*
Pho Van

## Salt Lake City & Mountain Resorts

*American (New)*
Bambara
Glitretind
Mariposa, The
Metropolitan
*American (Regional)*
Tree Room
*American (Traditional)*
Chez Betty
New Yorker Club
Snake Creek Grill
*Asian Fusion*
Wahso
*Continental*
Chez Betty
*Eclectic*
Log Haven
*French (Bistro)*
L'Avenue
*Italian*
*(N=Northern)*
Cucina Toscana (N)
Fresco Italian Cafe (N)
Lugano (N)
Michelangelo (N)
*Mediterranean*
Martine
*Mexican*
Red Iguana
*Seafood*
Market St. Grill
Seafood Buffet
*Southwestern*
Chimayo

## San Diego

*American (New)*
Arterra
Pamplemousse Grille
Region
*Asian Fusion*
Roppongi

*Californian*
A.R. Valentien
Dobson's
George's at Cove
*Continental*
Sky Room
*French*
El Bizcocho
Laurel
*French (New)*
Mille Fleurs
Pamplemousse Grille
Tapenade
WineSellar & Brasserie
*Japanese*
*(\* sushi specialist)*
Sushi Ota\*
Taka\*
*Pizza*
Sammy's Woodfired
*Seafood*
Rainwater's on Kettner
Star of the Sea
*Steakhouses*
Donovan's
Rainwater's on Kettner
Ruth's Chris

## San Francisco Bay Area

*American (New)*
Boulevard
Café La Haye
French Laundry
Gary Danko
Michael Mina
Terra
Town Hall
*American (Traditional)*
Lark Creek Inn
*Californian*
Aqua
Café La Haye
Chez Panisse
Chez Panisse Café
Fork
Frisson
Marinus
Rivoli
Rubicon
*French*
Aqua
Boulevard
Campton Place
French Laundry
Frisson
Le Papillon
Quince

# Cuisines by Area Index

*Steakhouses*
El Gaucho
JaK's Grill
Metropolitan Grill
*Vietnamese*
Monsoon

## St. Louis

*American (New)*
Arthur Clay's
Crossing, The
Frazer's
Harvest
Sidney St. Cafe
Zinnia
*American (Traditional)*
Annie Gunn's
*Asian Fusion*
Nippon Tei
*Californian*
1111 Mississippi
*Continental*
Kemoll's
*Eclectic*
Monarch
*Italian*
*(N=Northern)*
Dominic's
1111 Mississippi (N)
Giovanni's
Kemoll's
Tony's
Trattoria Marcella
*Japanese*
*(\* sushi specialist)*
Nippon Tei\*
*Mediterranean*
Remy's Kitchen
Restaurant Figaro
*Mexican*
Pueblo Solis
*Seafood*
Al's
*Steakhouses*
Al's
*Vietnamese*
Pho Grand

## Tampa/Sarasota

*American (New)*
Black Pearl
Mise en Place
SideBern's
*Bakeries*
Pane Rustica
*Continental*
Bijou Café
Michael's On East

Ophelia's
Six Tables
Zoria
*Cuban*
Columbia
*Eclectic*
Euphemia Haye
Zoria
*Floribbean*
Beach Bistro
*French*
Café B.T.
*French (New)*
Six Tables
*Hawaii Regional*
Roy's
*Italian*
*(N=Northern)*
Armani's (N)
*Japanese*
*(\* sushi specialist)*
Water, Unique Sushi\*
*Mediterranean*
Pelagia Trattoria
*Pan-Asian*
Water, Unique Sushi
*Peruvian*
Selva Grill
*Sandwiches*
Pane Rustica
*Seafood*
Salt Rock Grill
*Spanish*
Columbia
*Steakhouses*
Bern's
*Vietnamese*
Café B.T.

## Tucson

*American (New)*
Bistro Zin
Dish, The
Grill at Hacienda del Sol
Kingfisher
Ventana Room
Wildflower
*Continental*
Anthony's/Catalinas
Arizona Inn
Gold Room
*Eclectic*
Cuvée World Bistro
Feast
*French*
Le Rendez-Vous

*Italian*
*(N=Northern)*
   Vivace (N)
*Mexican*
   Cafe Poca Cosa
   Mi Nidito
*Nuevo Latino*
   J Bar
*Seafood*
   Kingfisher
*Southwestern*
   Fuego!
   Gold Room
   Janos
   Jonathan's Tucson Cork
*Steakhouses*
   Jonathan's Tucson Cork
   McMahon's Prime

## Washington, DC

*American (New)*
   Cashion's Eat Place
   DC Coast
   Equinox
   Eve
   Inn at Little Washington
   Kinkead's
   Majestic Cafe
   Melrose
   Nora
   Palena
   Restaurant 2941
   1789
   Vidalia
*Bakeries*
   Bread Line
*Belgian*
   Marcel's
*French*
   La Bergerie
   L'Auberge Chez François
   L'Auberge Provençale
   Marcel's
*French (Bistro)*
   Bis
*French (New)*
   Citronelle
   Gerard's Place
*Hamburgers*
   Palena
*Indian*
   Bombay Club
*Italian*
*(N=Northern)*
   Galileo/Il Laboratorio
   Maestro
   Obelisk
   Tosca (N)

*Japanese*
   Makoto
*Mediterranean*
   Zaytinya
*Nuevo Latino*
   Café Atlántico
   Ceiba
*Pan-Asian*
   Asia Nora
   TenPenh
*Peruvian*
   El Pollo Rico
*Pizza*
   Pizzeria Paradiso
*Seafood*
   DC Coast
   Johnny's Half Shell
   Kinkead's
*Southern*
   Majestic Cafe
   Vidalia
*Spanish*
*(\* tapas specialist)*
   Jaleo\*
   Taberna del Alabardero\*
*Steakhouses*
   Prime Rib
   Ray's The Steaks
*Thai*
   Rabieng

## Westchester/ Hudson River Valley

*American (New)*
   American Bounty
   Aubergine
   Bear Cafe
   Blue Hill at Stone Barns
   Busy Bee Cafe
   Cafe Tamayo
   Crabtree's Kittle House
   DePuy Canal House
   Equus
   Freelance Café
   Iron Horse Grill
   McKinney & Doyle
   Mina
   Rest. X/Bully Boy Bar
   Terrapin
   Would, The
   Xaviar's at Piermont
   Zephs'
*American (Traditional)*
   Lu Shane's
*Continental*
   Arch
   L'Europe

## AREA ABBREVIATIONS

## ALPHABETICAL PAGE INDEX

## Alphabetical Page Index

# Alphabetical Page Index

# Alphabetical Page Index

subscribe to zagat.com

# Alphabetical Page Index

# Alphabetical Page Index

# Alphabetical Page Index

# Alphabetical Page Index

# Wine Vintage Chart

This chart is designed to help you select wine to go with your meal. It is based on the same 0 to 30 scale used throughout this *Survey*. The ratings (prepared by our friend **Howard Stravitz,** a law professor at the University of South Carolina) reflect both the quality of the vintage and the wine's readiness for present consumption. Th[...] if a wine is not fully mature or is over the hill, its [...] has been reduced. We do not include 1987, 199[...] vintages because they are not especially recomm[...] for most areas. A dash indicates that a wine is [...] past its peak or too young to rate.

| | '85 | '86 | '88 | '89 | '90 | '94 | '95 | '96 | '97 | '98 | '99 | '00 | '01 | '02 |
|---|---|---|---|---|---|---|---|---|---|---|---|---|---|---|
| **WHITES** | | | | | | | | | | | | | | |
| **French:** | | | | | | | | | | | | | | |
| Alsace | 24 | – | 22 | 28 | 28 | 27 | 26 | 25 | 25 | 26 | 25 | 26 | 27 | 25 | – |
| Burgundy | 26 | 25 | – | 24 | 22 | – | 28 | 29 | 24 | 23 | 26 | 25 | 23 | 27 | 24 |
| Loire Valley | – | – | – | – | 24 | – | 20 | 23 | 22 | – | 24 | 25 | 23 | 27 | 26 |
| Champagne | 28 | 25 | 24 | 26 | 29 | – | 26 | 27 | 24 | 24 | 25 | 25 | 26 | – | – |
| Sauternes | 21 | 28 | 29 | 25 | 27 | – | 21 | 23 | 26 | 24 | 24 | 24 | 28 | 25 | 26 |
| **Germany** | 25 | – | 25 | 26 | 27 | 25 | 24 | 27 | 24 | 23 | 25 | 24 | 29 | 27 | – |
| **California (Napa, Sonoma, Mendocino):** | | | | | | | | | | | | | | |
| Chardonnay | – | – | – | – | – | – | – | 24 | 26 | 25 | 25 | 24 | 27 | 29 | – |
| Sauvignon Blanc/Semillon | – | – | – | – | – | – | – | – | – | 25 | 25 | 23 | 27 | 28 | 26 |
| **REDS** | | | | | | | | | | | | | | |
| **French:** | | | | | | | | | | | | | | |
| Bordeaux | 24 | 25 | 24 | 26 | 29 | 22 | 26 | 25 | 23 | 25 | 24 | 28 | 26 | 23 | 24 |
| Burgundy | 23 | – | 21 | 24 | 26 | – | 26 | 28 | 25 | 22 | 28 | 22 | 24 | 27 | – |
| Rhône | 25 | 19 | 27 | 29 | 29 | 24 | 25 | 23 | 24 | 28 | 27 | 27 | 26 | – | 25 |
| Beaujolais | – | – | – | – | – | – | – | – | – | – | 23 | 24 | – | 25 | 28 |
| **California (Napa, Sonoma, Mendocino):** | | | | | | | | | | | | | | |
| Cab./Merlot | 27 | 26 | – | 21 | 28 | 29 | 27 | 25 | 28 | 23 | 26 | 23 | 27 | 25 | – |
| Pinot Noir | – | – | – | – | – | – | – | – | 24 | 24 | 25 | 24 | 26 | 29 | – |
| Zinfandel | – | – | – | – | – | – | – | – | – | – | – | 26 | 26 | – |
| **Italian:** | | | | | | | | | | | | | | |
| Tuscany | – | – | – | – | 25 | 22 | 25 | 20 | 29 | 24 | 28 | 26 | 25 | – | – |
| Piedmont | – | – | – | 27 | 28 | – | 23 | 27 | 27 | 25 | 25 | 28 | 23 | – | – |